This book is the result of a lifetime love affair with France, with my late husband, John, and a VW camper van. It was written nostalgically *à la recherche du temps perdu*. It is dedicated to tomorrow and to Kate, Buzz, Alex and Gavin; my children of the road.

the
CHANNEL

the CHANNEL

Shirley Harrison

COLLINS
GLASGOW & LONDON

The author and publishers would like to thank all the staff of the following picture agencies for their help in the selection of the illustrations in *The Channel*: Aerofilms, Barnaby's Picture Library, BBC Hulton Picture Library, J. Allan Cash, Mary Evans Picture Library, Mansell Library, Paul Popper, Photo Source, Picturepoint, Ann Ronan Picture Library, John Topham Picture Library. Individual sources are credited in the captions accompanying each illustration.

Special thanks are due to the Department of Postal Administration, Jersey, Channel Islands for their permission to reproduce illustrations on pp. 17, 19, 159. These were originally published as postage stamps in 1982 when Jersey participated in a European publication of stamps with the common theme of historic events. With the professional advice of Dr John Renouf of Highlands College, Jersey, these stamps were designed by Alan Copp and complemented by the covers of the presentation pack. Enquiries about the stamps should be addressed to the Department of Postal Administration, Postal Headquarters, Mont Millais, Jersey, Channel Islands.

The genealogical tables on pp. 48–9 and 64–5 are by Reg and Marjorie Piggott.

Typeset in 10 point Ehrhardt by J&L Composition, Filey, N. Yorkshire
Reproduced by Arneg, Glasgow
Printed and bound by Collins, Glasgow

Acknowledgements

Along the 845 miles of French and English shoreline, the hospitality and kindness was never ending. Many of those who helped may be disappointed their contributions do not appear to be included – but without exception every conversation, every meeting has strengthened the foundations from which this book has grown. For the nitty gritty facts and figures and time beyond the call of duty my thanks to: Dr Brian D'Olier, B.Sc., Ph.D., F.G.S., Principal Lecturer in Marine Geology at the City of London Polytechnic and at the City University; Admiral Sir William Staveley; Rear Admiral Tom Bradbury; Monsieur Jean Marc of Affaires Maritimes and the staff of the French Embassy; Jan Ridley, researcher; Margaret Crosland for translation; Tony Watts, J.P. (Cherbourg Chamber of Commerce); Monsieur G. Lepelley and Monsieur Bouché of the Souvenir Normand; the Mallet family of Varengeville; H.M. Coastguards; Trinity House; the Economic Committee of Brittany; H.M. Customs and Excise; South Coast Shipping; English China Clays; Shell U.K.; Sealink, Townsend Thoresen, Brittany Ferries, and the Sally Line; British Caledonian; the Channel Tunnel Group and Bill Shakespeare, in particular; the R.N.L.I.; and to Kate Pawson, who typed it; Sally Evemy and June Creightmore, who checked it; and my agent, and all-weather navigator, Doreen Montgomery.

There are so many people whose help I have valued on my way – they are not forgotten and I am grateful. To the experts whose lifework I may have condensed into a paragraph I am humble. I must have made mistakes over some 10,000 years – if so, the fault is mine, not theirs. I have done my best to be accurate and hope they will bear with me.

Contents

Preface

Somewhere crossing the empty seas between Plymouth and Roscoff, the Channel ferry television fades. A snowstorm of atmospherics blurs England from the screen and for some minutes passengers cruise on, ghosts in no man's land – before the French programme appears through the haze and, like a mirage, lures them on to the excitements ahead.

It was at that moment, suspended in time and place, neither here nor there, on the wide waters of the Channel's Western Approaches that I decided to write this book. It is a tale of two peoples, on the south coast of England and the northern coast of France, bound together over 1000 years in an incestuous love-hate affair by the sea that links them. Their history has been shaped by a single family feud that began long before the Conquest when both shorelines were home to one race speaking one language – Norman French. Time has thinned the blood ties. Today's battles are concerned, not with land but with cauliflowers, milk and lamb. For though we are united once again, this time within the European Economic Community, Anglo–French bickering continues – despite Dunkirk. We face each other across one of the most unpredictable strips of water in the world, our friendships ebbing and flowing with the tide. The French have a wonderful word for it – *Méfiance Cordiale* – wary cordiality.

The English Channel is probably seen by more people in Britain than ever before. More of us squeeze on to the ferries for abroad each year. Eager children with clipboards, agog for the hypermarkets, teenagers and grannies on the booze-cruise, holidaymakers and businessmen. Of course, we have a proprietory claim to it – for us it is the ENGLISH Channel all the way to the shoreline of France, and we take it entirely for granted.

For the French – those who bother to make the journey in the opposite direction – it is usually a means to an end, no more. Those who live beside the Norman or Breton seaside tend, like the statue of Napoleon at Boulogne, to have their backs to Britain.

Yet, on every one of the crossings, coming or going, the view from the wide-screen windows in the observation lounge is littered with the flotsam and jetsam of the past. The whole of history is out there. West down Channel towards the Atlantic, where the colours change from dark blue to a disturbed green, east up la Manche, 'the sleeve', as the French unemotionally call it, to the Narrows between Dover and Calais, is concentrated adventure and romance, heartbreak and hope. This 'silver sea' has been infested with pirates, has run red with the blood of battle and has echoed to the sound of ships' sirens welcoming home the heroes. It has witnessed the conquest of Britain and liberation of France.

Think back as you stroll around the modern ferry with its perfumiers, shopping precincts and videos. Think back if you are a driver enjoying silver service in the RoRo lounge. Think back as you seek in vain for an open deck to stretch your legs – for today's shipping companies do not count sea spray and biting winds among their perks.

Remember the first car ferries, just after the Second World War, awash and smelling of sick. Before that – beyond memory – the packet boats dropping anchor offshore for passengers to be pick-abacked to the quay by wading porters. There were nineteenth-century sailing boats bringing escaped revolutionaries from the guillotine; large overcrowded eighteenth-century convict ships for Australia and the West Indies; the tiny over-crowded seventeenth-century craft that carried

Pilgrim Fathers to America; the cumbersome sixteenth-century Armada galleons, storm-wrecked and reeling up the Channel from Spain to meet the ghosts of the tenth-century Vikings in their open dragon ships. Queen Victoria, the Scarlet Pimpernel, Charles I, the infant Mary Queen of Scots, all suffered on the turbulent waters.

How many lost their way and foundered? How many are lying down there on the seabed alongside the victims of two World Wars, amongst the fossilized forests that only 8000 years ago united Britain to Europe across a swampy plain?

It was that final swirl of waters through the isthmus that made Britain an island, and though the North Sea and the Atlantic have had as much influence on our maritime history, it is the Channel which appeals most to our emotions.

The sea is always remote from the great mass of people, and this was especially so in the past. When very few ever saw the sea it was mysterious and exciting. Sailors, too, were isolated and glamorous. Sea power, for the British, became synonymous with liberty – and Protestantism. Whereas in France, a much larger country, land power and armies were more important for defence. Because Britain was never dominated by military rulers its people were free to develop an individuality and eccentricity not known in France – except, perhaps, amongst the Channel people of Normandy and Brittany.

The last War finally weakened British naval strength and changed our relationship to Europe as a whole. Like it or not we are now economically fused with the mainland. Today the nineteenth-century era of 'Rule Brittania' stirs our nostalgic hearts, for with the decline of our sea power, liberty also faded. We cling to its memory with fervent patriotism.

The Channel now has little strategic military importance but it is the high road to European trade for us, a link for all the major freight lines of the world. It is also fast becoming a leisure park. Tourism is such big business that the peoples from Kent to Cornwall, from Finisterre to Cap Gris Nez have a reason to exploit their historic relationship and the tourist boards along both shores are seeking to encourage interchange on a scale never known before. It is not an easy task. We have always been fascinated by the romance and lifestyle of France but are reluctant to like the French. They are indifferent to us. And there we are, with a common ancestry, glaring at each other – only a swim away.

It is the sea which often dictates events. It always has. It is the bond between us – a geographic and historic region in its own right largely unsung by the advertising moguls. So it is the sea itself which is the focus of this book and its effects on the communities along both shores. Of course, nothing ever happens in isolation and the story of the Channel is really the story of France and England. But I am not a historian and this is not a history. There are, inevitably, events I do not know of, places I have not seen and should you be tempted to follow the same path, you may well make different discoveries. I am simply an English traveller, with a love of France and I have taken a seagull's view across the waves of the waters that bind us to paint a personal, living portrait of the most traffic-jammed marine 'motorway' in the world – that Masefield called 'the grey highway of Britain'.

Shirley Harrison

Birth of an Island

Sailing in from the dark blue of the Atlantic to the disturbed green of the Western Approaches the pulse quickens and the stomach churns. For every returning British mariner, the emotional nausea and loss of appetite known as 'the Channels' means home. No sighting of land can match that moment; nor is it shared by the French whose relationship with the sea is a practical affair. Of all dangers faced in oceans around the world none is as thrilling or challenging or welcome as those now ahead within sight of journey's end. So many have survived far better-known hazards only to perish in that capricious water between the Scylla and Charybdis shores of France and England.

There is one way for the land-based traveller to understand a little about the special character of the English Channel or for the sailor to visualize better how it evolved. Somewhere, perhaps around the Hurd Deep in the Western Approaches, take out the plug and let the water drain away, leaving long-ago valleys, hills, riverbeds and forests exposed again to the seagull's eye. This is where the journey must begin. Then, seeing the way it once was, it is easier to see the way it is – how the rise and fall of submarine countryside has interacted with the waters that gradually flooded in some eight to ten thousand years ago, creating currents and tide patterns, carving cliffs and moulding headlands, often in mirror images from side to side. Where there were creeks and harbours men settled, where the waters ran deep they established great trading ports and where they were treacherously shallow people looked inland to become farmers. So it was that Brittany with its splintered, indented, vicious coastline, and Normandy with vast, unnavigable sand-flats were perhaps geographically handicapped from the beginning and the British monopoly of the Channel predestined.

There is not much sea in the Channel. At its shallowest point in the Straits over the Varne Bank a deep-draught tanker might clear the sand by five to six feet at the top of the tide; were St Paul's Cathedral to be sunk its dome would rise above the waves. The story of the formation of the English Channel over many eons of time is one of seas, warm and frigid, deserts and lakes, volcanoes and violent earth movements, uplift and subsidence, all of which have left evidence for the submarine explorer to chart. Though dredgers seeking gravel beds in the Straits have gathered acorns from where they fell on the ancient forest floor, few other remains have been uncovered along the shores of France or England to tell the story of those almost unimaginably faraway days before boats were even necessary, when the Paleolithic nomads of the old Stone Age wandered over the plains of northern Europe, across the chalky ridges now submerged by the English Channel into the arctic tundra of Kent and across the Northern Approaches into Devon from Brittany.

Overall, there has been a steady drift to the north-east of one of the world's great surface crustal plates. The entire surface of the earth is composed of seven large, and numerous small, internally rigid and relatively thin interlocking plates, moving slowly but continuously in relative motion to each other, like overlapping scales.

About 280 million years ago, at the close of the Carboniferous period when all today's continents were fused into just one land area, the Channel region lay deep within the Pangaean continental mass which included Africa, Australia and America. At that time there was no Atlantic Ocean, but a sea lay within its northern shores running east-west through southern Ireland, south Wales and southern England. The land we know as Britain lay only 15° to 18° north of the equator. There was probably no Mediterranean as we know it. There was a gulf known to geologists as Tethys which later became the Mediterranean. As the crustal plates gently rocked and rotated and slid sideways, Iberia moved away from the Grand Banks of America, forming the Bay of Biscay, Britain drifted away from Canada and Greenland and the Atlantic Ocean widened. The floor of this ocean developed tension in its crust running towards the Channel area, which was, millions of years later, to thin and cause a rift which would eventually create conditions for a new sea to nose its way between the continental mass towards the north and isolate Britain from the rest.

In the period from 195 million years ago up to some one-and-a-half million years ago the Channel was continuously affected by uplift and massive subsidence and invasion and retreat of the sea. Ice Ages came and went (the last was only eleven thousand years ago) and neither the land nor sea-floor levels have yet recovered what is known as their isostatic equilibrium. This is the geologists' term for what happens when, over hundreds and thousands of years, the weight of ice presses the surface down. When the ice melts the land rises. North of the Bristol–Humber line Britain is still rising while south-eastern Britain is still subsiding, perhaps thirty centimetres per hundred years. The Channel floor itself is an area of low relief, sloping with a gradient of 1.6000 from the Straits to the Western Approaches. The outward signs of these imperceptible yet gargantuan movements over hundreds of millions of years remain as witnesses to the story. The white cliffs of Dover themselves, symbol of Britain to travellers worldwide, are, in fact, a gigantic botanical cemetery. About 100 million years ago, during the Cretaceous period, a tropical sea covered Britain and France, teaming with zillions of free-floating algal plants, which as they died left skeletons to fossilise. Since then there has been uplift where the Dover Straits lie and subsequent cutting of the chalk by river and sea to leave the familiar cliffs exposed.

During the Ice Ages when sea-levels fell by up to four hundred feet, intense frost would have broken up the rocks of what is now the Channel floor. In the warmer phases ice-swollen rivers brought huge quantities of debris rolling and tumbling into the Channel basin to form the sea-bed sands, muds and gravels. High seas in turn formed, by erosion, a constantly changing cliff line and so provided more debris, whilst, at the same time, wave and tide action planed the sea-floor.

These, now submarine, cliffs may be traced from Eastbourne to St Catherine's Deep off the Isle of Wight where there is a break, across

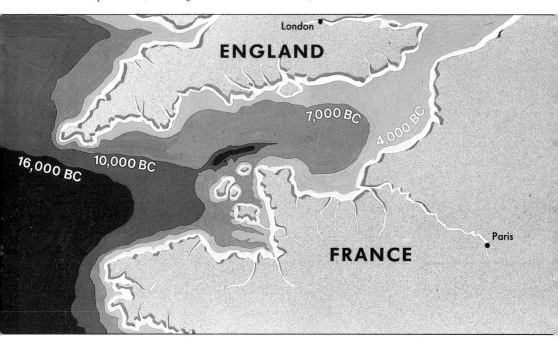

Lyme Bay, and past Portland Bill where they accentuate the tidal race. There is then another break before they reappear off Paignton to continue as far as The Lizard. Across the Channel the cliffs run from the Cherbourg Peninsula around the west and north of the Channel Islands and just offshore of the French coast all the way to Brest.

The floor of the Channel is also indented with deep continuous valleys, sometimes filled with sand, sometimes empty which were cut by rivers flowing off the high ground of England, France and Belgium. During the last two Ice Ages the Rhine and its tributaries, the Thames/Medway and the Scheldt flowed through the Straits of Dover cutting a deep channel through the chalk which can be seen off the Isle of Thanet to somewhere near Boulogne. There are buried channels for each of the present-day English and French rivers which

During the Ice Ages vast quantities of water were locked up in the ice which stretched from the polar region down into southern Britain. As the ice melted the sea level rose and the progression of the sea up the Channel – over thousands of years – is shown here. The final inundation which broke the land link with Europe may have been caused by a massive storm. (Department of Postal Administration, Jersey, Channel Islands)

run out to meet this main Rhine valley. The Seine has a well-developed drowned valley with terraces on either flank. They all converge on the Hurd Deep which is 94 miles long and plunges 787 feet deep before extending out towards the Continental Shelf and into the Great Shamrock Canyon.

From an aeroplane, above a calm sea on a spring tide, the outline of the Hurd Deep is there for the experienced eye to see, marked by ruffled breakers where the water rises over its edges. Far out in space British scientists are conducting satellite experiments to monitor changes in the sea-bed which show themselves in this way on the surface. It is similar to archaeologists who take aerial pictures to record the pattern of changing field systems through the ages.

The Hurd Deep itself may well give the lie to some geologists' belief that ice never moved further south than the line from London to the Scilly Isles. It has the characteristic boat shape of a sub-glacial valley rather like the melt channels found under the ice in Greenland and now exposed in Scandinavia. Beneath the Channel ferry route from Folkestone there is another deep channel which runs to about five miles off Sangatte and is thought by some to have lain between two large lobes of ice, one from the north and the other from the south-west. Saint Catherine's Deep near the Isle of Wight, the Fosse des Pluteurs and the Fosse de la Hague both lie between Hurd Deep and the Cherbourg Peninsula. The Fosse de l'Isle Vierge and the Fosse Ouessant could also be sub-glacial valleys.

In places, huge boulders known in the trade as 'erratics', like the Giant's Rock of Porthleven, Cornwall, weighing fifty tons, have been transported from north-west Scotland – and how else but by ice? Many of the boulders on the sea-bed at Selsey Bill weighing over ten tons have come from the Channel Islands and the Cotentin Peninsula. Further east they are much smaller and around Worthing, Lancing and Seaford the ten to fifteen centimetre 'erratics' originate from Ploumanach, north-western Brittany.

Much of the offshore gravel industry depends on these filled-in river beds and there is constant controversy between dredging companies, geologists and sailors over the way to harvest and care for the perpetually shifting Channel floor. It is, after all, a potential source of mineral wealth.

There are also many 'raised' beaches which are an indication of rising sea-levels, or perhaps of the uplift of certain areas during the recovery of isostatic equilibrium. Officially they are grouped into two sets known as 'Normanium One' which corresponds to a level some sixty-six feet above Ordnance Datum and 'Normanium Two' with a level of twenty-six feet above Ordnance Datum. Normanium One beaches can be seen around the Cotentin, and on the Channel Islands whilst on the British coast there is one on the chalk escarpment between Chichester and Arundel and thirty feet above sea-level at Portland Bill. You can crunch sea-shells underfoot along the path which runs high above the beach at Hope's Nose near Torquay,

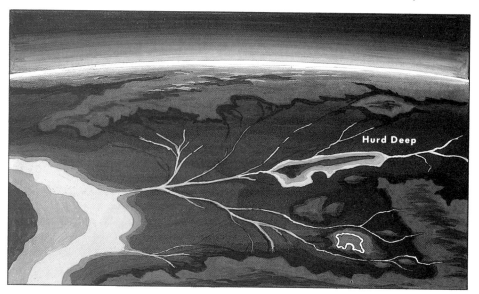

and further on there is High Beach at Plymouth and Penlee Beach near Mousehole which, they say, could be two hundred thousand years old.

The Normanium Two beaches which are only a hundred thousand years old, appear along many stretches of the north French coast near Le Havre, behind the Normandy beaches, inland between Étaples and Cayeaux and Sangatte near Calais.

These are beaches visible to all, though known best to the specialist. Chesil Beach, a defiant forty-five mile bank of golden pebbles, running dramatically separate from the shore between Portland and Bridport is a Nature Conservancy Council Grade I site. For, not only is it a geophysical phenomenon, it is also the only known British locality for the wingless cricket and one-sixth of the breeding population nests on its wild, bare slopes.

Today the Chesil Beach rises to about thirty-three feet above mean sea level. Its total mass is around 50 million tonnes and it is maintained by storm waves which can, as in 1934, overtop the bank.

It was probably pushed into its present position between eight and ten thousand years ago by the advancing sea as it moved through the marshes and Britain was being cut off from the mainland. As far as is known, it is hardly shifting any more. However, as the pebbles get smaller – the average size is two inches at Portland and one and a half inches opposite the Abbotsbury Swannery – they move along the beach to a position of equilibrium with the other constituent pebbles. It is a beautiful, perpetually-moving balance. Above the tide level the bank is composed mainly of flint shot with distinctive triassic sandstone, all available on the floor of the Channel. It is likely that the successive activities of frost action and sea-level rise have also

About 16,000 BC the Channel was a low river valley draining the higher lands of Britain and France. The last Ice Age still held most of Britain and the dry land here would have been frozen hard all year. The Channel Islands were then high ground in the low plain south of the deep lake now known as the Hurd Deep. The present area of Jersey is outlined. (Department of Postal Administration, Jersey, Channel Islands)

19

gathered material from offshore, though there are a few mystery stones from north-west Scotland, which seem to be more evidence of the advance of the ice sheets as they were most likely deposited by the ice. Below the well-rounded shingle of the surface, pebbles are less even and composed of local rock types which imply that this swept, offshore material lies over an older level.

The great Channel forests which once covered the land between France and England are visible still at certain tides around the coasts and along the shores of the ancient river beds where sand and shingle have preserved them. The twisted stumps and branches of silver birch, oak, ash and elder protrude from the sands at Little Galley Hill near Bexhill, Cliffend Hastings and at Dover. The treacherous quicksands around the Mont St Michel cover a huge forest, the Forêt de Scissy, which was drowned as late as AD 709 in a storm leaving the islands of the Chausey archipelago alone above the sea.

So, beneath the waves there are valleys, lakes, plains and hills, some rising like the banks which run for thirty miles parallel to the French coast off Calais and ten miles parallel to Britain off Dover to form treacherous shallows just below the surface. Many of the well-known coastal beauty spots of the Channel are in themselves a clue to what might be discovered if the imagination travels on down into the deep.

The eerie fossil graveyard that stretches along the beach from Lyme Regis marks the end of the Jurassic Age one hundred and fifty million years ago, when most marine and land life was extinguished. The bones of ichthyosaurs, dinosaurs, brachiopods and monster ammonites are here in a seemingly limitless supply for the eager schoolchild to discover. Fishermen have also hauled hundreds of these monster bones from their sea bed graveyard.

The cliff-path running between Lyme and Seaton is as exciting to the geological explorer as darkest Africa to the missionary, for, due to the way that porous rocks lie on impermeable rocks, the water percolates and greases the lower surface so that the top layers slip spectacularly towards the sea with an extraordinary rotary movement. Cracks have appeared which curve out and the section of the cliff between the sea and the crack tilts, its outward edge rising and its inward edge sinking. This has created a wild landscape of chasms and ridges over which the forest has grown, rich in plants and wildlife.

In Brittany the fjord-like 'abers' (*Aber wrac'h Aber Benoit*) which draw thousands of holidaymakers are, in fact, the drowned extensions of river-beds which run on out towards the Hurd Deep.

The great misty marshlands of the Bay of Avranches and the western Cotentin Peninsula, the endless beaches of Normandy, the precipitous chalk cliffs pleated like a kilt at Étrétat, facing the gentle curving chalk of the Seven Sisters at Eastbourne, and the extraordinary pink rock sculptures that rise so dramatically like Dartmoor tors from the sea around Trégastel, are all milestones in the story of the development of the shoreline.

The coastline of both countries changes imperceptibly every year

and in some places the changes are clear to see, especially in the softer rocks of the eastern Channel. The French cliffs are said to be retreating at about one hundred feet a century – Cap de la Hève near Le Havre is over four thousand feet further inland than it was eight hundred years ago. Hastings is the third town of that name – Saxon Hastings is under the sea!

Perhaps most spectacular of all in its wild eeriness is the no-man's-land of Dungeness, the largest shingle ridge in Britain, where four light-houses built in a line, much as children dig sticks into the sand to mark the edge of the tide, record the march of the growing headland into the sea. The most recent was built in 1792.

At the end of the Neolithic period three thousand to four thousand years ago, the area between Fairlight Head and Hythe was a large sandy bay into which the estuaries of the rivers Rother, Tillingham

'The village of Moonfleet lies half a mile from the sea on the right, near west bank of the Fleet stream. This rivulet ... loses itself at last in a lake of brackish water. The lake is good for nothing, except sea fowl, herons and oysters and forms such a place as they call in the Indies, a lagoon, being shut off from the open Channel by a monstrous great beach, or dyke of pebbles. ...' Chesil Beach from Moonfleet. (Aerofilms)

21

and Brede discharged. Much of the coastline of that time can be traced in the degraded cliff between Hythe and Winchelsea. At first a spit developed from Fairlight Head and ran north-north-east into the bay towards the Brede/Tillingham estuaries. The Camber ridges are all that is left of these. Eventually the spits were extended right across to Hythe either because of a fall in sea-level or an increase of dumped material due to stormy weather over a long period. The estuary deposits from the three rivers formed first a salting (marine) marsh, then a brackish swamp and finally a swampy forest. Later the sea invaded the whole marsh and submerged the forest. Later still Fairlight Head developed a slight bend due to erosion which trapped migrating shingle as it travelled along the coast.

Today the force moulding Dungeness is the up-channel, south-westerly induced waves, carrying shingle. But as the waves swing round the headland they are weakened and so drop their material which produces ridges overlapping the point, whilst storm waves from the east-north-east form ridges parallel to the eastern side. The Ness is moving east by perhaps eight to ten inches a year and, ironically, the CEGB who have built a massive power station too close to its edge are, it is claimed, paying huge sums of money to the landowner to transport gravel from one side to the other simply to maintain the status quo!

It is hard work scrambling across those shingle ridges or 'fulls' as they are known locally for there are no 'backstays' (like snowshoes) supplied today. From the road on the ridges left farthest behind by the sea, is an almost exotic profusion of plant life struggling to survive through the thin covering of soil. Nearest the marsh, which is the haunt of the largest European frog, grows clover, bird's-foot trefoil and fine grasses and moving out towards the sea the silvery spikes of sea-kale, sea-beet, sea-dock, sea-pea and the yellow-horned poppy. By the time the last bleak ridges drop sharply to the water at the point of the new-born Dungeness itself, there is nothing, and beneath it is all the clay that once nourished the forests which are in turn the source of coal for the nearby Betteshanger mine.

There is also one dramatic place on the Devon coast where, in the course of an afternoon stroll, it is possible to climb across a hundred and ten million years in a few moments. In 1839 a gigantic landslip of earthquake proportions left exposed a gulley, now known as Seaton Hole, which is almost tropically rich in vegetation. There on one side of the fault is the dark red soil of the Triassic desert two hundred and twenty five million years old, and on the other the shining white of cretaceaous chalk from only a hundred and fifteen million years ago.

Hundreds of thousands of years ago the climate was too cold to support a settled population and the only relics remaining from sporadic visits of the earliest men were the 'eoliths' – Dawn Stones – a rough-hewn tool found in such places as Kents Cavern near Torquay.

At least four Ice Ages came and went, but life for those restless little groups of people who hunted mammoths, avoided sabre-toothed cats, and gathered berries barely changed at all. Somewhere between

85,000 BC and 35,000 BC during the last Ice Age, a handful of slightly more advanced Neanderthal Men – they fashioned better tools and they buried their dead – reached Britain from Germany but they too became extinct. Homo sapiens, thinking man, emerged in Europe at least fifty thousand years ago. His were the first efforts at art and he polished his tools and carved his flints.

As the last Ice Age began to end about ten thousand years ago, the Mesolithic hunter-fishers, living in what is now Britain, must have been aware that their forays back and forth into what is now Europe were becoming increasingly damp underfoot. The rising sea was advancing up the river valleys and flooding across the land between them, reworking the broken, frost-shattered rock and redistributing the sands and gravels brought down by the rivers. The sand was re-sorted to form sand-banks usually at the edges of old river valleys such as the Varne Bank along the Rhine/Thames channel or the Hooe Bank along the Solent. The heavier material, the shingle and gravel, remained near the river channels that had often brought it in the first place from higher land. Some that remained in the advancing surf-zone of the sea on the flatter areas of the Channel floor were rolled inshore to form beaches such as Chesil and Dungeness.

There must have come a day about eight thousand years ago when the only way of getting across was by boat. So Britain became a sea-faring island with her future shaped by the geology of her coastline and France remained locked in the land mass of Europe.

At Seaton Hole, between Beer and Seaton in Devon, you can walk across one hundred and ten million years of prehistory in a few hundred yards – from the red soil of the Triassic Desert to the chalk of the Cretaceous Period. (Aerofilms)

Birth of a Nation

The Bronze Age fisherman from about 1000 BC whose upturned boat has been found on the sea bed in Dover harbour is, in terms of Man-on-Earth, one of us. In the context of the development of mankind, the three thousand years from the day when robbers wrecked that little boat to its discovery in 1980 is no more than the blink of an eye. Nevertheless, though historians may fuse whole centuries and forget individual heartbreak and hope, triumph or tragedy, it is these everyday happenings that bring history to life.

The first boats were not very ambitious – small scooped-out tree trunks suitable only for inshore fishing. These were soon followed by the currach, a wicker frame covered with skins, still used in parts of Ireland. On a good day, when the seas were calm these currachs almost certainly made it backwards and forwards across the western Channel. Where they landed and what they carried we may never know.

Around the year 3000 BC a population increase encouraged the first Neolithic Celts to move gradually up through Europe from France across the Channel and settle in Britain. There was no hostility because there was plenty of room for both the original inhabitants and the newcomers. Probably no more than a few hundred settled on the entire south coast. The Windmill Hill Culture, as it is now called, brought tremendous changes. These short, dark, long-skulled people built the first man-made structures in Britain: the wind-wild causeway camps such as those at Windmill Hill in Wiltshire, Cissbury Ring overlooking the sea on the Sussex Downs, and Whitehawk Hill Camp above Brighton. They were agriculturalists, the first crop growers, and they made leather pots. Even at this time the influences that flowed into Britain from Europe were clearly-defined. Most important, they built barrows to bury their dead communally in stone-lined tombs, or dolmen as they are called in Brittany, quoits in Cornwall.

They established the first religious centre in Brittany, some time before the building of the Pyramids in Egypt. These strange, weather-pitted stones, are the earliest of all signs of a religious bond between the remote west of Britain and France. No tourist crowds, or tatty bungalows can destroy their timeless magic and there is no need to be a mystic to feel their power. In such places there remains a spiritual force. Children in Cornwall today still understand that if a stone has a hole in it, it is best to climb through, seven times against the sun.

About 1800 BC the Beaker folk sailed in from Germany to Kent and from France to the west. They were a different stock, with round skulls, nicknamed by archaeologists because of their characteristic pottery. They certainly knew how to use metal and they bridged the gap between the Neolithic and the Bronze Ages.

The Channel of the Beaker Folk was a peaceful place. Although they were an aggressive tribe there is no archaeological evidence here of strife or territorial greed – there were probably not enough people. The land was inhabited by fairly stable, hard-working peasants living in small hut enclosures. The Beaker folk moved among them encouraging trade; they probably re-built Stonehenge and certainly exploited Irish gold.

From the beginning, the western end of the Channel was more important than the east as a staging post for the luxury import trade. While eastern Britain was a simple primitive land, the Celts in Cornwall already had their eyes on the riches of the Mediterranean. The blue beads of Crete, and golden jewellery have been found in their barrows. It is said the Phoenicians came for tin, though this may be legend.

The rate of progress was noticeably speeding up but the Channel was still a very domestic sea – like a country lane between villagers on either side. East–west traffic hardly existed, and Channel traders did not themselves venture far.

The Beaker folk were absorbed by the Wessex culture that followed them from Europe, a wealthy, aristocratic, trading community that knew well how to make gold and bronze ornaments and weapons. They brought with them fine jewellery and their settlements showed the first signs of an acquisitive society. No doubt the richness and strength of the early Wessex culture was founded in the desire to keep up with their neighbours in Europe and it is safe to assume that their ships were by now made of wood on metal frames, well-equipped for voyages to the Mediterranean in search of foreign goodies.

Modern harbours are not necessarily a reflection of the past because the primitive nature of ships, lack of nautical knowledge and, indeed, the different coastal pattern, dictated that ports were not in today's positions. The modern Etaples estuary of the River Canche, ten miles south of Boulogne, dries out completely nowadays. By the ninth and tenth centuries it had grown into Quentavic, a great European entry port. Even Cabourg, on the River Dives, where most of William the Conqueror's ships were built, is high and dry at low tide. In many places small, inland, handling ports grew up which could cope with ships that had been blown off course and might expect to land anywhere along the coast. One of the most popular crossing points from the very beginning was that between Cherbourg and the Isle of Wight, for the hills behind Cherbourg rise to 568 feet and those of St Catherine's Point to 785 feet. This meant that not only was the fifty-three-mile crossing tolerably short, but it was possible to have the 'loom of the land' in sight for most of the way.

Probably the most dangerous of hazards for those early sailors was west of the Cherbourg Peninsula where the Channel Island group and innumerable reefs and rocks are set in a sea where the tide runs at nine knots and legends of whirlpools and sea monsters encouraged captains to speed on their journey. The real reasons for the treacherous seas do indeed lie beneath the waves, but not in the shape of fabulous beasts.

The next wave of invaders, the Belgae, were refugees from European Roman expansion. Their arrival meant tremendous change, for with them came a knowledge of iron working, more sophisticated weapons, and – war. About the time when Greek civilization was at its height under Pericles, the people of the north discovered how to make iron at La Tène in France. This knowledge was soon taken up through Gaul, over the Channel and into the peaceful hill villages of Britain. The Belgae who actually made that crossing from the Normandy beaches were, in fact, cousins of the Celts already living here. The two cultures merged, adapting new ideas and improving the old, so that in the three hundred years before Julius Caesar attempted to extend the boundaries of the Roman Empire into Britain, a visitor to the coast of either Kent or Sussex or Gaul would have found the same mix of races and the same way of life.

No doubt there were group differences, and no doubt there were arguments over the cost of goods. In retrospect we are not aware of these local problems and see only four hundred years of quiet progress. The rest of the world knew almost nothing of the northern realms. In fact geographers believed the Ocean Stream encircled the earth and there were no islands. When Pytheas of Marseilles, one of the earliest true explorers, sailed right around Britain, Alexander the Great was expanding his empire into India. Pytheas described accurately what he saw, but no one believed him. He talked of the 'Pretanic Island of Albion and Ierne'. In Cornwall he met men driving chariots with wheels, living in wattle and daub thatched houses, and in Kent he tasted their bread, cake and mead.

Time has shown that Pytheas was right. These were already very far from the savages that Caesar expected to meet when he invaded three hundred years later. They lived in a simple but ordered society, building small towns on the site of the old hill villages, divided into freemen, slaves and serfs. Amongst the freemen were nobles, commons and Druids – the priests. Eventually they organized family communes under one ruling family which they called 'kins'.

In France and England these busy people were wearing bright, often gold-threaded, clothes. They introduced the first coins, called each other by the first recorded names in British history, ploughed fields with horses and used dogs to guard their expanding sheep flocks.

During those three hundred years, wave after wave of refugees from Roman expansion moved north and some were brave enough to flee across the Channel. Gradually the importance of the West of France declined, hit first by Caesar's destruction of its most important *entrepôt* – Corbilo on the Loire – and then by the increasing strength of ties with Europe over the shorter crossing at Dover.

By the time Julius Caesar made up his mind that the only way to secure the safety of Rome was to annexe the whole of Gaul and then Britain, there were many Gallic chiefs in responsible posts in Britain offering aid to their 'kinsmen' in France, against the might of Rome.

The roads Caesar built – *chemins haussées* – are still visible in the landscape, but the seaside villages along the length of the coast have long since crumbled into the sea. The names of many of the pre-Roman tribes of Normandy were adapted and are still recognizable in modern place names: Bajocasses (Bayeux), Caletes (Caux) and Abrincanthi (Avranches).

When Caesar came to Boulogne (Portus Itius) and questioned the local worthies he learned nothing, despite their constant cross-Channel contact with Britain. Even the advance party, a single boat sent to scan the shores, reported mistakenly that Deal was the best landing place. So at midnight on 11th August 55 BC Caesar himself set out for Britain.

In his own accounts Caesar has graphically described that exploratory landing in our country – and a Dad's Army affair it was! The beach on which he landed has long since disappeared under pasture inland.

> ... he himself [Caesar] reached Britain about the fourth hour of the day and there beheld the armed forces of the enemy displayed on all the cliffs [around Dover]. Such was the nature of the ground, so steep the heights that banked the sea that a missile could be hurled from the higher levels on to the shore. Thinking this place to be by no means suitable for disembarkation he waited at anchor until the ninth hour for the rest of the flotilla to assemble there. ... disembarkation was a matter of extreme difficulty for the following reasons. The ships, on account of their size, could not be run ashore except in deep water; the troops, though they did not know the ground had not their hands free and were loaded with the great and grievous weight of their arms, had nevertheless at one and the same time to leap down from the vessels, stand firm in the waves and to fight the enemy. The enemy on the other hand had all their limbs free and knew the ground exceeding well; and either standing on dry land or advancing a little way into the water they boldly hurled their missiles or spurred on their horses which were trained to it. Frightened by all this and wholly inexperienced in this kind of fighting our troops did not press on with the same fire and force as they were accustomed to show in land engagements.
>
> When Caesar remarked this he commanded the ships of war [which were less familiar in appearance to the natives and could move more freely at need] to remove a little from the transports to row at speed and to bring up on the exposed flank of the

enemy; and thence to drive and clear them off with slings, arrows and artillery. This movement proved of great service to our troops; for the natives, frightened by the shape of the ships, the motion of the oars and the unfamiliar type of artillery came to a halt, and retired but only for a little space. And then, while our troops still hung back chiefly on account of the depth of the sea the Eagle Bearer of the Tenth Legion, after a prayer to Heaven to bless the Legion by his act cried, 'leap down soldiers, unless you wish to betray your eagle to the enemy; it shall be told that I at any rate did my duty to my country and my general'. When he had said this, with a loud voice, he cast himself forth from the ships and began to bear the Eagle against the enemy. Then our troops exhorted one another not to allow so dire a disgrace and leapt down from the ship with one accord. And when the troops on the nearest ships saw them, they likewise followed on and drew nearer to the enemy.

The fighting was fierce on both sides. Our troops, however because they could not keep rank nor stand firm nor follow their proper standards, for any man from any ship attached himself to whatever standard he chanced upon, were in considerable disorder. But the enemy knew all the shallows and as soon as they had observed from the shore a party of soldiers disembarking one by one from a ship they spurred on their horses and attacked them while they were in difficulties, many surrounding few while others hurled missiles into the whole party from the exposed flank. ... the moment our men stood on dry land they charged with all their comrades close behind and put the enemy to rout. ...

Notes from *Caesar's Gallic War*

A year later he was ready for the real thing. The original fleet he had decided was not good enough so he persuaded workmen to construct a fleet of six hundred shallower vessels with oars – an astonishing demonstration of support for which he was openly grateful.

At sunset in midsummer 54 BC five legions (twenty five thousand men) and two thousand Gaulish cavalry and their horses, baggage, missiles, food and fortress material set sail to launch the first full-scale conquering invasion of Britain. They landed unopposed, and those men who had built the fleet in a year next set out on a twelve-mile night hike across roadless country. They had had an exhausting crowded crossing (eight hours at the oars) had constructed an entrenchment camp and yet still they were game to move on. Their stamina was impressive and it was unfortunate that that night an onshore wind blew forty of their boats onto the beach and wrecked them. Back they went and hauled every one of the hundred-ton ships up the beach into the shelter of the entrenchment.

... that same night, as it chanced, the moon was full, the day of the month which usually makes the highest tides in the ocean, a fact unknown to our men. Therefore the tide was found to have filled the warships in which Caesar caused his army to be conveyed across and which he had drawn up on dry land, and at the same time a storm was buffeting the transports which were made fast to anchors. Nor had our troops any chance of handling them, or helping. Several ships went to pieces and the others by loss of cordage anchors and the rest of their tackle were rendered useless for sailing. This, as was inevitable, caused great dismay throughout the army. For there were no other ships to carry them back; everything needful for the repair of the ships was lacking and as it was generally understood that the army was to winter in Gaul, no corn had been provided in these parts against the winter. ...

Notes from *Caesar's Gallic War*

Julius Caesar's second 'invasion' – more a raid in strength – achieved a considerable degree of acquiesence from the chiefs and kings in southern Britain. So much so that for almost a hundred years Britain was left unmolested by the Romans. Although Julius Caesar's successor, Augustus, was expected to invade Britain, and planned to do so, events elsewhere in the Empire conspired against this. British tribes paid tribute, acknowledged Roman authority and gave little cause for concern, until AD 43, when the Emperor Claudius decided it was time Roman authority was extended with real victories and a real conquest.

The third invasion was thoroughly planned. By now the Romans knew infinitely more about the coast line and tides than Julius Caesar and in the year AD 43 a powerful army landed at Lympe, Dover and Richborough. It was an army made up of merceneries from all parts of the Empire, but the British fought hard and it took four years before the Romans finally conquered the south, and twenty years before the whole of Britain submitted to the rule of the Emperor after bloody battles with Boudicca in East Anglia.

Tacitus described the people they found with sensitive understanding.

Those who are nearest to the Gauls are also like them, either from the permanent influence of original descent or, because the climate had produced similar qualities. ... The religious beliefs of Gaul may be traced in the strongly marked British superstition (Druidism). The language differs but little. There is the same boldness in challenging danger and when it is near the same timidity in shrinking from it. The Britons, however, exhibit more spirit being a people whom a long peace has not yet enervated. ... Their sky is obscured by continual rain and cloud. Severity of cold is unknown. The days exceed in length those of our world, the nights are bright. . . .

Quoted in
A History of the English Speaking Peoples
Churchill

The army was then garrisoned in the north and the Channel coast prospered without military intervention. It was one of the busier, more affluent and comfortable three hundred years in our history. Compared with Gaul at the time, life was securely provincial, but there were great building works afoot, engineering feats, plenty of food and local wine – the vineyard terraces can still be seen along the cliffs of Dorset. Christianity and idolatry flourished side by side. By the end of the Roman era 24,000 acres had been reclaimed from the sea around Rye. Engineers built an earthen bank which is where the Rhee wall now runs; there is a road along the top today, but the foundations are Roman. This wall was a frontier to the sea for seven hundred years.

Colourful galleys ploughed their way back and forth with merchandise and there was a constant interchange of travellers. Merchants, businessmen, and financiers flooded in from Boulogne, the streets were paved, the houses were warmed and there was hot water for baths. On the whole the people loved it.

The south coast of Britain, as far as Cornwall, along with France, as far as Brittany, shared a pride in being Roman. The two most westerly regions remained isolated and backward. Further north in Britain, too, there were hiccups, with local uprisings and rebellions; not so down south where they made the most of what Rome had to offer.

Small wonder when we look at what the Romans achieved. It is not too hard to visualize ships landing immediately in front of the great palace of Fishbourne near Chichester in Sussex. The sea is a mile away today, but when Cogidubnus, the local pro-Roman leader, built his house in AD 75, its colonnades and terraces looked straight over the water. Archaeologists discovered Fishbourne in 1960, one of the finest sites along either Channel shore; there too they found the garden trenches and so were able to reconstruct its surroundings, and fill the gardens for twentieth-century visitors with the scents and colours that would have greeted Cogidubnus's friends eighteen hundred years ago, as their ships anchored alongside on a business trip from France.

Modern audio visual techniques, a Roman cookbook, a Roman garden and guides in togas bring it all to life and curiously collapse the intervening centuries.

The town near the great palace of Cogidubnus, now known as Chichester, was at that time called 'Noviomagnus' and it must have been, what it says, a 'great new town' on the site of a previous development. Further down-Channel there seems to have been a fading interest in commercial expansion which was confined now

to London and the Straits. There is no evidence for a Roman Portsmouth, Dartmouth, Plymouth, Fowey or Falmouth and over the water no Roman Cherbourg or Le Havre. The Wild West of both Britain and France hardly benefited from the Roman invasion.

The great *Classis Britannica*, the Roman Navy, was largely based in the east and operated around the shores of Kent and Sussex in what they called the British sea. There is some doubt about the competing claims of Boulogne and Dover as its headquarters. These were by far the most important ports at the time (apart from London) and the path between was lit by identical lighthouses. The Dover pharos remains on the cliffs beside the castle; claimed as the oldest building in Britain, it stands proud on new-cut grass, sightless now, overlooking seventy miles of European coastline from Holland to Brittany.

Servicing the fleet, of course, employed a great many people who had to be housed. Tiles bearing the stamp of the *Classis Britannica* – CLBR could only be used for official buildings or staff housing – have been found as far away as the Isle of Wight.

The peaceful manoeuvres of the fleet saw a sea change at the start of the third century AD when the peak of Roman civilization was passing in the Mediterranean and there were signs of trouble already afoot in Germany. The south of England was more or less undefended, for

The remains of a great 'Roman' palace buit in AD 75 on what was then the Channel shore by a local leader, Cogidubnus. It demonstrates the extent of Roman influence on the people of southern Britain, and the wealth and importance of some native Britons. (Popperfoto)

PHAROS & ANCIENT CHURCH.

A Victorian couple contemplate the ruins of an ancient church beside the tower the Romans built to identify the harbour of Dover for the ships which sailed across from Boulogne where an identical lighthouse signalled back across the Channel. Today, the church of St Mary-in-the-Castle is fully restored and the Dover Pharos, said to be the oldest building in Britain, defies the passage of time as it still stares, blindly now, across the Channel to Boulogne. (BBC Hulton)

most troops were based in the north and it was clear to the people further south that the primarily merchant navy needed support from the land.

When the Romans first came to Britain it had been simply out of curiosity. Now they needed to retain this stronghold as their most northerly, and only, frontier. Moreover, they had come to depend on our British mineral wealth, especially the iron of the Weald.

So, somewhere around the year AD 220 the Romans began to build a series of forts along the coasts of both Britain and Europe. They were known as the Forts of the Saxon Shore – not because the Saxons had landed but because these were the coasts under threat from Saxon pirates. These forts have been extensively excavated and are a remarkable legacy to a complex network, under one commander, the Count of the Saxon Shore. The first fort in Britain was probably at Reculver in Kent and has been partially washed away by the sea. The last could well have been Pevensey, overlooking what was then a marshy estuary.

This system of forts is recorded in a remarkable document of the fifteenth century, which is itself a copy of a late Roman handbook and lists all garrison commanders and their garrisons. The *Notitia Dignitatum* has a section dealing with the *Comes Litoria Saxonici* (Count of the Saxon Shore) and lists clerical and military staff and illustrates the forts of the Saxon shore.

Whilst all this building was in progress the figure of Carausius bestrides the Straits. He is not a figure who looms large in the history books, if he looms at all. A pity, because Carausius was a real 'Channel man' – he *used* the Channel to make his fortune and to attempt from Rome the most audacious takeover bid for Britain. He caused history's first defensive sea battle in the Channel. Around the year AD 285 Carausius had been appointed by the Emperor Maximian to take charge of the *Classis Britannicus* which he did somewhat overzealously. Late fourth-century writer Eutropius says that he was a man of lowly birth entrusted with great power which he abused – he allowed the barbarians to land before seizing their spoils and confiscating them for himself. He became so rich that Maximian sentenced him to death and he escaped to Britain where he declared himself Emperor. He was clearly popular for he won considerable backing and then defeated Maximian at sea. He was no more than an adventurer but he reigned for six years, issued his own coins with the legend *Expectate veni* ('Come, we are ready') on the reverse and commanded complete control of the Channel until Maximian returned from his battles on the Rhine and put his mind to recapturing Britain.

He blocked the mouth of the river at Boulogne cutting the town off from the sea – and any hope of rescue by Carausius. He then attacked overland, took the town and established a base for his new invasion of Britain. But by the time he landed on the British coast three years later in AD 296 Carausius had been assassinated by his son Allectus who now reigned in his place. The usurpation was soon all over, and Maximian ruled supreme.

The nine forts shown here stretch from Norfolk to Hampshire. Othona and Dubris are Ithancester, near Bradwell in Essex, and Dover. Lemannis, Branuduna and Garianna are Lympne, Brancaster in Norfolk and Burgh Castle, near Yarmouth. Regullae, Rutupiae and Anderidos are Reculver, Richborough and Pevensey, and Portuadurm is Portchester. (Bodleian Library)

The next hundred years are a story of repeated horror; of invasion and counter attacks as the Romans clung to their British territory, and continued to build or rebuild their forts along the Saxon Shore. In the north the Picts and Scots were menacing, and from across the water came continual raids from the cruel Saxons. In AD 367 they all attacked together with such dreadful bloodshed and destruction that Roman Britain never really recovered. Rome withdrew military support because soldiers were needed to prop up the sinking Empire further south. So, left to look after themselves, they formed into areas which developed later as kingdoms.

Though the garrisons were withdrawn, the Romans never actually left Britain, any more than they left France, because they had long become Roman-Britons – a fusion of all the races that had gone before. However, their civilization collapsed, their organization was broken down and their homes vandalized. They did not escape or die, they simply faded away. We do not know how or when the last family left the deserted cities or where they went. We know only that the last of the forts was the isolated, windswept Fort of Anderida where the mighty forest – now only a remnant as Ashdown Forest, and thirty miles inland – once ran down to meet the swamps. That last Fort fell to the massacring Saxons in AD 491. All that was left of the theatres, the town halls, the forums and roads were the ruins and the plant life they had brought with them, growing – as it still does – amongst the ruins: the poppy, the chervil and, of course, the nettles.

Richborough, or Rutupiae to the Romans, is one of the best preserved of the Saxon Shore forts. The others which are well preserved are Burgh Castle and Pevensey. The remaining walls here are 12 feet thick and up to 24 feet high. This was the key fort on the coast, guarding the chief port of entry to Britain. Watling Street started here and led on to London and up to Chester. (Aerofilms)

The Mists Hide
Britain from Europe

When the Romans arrived in Britain they brought civilization to a peasant people. When the Saxons came they destroyed this Graeco-Roman culture of four hundred years with savage barbarity. A fog settled on the waters of the Channel which effectively hid Britain from Europe for over a hundred years during the 'Dark Ages'. During that time many Celtic refugees escaped from Cornwall into Brittany (Armorica – little Britain) and their peoples clung together protecting a culture which, because of its isolation, had been little affected by the Roman occupation and survives as a strongly individual ethnic group even today.

There was no single invasion, but a series of attacks, landings and finally infiltration over a hundred years until, eventually, the south coast grouped itself into tight, undisciplined regions, racially distinct, ruled by whoever was strongest. The Jutes were in Kent but then sailed on to the Isle of Wight. There was a Celtic-Saxon mix in the West Country which became Wessex – the most powerful of them all. Only the Celts in Cornwall – far-distant, uncoveted Cornwall – remained pure. It was the Breton-Cornish culture that created the greatest of all symbols of British folk heroes, perhaps the only light in those Dark Ages. Whoever he was, and whatever he really did in those dim distant days of struggle against pagan invaders in Britain, Arthur and his Knights of the Round Table became an international symbol of good versus bad and were finally immortalized by Breton romantic writers in the late Middle Ages. The knight in shining armour, the Round Table, the nobility of true love and the romantic concept of chivalry grew from the poetry of men like Chretien de Troyes and the Conte de Graal in the thirteenth century. It was poetry that carried the Celtic story of King Arthur right around the world, even to Japan. If the historic Arthur lived at all, he probably lived in Wales, but the legendary Arthur has so many homes; Camelot is everywhere, especially in Brittany and Cornwall, for the stories were embroidered backwards and forwards across the Channel and it is the people of south-west England and north-west France who have claimed them as their own. Tourists today in search of Arthur and the Holy Grail seek him here, seek him there – and find him everywhere.

In Brittany, the land called 'Armorica' meaning the land facing the sea, Celtic clans were welded into a kingdom by Nominoe after he defeated the Franks in 845. This was the 'first date of real importance in Breton history', claims Joseph Chardronnet 'and one scarcely found in the textbooks of France'. That monarchy lasted sixty short years, was taken over by the Normans and then in 937 Alain Barbe-Torte (Alan Curly-Beard) defeated them and established the independent Duchy of Brittany despite bitter struggles which lasted six hundred long years. Small wonder that many Bretons recall their heyday, before they were annexed by the nation of France in 1532, with such longing, sometimes nostalgic and sometimes violent – independent Brittany remains their dream.

The Breton-Cornish culture also formed the basis of modern Breton Catholicism, for, fleeing from the persecution of marauding tribes, Cornish priests escaped across the sea to Armorica and founded new churches amongst the superstitions of their Celtic cousins, in places which they often named, like the villages of their homeland, with the Celtic Landivisian, Lannion, but spelt with a single 'l'.

This mysticism which flows so strongly in Celtic blood, when fermented with the explosive mysteries of Roman Catholicism, produced in Brittany a powerful, brooding Christianity unlike any other. Even today Breton religion seems as close in spirit to the Druids as to the saints. There are 7847 saints, mostly unrecognized by Rome, and appointed to serve the individual needs of a community. There may indeed be as many in one village as there are parish councillors: a saint to look after wounds or madness or eye trouble or headaches and so on. Their relics – bones, fingers, clothes – are the focus of those macabre Breton ceremonial *pardons*, the elaborate, ritualistic processions with their flaming torches, grotesque statues and passionate pilgrims.

Thomas Adolphus Trollope, the brother of Anthony, described the *Pardon of St Jean du Doigt* when he wrote his *Summer in Brittany* in 1840. Saint John the Baptist's right forefinger had been brought from Normandy to the village ten miles north of Morlaix about 1437, having been taken there from Jerusalem by a Norman girl. There it is today in a box in a gloomy damp church; the line between belief, superstition and opportunism is delicate and who really knows the motivation behind the crowd-pulling and much photographed *pardon*?

> Just outside the moving circle thus formed, and constituting a sort of division between it and the rest of the crowd, were a row of mendicants, whose united appearance was something far more horrible than I have any hope of conveying any idea of to the reader. Let him combine every image that his imagination can conceive of hideous deformity and frightful mutilation; of loathsome filth, and squalid, vermin-breeding corruption; of festering wounds, and leprous, putrifying sores; and let him

suppose all this exposed in the broad light of day, and arranged carefully and skilfully by the wretched creatures whose stock in trade this mass of horror constitutes, so as to produce the utmost possible amount of loathsomeness and sickening disgust; and when he has done this to the extent of his imagination, I feel convinced that he will have but an imperfect idea of what met my eyes at St Jean du Doigt.

The best-known saint who links the two sides of Breton spirituality must be St Samson of Dol. With its vast, austere cathedral, Dol is the medieval gateway to Brittany. Samson was Welsh, born in AD 490, educated at Llantwit under St Illtyd 'a most wise magician who had knowledge of the future'. Illtyd may indeed have been a Druid with a foot in both camps, as he was such a great influence on Samson. Around 520 Samson went to Cornwall where he attempted to adapt local standing stone worship to Christianity and thoroughly upset the Cornishmen. So he crossed the Channel and founded a monastery at Dol, performing all manner of miracles until he died around 570. His world has been described by Gerhard Herm in *The Celts*.

> It was a copy of that known to us from the sagas; monasteries resembled large ring forts and became associated with others in centrally directed federations. Spear-carrying abbotts preferred the Johannes tonsure as well; they did not cut out a circular patch at the back of the head but shaved from ear to ear leaving the hair long at the back, Druid-style.

Everywhere along the coast of Brittany are the calvaries built by families in honour of their dead. Simple crosses or grotesque granite dramatizations of the Passion, they are to be seen on every cliff-top, by every lane and at every crossroads. Some ancient, many more the elaborately carved symbols of nineteenth-century prosperity. Trollope has described them too.

> A farmer's highest ambition is to place an enormous granite crucifix by the roadside with his name and that of his wife cut on the pedestal together with a request to the passengers to pray for the repose of their souls. Frequently the hard and careful savings of many parsimonious years are devoted to this purpose by men who have literally barely food to eat.

And according to Emile Souvestre in *Les Derniers Bretons*.

> Our cross-country roads are paved with saints. There is complete macadamisage of the heads, bodies and limbs of Christian statues.

For the rest of the people living alongside the Channel there was little romance about life in the three hundred years after the Romans left. Except in Cornwall, the Latin language gave way to Anglo-Saxon. Christianity had little part in the routine of daily life. Outside the Church there was no writing, no historic picture of the upheavals, the hopes and fears of men and women, though they must have been much the same as they are today. We know that the Odin-worshipping British King, Ethelbert of Kent, married the Christian Frankish Princess, Bertha. There must have been communications, meetings, emotions between them, but of this there is nothing.

In Gaul the Franks had invaded at about the same time as the Teutonic tribes battered Britain, but although they were extremely fierce, they did not destroy existing communities, and they assimilated Christianity. They left the Gauls with a foundation on which to rebuild civilisation some one hundred years ahead of Britain.

The upheavals that shaped Britain and prepared her for the divisive? mists to lift on a new era took place privately, from within. Neither the rest of Europe, nor history, will ever know the truth about the traumas of that re-birth. They went on throughout the sixth and seventh and even into the eighth centuries.

Saint Augustine came, at the instigation of Pope Gregory and Queen Bertha. He was the first Christian missionary from Rome to sail the Channel. He was an arrogant man and his mission ended in petty squabbling over such trivialities as the correct way for monks to shave their heads: Druid-influenced, Celtic-style, back from the forehead, or as in Rome, with a bald patch on top.

It was a period of feuding between rival local groups who rallied round their strongest member and made him King. Christianity spread very slowly and finally reached that last bastion of savagery – Sussex – in 681, when Wilfrid was preaching in Selsey.

By the middle of the eighth century the British Channel coast was Christian from end to end. In France Charles Martell had already unified Western Europe apart from Brittany and founded a system of government based on good relations with his subjects. He appointed counts in the main cities and laid the foundations of the feudal system which was eventually developed by the Vikings and taken to Britain from Normandy by Duke William.

So the waters of the Channel were clear and ready for the new French and the new Anglo-Saxons to face each other again. By one of those historic accidents two leaders emerged who were simultaneously to lead their countries into a vigorous new age.

In France, Charlemagne – grandson of Charles Martell – revived the title Emperor and created the Holy Roman Empire. In Britain, Offa annexed most of southern Britain and called himself the first King of Britain, *Rex Anglorum*, taking Britain once more into Europe. He and Charlemagne recognized each other's stature – though this did not prevent Offa enjoying the first confrontation with the mainland since the Romans had left. Charlemagne wanted his son to marry one of Offa's daughters – a sign of some respect – but Offa only agreed if his son could marry Charlemagne's daughter – a sign of temerity. They exchanged the first ever diplomatic letters, written for them, of course because, despite their shared interest in the revival of learning, neither could read or write. Charlemagne had a 'capitular' who kept all his chronicles for him. It was a lively and personal correspondence in which gossip-column history begins to emerge alongside more weighty matters, for Charlemagne also complained to Offa about the behaviour of British merchants. So they agreed that there should be some 'trades description' control – and the length of imported tunics be kept consistent.

An interchange of ideas and the sudden burst of creative fervour was carried back and forth across the water. We have no picture of the ships, but for those who sailed in them, explorers of the mind, philosophers, scholars and monks, the Channel was for a very short time a floating university. Alcuin, Charlemagne's recorder came from Wales. Aldhelm from Malmesbury, was a best-selling writer amongst the monasteries of Europe.

It was Charlemagne who prophetically, but subjectively, warned the future Kings of France from his deathbed that the Vikings would be the despair of the world.

The Vikings? The beleaguered coast-dwellers fishing off the Channel beaches had hardly time to draw breath when they caught sight of the very first Dragon Ship slicing through the waves off Portland in the summer of 789. So unsuspecting was the Reeve of Dorchester that he unwisely assumed these were merchants and went down to issue instructions. There on the harbour front they massacred him and his colleagues and the memory of those horrific murders was etched for the first time into the minds of the watching children.

Like most historical upheavals the Vikings did not just happen. There was no single swoop, it was a long, slow and in so many ways, even more agonizing takeover of the Carolingian and Anglo-Saxon worlds than anything that had gone before – all the more terrible to the people for its savage unpredictability.

They came, it seemed, from nowhere, in small numbers on smash and grab raids. They plundered churches and murdered indiscriminately. The Channel was terrorized by their slender longships with their sinister black and yellow shields atop the sides, swiftly flashing oars and merciless marauding crews. They were a restless, well-organized and in many ways intimidatingly legal-minded people. Neither Britain, weakened by an overdose of Christian piety, nor France, in the hands of squabbling nobles, was a match for them.

In such shallow narrow boats the Vikings terrorised and then colonised Britain and France and may have crossed the Atlantic to North America. (J. Allan Cash)

They left their own lands in Denmark and Norway because, amongst other things, the custom of polygamy meant life was overcrowded at home. At first they plundered and vanished again to the north, pushing further and further up the French river estuaries before returning home.

They landed on the long, desolate beaches that edge the rich farmland of Normandy, their drakaars ran up onto the sands which a thousand years later echoed to the huge invasion of allied soldiers in the Second World War. Almost painfully moving are these uncluttered beaches today, stretching endlessly along the Western Cotentin and Calvados. For, like the now treeless Downs in Sussex, there is little to mark the passage of time as you sit on soft sand your back to the beach huts. If your eye follows the seagulls' prints out towards the water's edge the ghosts of Vieul the Viking – or Eisenhower the American – merge. There is nothing to fix their places in history. They are there side by side in memory. And in the nearby hilltop village of St

Marie du Mont the Vikings live on – as they do in Appledore in Kent where Alfred fought them in the first sea battle. For even today there is a LeDanois and a Monsieur Ingouf – carrying forward the names their ancestors brought from the far north. Vieul became founder of the Norman family of Les Epaules, who, from St Marie were to play such an important role in Normandy for seven hundred years.

To some extent it is possible that the monks exaggerated tales of the ensuing horrors because it was they who suffered most. Imagine the nightmare of the nuns at Fécamp who, the story says, anticipating the worst, mutilated themselves rather than be ravaged by the Vikings.

There was a fair amount of local collaboration everywhere with the enemy. Even King Alfred's nephew became a King of the Danes, and it is certainly true that the Vikings were opportunists. Where it suited them they turned Christian.

Then in 851 they stayed over for the first time in Britain, wintering in Thanet, and gradually year after year the stays grew longer. All the time there was resistance but it was not until Alfred became King at the age of twenty-four when his brother Ethelred died in 871 that any effective resistance was mounted.

Not for nothing has Alfred been named 'Great' by history, for during his reign he consolidated all that was best in Britain. As King of the now powerful Wessex, which included most of the Channel coast, not only did he check the Danes, but he devised a way of allowing them to stay by creating a part of Britain, outside Wessex, in which they were allowed to live, known as Danelaws. Here the warrior turned farmer and merged with the agricultural Anglo-Saxons. It was a fusion of characteristics which laid the foundations of solid, vigorous indi-viduality and devotion to the land which has marked the English ever since.

The calm was shortlived for a new Danish leader, Guthrum, decided he must subjugate Wessex and launched a series of vicious inland attacks on Alfred from all sides. This was the period when Alfred, in hiding in the forest of Athelney, burnt the cakes. But eventually after many bloody battles, Alfred's men subdued the Viking Guthrum. In return for his agreeing to baptism, Alfred, with amazing magnanimity, once again allowed the Danes to settle and live in friendship side by side.

He was a remarkably civilized man. His, too, was the first vision of the need for sea power. He revitalized the design of his ships hoping that with fewer, better, boats he could command the seas. His new fleet had boats with at least sixty oars which were swifter and much more stable than their predecessors. But the sailors were not skilled enough to sail them. He set out a *Book of Laws* which blended the laws of Kent, Wessex and Mercia and which formed the basis for the legal system which William the Conqueror undertook to respect after the Norman invasion and upon which our Common Law was founded. He also encouraged the great *Anglo-Saxon Chronicle*, the first ver-nacular history in Europe.

When he died in 899 Alfred left the Channel still in turmoil but underpinned by a system of stable government and humane religious tolerance.

All was far from well in France where the degenerate descendants of Charlemagne, with such nicknames as 'the Stammerer', 'the Simple', 'the Pious' and 'the Fat' were ranged against 'Ironsides', 'Longsword' and 'the Teeth'. It was an unequal match. The Vikings had plundered far into Europe, plague was affecting them and they needed a new outlet – so they turned towards Britain.

Then in 911 the elderly, ailing Viking chief Rollo was defeated by Charles the Simple – much like Guthrum thirty years before – and agreed, at the Treaty of St Clair Sur Epte to become Christian and marry Charles's daughter in return for a tract of land in what is now Normandy. The area was not clearly defined and over the next twenty years the new 'Normans' extended their hold little by little, establishing strong danelaw on the other side of the Channel. But there was a difference. For the first time, the existence of that strip of water was to draw a line which marked the emergence of two distinctly different personalities – rooted on the same stock. The Anglo-Saxon Vikings became islanders, prospering but not rich, whilst the French Vikings, surrounded by the great upheavals of mainland Europe, were forced to develop an aggressive military system. Even while these changes were happening, through the hundred and fifty years up to the Conquest, the villagers who lived on the tenth- to eleventh-century Channel coast were certainly more aware of their counterparts thirty miles on the other side than they were of events a hundred miles inland behind their backs. Earls and dukes and kings were shadowy figures about whom little was known.

Coastal villages were incredibly isolated with wild tracts of untamed forest, marsh and moorland between them. The dangers were not so much of robbers or thugs, but of boar and wolves, and very few people ever travelled beyond the fence that surrounded their settlement. It was easier to cross the sea. This they did to carry merchandise to the little harbours of the Seine estuary. Long ships were replaced by round ships, a bluff, bowed vessel which was much more seaworthy. Fighting platforms or castles were added at either end.

In Britain, because there was no initial language barrier, the invading Danes had never felt foreign as they did in France. The Danelaw territories fixed by Alfred were largely in the Midlands and the North and merged anyway with the local indigenous communities, so that through the golden years of Alfred, Edward, Athelstan, Edmund and Ethelred, the Channel coast was largely Anglo-Saxon. England was ruled by one King based in Wessex and divided into earldoms with a social ladder of land tenure stepping down from thanes, to villeins, to cottars, to serfs. None of these, except the King, could claim absolute ownership of the land, and each was responsible to those above and below him; the countryside was organized into 'hundreds' of one hundred families.

In 958 Edgar formed a fleet of five thousand vessels by calling on every three hundreds along the coast to provide one ship and the crew to man it. The Channel share of that fleet was about twelve hundred ships, and Edgar himself went with them every year on manoeuvres. Democracy was emerging. Under this system the Danes and the Anglo-Saxons worked together to reorganize and revitalize the political, religious and cultural life of Britain. The countryside was undefended and there was no effective army.

In Normandy the invaders remained apart in a tiny one hundred and fifty-mile ghetto surrounded on all other sides by hostile warring countries – Brittany, Burgundy, Anjou and Flanders – with long indefensible boundaries. So although the people who farmed the countries still looked and felt much like their English counterparts, their overlords were more aggressive – they had to be for survival. They built castles and huge walled, fortified manor houses to withstand a siege. Moreover, the Channel protected England for many years from the disastrous effects of a new craze which swept across Europe – chivalry.

The twentieth-century, rose-tinted picture of chivalry is of the movement as it became, but at the beginning it was really an excuse for the illiterate young sons of noblemen to lord it over everyone and to ride around the countryside provoking trouble. Had they lived today we might have thought them degenerate hippies. At the age of seven a boy had to choose between being a churchman or a 'chevalier'. The chevaliers then went through a system of training – pages, squires, knights – and knew nothing but horsemanship, fighting and sex. Their existence marked a sharp dividing line between classes and it meant that instead of democracy, autocracy was emerging.

But despite – or perhaps because of – all this turbulent bloodshed, the Norman counts became the most powerful in Europe, and Normandy the richest state in a rich soil. This was the great age of cathedral building and the foundation of the great Channel families whose trees were soon to take root on both sides of the water. We hear now of the first use of family names.

1066 and all that

The story of the sixty years before the restless, energetic Normans looked north towards Britain for fresh lands to annexe unfolds like the telling of a television soap opera. For the invasion of England by William of Normandy in 1066 was just one episode in a complex quarrel during which the English Channel became like a private lake linking members of one family. This family was symbolized around the turn of the century by the powerful figure of Emma, sister of the Duke of Normandy.

Emma? Who was she? Perhaps Anglo-Norman history begins with her. So long forgotten, probably because we know so little about her appearance or personality. Yet she holds a key position in the intensifying drama of Anglo-French relationships. Emma achieved the unique status of having two husbands – first the unready Ethelred, then Canute, and two sons, Hardicanute and Edward the Confessor – who each became Kings of England. As great-aunt of the future William, Duke of Normandy, her role, if unwittingly, was to sow seeds for the eventual Norman claim to the British throne.

It was Emma, in fact, who began the infiltration of Normans into English life by appointing Normans at court and giving church lands to Norman bishops, such as that of Fécamp to Brede. She also seems to have organized the first bizarre exchange of Holy Relics, she certainly encouraged ecclesiastical twinning, and places such as the Mont St Michel and St Michael's Mount became a centre of Anglo-Norman exchange.

It has to be said that seen from afar St Michael's Mount in Cornwall is a curiosity. The Mont St Michel on the Normandy/Brittany border is a miracle. If your taste is for pure poetry, to recall Herman Hesse, the 'wild strains of fermenting nature', wonder at it from a distance lying amongst the sheep and golden buttercups outside Avranches and read its history later in the library.

The statue of St Michael, sword in hand, atop his granite rock rises fifty-two feet above the rosy mists over the vast Bay of Avranches, floating above the limitless quicksands and mirrored on the flood tide by a hundred rivulets sweeping their way across the flats, relentlessly

seeking victims who foolishly wander unguided from the causeway. At
high water the waves crash around its base. Stranded miles out on the
marsh, at low water it dramatically dominates every twist of the coast
road with its unexpected size and ethereal isolation.

Geologically the twin rocks share the same origins in a time some
350 million years ago. Only a few thousand years ago they were
outcrops in a great forest now beneath the sands. Historically, too,
they are related, for when William I came to Britain the Count of
Mortain in Normandy carried the banner of St Michael in the
invading army. Soon after the Conquest he made a grant of the Mount

*One of the titles of the abbey on
Mt St Michel is* la Merveille.
*The whole island is a marvel
as it rises from sea or sand.*
(Topham)

45

to the Benedictine Abbey of the Mont St Michel, with 'half a hide of land and a market on Thursdays'.

There is a Charter which may well have been forged by Norman monks at the time of the Conquest to back their cause and which states that St Michael's Mount had been granted to the French Abbey long ago by Edward the Confessor, who was so devoted to the land which had nurtured him as a child, and impressed by the symbolic similarity of these Channel sentinels.

By the time that a Priory was built on the Mount by Abbot Bernard of Le Bec, in 1135, the Mont St Michel was already a great centre of learning known as the City of Books. A sanctuary had been built on the rock as early as 708 after St Michael appeared in a vision, but it was Richard I, Duke of Normandy, who in 966 began a building programme that was to continue for five hundred years. At that time a busy town was already clambering up the base of the rock and then, in the twelfth century, the fourth Abbot, Hildebert, enlarged the summit of the Mount by constructing a vast series of crypts to provide a platform upon which a great Romanesque Abbey was built. From then on the story of the Abbey is one of war, destruction and rebuilding; it became at different times a prison, fortress and a place of pilgrimage.

There is a brutally commercial brashness about the overcrowded, narrow shopping streets of the Mont. But in the Middle Ages tradesmen sold holy medals and bulbs filled with sand from the Bay, much as they do with Alum Sands in the Isle of Wight today. The bawdy cockle-fishing residents fleeced pilgrims, much as pilgrims or tourists have been fleeced since time immemorial.

St Michael's Mount never achieved this magnificence or decadence. It was always a cell of its French Abbey though it had been important as a small trading port since it was safe haven for merchantmen anxious to avoid the dangers of Lands End. Diodorus, the Greek historian, has described the streaming of tin and how it was carried over to St Michael's Mount for export:

> They prepare the tin, working very carefully in the earth in which it is produced. The ground is rocky but it contains earthy veins, the produce of which is ground down, smelted and purified. They beat the metal into masses shaped like astralgi [knuckle bones] and carry it off to a certain island called 'Ictis' ... here then the merchants buy the tin from the natives and carry it over to Gaul. . . .

Probably St Michael's best-known legend is that which says that the Mount was built by a giant called Cormoran who waded ashore raiding villages and was finally destroyed by a Cornish boy who became known as Jack the Giant Killer. The pit in which Jack trapped Cormoran is there still, half-way up the hill.

Around the year 980 in England Viking raids had begun all over again – this time along the Channel. King Ethelred was more inclined towards 'back handers' than his great-great-grandfather Alfred had been, and time after time he bought the invaders off – to the point that he nearly ruined the country. He massacred the Danes living here, killed King Sweyn Forkbeard's sister which provoked a furious revenge attack on the Kent coast. Forkbeard then sailed on across the Channel and sold his loot in the Normandy markets. There was much bitterness at the way in which the Normans sided with the Danes, bought their booty and sheltered their armies. The Cotentin in particular, which was later to become the heartland of so much Anglo-French animosity, was a safe harbour for their ships.

In 1013 Sweyn Forkbeard with his son Canute attacked England, took over the north and was proclaimed King. So Ethelred fled over the sea and married the Duke of Normandy's sister, Emma, perhaps wishfully thinking that the union would give the ambivalent Normans a sense of responsibility to Britain. Far from it.

Ethelred took his new bride back to Britain and made a desperate attempt to save his impoverished country, but even while he was alive, Canute was declared his successor by the spiritual leaders of the land at Southampton.

In 1674 William Camden retold a story that had first been described in 1364 and for which there is no contemporary record, but for which Canute is best known.

> King Canutus, commonly called Knute, walking on the sea sands near to Southampton, was extolled by some of his flattering followers and told he was the King of Kings, the mightiest that ever reigned far and near; that both land and sea were at his command. But this speech did put the godly King in mind of the infinite power of God by whom Kings have and enjoy their power, and thereupon he made this demonstration to repel their flattery. He took off his cloack and wrapping round together sate down upon it near to the sea that then began to flow, saying 'See I command thee that thou touch not my feet', but he had not so soon spoken the word but the surging waves dashed him. He then, rising up and going back said 'Ye see now My Lords what good cause you have to call me a King that am not able by my commandment to stay one wave. No mortal man doubtless is worthy of such an high name, no man hath such command but one King which ruleth all.

Whether it was opportunism on the part of the handsome young warrior Canute or his love for the now aging Emma that brought them together, within a very short time he married her and so blocked any claim the Normans might have dreamed up on behalf of her children by Ethelred – one of whom was Edward, later to be called the Confessor.

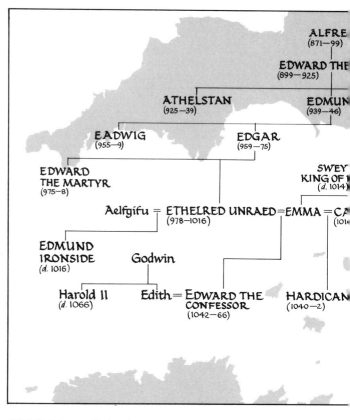

ALFRE
(871—99)

EDWARD THE
(899—925)

ATHELSTAN
(925—39)

EDMUN
(939—46)

EADWIG
(955—9)

EDGAR
(959—75)

EDWARD
THE MARTYR
(975—8)

SWEY
KING OF
(*d.* 1014)

Aelfgifu = ETHELRED UNRAED=EMMA = CA
(978—1016)   (101«

EDMUND
IRONSIDE   Godwin
(*d.* 1016)

Harold II   Edith = EDWARD THE   HARDICAN
(*d.* 1066)   CONFESSOR   (1040—2)
                         (1042—66)

This little boy, exiled and abandoned at the age of ten, for the sake of his mother's ambition, grew up a Norman in a Norman court. William of Malmesbury says of Emma: 'She had long mocked the needy condition of her son and never aided him, transferring the hereditary hatred of the father to the child'. His entire personality was shaped and warped by his mother's loss, his father's death and his need for affection. It is most likely he was homosexual. He never forgave his mother and though he finally married at the age of forty the marriage was loveless and childless – and so heirless. Not surprisingly he turned to excessive piety to cover his lack of manhood. A shy podgy albino, given to fits of petulant temper, it was perhaps a good thing that behind his throne loomed the ever-strengthening figure of Godwin, Earl of Wessex. Godwin was probably the son of a notorious British Channel pirate.

When Canute died and his disastrous sons Harold and Hardicanute followed him in very brief succession, Earl Godwin wisely revived the sleeping English veneration for the descendants of Alfred the Great, founder of the oldest ruling house in Europe. The obvious heir to that great line he said was the French speaking albino son of Emma and Ethelred.

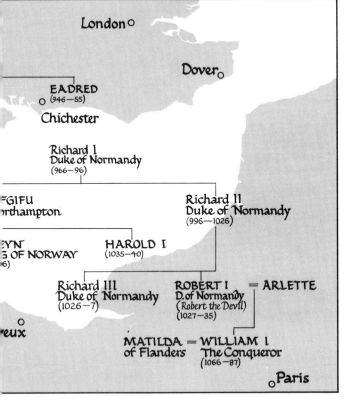

On Edward's coronation in 1042 the blood of the Vikings was united with the Anglo-Saxon royal house, Edward brought with him his childhood preference for France over Britain. The popular Godwin, the *éminence grise*, with son Harold at his side, parcelled out the land to his friends and relations. His six sons became Earls, his daughter Edith married the King and he was to all intents and purposes the ruler of the land.

The Godwins were everywhere. It was Harold, his second son, who became his heir, though not of blood royal acceptable to the British. Harold grew up at about the same time as another little boy in Normandy called William. Women still gather today at the public fountain in Falaise where Arlette, the leather tanner's daughter, caught the eye of Robert the Devil. Whilst Harold was learning to swim and hunt and fish in the ancient little port of Bosham (Boseham) in Chichester harbour, William was growing up in an atmosphere of violence and murder amongst the rival Norman Dukes. He was surrounded by bloodthirsty barons such as Roger de Toeni – who cut up and cooked Saracens – and Guillaume Talva, who strangled his wife and killed his tutor by blinding, emasculating and disembowelling.

The church where the child Harold worshipped is there, today, overlooking the creeks in which he paddled, and where one of Canute's little girls was drowned and buried in 1065 in the Church of the Holy Trinity – the oldest site of Christianity in Sussex. Her bones were discovered in 1865.

Bosham, which, today, is being left high and dry, as the sea retreats from its earlier shoreline at Fishbourne has the slurpy quality at low tide that those hunter-fishermen may have known in the long ago days when they walked across from France. Tufty grass, waterfowl and greenish mud flats surrounded by a picturesque ring of wood-clad cottages and inns, a millhouse and quaintly named Raptackle Barn now cluster round the former centre of the busy mediaeval port of Chichester.

Bosham has been left behind by the sea, and by history, a quiet little backwater beloved by artists, and all those who would let the world go by unnoticed. (J. Allan Cash)

So when Edward became King in 1042 Harold and William were aged about fifteen, young men heading unsuspectingly for the most famous confrontation in history.

Edward hated England. He spoke only French and his sole comfort was to surround himself with foreigners at court. Anyone was welcome – Normans, Bretons, French and Germans. William of Malmesbury wrote at the time: 'the English wore short garments reaching to mid-knee, they had their hair cropped, beards shaven, arms laden with golden bracelets their skins decorated with punctured designs [tattoos!]. They were accustomed to eat until they surfeited and drink till they were sick. These latter qualities they imparted to their Conquerors.' *Plus ça change?* It is places, not people, who are altered by the passing of a thousand years.

Despite all this, Edward was reputed, even as a child, to have healing powers which is presumably how he became a saint, in fact Patron Saint, until he was supplanted by George in 1416.

There is nowhere along the French coast that rings with such historical virility; nowhere more easy to pass by than that drowned remnant of Earl Godwin's estates – the Goodwin Sands, which were formed, they say, one day in 1097 when storms swept the south coast.

On a sunny day when the sea was calm and the tide was low on the Goodwins a group of daredevils in white have been known to cock-a-snook at providence and play cricket on the world's largest graveyard. Fifty thousand lives and at least £2100m of shipping had their end recorded on the Goodwins and there must have been many more than that. Here, off the bull-nosed, blunt end of Britain lies the most greedy, sinister man-eating monster of the Channel. No Loch Ness legend this, although the Goodwins are almost as elusive, the reality of the 27,000 acre sandbank has dramatically dominated life for the people who have grown up with the cries of a million ghosts ringing in their ears. Paradoxically, the existence of the Goodwins created the calm haven of the Downs. The men and women of Deal learned from the earliest times how to profit in times of calm by provisioning the waiting merchantmen from the shore, in times of storm they were there with a kind of blind courage ready to hurl their massive three-masted luggers into boiling water to save threatened ships in trouble in those merciless seas.

By the evidence of this Victorian line drawing of a well-prepared party of flannelled fools, the tradition of playing cricket on the Goodwin Sands is almost as old as cricket itself. (BBC Hulton)

This is the period in which the Bayeux Tapestry – the *Telle du Conquêt* – stretches the Channel with the two contenders in a symbolic tug of war standing on either shore. The tapestry was probably made in Britain on the orders of the hated Bishop Odo of Bayeux by a team of Anglo-Norman seamstresses, who never finished the job, for the *raison d'être* behind the entire heroic episode – William's coronation – is not shown. Perhaps this admission of defeat was too much to bear. The story unfolds in 231 feet of softly muted colours and is one of those rare tourist attractions indescribably the better for seeing. In the darkened cool of the lovely museum at Bayeux it rolls on and on and on, a cartoon strip of twelve years in the history of the Channel which finally brought together the Norman Vikings under William and the English Vikings under Harold.

The tapestry is alive with the sounds and smells of time. You can feel the water lapping on Harold's bare legs as he takes his dog aboard the boat at Bosham in 1064 for the trip that ended in shipwreck on the French coast and his first meeting with William. You can hear laughter and merrymaking in William's castle; for the two young men, so very different in temperament, liked each other well and Harold got on with William's wife. Harold even went with William to Brittany to help subdue Breton rebels.

For centuries after it was made, the tapestry lay unnoticed although it was displayed annually in Bayeux for the feast of the relics of St John. During the French Revolution there was a danger of its being turned into wagon covers. But in 1803 it was finally exhibited for the public in Paris and Napoleon, maybe seeking inspiration for his own invasion dreams, went along to admire it. He might well have enjoyed the contemporary exhibition at Bayeux.

Made for the Longest Day in 1066 the Bayeux Tapestry was, until 1973, the longest tapestry in the world. But in 1973 a team of seamstresses from the Royal College of Needlework in London completed the embroidered story of the other cross Channel invasion – D-Day or Operation Overlord. The Overlord Tapestry which was conceived by Lord Dulverton and designed by Sandra Lawrence is now housed in Portsmouth. It is 272 feet long, covering the years between 1940–44 in every graphic detail. There is a dreadful irony – an underlying sense of hidden satisfaction which is usually (perhaps rightly) unnoticed in the story, but which for the analysts of national psychology is unmistakenly summed up in a superlatively smug plaque at the British and Commonwealth Memorial for Bayeux, *Nos a Gulielmo Victi, Victoris Patriam Liberavimus*. One only hopes the people of Bayeux are a little rusty in their Latin, for the translation reads; 'We whom William conquered have freed the country of the Conqueror.'

There are dozens of different interpretations of what happened during Harold's stay with William. Historians are not sure whether Edward himself had promised the succession to his friend William when he was on a quick trip to England some years before or whether it was, in fact, Harold who in a fit of comradeship, reached an agreement whilst in France. If, as the tapestry says, he swore an oath to give William the throne with himself as vice-king he was probably not aware that the oath was sworn, by William's trickery, over some holy relics – a much more serious affair. Whatever the truth there is no doubt that when Harold set off for home William was sure that England was in the bag.

This is why, when he heard the news in 1065 that Harold had taken the throne, he was thrown into utter despair. He paced around tying knots in his tunic, was seen sitting with his cloak over his head against the cathedral arch and was, for a short time, completely overcome by the assumed treachery of the man he thought was his friend. Even then he tried to stay on good terms. He sent messages and even asked Harold to marry his daughter.

Never before had the Channel – its tides and its currents – played such an important role, nor the weather mattered so much to the peace-loving farmers and fishermen of the coast who suddenly found themselves caught up in an explosion of activity.

In France, William launched the most audacious, foolhardy, magnificent campaign ever conceived. He called it 'The English Adventure'. He would launch an attack on Britain – taking an equestrian army of some ten thousand men across the Channel. No one had ever attempted to transport so many men at one time, certainly not with horses. We see them peeping over the sides of the boats in the Bayeux Tapestry. To achieve his ends he had to rally support from all over the land, not just from Normandy, and he managed to convince them that this was not only a crusade to claim his throne, but also to reform the ailing English church.

He ordered a fleet to be ready within six months. This was not an easy task, for the Normans were not great seamen or shipbuilders and William himself had hardly ever been to sea. But they did it.

Imagine the overtime; the hammering, the swearing along the beaches that long hot summer. About three hundred and fifty ships were built, exact copies of the old longships but larger and designed for sail, to carry ten thousand men and three thousand horses.

At the beginning of August that year the last of the ships was complete and the fleet was assembling at the mouth of the River Dives. But then, as now, the Normandy coastline was impossibly difficult to navigate with huge forty-foot tides, a five-knot current and no safe harbours. Even small ships could only sail out and in on the ebb and flood or be grounded on the vast treacherous beaches.

The Duke's chaplain, William of Poitiers, described the scene as the fleet was stuck waiting for the wind to change.

> The Duke made generous provision for his own troops and those from foreign parts. Such was his moderation and prudence that he utterly forbade pillage and provided for fifty thousand soldiers at his own expense. The flocks and herds of the peasantry pastured unharmed through the province. The crops waited undisturbed by the sickle, without being trampled by the

pride of knights or ravaged by the greed of the plunderers. A weak unarmed man watching the swarm of soldiers without fear, might follow his horse singing where he would.

Meanwhile, back in England, news had spread along the south coast that trouble was afoot over the water. Most of the English army had to be made up of volunteers, the fyrd, called up for military service. Most of them were land workers who had never set foot on a battle field. The navy, too, was less than effective, relying almost entirely on the trading ships of the Cinque Ports. When Edward was King he had granted tax concessions to Romney, Hythe, Deal, Sandwich and Rye in return for fourteen days military service a year. They were cargo ships, quite unfitted for war, but at the beginning of 1066 they were ready and waiting. Even so, the battle that was to change the shape of British history remained a local affair with inland villages hardly aware of what was happening.

Then suddenly on the night of the Tuesday after Easter something happened which brought terror to every village in the country. Halley's Comet – as we now know it was – sped its hairy trail through the sky as a dreadful portent of tragedy ahead.

Whose was the tragedy? England for being invaded or France for the revenge blood that was to be spilt on her soil in the next three hundred years? The immediate problem was not William. It was Harold's foolhardy brother, Tostig, with a fleet of ships off the Isle of Wight. Tostig once a popular young man had been exiled and had turned schizoid. His pathetic invasion attempt ended in a forlorn drift along the south coast, blown by the southerly wind and watched with bewilderment by the fyrd who were waiting on the cliffs, as he was pushed from one harbour to the next. Eventually, he was left with only twelve little ships blown onward and then northward round the coast until he landed in Scotland. All this time preparations continued.

There was no question of trying to fight at sea. With fixed square sails, the ships were not able to manoeuvre against the wind and it would have been impossible for them to navigate within miles of each other. Harold's navy was used to ferry soldiers along the coast to assembly points – since the inland tracks and coastal paths were impassable. This is why he chose the Isle of Wight as his base. It was at the Western end of the only part of the coast where William might land, and it gave Harold a fair chance of sweeping his men along the shore with the wind in advance of the oncoming invasion.

But all that summer along the cliff tops boredom set in. Apart from the diversion of the comet and Tostig's folly there was not much to do and the men were getting restless. They were not even sure they believed the invasion threats. Harold himself enjoyed some of the summer in the old haunts of his childhood at Bosham, with his own small sons. The wind stayed northerly and they all knew that William could not sail against a northerly wind.

The men of the fyrd, separated from their families, must have behaved much like soldiers billeted anywhere. No doubt their presence brought some light relief to the inhabitants. Everywhere meals were cooked on the beaches, every day the sun shone, every day they sat and talked of tactics and weapons and old battles, and peered out across the Channel millpond. It was a fool's paradise, for over on the other side of Europe the sorry Tostig had turned up again, rallied the King of Norway to his side and prepared to invade England from the North. Harold had been caught napping.

Suddenly everything began to happen at once. The men of the fyrd ran out of food and on 8th September were allowed to go home. Four days later, after a record month of quite extraordinary, unchanging weather, the wind switched. The summer was nearly over and Norman tension was mounting, for they knew that soon they would have to give the entire project up and face humiliation.

At high water the Conqueror's navy set sail for Britain and within twenty-four hours the treacherous Channel played them another trick – the wind changed to a westerly and whipped up into a gale. The fleet was completely disorientated; there were no charts or compasses, no coastal lights along the harbourless shoreline that runs up the bleak, empty coast to St Valéry. Many were wrecked, others took shelter in St Valéry and with the storm summer ended. All, it seemed, was lost.

The same storm broke up Harold's navy on the Isle of Wight and then the remainder decided the invasion season was over, so it was safe to go home – and home they went to the Cinque Ports.

Harold went up to London where he heard that King Harald Hardrada had landed in Northumbria – and he set off to stop the real invasion, rather than wait for one he thought now would never come. But William could not face defeat without a fight. He prayed for help over the bones of St Edmund at St Valéry – and help came.

The Conquest is finally under way. William's ship, the Mora, leads the fleet with a light at the masthead and a carving of William's son Robert on the sternpost. This was the first-ever invasion fleet which carried its own transport. As well as thousands of men the ships were packed with horses; specially bred and trained chargers for William's knights. (Topham)

At the Battle of Stamford Bridge, Yorkshire, on 25th September, Harold defeated Harald. The wind changed again on 26th September and on 27th September William's navy followed the lights on his own ship *Mora* out of the harbour of St Valéry on the twelve-hour crossing to England.

The harbours which were then accessible have long since been swallowed up by silt and are now the inland villages of Pevensey, Bulverhythe, Rye and Romney. William knew nothing of the coast beyond what he had learned from the monks of Fécamp – when Edward was King he had given parts of the coastline from Hastings to Winchelsea to the Abbey of Fécamp and William certainly discussed his plans with the Abbot . So he decided on Hastings – or rather the little port of Bulverhythe – as a landing place. But how to get there was more difficult. It was really a case of trial and error. Bulverhythe today is a desolate shingle beach, edged with bijou beach huts and a lone timber café; hardly a draw for crowds in nearby Hastings. The port has long since disappeared in the perpetual pebble drift.

How their hearts must have sunk in the morning when the sun rose and the men on the *Mora* saw no white cliffs, no land at all and not another ship in sight. Morale must have plummetted and it is a real credit to William that he rallied his men, ate a good meal and whiled away the nail-biting hours whilst the pilots peered anxiously out across the sea. Eventually the rest of the fleet caught up; the relief must have been indescribable. Within hours they were sailing into Pevensey watched from the shore by hundreds of helpless civilians. There was nothing they could do, and the invading army, without a battle to fight, went on the rampage for food. It is all there on the tapestry – the exuberant, probably over-excited, feasting, presided over by the infamous Bishop Odo. It was so festive, in fact, that William, it is said, put his tunic on back to front! There were five times as many soldiers as there were local folk and in no time food became short. There was no news of Harold and after the first flush of success must have come a sense of anti-climax.

But Harold was already returning. He made that amazing two hundred and fifty mile journey from Stamford Bridge to London in about eight days. On Friday 13th October, Harold met his men at an ancient apple tree outside Battle – 8 miles from Hastings. On 14th October battle began.

The story of that battle has been told so many times, though the tales have to be based on contemporary French accounts for the British seem to have been so crushed by events that no one bothered to record their interpretation of what happened. It is strange that the battle – the sounds of which must have echoed through history – must have been a very quiet affair, just the sound of clashing steel and the cries of the soldiers. No cannon or guns. It would hardly have been heard a few miles away. But within the next twenty years several thousand Normans and French men moved in to take up the lands William had given to them, whilst many thousand Englishmen were jailed or killed. The effect on the countryside was completely devastating.

William did not like England, he never learned the language and the English, in turn, bitterly resented what he did to their land. For in place of the Thanes, who understood the people and had cared for their serfs, came Norman-speaking rulers to lord it over the villagers.

Worst of all, and an affront to the peaceable English, the Normans built their hated castles. Those beautiful expensive rounded stone fortresses that epitomize story-book romance, Arundel, Dover, Pevensey, were resented by people who were now so short of food they saw them only as an overbearing means of suppression, a place of punishment if they did not toe the line. But the Normans were here to stay, and as they had done so many times before, the people of the south made the best of it. Eventually the intruders were absorbed, much like the Saxons and the Danes, to become Englishmen, simply adding another ingredient to the cake.

It was a long struggle however. All along the south coast the bloodshed was terrible, William was ruthless in his conquest. In fact when he died and William Rufus his son succeeded him, he was amazed by the extraordinary amount of plundered treasure which his father had stockpiled at Winchester.

Long-term, of course, we can see that William's victory turned the face of Britain forever towards mainstream Europe – rather than to the outer edges of the northern continent. But it made very little difference to either French or English attitudes to the sea, or the development of shipping. The Channel was still merely an obstacle to be crossed, a tool. The sea didn't stir the hearts of men.

We can appreciate the order and new life that was injected. On one level there was the Domesday Book which imposed French feudal law and order on our society. On the more simple day-to-day level, diet became more varied. To the English mutton, chicken and fish, the foreigners added their favourite delicate meats, veal, lamb and game. They introduced cider-making too in Kent, as a change from the gale brew which the locals made from the bog myrtle plant (also used for mead). Traditionally claimed for the West Country, it is more likely that cider apple orchards were first tended in Brittany by Celts – the knowledge passed to Normandy and to Britain via Kent and Sussex.

Whilst the Norman knights were living it up over the water in the early days, their wives and families were left to keep the home fires burning. They could see no reason why their men did not come home, and they made a great deal of fuss.

Orderic Vital, the monk, was obviously aware of the problem. He wrote 'some of the Norman ladies were becoming extremely frustrated'.

The Conquest,
and the Loss of Normandy

So there William was – King of one country but only a Duke in a province of his own native land. The trouble this caused within his family was to turn the tide of events on their head; for England, having been conquered and made immensely powerful by the Normans, became the aggressor.

William had nine or ten children, four of them important. Robert, the eldest (nicknamed Curthose because of his short legs!), was made Duke of Normandy, whilst William (Rufus) was allotted the throne of England. Robert and William never saw eye to eye and had even had a duel in France. This immediately meant that half the Norman Barons in England, who hated the disagreeable William Rufus, were set on causing trouble. The problem was not helped when Robert pawned Normandy to him in 1096 in return for 10,000 marks to finance one of the first Crusades to the Holy Land. Robert was away when William Rufus died in 1100, so yet another brother, the learned but cruel Henry Beauclerk, stepped in and whisked the crown from under his nose. He was a clever man who ruled for over thirty years. For most of the people these were peaceful times. Robert and Henry sailed back and forth over the Channel squabbling and fighting. Their feud was aggravated by Henry's decision to consolidate his Englishness by marrying Matilda, the niece of the last Saxon claimant to the throne, and finally ended in the pastoral countryside of Tinchebrai near Avranches in 1106. Robert was kept prisoner for twenty-eight years and control of both realms passed to London.

Henry's only legitimate son William, a young man of seventeen, was drowned when his ship was capsized off the coast of Normandy. William of Malmesbury in his *Gesta Regum Anglorum* has described the tragedy of the White Ship:

> On 25th November the king gave orders for his return to England, and set sail from Barfleur just before twilight on the evening of that day. But the young man who was just over seventeen and himself a king in all but name, commanded that another vessel should be prepared for himself, and almost all the young nobility, being his boon companions, gathered round him. The sailors, too, who had drunk overmuch, cried out with true seamen's hilarity that they must overtake the ship that had already set out since their own ship was of the best construction

and newly equipped. Wherefore these rash youths, who were flown with wine, launched their vessel from the shore although it was now dark. She flew swifter than an arrow, sweeping the rippling surface of the deep, but the carelessness of her drunken crew drove her on to a rock which rose above the waves not far from the shore. All in consternation rushed on deck and with loud cries got ready their boat-hooks in an endeavour to force the vessel off, but fate was against them and brought to naught their efforts. The oars, too, lashing ineffectively, crashed against the rock, and the battered prow remained fixed. Then the waves washed some of the crew overboard and the water entering the vessel through chinks in its side drowned others. A boat was, however, at last launched and the young prince was taken into it. He might easily have reached the shore in safety had not his bastard sister, the countess of Perche, now struggling with death in the larger vessel, implored his assistance. She cried out that her brother should not abandon her so heartlessly. Whereupon, touched with pity, he ordered his boat to return to the ship that he might rescue his sister, and it was thus that the unhappy youth met his death; for the boat overcharged by the multitude that leapt into her capsized and sank and buried all indiscriminately in the deep. One rustic alone, floating all night upon a mast, survived until the morning to describe the dismal catastrophe. No ship ever brought so much misery to England; none was ever so notorious in the history of the world.

The treacherous waters off the coast of Normandy claim a royal victim, among many other victims, as William, son of Henry I, is drowned while trying to save his sister after their ship was wrecked on rocks outside Barfleur. (BBC Hulton)

Henry's daughter Matilda (or Maud), the direct-line grand-daughter of William the Conqueror, was living in France, married to Geoffrey of Anjou. She should have become Queen – Henry had tried to comfort himself and make her Regent on the death of Prince William – but instead Stephen, son of the Conqueror's daughter Adela, won favour with the barons over a woman, and when Henry died of lamprey poisoning in 1135 Stephen became King.

Matilda would not give up. She sailed over to England and, a formidably proud, turbulent princess, she instigated numerous battles until eventually she fled to France in the dead of winter camouflaged in white. But she won a dynastic victory for her son, Henry of Anjou. He was acceptable and when Stephen died in 1154 with no heirs, Henry (who had with great presence of mind, in the meantime, stolen Louis VII, King of France's wife, Eleanor of Aquitaine) became King Henry II of England and the Channel became a mere river running through land united from the north of England to the Pyrenees.

Churchill has called this time one of 'growth amid turmoil'. These were the people who, for a hundred years after the Conquest, dominated England, Normandy and gradually the European scene. On the whole the ordinary folk were quiet, subdued and busy about their humdrum lives. Farming didn't change much, saltpans sprang up all along the coast. The iron workings in Sussex stripped Ashdown Forest of its trees and earned the name of 'The Black Country'. Boats were busy carrying creamy-coloured, cathedral building stone from Caen to various parts of the country for this was the great age of construction – what the Benedictine monk Raoul Glabert called *une robe blanche d'églises*. Coutances, Winchester, Canterbury, Bayeux, Battle all belong to this period. Southampton became the centre for cross-Channel traffic of all kinds – though there were still no major ports further west.

It is hard to imagine the confusion caused by such fundamental difficulties as who spoke what to whom. Gradually Norman French took over; names like William, Robert and John replaced Bugge or Ragge or the norse Sweyn or Harold; the English vernacular and its literature died out. But there arose at the same time, both here and in France a strongly romantic yearning for the past, and a literature that linked the down-trodden peasants with a golden age.

The *Chanson de Roland*, written at the end of the eleventh century was a story of superhuman courage and piety unattainable by ordinary men – Roland was a medieval superman. It expressed the picture of idealism *versus* reality; idealism won, and laid the foundation for a spirit that eventually gave birth to the French nation at the end of the Middle Ages. *The Song of Roland* expressed for the first time the uncompromising characteristics that are still latent in the French today: love of *La Gloire*, *L'Honneur* and of course *L'Amour*.

The earliest known French poetess was a lady called Marie de France who lived and wrote in Devon towards the end of the twelfth century. She wrote the sad story of Eliduc, a tale that was carried many times between her native and adopted lands. Eliduc is a Breton who escapes to Totnes in Devon after a disagreement with the King, and falls in love with the local lord. His own wife tragically, and nobly, enters a nunnery so that he can wed his new love.

The literary bond between the ordinary folk around the Channel at that time was strong, and grew stronger as time wore on. It was symbolized by the revival of the Arthurian legend in the twelfth and thirteenth centuries, Geoffrey of Monmouth, Chrétien de Troyes and the Conte de Graal with the Morte d'Arthur stirred the imagination of everyone with Europe's first 'best-selling' romances. People gave Christ-like qualities to Arthur, were convinced of his reincarnation, especially in Brittany, and fought physically over the truth of his birthplace.

The cultural affinity was increased by the patricide of noble Norman families in England sending their sons across the Channel to study in France where they picked up the growing French feeling for chivalric romanticism. The Crusades were an expression of this.

It was the concept of chivalry and love of horses with its attention to personal combat and horsemanship that may well have helped restrain the English nobility from an interest in sea fighting. The foundation for British skill at sea was laid not by the upper classes, but by seamen in small boats around the shores, the men, especially of the Channel – adventurers, pirates and fishermen. When, eventually, chivalry gave way to the Reformation in Tudor times and the nobility began to realize the priceless asset of the Channel at their feet, the names given to the upper ranks were in chivalric French and the seamen in Saxon. Admiral – from the Arabic Amir al Balir – captain and lieutenant are all from Norman French, while seaman, coxswain and boatswain are from the Anglo-Saxon of the commoners.

But throughout the century after the Conquest the problem was dynastic – of divided allegiance, family friction on a noble scale.

When William died there was no attempt made to bring England and Normandy within the same system. The Norman nobles inherited their estates by right of birth; in England it had become by right of conquest. So there were families where one son inherited British land acquired by his father at the Conquest and another took land in France inherited through patrimony. The inevitable ructions were disastrous. Odo of Bayeux is supposed to have said, 'How can we give proper service to two mutually hostile lords. If we serve Duke Robert of Normandy properly we shall offend his brother William, and he will deprive us of our revenues and honours in England'. It was impossible – a problem that must have beset nearly every Norman manorial lord in Britain.

In fact Normandy probably suffered most from the invasion of England at first, for the countryside was neglected in the efforts to establish a sound foothold in England. But by the reign of Stephen in 1135 the Barons on both sides were getting dissatisfied with their lot. The divisions became acute, and the reign was marked by a great deal of distress, although Stephen himself seems to have been a good man. Backwards and forwards they sailed – Stephen's Geoffrey of Anjou captured Normandy, his wife Matilda seized Dover, then Stephen seized Matilda ... and so on.

Nowhere did civil war affect the people more than the Fens and the Channel coast. They were caught in a tangle not of their making. In *Gesta Stephani* a Winchester monk described life there in 1143.

> With some men the love of the country was turned to loathing and bitterness and they preferred to migrate to distant regions. Others, in the hope of protection built lowly huts of wattle work round about the churches and so passed their lives in fear and anguish. Some, for want of food fed upon strange and forbidden meats – the flesh of dog and horses, others relieved their hunger by devouring unwashed and uncooked herbs and roots. You might behold the villages of famous names standing empty because the country people, young and old, had left them; fields whitened with the harvest as the year verged upon autumn but the cultivators had perished by famine and the ensuing pestilence.

No wonder that by the time Stephen died in 1154 the devastated Channel people were overjoyed at the prospect of change.

The change was Henry II. It is in the ancient hill town of Avranches in southern Normandy, where the colourful stalls straggle up the church steps on market day, just as they did eight hundred years ago, that Henry II has his most poignant memorial. There is a panoramic square at the top of the town, shaded by plane trees, a refuge for the elderly from the dusty heat of a summer day. They congregate around a small, unremarkable column, guarded from people, but not from dogs, by a protective chain. The plaque set in the yellowing grass is almost unreadable. Its historic twin is in the floor of

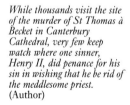

While thousands visit the site of the murder of St Thomas à Becket in Canterbury Cathedral, very few keep watch where one sinner, Henry II, did penance for his sin in wishing that he be rid of the meddlesome priest.
(Author)

the mighty Canterbury Cathedral in Kent and is gazed upon with reverence by thousands of tourists every year. The latter marks the spot where Thomas à Becket was murdered. The first, with an equally moving story to tell, marks the spot where King Henry, barefoot and in white, knelt to do penance for that murder. It says simply: 'After the murder of Thomas à Becket, Archbishop of Canterbury, Henry, King of England, Duke of Normandy, received on his knees from the Papal Legate apostolic absolution.'

The murder of Thomas à Becket, his former friend, is probably the best – and often only – remembered event in Henry's reign. Yet the accession of this remarkable Frenchman really saw the crowning of all that William the Conqueror could have hoped for – and more. For when Henry became King, England was, in fact, just one of his provinces, and he spent only half his reign here. He was ruler of lands that ran from the Arctic Ocean to the Pyrenees, right down the middle of what is now the nation of France. To the east the Kingdom of France to which as Duke of Normandy he owed, but never gave, allegiance and the independent Duchy of Brittany to the west. His daughters married rulers of Castile, Sicily and Saxony, his cousins ruled Champagne and Flanders. He made the best of past systems and laid the foundations for central government and judiciary which still exist today.

The day of Henry's coronation meant that Louis VII was overnight confronted not with a lot of feuding barons, but with a single imperial and very ambitious power, the Angevin (English) Empire. Even his ex-wife had married Henry and later bore him sons: by Louis she had daughters. But Louis's loss was not entirely Henry's gain, for those barons were to prove difficult to control. He tackled the problem by a superhuman programme of travel. No absentee monarch this. He was everywhere – and normally when least expected. When they thought he was in France he would turn up in Scotland, the entire court breathless behind him; he carried dozens of rolls – the modern despatch box – wherever he went. He must have been one of the best publicized of all monarchs, and there are no shortages of contemporary profiles.

Gerald of Wales says:

> ... a man of reddish, freckled complexion, with a large round head, grey eyes which glowed fiercely and grew bloodshot at anger, a fiery countenance and a harsh, cracked voice. His neck was somewhat thrust forward from his shoulders, his chest broad and square, his arms strong and powerful. His frame was stocky with a pronounced tendency to corpulence due rather to nature than to indulgence which he tempered with exercise.

However, Henry made no real attempt at a universal government and each province, including England, developed its own identity. There was no cross-Channel merger. For England, Henry II paved the way

THE PLANTAGENET LINE

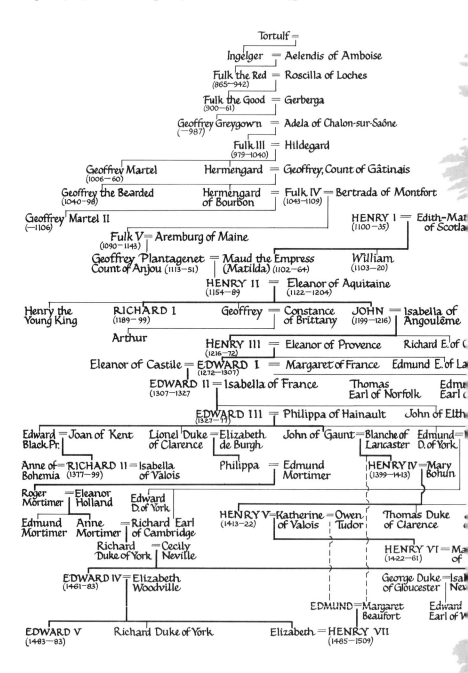

Tortulf =

Ingelger = Aelendis of Amboise

Fulk the Red = Roscilla of Loches
(865—942)

Fulk the Good = Gerberga
(900—61)

Geoffrey Greygown = Adela of Chalon-sur-Saône
(—987)

Fulk III = Hildegard
(979—1040)

Geoffrey Martel   Hermengard = Geoffrey, Count of Gâtinais
(1006—60)

Geoffrey the Bearded   Hermengard = Fulk IV = Bertrada of Montfort   HENRY I = Edith-Mat
(1040—98)   of Bourbon   (1043—1109)   (1100—35)   of Scotla

Geoffrey Martel II
(—1106)

Fulk V = Aremburg of Maine   William
(1090—1143)   (1103—20)

Geoffrey Plantagenet = Maud the Empress
Count of Anjou (1113—51)   (Matilda) (1102—64)

HENRY II = Eleanor of Aquitaine
(1154—89)   (1122—1204)

Henry the   RICHARD I   Geoffrey = Constance   JOHN = Isabella of
Young King   (1189—99)   of Brittany   (1199—1216)   Angoulême

Arthur   HENRY III = Eleanor of Provence   Richard E. of (
(1216—72)

Eleanor of Castile = EDWARD I = Margaret of France   Edmund E. of La
(1272—1307)

EDWARD II = Isabella of France   Thomas   Edmu
(1307—1327   Earl of Norfolk   Earl o

EDWARD III = Philippa of Hainault   John of Elth
(1327—77)

Edward = Joan of Kent   Lionel Duke = Elizabeth   John of Gaunt = Blanche of   Edmund =
Black Pr.   of Clarence   de Burgh   Lancaster   D. of York

Anne of = RICHARD II = Isabella   Philippa = Edmund   HENRY IV = Mary
Bohemia   (1377—99)   of Valois   Mortimer   (1399—1413)   Bohun

Roger = Eleanor   Edward
Mortimer   Holland   D. of York

Edmund   Anne = Richard Earl   HENRY V = Katherine = Owen   Thomas Duke
Mortimer   Mortimer   of Cambridge   (1413—22)   of Valois   Tudor   of Clarence

Richard = Cecily
Duke of York   Neville   HENRY VI = Ma
(1422—61)   of

EDWARD IV = Elizabeth   George Duke = Isab
(1461—83)   Woodville   of Gloucester   Nev

EDMUND = Margaret   Edward
Beaufort   Earl of W

EDWARD V   Richard Duke of York   Elizabeth = HENRY VII
(1483—83)   (1485—1509)

64

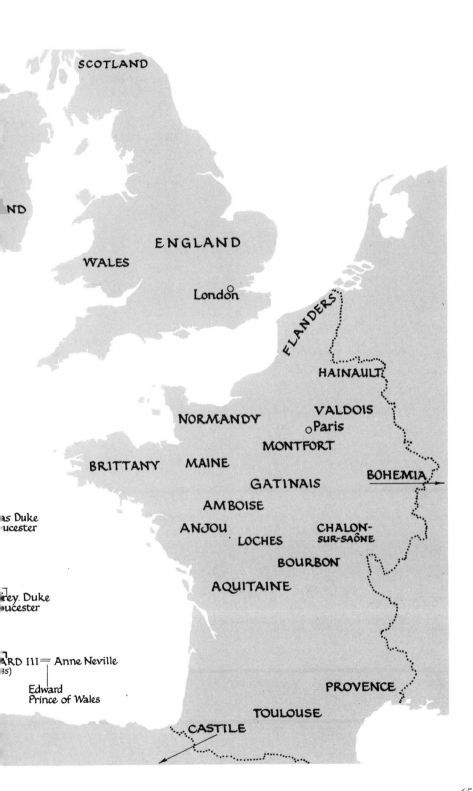

SCOTLAND

ND

ENGLAND

WALES

London

FLANDERS

HAINAULT

NORMANDY

VALDOIS
Paris

MONTFORT

BRITTANY   MAINE

GATINAIS

BOHEMIA

AMBOISE

ANJOU

LOCHES

CHALON-
SUR-SAÔNE

BOURBON

AQUITAINE

PROVENCE

TOULOUSE

CASTILE

as Duke
ucester

ey. Duke
ucester

RD III = Anne Neville
35)

Edward
Prince of Wales

in fact for the emergence of a country with a sense of national identity. He drew the best from the past and grafted it onto a framework for a stable future. French-speaking Henry was responsible for the fact that English-speaking nations everywhere are governed by English Common Law. It was his efforts to keep the Church in its place, alongside but not dominating, the State, that led to the eventual confrontation with his friend Becket. He was responsible for granting the Cinque Ports their first official charter in 1297; he established the jury system (from the French *jurer*, to swear) and initiated the concept of the King's Peace – instead of relying on Barons' courts, and a single form of justice.

He was less successful at controlling his sons, Henry, Richard and Geoffrey, who enlisted the help of their mother Eleanor and her ex-husband King Louis of France, to organize rebellions. It was a clever ruse on the part of Louis who always seemed so much weaker than the powerful and charismatic King of England. He set the boys to cause ferment within Henry's domain and to weaken it by encouraging local uprisings. These battles and sometimes bloody squabbles were fought on the soil of France, not of England. For three hundred years – not just the well known one hundred – the ordinary villagers of the Channel shore were to suffer for English determination to protect, at all costs, its hold over northern Europe. Their menfolk crossed the sea to die on the plains of Normandy, just as they did later in the First World War. The English came first to conquer and then to liberate, and since no one likes to feel obligated in either role they were not much loved by the people whose land they desecrated. By giving England her national identity, Henry the Frenchman turned the tables and started a process of almost perpetual hostility between the two countries.

Henry died in France in 1188 after a war in which his son and heir Richard sided with the new King Philip. He died in Chinon from illness, not wounds, after the battle of Le Mans; amongst those on the list of conspirators against him was his favourite son, John. His last sad words were 'shame, shame on a conquered King'.

Just as Henry could always be found somewhere within his Empire, Richard *Coeur de Lion* could not. He spent only ten months of his reign in England. The remainder was spent at the Crusades: wonderful, historically, for his romantic image, but not good for the country. What spare time he had he spent fighting in France, but his need to travel did provide a stimulus for shipbuilding to carry the Holy warriors. The new ships were known as 'dromons' and 'busses', and for the first time they had 'engines' for hurling stones and Greek fire (nitre, sulphur and pitch) at the enemy.

The journey to Jerusalem which pilgrims undertook from both sides of the Channel was long and arduous. The fifteenth-century verse which has no title and is usually known by its first line 'Men may leve all gamys' describes the hazards of travelling through the Western Approaches.

> Men may leve all gamys
> That seylen to Seynt Jamys
> For many a man hit gramys
>   When they begyn to sayle.
> For when that they have take the see
> At Sandwyche or at Wynchelsee
> At Bristow or where that hit bee
>   Theyr hearts begyn to fayle.

As the journey continues the pilgrims begin to 'cowgh and grone' though those with stronger stomachs 'layde theyr bookys on theyr kne and rad so long they myght net se'. They had their 'bolys fast them by, and cry aftyr hote malvesy, theyr helthe for to restore'. In fact all they could face was 'saltyd tost'. The worst place of all in the ship was the cabin through which the bilge pump worked 'a man were as good as to be dede, as smell thereof the stynk'.

For the first time a disciplinary code was worked out, the 'Ordnance for the Great Crusade' from which our own less ferocious Articles of War are based. A murderer was to be tied to the body of his victim and thrown overboard; for stabbing the punishment was the loss of a hand, for fist-fighting a ducking. Pitch was to be poured over the head of a thief followed by feathers and he was then to be thrown overboard at the first point of land.

King John was not entirely bad. He appointed the first keeper of King's ships, galleys and seaports, William Wrotham, and he made Portsmouth the navy headquarters because the Cinque Ports were silting up. Two-masted ships, with room for some four hundred men were being built there. In 1213 when the British defeated the French after the first Anglo-French battle in the Channel, King John himself assumed the title of 'Governor of the Seas' and commanded all foreign ships to salute him.

He was succeeded by Henry III who managed wisely, to consolidate his position and keep the peace too and few changes were recorded on either side of the Channel during his long reign – fifty-six years.

Geographically 'France' now meant most of the land we know as France, but this was not ruled directly by the French Kings from Paris. For two hundred years the Kings had been trying – as they had done in Normandy – to extend control over the Duchies. But there were still large areas, such as Aquitaine, ruled by King Edward III from England, who acknowledged the King in Paris as overlord, but who possessed all the real power.

The causes of the Hundred Years War were complex. For the English it was about Edward III's claim to his uncle Charles IV's French crown, and his quarrels with Charles's successor Philippe VI, the first de Valois. So far as Philippe was concerned, Edward's claim through his mother, Charles's sister, was invalid. No King's title had yet been derived in France through the female line. Moreover,

Philippe confiscated Aquitaine. It was also a struggle by the English nobility to claim large chunks of the land of their Norman roots.

The French have bitter memories of the Hundred Years War; a bitterness that is rooted deep among the ordinary people of Normandy even today. It was a war that drew in the Dutch under Spain and the people of Flanders and Brittany, but for them, as for the British, that is history long ago. Yet it is not an exaggeration for the English traveller in the Cotentin peninsula of Normandy to sense the very slightest shiver of unease even today. For the memory of the villagers in such places as St Marie du Mont threads surprisingly unbroken through six hundred years. It is undeniable. Sit in the sun in the evening when the calvados has reached the soul and there they will talk, as though it were yesterday, of the atrocities at the hands of the British.

The people of Plymouth, Dartmouth, Winchester and the Cinque Ports also suffered, but life was cheap and the rapidly rising birthrate was either checked by war, or plague. Houses were cheap too, and easy enough to rebuild to the unsanitary standards of the time. For much of the time the people of both shores played cat and mouse, pillaging churches in the dead of night only to find looted treasure reclaimed in a reprisal raid weeks after.

This was the time during which France and England grew into nations. The seeds planted before the Conquest when single families first split into factions on either side of the Channel, finally germinated. The saplings from the original tree began to flourish on soil that was entirely their own and a dynastic feud became a national conflict. Ironically the wars brought a kind of peace to inland Britain; for many of the nobles who might have made trouble, or raised rebellions, were otherwise occupied in France. This is the pattern of history. Wars abroad have often been a useful diversion for kings and politicians in trouble, and it was Normandy which bore the brunt of British determination to keep a foothold in France, because she was a natural fortress on the main road to the King of France.

Parisian writer Gilles Perrault has for twenty years lived in St Marie du Mont. He talks with passion in *Les Gens d'ici* of his study of that village and its traces of the past in the mentality of the inhabitants today – especially their suspicions of England. Present attitudes are only explicable by a collective memory, he believes.

At the beginning of the Hundred Years War France itself was *une petite chose* and was nothing to match the powerful richness of its Duchy of Normandy. At the end, Normandy emerged ruined. She did not exist – and the ordinary people have never forgotten. Brittany, on the other hand, was ruled for much of the War by Jean le Sage, who managed to walk a skilful tightrope of non-alignment between the two contenders. He was married to Jeanne, whose father was mad Charles VI of France, and sister to Katherine who married Henry V. (Arriving too late at the Battle of Agincourt in 1415, Jean adroitly changed sides and joined forces with Henry.)

Gilles Perrault explains with deep sensitivity: 'The first and last acts of the Hundred Years War happened here. At first we welcomed the British – after all those who came were our cousins – the descendants of William's army, the Montgomerys and the D'Arcys and we had no special love for Philippe VI.' But as the years went by and French nationalism began to take over, families were divided. They played a double game.

> During that War we in St Marie changed sides twenty-five times. We would go to bed subjects of the King of France and wake up subjects of the King of England. Three-quarters of the population died – you can see today the Vallée de la Misère and the Bois de la Famine where peasants hid from the reprisals of one side or the other. They say that this is the origin of the traditional Norman ambivalence *'peut être ben qu'oui, peut être ben qu'non'*, they still say today, 'maybe yes, maybe no'.

It was a war with no real beginning and no real end, and many of the years in between battles were tolerably peaceful. In fact, the British did not finally renounce their rights to the throne of the de Valois until 1802, by which time France was a republic and the pretender to the French throne was living in London!

Alongside it all lay internal unrest in the outlying provinces of Scotland and Brittany, both of which were used by France and England for their own purposes. Churchill claims that it was in Scotland's fight against the English that the standard of nationalism was first raised one hundred years before Joan of Arc, during the reign of Edward I. The Scots, allied with France, under Robert the Bruce defeated the English at Bannockburn and it was to France that the Scots turned for help. The befriending of Bruce's son David, as a refugee, by Philip the Fair, was yet another irritation, and eventually Robert the Steward (Stuart) was to conclude a treaty with the French in 1371 which was to last for several hundred years.

The catalyst which finally provoked hostilities was probably the English sheep upon which the economy of France, the Netherlands and Flanders greatly depended. There were many more sheep than people in Britain and most British wool was exported in its raw state to Flanders where it was woven by skilled craftsmen into fine cloth.

All kinds of inducements had been offered by Edward to persuade the weavers to settle in Britain, mostly unsuccessfully. But in Flanders the aristocracy, who were very sympathetic to France, were most uneasy about the blossoming wealth of their middle-class weavers. They saw this as a threat to their power, and so they interfered with trade until, in 1366, in a fit of anger, Edward put an embargo on exports and provoked a crisis.

Jacques Van Atreveldt of Ghent led the weavers in revolt against the lords and having won over much of the countryside appealed successfully to the English for help.

Edward's first move, in January 1340, was to assume the title King of

An early naval success for the English fleet. In 1340, off the coast of Flanders, near Sluys, the English under Edward III destroyed the French fleet of Philippe VI. (BBC Hulton)

France and quarter his arms with the Fleur de Lys. He gathered together the best army England had had for years, issued the first gold coin with a ship on it and himself standing on deck.

The French King had dreams of a second Conquest and he too rallied a huge fleet from all around the coast. But Edward had earned himself the title 'King of the Sea' for his keen interest in the navy and when the two fleets met off the coast of Flanders in June for the Battle of Sluys, there was, according to Froissart, a curious and horrible battle.

> The next day, being the Feast of Saint John the Baptist, early in the morning the French fleet divided themselves into three parts, withdrew about a mile, and then approached the King's fleet. When the King saw this, about nine o'clock, having the wind and sun on his back, he set forward and met his enemies as he would have wished; at which the whole fleet gave a terrible shout, and a shower of arrows out of long wooden bows so poured down on the Frenchmen that thousands were slain in that meeting. At length they closed and came to hand blows with pires, poleaxes, and swords, and some threw stones from the tops of ships, wherewith many were brained. ... The French ships were chained together in such a way they could not be separated from each other, so that a few Englishmen kept that

part of the fleet. They then set upon the second part and with great difficulty made the attack; but when this had been done, the second part was sooner overcome than the first because many of the Frenchmen abandoned their ships and leapt overboard.... The fight continued all night, and in the morning, the Normans being overcome and taken, there were found in the ship four hundred men slain.... The number of ships of war that were taken was about two hundred and thirty barges; the number of enemies that were slain and drowned was about twenty-five thousand and of Englishmen about four thousand among whom were four knights....

At the centre of hostilities on land and from the Norman point of view, the *agent provocateur*, was Godefroy d'Harcourt, descendant of one of the original companions of Rollo the Viking. He is hardly known to English history but Froissart says he was a man of much courage who never fled from battle.

Godefroy's castle was in the centre of the Cotentin at St Sauveur le Vicomte near St Marie du Mont. He had quarrelled with a neighbour over his daughter's marriage plans and was about to make war on him when King Philippe forbade it. Presumption indeed! For, what right, thought Godefroy, had the King of France to interfere in the affairs of a Norman noble? In a fit of pique he went over to England and persuaded Edward to fight the King of France in Normandy. Edward needed no further excuses. Godefroy offered to lead the invasion himself and in 1346 he disembarked at St Vaast, with twelve thousand archers and two thousand four hundred cavalry. Their objective: the capture of Paris.

There was complete confusion. Godefroy's brother Jean was fighting with the French. The battle was a family gathering, for the English army was led by Thomas de Beauchamp, Guillaume de Bohun, Jean de Moyon, Riber Bourchier, all descendants of the Conqueror's first army in Britain, all with relatives in France.

The army possessed a weapon which was to prove to the French as initially devastating as German doodlebugs were to the British in the Second World War. It was the longbow, the deadly long-range weapon against which there was no defence.

The English marched across Normandy rioting and killing, failed to take Paris and eventually, in thick fog, on Sunday morning 27th August 1346 met the French army at Crécy – one of the great British victories. Fifteen thousand French knights and their esquires were slaughtered and the French idea of chivalry defeated for ever. Ironically, only two years later in 1348 the Black Death swept across the Channel from Europe having devastated northern France. The first plague-carrying boat anchored in Portsmouth Harbour and within about two years nearly half the population of England was dead. From Crécy Edward went on to Calais and beseiged it.

The seige of Calais has been recorded in verse and in oils. It lasted a year and no attempts at relief succeeded. Sea piles were dug into the

Channel bed to stop small craft from threading their way inland and all kinds of new weapons were hurled at the city. In the end, as so often before and since, it was famine that won. Eventually a truce was declared. Edward renounced his claim to the French throne and England's right to all land north of the Loire except for Calais and Pointheu.

The story of the six brave burghers of Calais who offered themselves as hostage–martyrs to the English – and were in fact spared by Queen Phillipa's compassion – is best remembered in Rodin's powerful sculpture and in Froissart's account of the end of the siege.

> Then the king said: 'Sirs, I will not be alone against you all; therefore sir Gaultier of Manny, ye shall go and say to the capitain that all the grace that he shall find now in me is that they let six of the chief burgesses of the town come out bare-headed, bare-footed, and bare-legged, and in their shirts, with halters about their necks, with the keys of the town and castle in their hands, and let them six yield themselves purely to my will, and the residue I will take to mercy'.
>
> Then sir John went into the market-place and sowned the common bell: then incontinent men and women assembled there: then the capitain made report of all that he had done, and said: 'Sirs, it will be none otherwise; therefore, now take advice and make a short answer'. Then all the people began to weep and to make such sorrow, that there was not so hard a heart, if they had seen them, but that would have had great pity of them; the capitain himself wept piteously. At last the most rich burgess of all the town, called Eustace of Saint-Pierre, rose up and said openly: 'Sirs, great and small, great mischief it should be to suffer to die such people as be in this town, other by famine or otherwise when there is a mean to save them. I think he or they should have great merit of our Lord God that might keep them from such mischief. As for my part, I have so good trust in our Lord God, that if I die in the quarrel to save the residue, that God would pardon me: wherefore to save them I will be the first to put my life in jeopardy'. When he had thus said, every man worshipped him and divers kneeled down at his feet with sore weeping and sore sighs. Then another honest burgess rose and said: 'I will keep company with my gossip Eustace'. He was called John d'Aire. Then rose up Jaques of Wissant, who was rich in goods and heritage; he said also that he would hold company with his two cousins. In like wise so did Peter of Wissant his brother: and then rose two other; they said they would do the same. Then they went and apparelled them as the king desired. . . .

Rodin was commissioned to create a statue in 1884 at the request of a Monsieur Dewarvin, Mayor of Calais. But he became so obsessed by the heroic expression and emotion of the subject that he designed not one monument but a group of six for a fee of thirty-five thousand francs. A long tussle ensued between Rodin's powerful vision and that of the bureaucracy who preferred to honour their heroes in a more conventional way, and thus, according to Rodin, 'emasculating them'. It took seven years to resolve the problem and the monument was finally unveiled in 1895 – an extraordinary work of tragic grandeur. In it the personalities of the men shine out: Eustace de St Pierre a tired old man, shoulders drooping, hands swollen; Pierre de Wissant with eyes half closed and brow furrowed, a young man, courageous and handsome, with the keys of Calais in his hand. It was triumphantly acclaimed as an immortal masterpiece.

All developments, all battles, had been on land, none were fought at sea during the three hundred years after the Conquest. Even the Battle of Sluys took place with the French fleet at anchor. What changes took place in ships were all in the cause of trade. When the King needed a navy he borrowed merchantmen and they sailed under the instruction of his knights. How history repeats itself. In the NATO exercise *Lionheart* in September 1984 some 7,000 territorial army troops and 4,600 vehicles were transported to the Continent by Sealink ferries.

They added brightly-painted castles (which made them top-heavy) and which appear, as they may well have done to the fisherfolk and merchants of Plantagenet days, like the phoney extravagant follies of the *nouveau riche*. There is perhaps a parallel in the home-from-home mansion tents into which many twentieth-century campers pile all their worldly goods. For to those soldiers, more at home on a horse than a rolling ship the castle was probably a symbol of security too. At first these castles (forecastles or 'fo'c'sles') were dismantled after use, but eventually they were constructed with the ships and used for defence.

Towards the end of his reign, King Edward founded the Court of Admiralty and appointed a Lord High Admiral responsible for administration and maritime law. Today the executive powers conferred on the Lord High Admiral are exercised by the Ministry of Defence, the judicial power by the High Courts of Justice.

One of Rodin's six Burghers of Calais *with the keys of the city in his hands.* (Burrell Collection/Glasgow Art Galleries and Museums)

There are Granville avenues, Granville streets and Granville squares all over Britain – named after the granite fortress town on the western

Cotentin coast which was the medieval British Gibraltar. For during the Hundred Years War they turned the original little fishing village on a rock into a base from which to attack the Mont St Michel. They isolated it by cutting a ditch (now known as La Tranchee aux Anglais) across the isthmus joining it to the mainland and so dividing the town in two. Granville has always attracted the British and supported a strong British colony, though many modern tourists who discover the town are part of the overflow from the Mont St Michel and do so by chance. It is a town of cobbled streets, spectacularly varied architecture, exhilarating ramparts and walks overlooking the waters which once provided anchorage for the huge fleets of fishing boats bound for the Grand Banks of Newfoundland. From that harbour today small boats take visitors out through the reefs and rocky outcrops towards the lonely Chausey Islands archipelago to the part of the Channel Islands which belong to France.

Time has been frozen in the medieval streets of Dinan in Brittany where the black and white timbered houses, senior citizens that they are, lean in quiet nostalgic reverie towards each other across the alleys. Here, in the church of St Sauveur, in the tree-shaded Jardin des Anglais, lies the heart of Bertrand du Guescelin, a symbol of the curiously ambivalent attitudes during the Hundred Years War see-saw. The inscription on the tomb reads 'Here lies the heart of Messire Bertrand du Guescelin, some-time Constable of France who died on the 13th day of July 1380 and whose body lies with the Kings at St Denis *in France*'. For Bretons, France was a place apart in those days – another country – and du Guescelin chose to side with the French king against the English king.

Paradoxically, Bertrand liked the English; they had a soft spot for him. Over the years he harried their soldiers throughout Brittany. During the Wars of Succession (1364–1391), he was captured and crossed the Channel to enjoy his 'captivity' at the English court, for he was never kept in gaol, and was always well entertained in the homes of noblemen.

Bertrand du Guescelin was born in La Motte Broom, north of Dinan – a snub-nosed, swarthy, scowling child, hated by both parents. But as a young warrior he avenged his unhappy childhood, stole money and jewels from his mother and became a hero. There is a café in Dinan today – Canterbury Café – to mark the spot where Bertrand fought and killed Sir Thomas Canterbury in single combat. Many of his best friends were Englishmen – people like Robert Knollys and John Chandos. His one wish was that they would stay put, on their side of the Channel. The sentiment was returned – the English actually admired the warrior, who was married to a beautiful astrologer, Typhaine, and who sent her for safety's sake to live and study on the Mont St Michel.

Du Guescelin was one of those young warriors who thrived during the tragic role of Brittany, as a pawn in the game of political chess, between France and England. Rival families, the English supporting de Montforts and the French backing de Blois, contested the succession and Brittany became a battleground for twenty years within the Hundred Years War. Du Guescelin backed the wrong side and for him it was checkmate.

In 1360 the Black Prince, son of Edward III, sailed home to England after his victory at Poitiers with King Jean of France as his hostage. That same year Du Guescelin was knighted and formally entered the service of his exiled monarch. With Jean in the Tower, Edward signed the Treaty of Brétigny and fixed a ransom of three million gold crowns – eight times the peacetime revenue of the British monarchy. Edward acquired or re-acquired Gascony, Aquitaine, Ponthieu and Calais, but by the time he died in 1377 only Calais and a strip of coastal Gascony remained to England.

In 1364 the pro-English Jean de Montfort became Jean IV, Duke of Brittany, on the death of Charles Dubois, and Bertrand went off on the orders of the new King of France Charles the Wise to fight the English in Spain. He returned in 1370, became Constable of France and began to fight English supporters amongst his own people in an

A remarkably realistic portrait in stone of the 'hero' Bertrand du Guescelin, a French patriot but a traitor in Brittany.
(Popperfoto)

effört to shake off English interference in Brittany. Duke Jean escaped to England, but when eventually in 1379 he returned home to a hero's welcome, Bertrand's own army refused to fight fellow countrymen and he was considered a traitor in his own country.

> And where the Frenchmen fall, they'll stay
> Until the final judgement day
> Until they are judged and punished all
> But most their traitor general
> Rain dripping from the trees he'll have
> As Holy Water for his grave.

It was hardly fair, for Du Guescelin really loved Brittany and wanted it to be a part of what he now saw as the great nation of France. He was a man ahead of his time. In 1946 Breton nationalists blew up his statue in Rennes, in an attempt to put the clock back.

The English 'hero' of the Hundred Years War was, of course, Henry V, the first King to speak and use the English language in his letters, the first King to fight in the name of St George for England. Saint George was a somewhat bloodthirsty and doubtful character from the Cappadocian area of what is now Turkey, whose exploits were extolled by the Crusaders and whose legend was brought back by them to England in the thirteenth century.

The young King took over the throne of a war-weary country in 1413, the year after a baby girl was born in the faraway village of Domrémy in Lorraine. She was toddling around the fields of her father's farm the day of Agincourt – one of the most spectacular of all English victories over the French, which made the English monarch once again one of the greatest monarchs in Europe. This unpalatable situation was eventually to provoke the adolescent Jeanne d'Arc to galvanize the French in a patriotic stand against the unwelcome intruders – and to bring her martyrdom.

The dashing young Henry V had reorganized the fleet but instead of commandeering private ships, like all the kings since Alfred, he commissioned specially built vessels. Six great ships and fifteen hundred smaller craft were built in harbours all along the Channel, before Agincourt.

There is an eternal magic in the size and grace of great ships manoeuvring in confined space which has always drawn spellbound crowds. Even in these days of supertankers the arrival of the *Queen Elizabeth II* in the tricky Southampton waters, the skill of her pilots moving an intricate path through the congested water still draws a hushed crowd. The great *Queens* before her have also had this magic of sheer size moving with such grace.

Spectators wandering along the quay by the wool house of five hundred years ago would also have been spellbound by the size of the elegant three-masted Venetian boats bringing luxuries into the town from the Mediterranean. They were far bigger than any other Channel craft, but before Henry V began preparations for Agincourt no one had thought of copying them.

Until then the development of the navy during the Hundred Years War seems to have gone in fits and starts – the little craft of Edward III at the Battle of Sluys were of two hundred tonnes or less. Henry V ordered boats six times that size and nearly as large as Nelson's *Victory* and *still* they were dwarfed by the Venetian carracks.

In the two years before 1415 Henry ordered four even bigger craft, which had to be built abroad because British yards were, even then, unable to cope! The *Andrew*, the *Peter*, the *Trinity* and the *Holighost* with their two masts were assembled, with fifteen hundred single-masted craft, in Southampton Water during the summer of 1415. The *Christopher* was the first British ship to carry guns, though she was a single-mast.

All this ship-building enterprise must have stirred British yards into action. In Southampton, when the fleet set sail for France, Henry's master carpenter began laying the keel of a monster ship that was to become the largest in the world. Three years later, the *Grace Dieu* was completed; she was fourteen hundred tonnes, a rush job, on dangerously old-fashioned lines, with three masts. Her clinker-built skeleton can be seen still at certain tides in the Hamble Estuary, for the *Grace Dieu* never went to sea. She was redundant before she was launched; a useless white elephant, she leaked and was laid up with the other warships after Agincourt to rot in the mud of the river-bed where she lies today. There are not even any pictures of her. But all was not in vain, for Henry's interest in shipping had encouraged a move forward – from one, to two and then to three masts – so that by the time that Henry Tudor was on the throne, at the end of the century, there was talk in the seaside inns of venturing far beyond the boundaries of the Channel.

The Battle of Agincourt itself belongs rather to the history of France and England than the story of the Channel. But the preparations, the departure and the homecoming took place to the sound of the sea and the crying of the gulls and this part of the adventure is shared between the towns of Southampton and Harfleur.

It was a long hot summer. The French sent a deputation to see Henry, but in true negotiating style he could not be moved. Charles VI agreed to cede certain territories and give him the hand of his pretty daughter, Katherine de Valois, with an unprecedented dowry of eight hundred thousand gold crowns. But Henry wasn't satisfied. He wanted the crown of France.

By July every creek along the south coast of England was bright with the colourful craft of the King's Navy. He was a tireless supervisor himself – rising before dawn, sleeping little, eating little and keeping in close personal contact with all his craftsmen on the quay-sides. There was a theatrical touch which Hollywood at its most lavish would not have bettered: the serpent embroidered sails, the gilt decorations and flags and pennants flying proudly.

In the bright sunshine of 7th August, the huge fleet began to move slowly down the Solent. As they manoeuvred for position three ships caught fire, which meant that many horses and much equipment had to be left behind. It took all day to position the boats, then at three o'clock, to much drum beating, trumpeting and shouting, the *Trinité Royal*, with the King aboard, weighed anchor and sailed for France. A good omen, a flock of swans, followed them out to sea.

Thanks to William Shakespeare and Laurence Olivier all the world knows what happened next.

> *Chorus:* Suppose that you have seen ...
> The well appointed King ...
> Embark his royalty; and his brave fleet
> With silken streamers the young phoebus fanning
> Play with your fancies and in them behold
> Upon the hempen tackle ships boys climbing
> Hear the shrill whistle which doth order give
> To sounds confused; behold the threaden sails
> Borne with the invisible and creeping wind
> Draw the huge bottoms through the furrowed sea
> Breasting the lofty surge. O! Do but think

You stand upon the rivage and beyond
A city on the inconstant billows dancing
For so appears this fleet majestical.

And so to Harfleur, and the white cliffs of the Seine estuary known as
the Chef de Caux. The village they could see, Leure, has long since
disappeared under the sand that eventually plugged the entrance to
Harfleur and necessitated the building of the French Newhaven (Le
Havre in 1517).

But in 1415 Harfleur 'the key to the sea of all Normandy' was one of
the most prosperous and thriving of the French Channel ports. A
fairy-tale town – a smaller version of the Sleeping Beauty city of
Carcassone near the French Pyrenees, with its undulating walls,
and its turrets with blue-gold painted stone figures atop.

The approach by land today is over the perilously slender Pont de
Tancarville. From any standpoint this free-flying elegant suspension
bridge is one of the wonders of France. Built in 1957, it straddles the
beautiful estuary of the Seine, fifty feet above the water and nearly one
kilometre long. Harfleur has almost been gobbled up by the impressive sprawl of Le Havre itself: impressive because, despite the miles of
flare stacks, chimneys, cranes and the approaches to France's leading
container port, there is a pleasant sense of compromise with the rich
tree-banked countryside around. Had Henry V arrived today this
would have been a stirring spot from which to deliver that speech of all
speeches, set by Shakespeare, outside the walls of Harfleur: 'Once
more into the breach. . . .'

*The film version of
Shakespeare's* Henry V *was
made in 1944 to inspire a
nation at war. Shakespeare's
words, Olivier's acting and
direction, and William
Walton's music combined
successfully to inspire
audiences then, and now.*
(British Film
Institute/Rank
Organisation)

But Henry V arrived in Harfleur by sea – landing on a beach swallowed now by the docks – in an armada of small rowing boats. He surrounded the town and made strenuous efforts to stop his men from raiding the nearby hamlets for plunder and women. After some weeks of siege he decided to attack. From inside Harfleur that initial onslaught must have been terrifying. For although guns had been used in various forms for about a hundred years, the 'gunnys' which Henry had transported over the sea were of cast iron and 'blew forth stones by the force of ignited powers'. They were given nicknames: 'the messenger', 'London' and 'the King's Daughter'. According to C. Hibbert in his *Agincourt* they hurled entire millstones at the town and soon the masonry of the towers and the earthwork in the bulwarks began to crumble and great hunks of stone were knocked out of the walls. Day and night they fired for over a week and Henry became confident of victory.

He was almost thwarted by a more silent and more devastating disaster: dysentery. The weather was stiflingly hot, and the sweating men were exhausted by the weight of their airless armour. Over the salt marshes, tainted air polluted the camps which were themselves filled with the stench of men and animals. Flyblown grapes and fetid fish, washed down with the new *vin du pays* did not help. It was no comfort to know that the French were suffering too. But by the end of September Harfleur gave in, and twelve citizens left to inform the King of the events. Inertia set in: over two thousand men had died and far more were ill – many more than died at Agincourt itself – and they waited in the stifling heat for news from Paris. Charles wrote:

> As none of your predecessors ever had any right, and you still less, to make the demands contained in certain of your letters presented to us by Chester, your herald, nor to cause us any trouble, it is our intention, with the assistance of the Lord, in whom we have singular trust ... to resist you in a way which shall be to the honour and glory of us and our kingdom, and to the confusion, loss and dishonour of you and your party.

They were brave words, but without meaning, for Charles had no way of sending relief to the people of Harfleur and on Sunday afternoon 3rd September they surrendered.

Henry sat on a throne draped with cloth of gold in a silk tent, waiting for the keys to be delivered. Humiliation was complete when the twenty-four hostages, and knights with ropes around their necks over shirts of penance were forced to kneel time after time before the English lords before they were allowed even to see the King.

In retrospect, Henry's behaviour falls rather short of the heroic picture Shakespeare painted years later, though by all contemporary accounts both French and English accepted it. He announced that merchants and tradesmen would be invited to come across from England and would be granted accommodation and aid to set up businesses. Only the old and infirm of Harfleur would be moved out. And so it was: on the day after Henry rode into Harfleur, two thousand pathetic refugees, each carrying a small bundle and five sous, walked away from the town 'under much lamentations, wretchedness and tears'.

On 15th October, two hundred and fifty miles away, Henry massacred the French army. With his remaining men – outnumbered four to one – he slaughtered around seven thousand, many of them not in battle but whilst they lay wounded. His own losses were a mere hundred men. The bodies were piled into a barn, which was set on fire.

Four years later, at the Treaty of Troyes, Henry was made heir to the throne of France. He married Charles's daughter Katherine, the mother of the future King Henry VI. Henry V died in 1422 and Charles of France a few months later, leaving the seven-month-old

Henry VI King of France and England. His uncle, John Duke of Bedford became Regent in France, and Gloucester took over in England.

The course of events in the next few years which really led to the end of the Hundred Years War was dictated by the existence of three children: the baby King Henry VI, the adolescent Joan of Arc, and her protégé, the weak-willed, simple-minded Dauphin.

Joan of Arc never saw the sea; she was a soldier, not a sailor, but she did for the French what Henry V had done for the English: she created a national spirit of 'France' on one side of the Channel, as he had created 'England' on the other. Hostilities rumbled on for some time but, inspired by her death in 1428, Normandy, within twenty years, was again under the French crown. Only Calais was left to the English, to garrison at phenomenal cost, and both sides retreated behind the sea walls of the Channel to lick their wounds in private and generally to pick up the pieces of their shattered social order.

The twenty-year period after the Hundred Years War marked a virtual reoccupation of Normandy by the British, under the house of Lancaster, first by soldiers but then by farmers, traders and landowners. Families such as the Umfrevilles, and the FitzWalters, established in Britain under the Conqueror, now returned to fight and repossess estates in Normandy. Thomas Walsingham wrote his book *Ypodigma Neustriae* to emphasize the historic link between the lands facing each other across the Channel.

Merchants were offered houses in Calais, Harfleur and Caen in order to stimulate business, and members of entire families, tending to settle within easy reach of each other, established British ghettoes. At one time in the southern Cotentin, in the area around Avranches there were Nessfields from Yorkshire, Entwistles from Lancashire, Paldeys, Oldhalls and Tisdalls, all tending at first to marry within their community and so to preserve its strength and unity.

Caen was the first town to come completely under British control and they were to found a University there in 1429 on whose roll the first names were British: Nilcent, Holme, Apwell and Gough. The founding of Caen University was one of the few creditable achievements from the Hundred Years War, and it is at Caen University today that research into the history of the Norman language is revealing many modern French words which are the left-overs of British influence.

On the whole the nobility and the clergy were supportive of, and cooperated with, the occupation because it brought them some stability at least. But amongst the peasants and ordinary folk reactions were different: a difference reflected in attitudes today.

C. T. Allemand in his *Lancastrian Normandy 1415–1450*, says: 'There is every reason to believe that over the years passive aquiescence in the countryside came to be replaced by a sense of indignant resistance'. It was this resistance which grew, gradually, into the

Brigand movement which was a grass roots, anti-British organization founded for the first time on national pride.

When eventually the British left Normandy in 1450 there were celebrations which were to continue annually in the villages until well after the Revolution. In fact, whatever the truth at the time, local officials, mayors and dignitaries have used the defeat of the British mercilessly in their propaganda. In the late nineteenth century the French were constantly reminded of the glorious patriotism which had ended that war in order to strengthen their resolve against Germany. Streets were renamed: Jeanne d'Arc, Domrémy or La Hire. The words of M. Leon Puisseux were recalled, when he had stated that sacrifice and blood had made a nation and that common danger had united France against England *usurpateur du sol national* (usurper of our national soil). Plaques, historic tomes and statues were produced all echoing the sentiments expressed at the unveiling of a plaque to commemmorate the fifteenth-century patriot Ambroise de Loré, who was they said,

> au premier rang de nos gloires de France, avec tous ceux qui ont lutté sans trève et sans défaillance, dans ce duel gigantesque avec l'insatiable Angleterre, pour l'indépéndence de notre sol et le maintien de notre intégrité nationale contrel l'eternel adversaire toujours armé, sur notre route contre le réel, implacable et héréditaire ennemi de notre race et de notre sang.

Translation.

> Among the greatest glories of France, with all those who have struggled without respite and without weakening in this monstrous duel with the insatiable England, for the independence of our national integrity against the everlasting adversary always standing armed, in our way, against the real, implacable and traditional enemy of our race and of our blood.

Strong words in 1901 – three years before the *Entente Cordiale* put an opaque plastic covering over such sentiments, tucked them away and presented the world with a rather rosier picture.

The Breton towns of Roscoff and inland St Pol de Leon are contestants in a curious historical dispute over a little girl who, in 1548, at the ripe old age of eight, reached their shores in 1548 after a horrendous eighteen-day journey from the outer edges of the world – Dumbarton in Scotland. She was Mary, Queen of Scotland, on her way to marry the Dauphin and spend there the happiest years of her life. Today, the exact place where she landed on that still wild, rock-strewn coast has become a commercially hot property, and since the records are ambivalent the local syndicates are anxious to establish who has the greater claim to Stuart patronage. It does not really matter, of course, because tourists, too, like an argument.

Two houses stand opposite each other in Roscoff. At the turn of the century one belonged to a blacksmith who was accustomed to working with his doors open so that visitors could admire his inner courtyard. One day he overheard a tourist say that Marie Stuart must have lodged in 'just such a house' – and being an opportunist he began to charge entrance for the privilege of looking at 'Mary Stuart's House'. But his neighbour would have none of that – his house was more beautiful and older to boot. So, knowing a little English, he put a plaque on the wall, which is there today: 'Mary Stuart's House'.

Even the Church of St Ninian which claims to have been built on the spot where the Royal feet touched French soil was, in fact, built some years before she was born!

What was Mary doing there at all? James V of Scotland had married the daughter of Francis I. She died and he married Mary's mother, Marie de Lorraine. When James died Mary was eight days old and as Queen of Scotland was a good catch for France. At the age of six she was engaged to the Dauphin – and despatched to Roscoff by her young mother.

The voyage would have taxed a hardy sailor, and it is hard to imagine the stamina and maturity of children in those days. What did they do on board, how did they amuse themselves, five aristocratic little girls, all called Mary, who had been appointed as her Ladies-in-Waiting, leaving home, and mother, for the first time for a foreign land. We shall never know for the records are tantalizingly thin.

On 18th August, de Breze who had been entrusted to care for Mary wrote home to her mother:

> Madame,
> In the knowledge that you will be comforted by news of The Queen, your daughter, and her suite, I am not failing in my obedience to the orders you gave me on our departure and I am pleased to inform you that she is in as good health as she was when you last saw her. She was less seasick than anyone else in her suite – so much so that she teased those who were ill. We disembarked here at St Paul de Leon 15th August after a stormy crossing of eighteen days . . .

On the other hand King Henri II of France wrote on 24th August: 'I have news of the arrival in good health of my daughter the Queen of Scotland, in the harbour of Roscoff near to St Paul de Leon in my Duchy of Brittany'.

Sixteenth-century Roscoff may well have been reminiscent of her Scottish home to the little Queen, its approaches spiked with a thousand crags and rocks lurking just on the surface of the sea. It is a no-man's-land, where the occasional bullock still levels the fields, and families farm on their knees. They didn't like the English then – the guns on the three-tiered wedding cake of a church point out to sea – and they are no more enthusiastic today, because they say the English are not big spenders. An apple a day does not please shopkeepers in a poor region which still depends on its produce for survival. To the Breton, thrift (on the part of someone else) means meanness.

Mary married Francis in 1558 when she was sixteen years old, and returned to Scotland after his death in 1561 broken-hearted at leaving the land 'where misfortune left me and good fortune took me by the hand'. As the ship sailed away she leaned for five hours on the poop, her eyes full of tears crying 'Adieu France, adieu' and at dark she ordered a hammock to be stretched over the deck so that she could remain there all night. At daybreak, having refused to eat she was still distraught 'Adieu dear France, I shall never see you more.'

Growing Trade
Means Growing Ports

A worthy merchant is the heir of adventure whose hopes hang much upon wind. Upon a wooden horse he rides through the world, and in a merry gale he makes a path through the seas. He is a discoverer of countries and a finder out of commodities, resolute in his attempts and royal in his expenses. He is the life of traffic and the maintainer of trade, the sailor's master and the soldier's friend.

Nicholas Breton
The Good and The Bad

The sea carries, not only luxuries for the rich from afar, but also the essentials for the survival of communities unable to be completely self-sufficient – both in peace and war. Because they are vital to the movements of goods the ports which handle them can usually boast they are open for business whatever games kings and politicians are playing. So it was at the time of the Conquest, through the Hundred Years War, and through all the Tudor troubles: merchants continued to ply their trade. There were disruptions, peace came and went, treaties were made and broken; there were embargoes, such as the ban on wool exports from Britain which led to the Hundred Years War. But by and large the story of Channel merchantmen is one of gradually increasing trade and it was on the skills of merchants that the British Navy eventually built its international reputation and established sea-power world-wide.

Long before there were any written reports, we know there was a simple trade, first in flints, possibly in tin and then in gold. Because Cornwall was a staging post for ships carrying gold from Ireland, the western end of the Channel became far more important in pre-Roman times than the undeveloped east where there was virtually no ex-change either way between Britain and the Continent. Jewellery was carried from Wicklow and Kerry via Cornwall to Spain and probably Italy. Some was taken to Brittany and then overland; other ships took the western coast route of France. But we have no certain record of the ports they used or of the ships that made the journey.

By Roman times the use of metal and more sophisticated building techniques meant better boats with room for human cargo. Around the year 30 BC Strabo noted in Rome that slaves and hunting dogs were being brought with cattle and Wealden iron from Britain. Roman ports such as Richborough on the Wantsum canal (now silted up and crossed by roads) were lively, colourful places, noisy with the clatter of wheels and cobbles, though quayside bargaining concerned mainly sale rather than purchase. At Winchelsea, as in many other places, the local inhabitants were too poor to buy from traders who came loaded with ballast which they emptied into the harbour when ready to load up with goodies. This habit contributed, ironically, to the silting of Winchelsea and the end of the port.

As the Dark Ages came to an end trade increased and so did the size of the ships to carry it. It is hard to imagine how those first brightly-painted little boats with their single mast and square sail could be paddled through the menacing teeth of the unlit Brittany shore. Not for them the luxury of compass and rudder. These came much later in the thirteenth century and even then the badly-made ships continued to leak salt water. By about three hundred years after the light of Roman civilization faded around the Channel the heyday of the western end was over. The rapidly increasing population of Kent and north-eastern France and the rising importance of London drew the emphasis towards shorter sea-crossings. The natural creeks of Cornwall and the Breton coast lay lurking for their later revival of glory as smugglers' and pirates' havens.

The Normans had introduced a population of several thousand extra people which meant a massive increase in demand in Britain for food, jobs and clothes. And so, along the English shoreline, new ports grew to cope with this trade. Wheel-makers, sail-makers, carpenters were all busily at work. Beautiful, creamy-coloured stone from Caen in Normandy was carried across in open boats to build great cathedrals and many castles within ten years of the invasion. Wine, cider and garlic were brought in to lighten the labour. The agriculture of the coastal regions was given a tremendous boost: 1,900 Kent chickens were ordered for William's coronation, 2,217 pig carcasses were sent to feed the troops in Normandy in 1203 (how, in those days without freezer ships, does not bear thinking about!)

Southampton owed its rise after the Conquest to many factors. Navigation was still in its infancy, so imagine the delights of a vast stretch of inland water with two tides a day which meant that a ship need never wait to enter harbour. The same distance from the open seas that was such a boon to the twelfth-century captain was, in the end, to create problems for the speed-needy twentieth-century port and to present great opportunities for Portsmouth at the Channel end of the Solent. Centrally placed in the middle of the south coast, Southampton became a reassuring safe harbour for pirates.

In 1297, together with the beautiful old town of Sandwich in Kent, she became the first 'staple' town with special trading privileges and proudly linked with the violent trade which had such peaceful origins in the southern meadow lands of medieval Britain and was to bring wealth and bloodshed to both sides of the Channel – wool. Woven into the story of wool, of course, is the rise and fall of the Cinque Ports, that curious maritime brotherhood for which there is no parallel in France.

Wool 'so fine it was comparable to a spider's web' had been woven in Roman times. But it was with raw wool, exported especially to Flanders and to Holland, that the real profits were made. Merchants drew together, established guilds and certain ports through which the wool could be exported and tax levied by the King (Edward I). Eventually, Winchester, Exeter and Chichester all became 'staples' but the honour was moved from place to place and was sometimes given short-term as a protection – such as that to Calais over the water. Soldiers' wages in Calais were paid for by the revenue raised from the 'staple'.

Foreigners began to settle in England in large numbers – Jews, Dutch, Germans – so there was much brawling around the south-coast waterfronts. Most powerful of these were the dynamic and efficient merchants of the German Hanseatic League (known as the Easterlings) who set up branches in a number of Channel ports with headquarters in London and ferried goods between Spain and the west coast of France to England and northern Europe. For many years they were a wealthy, powerful – and so, much resented – presence in the Channel. They were greatly opposed to piracy, but even they had succumbed by the fifteenth century, when, to avoid the laws of their own rulers, merchants banded together and a kind of civil piracy broke out in the Channel. The Channel was now a link-line between the two most important French exports: wine, especially from the English territories around Bordeaux and salt from the Bay of Biscay. Salt was vital to medieval fish and meat preservation and the great Hanseatic Bay fleets were a prey to all manner of attacks.

The Channel was a rowdy, chaotic place and the wrecks that were sunk were a source of revenue to the waiting vultures on the beaches. The Counts of Leon in Brittany preferred to sacrifice the ports of Brest and Morlaix to the Duke of Brittany rather than lose control of their coastline *fertile en naufrages* (rich in shipwrecks).

Efforts were made to protect merchants, not very satisfactorily, because there was much profit to be made in lawlessness. Remember Chaucer's Shipman who was a trader and a pirate who threw his opponents overboard wherever they came from:

> Of nice conscience took he no keepe.
> If that he faught and hadde the hier hond,
> By water he sente him hoom to every lond.

Our Lady of the Shipwrecked, at Pointe du Raz, Brittany. A different attitude to the shipwrecked now prevails among the Bretons. They pray for them, rather than prey upon them. (Picturepoint)

In 1353 a new statute was enacted which gave any merchant robbed at sea the right to recover his property from the port which had taken it, provided he could prove ownership. A forlorn hope. It was from these early efforts to protect the merchant trade that the great corsairs of St Malo emerged and the legalized mafia of the Cinque Ports at the other end of the Channel in Kent and Sussex.

The story of the Cinque Ports is cloaked in the traditional red robes of history. When Queen Elizabeth, the Queen Mother, became their first woman Warden in 1978, these little Kent and Sussex coastal towns had already woven for themselves a unique place in English ceremonial – which has been embellished over eight hundred years. Being a member of the Cinque Ports today gives a certain privilege such as that of carrying the canopy over the Monarch at coronations and having their own Courts of Justice. On the other hand it costs an official £1,000 for the honour of buying the robes. Between them they now own a vast treasure trove although the amount is discreetly unobtainable.

When the Confederation of Cinque Ports were at their greatest they were justifiably known as the *King's Pirates* and they ruled the Channel from behind the safety of the Goodwin Sands which they, at least, knew so well. They were isolated geographically from the rest of Britain by unmade roads, marshes and the great forest of Anderida (the last remnant of which is now known as Ashdown Forest) which was infested with wild boar and ran down to the sea.

Long before the Conquest the people of the original five ports – Romney, Hythe, Rye, Dover and Sandwich – clung together in the face of Viking attacks. They drew up an alliance and offered their service to the King (Edward the Confessor) in return for exemption from certain dues. According to this Charter they then had the right to 'soc and sac, tol and team, bloowit and fledwit, pillory tumbril infangentheof, outfangentheof, mundbryce waives and strays, flotsam and jetsam and ligan'. In other words they could do what they liked – and mostly did. They established their own courts to mete out their own form of justice, were allowed to get away with outrageous piracy, plunder and wrecking, all for just fourteen days' service to the King a

The last stage in the ceremonial installation of Queen Elizabeth the Queen Mother as Constable of Dover Castle and Lord Warden and Admiral of the Cinque Ports. The ceremony starts in the Church of St Mary-in-the-Castle with a hallowing ceremony, takes in the Constable's Tower, and ends with this scene, the Grand Court of Shepway on the site of the ancient priory of St Martin. (Photo Source)

year. A little rape and pillage and a quick smash and grab became the sport in which the coastal ports of France were fair game. People were replaceable, the birth-rate was booming, and houses and churches destroyed meant more people in work.

It is hard to imagine much organized thought or high-minded intention behind this primitive roistering. Scenes such as that at the Battle of Sandwich when portsmen hurled pots of quicklime at the approaching French must have been all too common.

The definition of 'policing' was greatly fudged around the edges and almost anyone could attack and rob in the name of the law.

This was the age that saw the birth of the petty pirate which really reached its zenith with the swashbuckling Tudor buccaneers of the Spanish Main – Drake (El Draque) – and later still with the seventeenth- and eighteenth-century corsairs of St Malo, Duguay Truin and Surcouf. It is strange how so much blood, pain, torture and unremitting, drenched despair are glorified by time and recalled only through the technicolour eyes of Errol Flynn or Douglas Fairbanks. Everyone joined in, only the English were rather better at it: 'the greatest rovers and the greatest theevis that have been in the sea many yeeres'.

Some were ruffians whose daring mastery of the Channel trained the seaman's indomitable spirit which was the bedrock on which British naval supremacy was founded. This was not smuggling, there was nothing in the law agin it. Smuggling reached its heyday in the eighteenth century as an evasion of duties and was an internal affair not fought out on the high seas.

One of the most notorious pirates was Eustace the Monk who was, in fact, French. The son of a nobleman, he had been in a monastery, joined the army and when outlawed for murder became a mercenary pirate selling his superb skills to the King of France and England in turn. Eventually the King's Pirate defeated him on the Feast of Bartholomew in 1217, cut off his head and paraded it along the English coastal towns. The tale has, in the telling, acquired a certain fantasy for Eustace, so said local folk, was a magician who could make himself invisible, but he was overcome by one Stephen Crabbe, a portsman, who was himself a student of magic, and so could see his foe. When it was all over, St Bartholomew raised a storm which scattered the French but not the British ships. Pirates sometimes took the 'knees' which joined the frames to the deck beams out of their ships to make them more flexible and therefore faster 'like a man that is tight trussed and hath his doublet buttoned that by loosening it he is able to run the faster'. It didn't matter that the ships didn't last, there were more where they came from.

There is no clear difference between privateers and pirates, both were robbers and equally bloodthirsty. The privateer however operated officially with a 'letter of marque' which permitted him to plunder the ships of the enemy, especially in wartime. The pirate was a ruffian, an outlaw who could only expect to hang.

Cargoes that did arrive legally in the Channel during the medieval period reflected the feudal system for they were almost entirely satisfying the extravagant tastes of the rich. Living in filth and squalor, the stench of most castles must have been appalling even for those hardened stomachs. There was no sanitation, sewage flowed free in the streets and cleanliness was considered incompatible with godliness by the Church. Monasteries and castles smelt to high heaven. (There is a report that when Thomas à Becket was murdered his hair shirt was alive, but as Francis of Assissi had said lice were God's creatures this was indeed a blessing!)

So the medieval love of spices, herbs and erotic perfumes which the crusaders discovered in the East is understandable. This rich merchandise disguised many an unpalatable meal and many an undesirable stench. It was these goods which had for centuries travelled along the 'silk road' across Asia into Europe which provided the *raison d'être* for the medieval merchant to leave the Channel ports and go adventuring. Not till the sixteenth century, however, did the Channel folk of France and Britain go 'shopping' themselves on any scale. For hundreds of years they sold, and occasionally bought, only in their own harbours.

New ideas were always slow to catch on amongst ordinary people which is why in 1436 Adam de Moleyns wrote his tract the *Libelle of English Policy* in a popular doggerel that was easy for everyone to remember in days when there was no printing or mass communication. The *Libelle* was the first attempt to urge a system of mercantile protection and to argue the doctrine that England could only live by sea power. It was propaganda for a new mercantile class that was emerging throughout the Middle to Tudor Ages, and no one took much notice of it for another fifty years. The time was not quite ripe.

> Four things our Noble sheweth to me,
> King, Ship and Sword, and power of the sea.
> Where be our ships, where be our swords become?
> Our enemies bid for the Ship set a sheep.
> Alas our rule halteth, it is benumb.
> Who dare well say that lordship should take keep?
>
> I will assay, though mine heart gin to weep,
> To do this work, if we will ever see,
> For very shame, to keep about the sea.
> Shall any Prince, what so be his name,
> Which hath nobles much like ours,
> Be Lord of Sea? And Flemings to our blame
> Stop us, take us, and so make fade the flowers
> Of English state, and distain our honours?
> For cowardice alas it should so be.
> Therefore I gin to write now of the sea.

The Golden Age
of the Tudors

It is probably true that for most British people 'history' is *Tudor* history – the period when national pride sailed majestically out to sea and when, with the sinking of the Armada and the success of Shakespeare the Channel finally became 'English' once and for all. By the time Henry VII sailed across from his childhood exile in Brittany to claim his rather doubtful crown, the intellect of Europe was already on the move. The great Renaissance movement in literature and art was stirring new perspectives in the minds of the people of Italy, Germany, Spain and France; pure thought was fashionable, and scientific developments brought better navigational aids, better ships and most exciting of all, the restless exploring will to seek adventure on the high seas.

Much of the credit for this goes to a man who had seldom been to sea but who in the early fifteenth century built an observatory to study seamanship on a remote peninsula in Sagres, Portugal within easy reach of eastern trade routes. He was Prince Henry the Navigator, whose mother was Philippa, sister of Henry IV of England. With his love of astronomy and mathematics he acted as a catalyst between scholars who knew how to use the moon and stars in navigation and mariners whom he persuaded to study compasses and map-making at his school. Under his patronage the Portuguese led the way south and east in search of exotic perfumes, silks and spices from the East. The tools of their trade comprised a compass, a leadline, a log, a cross-star or an astrolabe, a table of the sun's declination and a mental formula for correcting the elevation of the pole star. This was a way a captain could find his latitude, but not his longitude. As usual the English lagged behind. The knowledge Henry passed on was slow to reach either British or French shores and it was some fifty years before John Cabot left Bristol for America, in 1497, on the first voyage of pure exploration.

England was to make a spectacular and dramatic entrance onto the world stage with such remarkable 'players' as Henry VIII, Walter Raleigh, Francis Drake – and Erasmus, who crossed the Channel to talk with his friends Colet and Sir Thomas More, and discovered another pleasure: 'when you go anywhere on a visit the girls will kiss you'!

Dwellers along the Channel shore looked out over a colourful waterway which now served not only to transport soldiers between

Europe and France but also to give them their first vision of far-distant lands as explorers returned with treasure 'beyond the dreams of avarice'. Eventually, in the reigns of Catherine de Medici and Elizabeth, compelled by the desire to see for themselves people began to venture away by land and sea to live, work and travel.

The fate of England and France, of course, was still inescapably locked, but the pattern was changing as the consciousness of the two hardened into nationhood, and European ambition exploded. The sea between them became the gateway to the world. But for the English it was much much more. The very waves were English and they also lapped on shores which they felt were rightly theirs – France.

Henry VII had arrived in 1485, appropriately by sea from France, backed by French money, and it was he who laid the foundations of English sea power. He was a diplomat, a serious man, a statesman in his dealings at home and abroad, playing France and Spain off against each other rather than fighting either. But though he did not like to fight when, in 1489, he saw independent Breton fishing villages, and Calais itself, threatened by French invasion, in the war of Breton succession, he sent English soldiers across to help the Duchy that had sheltered him during his adolescence.

For fifty years since Adam de Moleyns had written his *Libelle of Englishe Policy*, English trade had taken a hammering from almost everyone. Henry VII did his best to put a stop to all that.

The first naval dockyard was built at Portsmouth and all along the south coast those who were not needed on the land found work in the thriving shipbuilding industry.

With a keen business sense Henry determined to protect British trade, so he passed the Navigation Acts which established that ships should carry only the goods of their country of origin – which caused considerable concern to the cutting and thrusting Hanseatic League members. The *Intercursus Magnus* was negotiated in 1496 and established more secure trading arrangements.

Above the gorge of the Tamar, looking over towards Devon and England, is 'Cotehele', the beautiful house built for Sir Richard Edgecumbe, owned now by The National Trust. Friend of Henry VII, founder of one of Cornwall's most powerful families, his body lies faraway in a simple grave in Roscoff. Sir Richard and his family are part of the foundation of Tudor England but even more of the Tudor Channel and its links with Tudor Europe. It was the crack in the chess board across which Franco-British pieces moved backwards and forwards in a gripping game of noble intrigue. Checkmate was probably the loss of Calais, England's last toe hold in France, in 1558.

In 1487 Sir Richard was Sheriff of Devon and had many favours heaped upon him by the King; he was a Controller of the Household, a Chamberlain of the Exchequer and a member of the Privy Council – the kind of reliable, loyal diplomat upon whom Henry leaned heavily. Just the man to send across the sea on sensitive missions such as that to Cornwall's much troubled cousin, Brittany.

A Victorian view of one of the finest Tudor houses in England. Cotehele House was built over a period of fifty-four years from 1485 to 1539. The interior is richly decorated with tapestries, and collections of armour, weapons, hunting trophies and furniture. (BBC Hulton)

Louis XI, powerful King of France, had died in 1473 and his daughter Anne, acting as Regent, was determined to bring the Duchy to heel. Equally determined to maintain her independence was another strong-willed Duchesse, Anne of Brittany, who at the age of eleven was capable of handling her own affairs. Sir Richard met her in Rennes at the end of 1488 just after she had become a duchess and Henry wrote 'our right trust knight and counsellor Sir Richard Edgecumbe is there also, having chief rule about her'. He managed to effect a treaty of help conditional on Anne giving pledges of land as security and agreeing to submit her marriage plans and foreign policy for Henry's approval.

The same year Henry, rather reluctantly, sent troops over the Channel to lay seige to Boulogne – but they stayed only two weeks and a treaty was drawn up at Etaples. Sir Richard returned for further talks at the end of the year but became ill and died in Morlaix – before the little girl Anne was crowned Duchess. Henry did send troops later to help her but Brittany was then in chaos, French troops ravaged everywhere and everyone, and when eventually Anne signed a treaty with Charles VIII, the new French King, in 1491, there was much relief.

But then Anne acted in a way that today would be put down to adolescent unpredictability. Within four days of the Treaty she agreed to marry Charles and become Queen of France. It was to be a happy, if odd marriage, between a twenty-two-year-old 'ill-formed person, with an ugly face, large eyes with which he sees rather badly than well, an aquiline nose much out of proportion to the rest of his face and certain nervous movements of his hands which are not pleasant to see' and a girl of seventeen, 'small and thin in person, visibly lame in one foot although she uses a false heel, very determined for her age so much so that if a wish enters her head, by smiles or teases at any cost she will obtain it'.

Not so. For despite Anne's dedicated love of her native province and her determination as Queen that the Duchy would remain independent, she failed. After her death in 1514 the three-hundred-year struggle came to an end with the union of Brittany and France in 1532 when most Bretons came to terms with the truth that their only hope of survival was to align their interests with those of the French nation.

As in the Celtic fringes of Britain there remained a strong nationalist element symbolized by the fate of the statue which was erected in Rennes, the capital of Brittany, in the twentieth century, showing Brittany on her knees pleading for union before France. The separatists called it a monument to national shame and blew it up.

Meanwhile in the year that Anne was crowned Duchess, another Cornishman, Sir Richard Nafan, was sent by Henry on a diplomatic errand to Spain and Portugal and to arrange the marriage of his son Arthur to the little Catherine of Aragon.

Travel for the Tudor diplomat was hard. The party left Southampton on 19th January but was forced to land next day in Plymouth and to stay there until 1st February, only to land at Falmouth on 3rd February 'in a great tempest of wind, rain and bad weather'. Falmouth was not inhabited then, so they lodged in Penryn with various local families who were doubtless thrown into a spin by the unexpected needs of such colourful company in a poor fishing village. It was a far cry from the welcome they received when eventually they reached Spain some three weeks later and were treated to a right royal reception, with bull fights, feasts, jousting and presents all round.

Some years later the King Ferdinand and Queen Isabella of Spain no less, were forced by storms to anchor in Falmouth after a return visit to Henry. Their observations were somewhat unfair and the miseries that lay behind them are not difficult to imagine!

> We are in a very wild place – which no human being ever visits in the midst of a most barbarous race, so different in language and customs from the rest of England that they are as unintelligible to these last as to the Venetians.

> Pollard

Tudor Cornwall must have been a wild place, inaccessible except by sea, where Cornish was still the native language:

Where fragments of forgotten peoples dwelt
And the long mountains ended in a coast
Of ever shifting sand, and far away
The phantom circule of a low moaning sea.

The people who lived there were indeed poor and forgotten except as providers for the Royal Purse, which is probably why so many of them rose against Henry in the rebellion led by the flashy young Frenchman Perkin Warbeck in 1497 the name is anglicised from de Werbecke. Mainly fishermen or tinners, there was not much comfort in their lives. The Duchy grew rich on the sufferings of the tin miners but they had nothing to show for their dangerous, ill-paid labour.

Under the white volcanic shapes where today's china clay industry has sculpted the moors above St Austell into craters and peaks like a Dali moonscape, there is a warren of tunnels, empty and black. They echo with the memories of 'the roughest and most mutinous men in Britain' according to Thomas Cely. Gwethenbarra, Will Gunmow's Work, Good Fortune, Little Good Fortune – the mines in which so much resentment and anger against England and the crown was bred.

Like a ski-lift on the snow slopes (opposite), a rail track runs from pit to peak of a great heap of china clay dug up from just below the surface near St Austell. Cornwall's men have dug much deeper to supply the world with raw materials buried in this strange land. The Ding Dong mine's wheel house (below), near Penzance, overlooks the Channel through which Cornwall has exported tin and copper, and finally miners. (Picturepoint, p 96, Popperfoto, p. 97)

To understand something of the lives they led, the tourist today can do worse than visit the Poldark Mine – inland it is true but much like those along the coast itself where the shafts sometimes ran out under the sea bed. Some thirty thousand gallons of water a day are pumped out of the Poldark workings to keep them free for the millions of visitors in hard hats who slip and slide along the corridors where so many men lost their lives. They worked by candlelight in these cold, wet tunnels, sometimes at fifty fathoms underground.

During the sixteenth century, Cornwall played host to many German engineers who were brought over to advise the mine owners on new developments. Since the Bronze Age when explorers from the Mediterranean had settled in Cornwall and began to work what proved to be the largest deposit of ore in Europe, tin had literally flowed from the soil. It was 'streamed' like gold and was panned by men working out in the open amongst the 'furze' or broom, and used to line pots and make weapons and domestic utensils. In those days the tinner took the profit. Then in the fifteenth century when the shafts were sunk and the tunnels probed further into the ground, the work became more dangerous. Moreover, middle men began to take the profits and mining companies were formed which yielded rewards for their owners and little comfort for the men. Small wonder that living, breathing, and spitting black dust, their sports and pastimes were often violent: wrestling, quoits, cockfighting.

The skeleton engine houses which stand memorial to their bravery along the clifftops of Cornwall today, with the sea thundering below over many a submarine grave, belong to a later age, the eighteenth and nineteenth centuries. By then mining, though no less hazardous, had

become a thriving industry employing some fifty thousand men and supplying most of the world's copper. Then at the end of the nineteenth century with the discovery of tin and copper in other parts of the world, production plummetted. Families starved and a third of the mining population emigrated to America, Australia and South Africa. In Cornwall today they still say that where there is a hole in the ground, anywhere in the world, you will find a Cornishman.

> Houses of the Husbandmen
> ... walls of earth, low thatched roofs, few partitions, no planchings or glass windows, and scarcely any chimneys, other than a hole in the wall to let out the smoke; their bed, straw and a blanket: as for sheets, so much linen cloth had not yet stepped over the narrow channel, between them and Brittaine [Brittany]. To conclude, a mazer [drinking cup] and a pan or two, comprised all their substance: but now most of these fashions are universally banished, and the Cornish husbandman conformeth himself with a better supplied civility to the Eastern pattern.
>
> Richard Carew, *Survey of Cornwall*, c.1580

Geology made Cornwall a bleak forgotten land, with sea on three sides and not much in between: a place where the granite protrudes like bones on an undernourished frame. There was little room for the building of cities or the growing of crops as in Brittany. There, although the peasants were downtrodden and forever pawns in a power struggle between the French and Breton noble families, there was no sea between them, new ideas reached them faster and they were more adept at adapting the old while withstanding pressures on their Celtic heritage. There were many more of them too. The Breton language is still spoken in a few places even today; her costumes, music and folklore are there for the inevitable tourists, but have survived in their own right as a way of life and did not become purely a tourist attraction until the Second World War. The last Cornish-speaking native died in 1777; she was Dolly Pentreath, aged 102.

It has largely been through music that the Celtic bonds between Brittany and Cornwall have been strengthened. Brenda Wootton and Alain Stivel sing with pride and passion of their native lands. Though she had sung in Cornish folk clubs all her life, Brenda's rich and tuneful music only became known in France at an age when most grannies are settling down to knitting toddlers' clothes. As the only person in the world singing in Cornish she became an international star, loved in Australia, Canada and America too – and, significantly, hardly known across the border in a more philistine Britain. She broadcasts, talks and sings to packed stadiums in France where they call her *la Grande Cornvaillaise*. She and Alain Stivel have independently but together focused the attention of a world hungry for poetry on the Celtic culture that links their lands.

The handsome eighteen-year-old Henry VIII exploded on the Channel with great style and gusto. The contrast between his virile good looks, with the syphilis-ridden Louis XII (who died the year after), the pig-faced Emperor Maximilian and shifty Ferdinand of Spain were lost on the great mass of people. The villagers of Devon, or Calvados were hardly aware of the appearance of these remote beings; they felt change in a much more practical way – and in the countryside of sixteenth-century northern France and southern England such change was caused by the insatiable demand for shipbuilding timber. Forests were felled to build great ships and in many places wood fuel became short and peasants faced winters without fires with which to cook or keep warm. As they grew thin the coastal ports grew fat.

> The Mayor of Rye in 1581 tells the Mayors of Winchelsea, Hastings, Romney, Hythe, Dover and Sandwich about the Iron Industry
> By sundry iron works and glass houses (for glass blowing) already erected, the woods growing near unto the three towns of Hastings, Winchelsea and Rye are marvellously wasted and decayed; and if speedy remedy be not had the said woods will in short time be utterly consumed, in short as there will not any timber be had for shipping, waterworks, house building, nor wood for fuel.
>
> Rye MS, 1581

Henry really loved the sea and enjoyed the company of mariners. He lavished on his ships the kind of heraldic magnificence that had before been associated with medieval palaces and commissioned some of the most exotic ships England had ever seen. Even the ladies of the Court sat sewing streamers and pennants with which to deck them out.

He was the first King to establish a permanent military Navy separate from the merchant fleet; he encouraged the expansion of docks and building yards, created an executive Navy Board, and he built a superbly aesthetic necklace of forts along the English coast to defend them, of which the single-storey, Tudor rose-shaped castle at Deal is perhaps the prettiest. Undecorated and simple in construction these were not the castle–homes of William the Conqueror, but purpose-built fortresses, compact and cost effective for they were designed to be stocked with the maximum possible artillery. Due to Henry's insistence and encouragement the ironworkers of the Weald produced for the first time a method of casting iron guns and so commanded a greater range out to sea. The building of the castles and blockhouses produced employment for artisans and craftsmen over in Calais and all along the coast from Sandown in Kent round to Pendennis in Cornwall and was financed by money from the dissolved monasteries. Much of the stone used to supplement poor quality local material also came from the monasteries which had long ago imported it across the sea from Caen in France.

The fortifications were never tested in war, any more than were those created later by Palmerston against Louis Phillipe in the nineteenth century. It was said of those that they were built 'not so much to resist as to deter' and this they have all seemed to do effectively.

Surrounded by the sea as she was, England was still slow to develop her naval prowess and the young King was, in truth, tasting salty breezes that were already blowing across the sea from France. His ships were the achievement of an envious ruler anxious to keep up with the French Jones's who were by now fifty years ahead. Anything one could do, the other tried to do better.

When Henry inherited his father's quietly stable and securely prosperous country he faced a Europe that was now immensely powerful and bursting at the seams. France had pulled herself together after the Hundred Years War, her Channel fleet was growing fast, and her new King, Francis I, was as tall, dashing and extravagant as Henry (and with the prestige that Leonardo da Vinci had died in his arms). Spain under Ferdinand had a rush of blood to the head with her new-found wealth in South America, the Holy Roman Empire under Maximilian was almost everywhere else including the Low Countries and to the north of Calais. But frontiers were changing yearly; everyone was eyeing everyone else. Ferdinand died in 1516 and Maximilian died in **1519** and Charles V of Spain inherited both crowns to become Holy Roman Emperor; so France was surrounded. England was, as ever, tied economically by her proximity to Europe but because of her insularity was as usual behind in many areas of development. She had no army to speak of – since the moat around her made invasion improbable.

Henry had to decide whether to stand aloof and independent. The idea of playing toy soldiers for ever must have been altogether too tame for this hot-blooded young redhead. He dived headlong into the changing Europe and took England with him. During his reign the Channel ports of England and France saw the departures and arrivals of some of the greatest cavalcades in history, for everything that Henry did' was tackled with flair – whether it was royal weddings, kingly conferences or war. Because his naval build-up around 1545 coincided with the start of the national drift away from Catholicism when the now-Protestant British sea-power finally did eclipse that of the rest of the still-Catholic Europe in his daughter Elizabeth's reign, the British Navy became popularly associated with the defence of 'The Faith' – Protestantism.

But at the beginning of Henry's reign he was a Catholic. He married his brother Arthur's widow, the beautiful Catherine of Aragon, to secure the friendship of the Catholic Ferdinand of Spain and in 1511 threw in his lot with the Holy League of Venice, and the Pope and Spain, against France.

In the following year in Brittany the now-ageing Duchesse Anne watched, with pride, the trouncing of the British fleet in the Western Approaches; it was part of Henry's first attempt at flexing his muscles but one of France's greatest successes. The pride of the French fleet, a huge ship called *La Cordelière* had been launched some ten years before in Brest, and died a glorious death on the rocky island of Ushant. The French were outnumbered three to one but because the wind lay in their favour they sank half the British fleet before *La Cordelière* caught fire. Her crew escaped in lifeboats, but the Captain, a Breton named Hervé Porzmoguer, stayed on board and drove the huge vessel straight into the English flagship *The Regent*, until then the largest ship in the British Navy. The skies, and the sea ablaze, the two ships grappled, exploded and sank.

Two years later Henry commissioned the biggest and best so far – or so he thought – the *Henry Grace Dieu*. She too, like his father's dreamboat the *Grace Dieu*, lies rotting, somewhere in the Solent.

The fifteen-hundred ton, four-masted *Grace Dieu* or *Great Harry* was a golden ship – as painted by the Flemish artist Volpe, in her golden heyday at Dover, with Henry heading aboard for the Field of the Cloth of Gold. In fact, the *Henri Grace Dieu* was never there. No matter, the picture's glorious lavish extravagance reflects the age's vibrant energy.

The Embarkation of Henry VIII for the Field of Cloth of Gold *by Volpe is a grand panorama of Tudor naval splendour and a figment of artistic imagination. Henry VIII's great ship* Henry Grace à Dieu *did not carry its sovereign across the Channel but this detailed painting illustrates much about Tudor naval architecture while ignoring historical fact.* (Reproduced by gracious permission of Her Majesty The Queen)

The Ship *HARRY GRACE a DIEU*, from an original Drawing preserved in the PEPYSIAN Library in Magdalen College Cambridge. Nº 991.

Vol. VI. PL. XXII. p. 208.

Tunnage ... 1000.

MEN
Soldiers .... 349 ⎫
Mariners .... 301 ⎬ 700
Gunners .... 50 ⎭

The Henry Grace à Dieu *by Anthony, from an original in the Pepysian Library, Magdalen College, Cambridge.* (BBC Hulton)

To the expert, the *Henri Grace Dieu* was doomed before she set sail, for she showed off the enthusiasm of her monarch at the expense of her sailors. She was built – like so many Tudor ships – of unseasoned wood, for knowledge of timber was primitive, and they were prone to rot. The *Great Harry* was a carvel-built wooden dinosaur with seven decks one upon the other in the medieval style but, looking to the future and the changing shape of naval warfare, she had twenty-one guns placed low down which could be fired through closing portholes. This had been done in the Mediterranean for over fifty years, but the idea was new to Britain. Over the next one hundred years British seamen were to acquire more confidence in the knowledge and expertise they gained from much voyaging, in particular to the Newfoundland cod beds. By the death of Elizabeth, ships were purpose-built for defence, ready for battle at sea, and had outstripped their European rivals in guns and manoeuvrability.

France and England were still pitting their wits against each other and Europe. The discovery of the mariner's compass in the mid-fourteenth century made an immediate impact: the invention of printing meant villages were better able to keep up with the news. But long-distance travel was still in the hands of the Portuguese and Spanish. The horizons were wider but neither England nor France was ready to explore them. All that was a long way off.

We may be awed today by the colourful sight of a thousand sails in Cowes week, dipping and diving around the Solent for the sheer pleasure of boating. How much more awesome a sight must have been presented by those huge, richly-decorated, Venetian galleys that arrived every year in the same waters until Henry VIII's reign, sometimes two hundred at a time carrying spices, damask, velvet, gold and rare gilded armour from Italy. Although freight charges were higher for these huge galleys than for more mobile craft, they were equipped with two hundred rowing crossbowmen to protect the cargo. But crossbowmen could not protect them against the treacherous currents and village vultures who watched hopefully along the coast for the chance of wrecks to plunder.

The Venetian trade ended because new routes were being explored to the East, and the Italians lost their monopoly of the spice trade. The quality of their merchandise declined and though Henry VIII himself made a personal visit to Southampton to welcome them, he was no longer happy to allow valuable British wool exports for second-rate goods. Their welcome grew cooler and eventually after one terrible voyage the crew mutinied, the townspeople of Southampton joined in and there was a riot which put an end to further trade.

All through the British occupation of Calais – and indeed long after – mercantile interests were represented by a thriving community. Richard and William Johnson who settled there were fairly typical. Their father had been a Dutch settler in London and the two boys decided to try their luck in turn in Calais, where they imported broadcloth and kerseys from England and silks, velvets, damask and grosgrain from Flanders. William became an alderman of Calais and, as representative of the Crown, was one of the organizers of the Field of the Cloth of Gold. Their children in turn grew up as citizens of the city.

Thomas Pettyt's delicate drawings of the Calais of that time capture the smells and sights. In them Calais rises sheer from the sea prettily encircled by its walls. Barbara Winchester has described it all in her biography of the Johnson family, *Tudor Family Portrait*.

> Inside are wooden houses with crow-step gables and pleasant gardens set close together in the winding streets. Here stood the ancient church of St Nicholas – the mariner's saint – and the tall spire of Our Lady Church where the merchants of the 'staple' knelt to pray. Here was the schoolhouse behind William Steven's place; taverns like 'The Sign of the Ship' and 'Crosskeys'; the leather, swordsmith and goldsmiths shops down bustling Lantern Gate Street; the fish and vegetable stalls in the market place where 'Flower Mary' sold her cabbages and pot-herbs and delicious early fruit that came from France. Every week the clumsy market carts came rumbling in from Oye and Sandgate,

villages set among the farms and orchards of the lowland countryside with its landscape of willow-hung canals against the line of wooded hills. A stream of clear water flowed through the town falling into the haven at a place called Paradise.

Such wares as the town lacked came in by sea, for Calais was a flourishing port, with the finest harbour on the Artois coast. All sorts and conditions of ships lay anchored in the Roads or moored at the wharves along the foreshore: great hulks bound for Antwerp with cargoes of ebony, spices and silk; pirate vessels in the guise of honest merchantmen; herring catchers, slow cogs and slender barques, their pennants streaming in the wind. The quayside was always crowded with merchants and mariners, arguing and gesticulating as the bales of goods were swung ashore, and carried into the warehouses that were only a stone's throw from the Watergate.

In 1514 Henry was busy playing one European power off against the other – and, when Ferdinand of Spain suddenly switched allegiance and signed a Treaty with France, Henry too negotiated peace. His beautiful, eighteen-year-old sister, Mary, yet another pawn in history's power struggle, was sent to marry the ugly, fifty-two-year-old future Louis XII.

In Boulogne that day in 1514 there was great public rejoicing. The young princess was welcomed by *La Vièrge Comtesse* in verse and in front of the portcullis of les Dunes young girls dressed as virgins, accompanied by two angels, waited beneath a boat full of roses and lilies suspended from the portcullis. The girl who married first for duty, was eventually married for love to the Earl of Suffolk and became the mother of Lady Jane Gray.

And so the Royal game of 'tennis', which Henry loved, was played on a grand scale across the Channel. Henry had built a bigger and better boat for himself, so Francis now built a port to outmatch Portsmouth. In 1517 the first warship sailed into the Bassin du Roi in the brave new port of 'Franciscopolis' (Le Havre). But it was built on shifting sands and salt. On either side the life of Honfleur and Harfleur were already being strangled as their harbour entrances filled up and the harbour walls of Franciscopolis kept crumbling. On a high tide the water poured in – the priest at the Church of Notre Dame habitually had to stand on a chair for Mass. Why was he privileged? Were wet feet the congregation's penance? The new town had a stormy start: a freak tide destroyed it in 1525 and drowned many people; the two-thousand-ton ship *Grande Nef Françoise* was smashed on the rocks there, the warship *Philippe* caught fire and sank in the King's presence. Not until 1540 when it was redesigned and reborn under the Italian architect Bellamarto did Le Havre really set out on the road to fulfilling Francis's dream. Le Havre is safe today – France's second largest port after Marseilles – but still around the estuary of the Seine the cows graze, moving ankle deep across a swampy mirror where the sea and silt silently struggle at every tide.

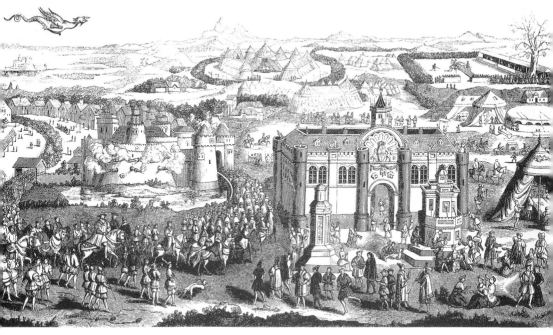

Compared with twentieth-century political jamborees and gatherings of heads of state, the events of 1520 in the little towns of Ardres and Guisnes, have never been matched. This was their moment of glory – for a few brief glorious months the villagers in the stretch of land beyond the back of Calais were caught up in preparations for a spectacular meeting of Kings that would have delighted Cecil B de Mille. This was the chosen site for the Field of the Cloth of Gold – the grandiloquent name that has been given to the most colourful summit meeting in history – the most spectacularly futile attempt to reconcile the French and the English. It was a great party under canvas – but, like holiday friendships, it was a non-starter.

However gracious was the outwardly royal *entente*, that of the French and English workers on the site was less than cordial! Competition between them was intense and the night a gale blew the roof off the pavilion the French were building for their King at Ardres, there was much rejoicing and *vin ordinaire* amongst the English at Guisnes. From beginning to end it was an exercise in one-upmanship, with a little crafty manoeuvring on the side by Henry. Only a week before his departure date, when most of the royal officials had already left Britain to supervise the planning in France, Charles V of Spain arrived for secret discussions in Dover. This clandestine move doomed the prospects for the meeting between Henry and Francis before it began.

This etching of the Field of Cloth of Gold is based on the painting by an unknown artist and shows the arrival of the two sovereigns with displays of extravagant splendour in an attempt to impress one another at the start of the most ostentatious summit meeting of all time. (Mansell)

Charles never did draw Henry into his battle with France, but it is not surprising that Francis was concerned.

This was the last nostalgic fling of medieval romanticism. An army of English workmen laboured under ridiculous pressure to prepare the site. They built a colossal ornate tent, connected with the castle by a secret passage. All the buildings were painted blue and gold and richly decorated with heraldic artistry; the canvas was gilded inside and out. Into the state 'apartments' went Turkish carpets, statues and beautiful tapestries. Two fountains flowed with claret and malmsey – free for all – and all around were about four hundred tents for the courtiers and staff. But most wonderful of all was the banqueting hall – canvas painted outside to look like brick and inside hung with cloth of gold and silver and interlaced with white and green. It was an *Arabian Nights* fantasy on a windy northern plain. When the day came and His Majesty arrived all this splendour was no more proof against the wind than the humble camp sites at Guisnes and Ardres which straddle those very same Fields of Gold. All the glorious tents were blown down and the dust blew into the jousters' eyes.

Tents of a more humble orange and blue shelter the holiday-making, middle classes of the twentieth century, where gold has given way to plastic and the sound of portable television has replaced the sound of music. But the wind blows still and the dust rises just as it did for those jewel-laden monarchs and their all too merry men and women.

On that May 31st, 5172 people and 2865 horses crossed the Channel to the still English port of Calais, including 70 grooms, 12 chaplains, 114 nobles and 200 guards. The Queen's retinue stood at 267 – including the former Queen of France, Henry's sister Mary, now married to the Duke of Suffolk. The problems of etiquette and protocol were insoluble from the outset and tempers were fragile. It is not hard to imagine the relief that must have shivered through the organizers on both sides when eventually the two monarchs galloped out to the edge of the Val d'Or, waited and then charged, to meet in the middle and, still mounted, embrace. Then the fun really began.

All that free-flowing wine must have dimmed the memories of many who were there. Henry asked Francis to wrestle with him and to his chagrin was tactlessly upended by the French King and thrown to the ground. Never a good loser, Henry turned white with anger. He was not amused.

Nor were the ladies exempt from the merrymaking. They appalled the elegant-mannered French by drinking from one cup, passed round time and time again. But King Francis, with Gallic charm, made great efforts to please his guests and at one banquet managed to kiss all the ladies in turn 'save four or five that were old or not standing together'.

The cost of this pantomime nearly wrecked Henry. The bill for jousting clothes alone came to £3000, provisions costing £8839 were shipped across from Dover and another £15,000 worth of wine and beer collected at Calais.

In terms of Anglo-French relationships although it kept a great many people in work throughout the year it achieved nothing! It certainly did not bring Henry any nearer to his private hopes of regaining his foothold in France.

In fact there are many aspects of Henry's relationship with France which the English textbooks tend to gloss over and which reveal, sadly, why French history is a little tender around its Channel edges.

In human terms, for instance, the siege of Boulogne of 1544 which rates one line in Churchill's *History of the English Speaking Peoples*, was a disaster which is inescapably displayed for all the thousands of no-passport day trippers if only they knew what they were seeking.

The background to the siege, as usual, was the complex manoeuvring of the rulers of Europe. Charles V of Spain with his eye on Paris, persuaded the new ageing, bad-tempered Henry to cross the Channel to fight against Francis, who, from a French point of view had tried too hard to be friends with England. The siege is recorded by Churchill in one line, but in the *Histoire de Boulogne* by Jules Paublan it is linked with the better-known seige of Calais, and its brave people praised.

After a three-month siege by forty thousand troops, the Commander of the Garrison weakened and talked of 'parley'. But the mayor of the town, Eurvin, offered to let him escape and to take on, with his citizens, the defence of their town rather than let it fall to the enemy. His courage is displayed in the *Salle des Fêtes* in the Town Hall. The aftermath was painted by Tattegrain and hangs proudly in the *Salles des Pas Perdus*, also at the Town Hall, at the top of the old walled town.

> The King of England, having captured the higher and lower parts of the town allowed the inhabitants to leave. During the last week in September, 1500 on foot, 77 on horseback, 1927 women and children, and 87 wounded left their elderly and their sick and carried away from the town all they possessed. But the English were waiting. Those who resisted were torn to pieces. It was terrible to see young girls and women escaping from these savage dogs, barefoot, their clothes torn, dragging their little children. On the road to Etaples a dreadful storm completed the agony of these tortured, half-naked people.

Henry had won Boulogne for six years, but by keeping his men in the north he had inadvertently allowed the French the opportunity of saving Paris from Charles. He took over an empty, destroyed city – nothing was left but a shell. Unlike Calais its value was negligible, and although he built some forts the place was isolated and indefensible. To Edward VI fell the task of selling it back to Henri II for four hundred *écus d'or*. Henry VIII and his colourful adversary Francis I died within two months of each other in 1547. Eleven years later Calais, too, was lost and his dispairing daughter 'Bloody Mary' declared that when she died the name of Calais would be found engraved on her heart.

The Tudor warship Mary Rose, *sunk accidentally due to bad design, passes Britain's most famous warship, the* Victory, *while in the background a modern warship, a frigate, is moored at the dockside in Portsmouth. The inset shows the* Mary Rose *being preserved for posterity.* (Topham)

Somewhere beneath the seas off the Isle of Wight lies a ship whose name has long been forgotten and whose secrets are likely to remain forever hidden. She is *La Maitresse*, flagship of the French Navy who sank on the treacherous St Helen's Shallows the day before the now celebrated *Mary Rose*.

The history of the *Mary Rose*, pride of Henry's fleet, is well-known. Her end was caused by the very innovation of which he was so proud – the low, open gunports for the new-style cannons. A squall caught her as she left Portsmouth and, to the distressed horror of the onlooking crowds, while the helpless King himself wept and comforted Lady Carew (wife of the Vice Admiral), she heeled over and sank. Nearly everyone was drowned. There she was to remain, until in 1982, after huge international fund-raising efforts, she was brought to the surface and is now on show in Portsmouth – the earliest example of a complete Channel fighting ship.

It is curious how, time and time again, the pattern of history is mirrored across the Channel.So it was during the later sixteenth century when the slow-starting English zest for the sea finally took off, that two women shone above all others. On one side the ambitious, childless Protestant, Elizabeth I. On the other, Catholic Catherine de Medici. Catherine, mother of nine children, had been a back-seat Queen for twenty years when the eighteen-year-old Elizabeth came to the throne. At the age of forty, as a widow, she was about to emerge, and make her royal mark in a country once again torn by internal torment – this time the holocaust of religious wars. They were two colourful, powerful monarchs in whose time the Channel was to experience its greatest drama – the defeat of the Armada, which swept the sea clear for Britain's future domination of the world's oceans.

The story of the Armada has been told a thousand times, for it opened the flood gates which had blocked the rising tide of English sea power. There was never again in the minds of the British at least, to be any real doubt about who ruled the waves.

During the first two thousand years of Channel history, control of land, not sea, was the driving force for its people. Ships were transports for armies, they looked like floating castles and men fought on board as though they were ashore. But during the sixteenth century the restless seeking of the Renaissance crossed the sea. It seemed as though all Europe was afloat – in search of treasure, slaves, new ideas and especially new lands to conquer. This drew a new breed of adventurer through the Channel: ambitious seamen who spent their lives pitting their wits against its diabolical moods. The Renaissance itself did not celebrate the sea which was not a matter for poetry or music – that was to come later. To these men it was an adversary still, to be mastered, not romanticized and though they ventured further afield in greater numbers than ever before, from all over Europe, so many of the names that still echo through the Western Approaches were Channel men through and through. They were mostly trained professionals: there were merchants anxious to extend trade routes, adventurers out for personal glory and privateers with a touch of both.

Jacques Cartier from the dark streets of St Malo claimed Quebec for the French; there was Humfrey Gilbert from Dartmouth whose exploitation of the apparently limitless herring beds off Newfoundland was to provide work and training for thousands of French and British Channel seamen. This was the age of the East India Company, from whose trading eventually grew the British Empire. It also saw the foundation of that august body Trinity House, to control and pilot the rapidly-increasing traffic past British shores. But above all, with the Spanish having long adventured in the South Atlantic and threatening to annex much of Europe, for the French and British this became the age of Spain-baiting – of the slave trading Hawkins family, the tub-thumping Protestant pirate, Drake from Plymouth, and Raleigh. Sir Humfrey Gilbert was Raleigh's lesser-known older stepbrother and was perhaps the first Englishman to realize that gold was not the only prize to be found in foreign parts and that with the rising population, land was a prize in itself, to be gathered in the name of the Queen.

He obtained a charter from the Queen which allowed him to 'discover, finde search out and view such remote, heathen and barbarous lands countries and territories not actually possessed of any Christian prince . . . and the said Sir Humfrey . . . shall goe and travel thither to inhabite or remain there, to build and fortifye . . . '

Leading up to and then beyond the Armada the Channel ports of both England and France were busy with shipbuilding families designing new craft to keep pace with the improvements afoot in other maritime areas. The spread of printing and education, for instance, encouraged the production of charts and maps so that it was easier for sailors to follow the new Trinity House pilot books for coastal navigation. Out at sea they were helped by the introduction of very simple instruments, the quadrant and the astrolabe.

The navy was still controlled by soldiers and her ships retained their imposing unwieldy design. Ships were constructed around a skeleton and then clad with overlapping unjoined planks (carvel-built) and they were fitted with three masts which made them better for longer voyages. But the greatest step forward was, in Britain, the simplification of the upper decks and the introduction of guns. The old-fashioned forecastle was abandoned and the aftercastle lowered so that the whole craft was much more manoeuvrable. In Spain and France on the other hand, where Catholics and Protestants were massacring each other, there was little time for naval enterprise.

When Elizabeth appointed John Hawkins of Plymouth as Controller of her Fleet in 1577 she knew exactly what she had done, for John, son of the redoubtable sea-dog slaver William Hawkins, had learned to loathe the Spaniards when serving with his father and was unswervingly dedicated to their destruction. John and his brother were not prepared to wait and began a massive naval build-up. He attacked corruption and cut naval costs whilst improving standards.

The Queen did not want to fight. Neither did Philip. They both worked to the end for some kind of external compromise. Philip watched the British becoming more and more strongly Protestant and he was torn between his father's exhortation to preserve his religion and his own desire to retain the alliance. The two were becoming increasingly incompatible. Meanwhile Elizabeth watched uneasily as Spanish might grew throughout Europe and the world, encircling the war-torn France, and so also threatening England.

In the early part of Elizabeth's reign John Hawkins tried time and time again to establish a regular trade route with the Spanish West Indies and in 1567 all Plymouth was agog with preparations for the biggest expedition so far. Two of the Queen's ships, the *Jesus* and the *Minion* were being laden with supplies including beans for the slaves. Whilst they were anchored in the Cattewater, eleven Flemish trading ships under the Spanish flag sailed in and cocked a snook, refusing to lower their flags. So Hawkins opened fire. He knew that despite protestations, the Fleet was there to catch him unawares and prevent him sailing. The Queen, diplomatic as ever, was officially 'displeased' with her Controller, but on St Andrew's Day in October all the waiting seamen were assembled in St Andrew's Church for the familiar service of blessing. Four hundred of them left that day for Africa and Brazil. In the sixteen months before their return, the Channel became a ferment of aggression, with Protestant 'privateers' legitimately plundering French, Flemish and Spanish Catholic shipping.

In France the Protestants were led by the old soldier Admiral Coligny. The young King Charles IX was dominated by his love for his power-hungry mother Catherine. It was her choice to face civil war, rather than war with Spain that made her urge him to massacre every Protestant in France on St Bartholomew's Day in 1572. His reply, 'kill them all, so that none will be left to reproach me'. No wonder they had little time for affairs of the sea.

Coligny turned the Channel town of La Rochelle into a Protestant Huguenot fortress and appealed to the young blood of England for help. Before long the Channel was alive with his Huguenot ships attacking, harrying, plundering every Catholic vessel that dared to enter its waters. Coligny was a genius, for he realized that so long as the sea was Protestant, he would hold the upper hand. Both William Hawkins, brother of John, who then was Mayor of Plymouth and the Vice Admiral of Devon, Sir Arthur Champernowne, joined in the assault from headquarters on what is now Drake's Island (it was St Nicholas Island then). In Holland where the people were revolting against the persecutions of the Duke of Alva, they pinned their hopes on their own 'Sea Beggars' who joined in the bombardment of Catholic shipping.

At the height of this upheaval when the hearts of ordinary folk strolling along the cliffs of Torbay thrilled at the sight of this reassuring, Protestant, police force patrolling far out at sea, Philip of Spain made a strangely reckless error. He assumed that the Channel was as free as it had been before when his ships sailed through *en route* for the Netherlands. He seemed not to realize that this was no longer true and he sent six, small, unarmed ships up-Channel with £100,000 in silver destined for the Catholic butcher, the Duke of Alva, to pay soldiers in the Netherlands. They sailed, unsuspecting, through the Western Approaches in the autumn of 1568 – into 'a sea of sharkes'. the Huguenots chased the ships into Southampton, Plymouth and Fowey. Somewhat amazed at the Spanish Ambassador's request for safe conduct for his vessels to the Netherlands – especially as their contents would doubtless have financed an invasion of England – Elizabeth commanded that the treasure be safeguarded behind her own guns and battlements.

To Spain it looked like the greatest robbery of all time. To the people of Plymouth, eager to see what was happening, it must have been a day of wonderful excitement. But, as a consequence, all British goods in Spain and the Netherlands were confiscated.

This Tudor map, in the library of the Marquess of Salisbury, is one of the earliest surviving charts of the entire Channel. While the detail is intricate it is not quite accurate but a similar chart would have been used to create the illustration on p 115. (Marquess of Salisbury)

In the following year John Hawkins returned to moor in Mounts Bay, Cornwall, after his foray to the coast of South America and news spread that of the four hundred who had left in such high spirits the year before only seventeen were still alive. Hatred of Spain grew near uncontainable, and the Channel temperature was near boiling point. To their credit Elizabeth and Philip kept their cool and tried for a further fifteen years to avoid an out-and-out war.

Farewell and adieu to you fair Spanish ladies,
Farewell and adieu to you ladies of Spain.
For we've received orders to sail for old England
But we hope in a short time to see you again.
We'll rant and we'll roar o'er all the wild ocean,
We'll rant and we'll roar o'er all the wild seas
Until we strike soundings in the Channel of Old England.
From Ushant to Scilly is 35 leagues.   contemporary song

Flying in a small plane from the Ushant coastline zigzagging across that still narrow stretch of sea between France and England the scene is so easy to visualize – an aerial camera could have taken in the entire Armada fleet as it moved into the Western Approaches. More than two hundred and fifty English ships – with dozens of others ferrying food and supplies back and forth were there to harry some one hundred and thirty magnificent Spanish galleons, that, after months of expectation, had finally been sighted off The Lizard. This was the mightiest fleet the world – let alone the Channel – had ever seen, and because he wanted to frighten the English in advance Philip of Spain made a detailed reckoning of exactly what it comprised. There were copies of these lists in England before the Armada sailed.

There were to be 8052 sailors, 18,975 soldiers, and 2008 convicts at the oars. Amongst the soldiers were 178 gentlemen who demanded cabins of their own. There were 6 surgeons and 6 doctors – whereas there were 180 priests, obviously to cater for the souls the surgeons did not save. All these men required 14,000 pipes of wine, 11 million pounds of biscuit, 600,000 pounds of salt, 800,000 pounds of cheese, 18,000 bushels of chickpeas and 40,000 gallons of olive oil. For the army that was to land in England there were 5000 pairs of shoes, 11,000 pairs of sandals, 10,000 pikes, 20 gun carriages and 40 mules.

Yet the man in charge of it all, the Duke of Medina Sidonia, had hardly ever been to sea and had no with at all to do so.

Compare all this with the usual ramshackle, raggle-taggle disorganization of the English – always ill-prepared and late. There had been the usual reluctance of poor coastal towns to spend money for defence – they did not want a war that would spoil their trading. Nicholas Danthey, sent by Her Majesty to the Isle of Wight, said troops were 'furnished' and missing equipment. Seamen were in rags, unpaid and hungry. John Hawkins raised their pay in order to enlist 'decent, respectable, god-fearing sailors such as could make shift of themselves and keep themselves clean without vermin'.

Once the Armada sailed the campaign was conducted in almost complete ignorance on either side. The 20,000 Spaniards had very little idea why they were there or what was happening. Indeed they believed they were on a mercy mission and would be welcomed with open arms by the English. They were also hungry and sick. The Spanish ships, unlike the English, still sported unwieldy castles of medieval warfare and were not designed to cope with Channel winds. Nor could the Spaniards get a message back to Spain for help.

The English, though backward, now had a few much faster 'race' built ships and, on the insistence of Drake and the Admirals, were sailors' weapons, not merely transports for soldiers.

Admirals could only report as far as the eye could see, the clifftop watchers in France and England could not possibly guess the movements of so many ships over the course of seven days.

For months Drake had urged the Queen to let him go to Portugal and lie waiting for the Armada outside Lisbon. Three times the English

Fleet left and three times was driven back by foul weather and lack of food. When eventually the Spaniards with the wind in their favour reached British waters, nearly all the might of British naval power was assembled in Plymouth waiting for a chance to sail again. Lord Howard in the *Ark Royal*, Drake in the *Revenge*, John Hawkins in the *Victory*, Frobisher and 'the gallantest company of soldiers and mariners that I think was ever seen in England'. The Royal Fleet itself numbered only 34 ships; the rest were merchantmen, called up as usual from the Channel ports.

Drake's somewhat deflationary decision to continue his game of bowls on the Hoe when the Armada was sighted is one of those unproven legendary acts that sums up what it was all about: the wind. He knew that the Fleet was marooned in Plymouth Sound and there was time. What he did not know was that the Spaniards were planning to attack with fireships. That afternoon, sixty-five of the English galleons sailed down the Sound and accomplished a feat of seamanship that would have made headline news in later years. It was nigh impossible, but, by tacking inshore along the shoreline into the wind, they worked their way along the coast, whilst the rest of the Fleet worked up to windward through the night. By dawn both parts of the Fleet had gained the weather gauge. They could not sink such a huge, closely-formed Armada, so they began to herd it up the coast,

The imagination of the artist soars above the Channel as the English fleets begin to shepherd the ungainly galleons towards their destruction. (BBC Hulton)

115

like wily sheep-dogs, keeping out of range of the grappling irons; past Plymouth, Torbay, and the Isle of Wight they crept, at the rate of about two knots a day.

The Spaniards, blown out of touch with their Commander and in heavy seas, began to despair. One Spanish captain wrote: 'The worst of them, without their maincourse or topsails can beat the best sailors we have'.

On July 27th, eight days after its arrival off Plymouth, the French got their first sight of the Armada as the entire fleet anchored off Calais with the English no distance away.

It was a horrendously dangerous position: 'We rode there at anchor all night' wrote a Spanish seaman, 'with the enemy also anchored half a league from us. We made up our minds to wait for there was nothing else to be done, but with a great presentiment of evil from that devilish people and their arts'. Spanish morale was abysmal – and the weather was turning.

What happened then has been reported in so many places – and every tale is different. The English sea captains squabbled amongst themselves and were furious not to have taken any prizes – Drake was even called a cowardly knave by Frobisher. No one really knows what took place. But the men who left home in the heat of a Spanish summer day all those weeks before were finally defeated in the sleeting cold and rain of a Channel storm. The English seamen behaved like a disorderly rabble. There was looting and some even swarmed into Calais to rob spectators on the beach.

On the turn of the tide at midnight on July 28th the English sent 8 fireships amongst the sleeping fleet. They were 'spurting fire and their ordnance shooting, a horror to see in the night'. There was no time to weigh anchor or retaliate: the Armada was shattered and by dawn the people of the white cliffs of Dover and Cap Gris Nez could see the ships scattered out to sea. Then the English charged again amidst the blinding gunsmoke: There was no strategy or co-ordination – how could there be when the only way of receiving orders from the flagship was when you came within earshot?

By afternoon sixteen Spanish ships were crippled, no English. Hundreds of bodies were thrown in the water. Then it began to rain; the British held off to shorten their sails and the fleets were driven apart by gusting winds. It was all over – but the nightmare for the Spaniards had only just begun as they drifted helplessly towards the shallow sandbanks of Flanders. They drifted together through a night of terror, no lights, bar the menacing reminders that the English were not far behind; the soundings became shallower and keels began to stir up mud from the bottom. 'Everyone was in utter despair and stood waiting for death' wrote a Spaniard aboard the *San Martin*. Then once again the wind intervened and blew them off the immediate danger and out to the North Sea where they drifted on for weeks and weeks further and further towards the ends of the earth, until one by one they were wrecked around the wild coasts of Scotland and Ireland.

Sir Francis Drake by the miniaturist Isaac Oliver (BBC Hulton)

Golden Hind. (Mansell)

The sixteenth century had been larger than life on both sides of the Channel for although the names of the English sea-dogs are better known, France had her share of colour.

The English, according to Paul Hentzner, a foreign visitor of the day, were 'good sailors and better pirates; cunning, treacherous and thievish. They are powerful in the field, successful against their enemies, impatient of anything like slavery, vastly fond of noises that fill the ear, such as the firing of cannon, drums and the ringing of bells … If they see a foreigner very well made or particularly handsome they will say "it is a pity he's not an Englishman".'

Drake, Sir Richard Grenville, Sir Humfrey Gilbert, Hawkins and many others less well-known left Plymouth in a programme of exploration which was to claim huge chunks of the world for Britain. Most famous of all those voyages, of course, was Drake's around the world in the *Golden Hind* in 1577–80.

One of the characteristics of the twentieth century is a nostalgic curiousity about the past. Centuries ago people were far too busy looking to their present to be concerned with 'heritage'. The *Golden Hind* lives on in two, somewhat smarter, privately and probably better built reconstructions. One, moored in Brixham harbour is open to the public. The other, which is itinerant and is often seen in Channel waters, completed a celebration round-the-world voyage on the 400th anniversary of Drake's voyage in 1973. This was the ship used in the television series *Shogun*.

With its twentieth-century statutory lavatories, bunks, well-equipped galley, radar, and shame of shames, an engine in the hold, this *Golden Hind*, is a far cry from the original in which some sixty men were crammed, sleeping on decks between eighteen gun emplacements. Headroom was less than five feet in many parts of the ship and though Tudor sailors were shorter than we are, many of them spent much time bent double. She was built in Appledore, on the north coast of Devon, as far as possible from authentic materials, and the flax and hemp rigging were raised by manpower when she made that celebration voyage. Clare Francis was with her then and reported that 'a three-masted square-rigger is a far cry from a small single-masted yacht, but it didn't take an expert eye to see that this ship was bulky, heavy and squat for her short length.'

Hakluyt, the prolific chronicler of Elizabethan sea adventures recorded Sir Humfrey Gilbert's gallant end in 1583.

> We had got into the height and elevation of England ... we met with very foule weather and terrible seas, breaking short and high, pyramid wise. The reason whereof seemed to proceede either of hilly grounds high and low within the sea (as we see hilles and dales upon the land) upon which the seas doe mount and fall; or else the cause proceedeth of the diversitie of winds, shifting often in sundrie points; all of which have power to move the great ocean ...

> Monday the ninth of September in the afternoone, the Frigate (on which Sir Humfrey had stayed despite entreaties from Drake on the Golden Hinde) was neer cast away, oppressed by waves, yet at that time recovered; and giving forth signs of joy the Generall sitting abast with a book in his hand cried out to us in the Hinde (so oft as we did approach within hearing) 'We are as near to Heaven by sea as by land ... ' The same Munday night about twelve of the clock the Frigat being ahead of us in the Golden Hinde, suddenly her lights were out whereof as it were in a moment we lost the sight and withall our watch cried the Generall was cast away which was too true. For in that moment the Frigat was swallowed up of the sea. Yet still we looked out all that night and ever after until we reached the coast of England.

Plymouth, the home of so many of these rough, tough men was, according to the Tudor traveller, Leyland, a 'mene thing, an inhabitation of fishers', even so it was the fourth largest town in Britain, after London, Bristol and York. Almost totally destroyed during the last war, it was rebuilt as a brand-new town and the town that Hawkins knew has been swallowed up in the great ugly sprawl of the industrial development allied to a naval dockyard. The corpses of rusting submarines lie near the motorway bridge into Plymstock where once the quayside inns smelt of tar and canvas, and were rowdy with drunken brawling, shanties and the rattling of barrels on a cobbled front.

Like the great railway junctions of later ages, Tudor Plymouth must have been a town where tears of pain and pleasure mingled all too often with the salty air. Down by the slippery harbour steps a plaque and a map mark, unemotionally, some of the human dramas, the departures and arrivals that have been witnessed here, from the landing in happier days of Queen Catherine of Aragon to greet her husband Henry, to the arrival in England of the very first American 'tourist' in 1528.

This visitor was a South American Indian chief – a valuable prize for William Hawkins senior after his trading journey to Brazil. He brought him home to Plymouth where Hakluyt described his first impact on the amazed locals.

> In his cheeks there were holes made according to their savage manner and therein small bones were planted, standing out an inch from the said holes, which, in his own country was reputed for bravery. He also had another hole in his nether lip in which was set a precious stone about the bigness of a peg. All his apparel, behaviour and gesture were strange to the beholder.

One wonders what that warrior made of the people of Plymouth. He stayed in England for a year but when he left to go home 'it fell out in the way that by change of air and alteration of diet the savage King died at sea'.

From Plymouth the Tolpuddle Martyrs were sent to the despair of Botany Bay and hopeful families watched the brave departure of one hundred Pilgrim Fathers on their sixty-six day nightmare journey to America. Drake sailed in here with enough silver and gold to clear the National Debt. And three hundred and fifty years later the wheel went full circle on the triumphant return of Francis Chichester – first person to sail around the world alone. The people of Plymouth are well used to cheering their heroes, in a town where sea pride flows freely in the veins!

Dartmouth had once been the equal to Plymouth – its harbour in many ways was better – but it is the reputation of great men that builds a town, and Elizabethan Dartmouth had no Hawkins family, and no Drake. Its only moment of uplift came colourfully later, when in 1592 a privateer crew brought the East Indian carrack *Madre de Dios* into the town. She was richly loaded with spices, perfumes, gold, precious stones and pepper which were all looted by the sailors, leaving the Queen with nothing but pepper. She dispatched Robert Cecil and Raleigh to retrieve what they could but they met with men, their pockets loaded, rampaging around the town and little could be done.

The old city of St Malo known as the City of Corsairs is host today to adventurers of another sort, yachtsmen – *plaisanciers* – from all nations, who shelter in the huge marina in the shadows of the ancient walls. There is nowhere like St Malo on the Channel – its history reads like an adventure book . . . for the Malouins have always been an independent, stubborn breed. In the middle ages they trod a delicate anarchical tightrope between the warring Kings of France and Dukes of Brittany. In 1395 the King of France issued a declaration which was to prepare the ground for the evolution of a very special kind of resident.

The massive walls of the port of St Malo deliver a message much older but just as blunt as the graffiti on the sea wall. (Barnaby)

Any man or woman from any nation or country seeking refuge in our town and demanding franchise will enjoy immunity whatever misdeed or crime they have committed outside the said town and thenceforth may not be detained or arrested if they submit to the usual civil laws and rules.

St Malo deserves all the spectacular, dramatically scenic effects in which the sea and sky can frame it. It is a spectacular town in design and has produced men of spectacular spirit. Caught in the crossfire at the end of the Second World War, it was almost totally destroyed and was recreated brick by brick to recapture exactly the ancient city, floating within its walls like an island in a wild and rock-strewn sea. The cobbled streets, too narrow for cars, bustle with the passing, overcrowded twentieth century – the clothes are different but perhaps not the character within. Fat ladies in too-short denim skirts, bronzed beauties in bikinis, matelots in striped tee-shirts and old men in plastic sandals sucking lollies, busy going nowhere in particular. It is a safer place than it was when Jacques Cartier sat looking out over the harbour in 1534 – and much less smelly.

In the dark cool of the museum the show cases are warm with mementoes brought home by those brave crews who had sailed from their Channel homes on voyages long ago to fly the French flag in Canada, the West Indies and West Africa. The rolling pins, decorated for luck, Bristol glass, carved mother of pearl ties and purses. And in one surprising corner of this French museum is the yellow, torn record of an event that ignominiously marked the end of an era: the death of Drake in 1596 who died, it says, 'of the bludie flixe'.

By the time of Drake's death the Channel had become – at least in the British view – English. The sea itself became the great divide between Britain and the rest of Europe, and so a bulwark to be defended and to be used for defence. A fact which most foreigners chose to ignore. Because it was a Protestant navy which had sunk the mighty Catholic Spain, naval power became synonymous for the British with Protestantism.

All this was aided and abetted by the huge popular success of an inland playwright, William Shakespeare. What Shakespeare had to say about England and its surrounding sea, did for that offshore country what the Beatles did for Liverpool. Tudor England seized the opportunity. Shakespeare underlined what, by the turn of the century, ordinary people had come to assume. The words he wrote were said by John of Gaunt, but they were the sentiments of the Elizabethan people.

> This royal throne of kings, this scept'red isle,
> This earth of majesty, this seat of Mars,
> This other Eden, demi-Paradise;
> This fortress built by Nature for herself
> Against infection and the hand of war;
> This happy breed of men, this little world;
> This precious stone set in the silver sea,
> Which serves it in the office of a wall,
> Or as a moat defensive to a house,
> Against the envy of less happier lands.

121

Trade is Simply
Nations Going Shopping

Trade is simply nations going shopping. The French word for both is
the same: merchants and housewives alike go out and '*faire les courses*'.
What you buy depends greatly on the size of your basket, the service
offered by the 'shopkeeper' and, of course, how much money you have
in your purse. The Channel today is much like any high street, but
customers come from all over the world. East-West juggernauts,
container ships bring cars from Japan, supertankers glide in from the
Gulf, freight craft and roll-on-roll-off ships thread their shorter
routes backwards and forwards between France and England. Local
'shoppers' potter with their wares along the coasts. From the British
point of view since 1973 the Channel has become the *entrée* to the vast
European hypermarket, exporting £38 thousand million of goods a
year to the mainland and importing £44 thousand million – a far cry
from Napoleon's Continental Scheme for a Europe dominated by
France, with British goods banned from every port. It is six hundred
years since Britain was emotionally part of Europe, when the main
links were for exchange of wool and wine – and even then we fought
over those.

The death of Elizabeth I, the evolution of constitutional monarchy,
the rise of the middle classes and the French Revolution meant that
the personality of the Channel from the seventeenth century to the
present was shaped more by the activity of the people than by their
monarchs. From this time it is easier to portray the style of each
century through social and commercial trends. This was the heyday of
fishing, of smuggling and of a developing bureaucracy as it struggled
to establish order.

As inland France and Britain prospered with the early industrial
revolution, the coast was left comparatively undeveloped, to become
first a health attraction for the rich, then a playground for the smoke-
weary Victorian masses until today the sea itself has become a pleasure
park for the well-to-do, and the ancient skills, fishing, boatbuilding,
net repair, have largely moved over to make way for the great new
industry of the Channel – play.

The motivation in the seventeenth and eighteenth centuries was a
hunger for new land and a thirst for trade expansion to offer hope to
a rapidly increasing population. The national mood was one of
confident exuberance. History sailed out into the Channel as never
before, in merchant fleets bound for the New World and the East,

from France, Holland and England. Commerce became all-important to an increasingly consumer society, and sea power grew to protect it.

By the end of Elizabeth's reign the emotional break with Europe was total and it is this idealist sense of separateness which Europe now is trying hard to understand. We voted 'yes' with our feet in 1973, but not really with our hearts – they were still with those faraway dominions we had settled so long ago. Maybe there was an intellectual excitement at the concept of a united Europe but the British are not willingly a part of anything: as Churchill said 'In Elizabeth's reign we ceased to be the anvil and became the hammer'. When Spanish domination ended the way was clear for the great trading and colonial enterprises of the seventeenth and eighteenth centuries. This time it was the sea-faring Dutch who vied with the British and the markets that were important to them both were those of the East. Amsterdam became the economic capital of Holland and there was to be nearly one hundred years of close co-operation between the Dutch and the British, with large numbers settling in each other's country to found businesses.

For the first time two great maritime powers were jostling for commercial control of the Straits at Dover: wars were to be fought for trading rights rather than in defence of land.

The work of Trinity House continued to improve buoyage, and charts helped to establish London as by far the most important of British ports – but the poor people scratching a living in primitive agricultural and fishing communities were still accustomed to seeing the great ocean-going ships from the capital and from Holland pass by with cargoes that were rarely meant for them. Nevertheless, on both sides of the water, the early part of the seventeenth century was peaceful. The inland economic boom gave rise to gentle growth; there was increased work, and new ships were built. However, the rise in prices was six times that of wages and the workforce was terribly poor.

Privateering was banned by James I, which meant that many of the gentlemen who had invested in privateering now became pirates. Efforts were made to control piracy in the Channel but there was a new danger, from which no one in the Western Channel was safe – the savage corsairs from the Barbary Coast of the Mediterranean. They swept in on the villages and ports, captured ships in quite incredible numbers, and far worse, dragged men from the fields or small boats, in sight of their own homes and families, to a cruel death under the whip of a galley slave master. Those men whose fathers had once sailed from Dartmouth, Fowey and St Malo in search of human cargo in Africa now found the tables turned. For men of substance there was always hope of ransom, but for the labourer the sentence was a slow and cruel death as an oarsman in the stagnant, stinking bilges of Moslem ships. Beautiful Torbay was a favourite refuge of Algerian freebooters. Between 1609 and 1616 they captured 466 British vessels alone, and held a Dartmouth ship owner slave for a year in Tunis. The only official attempt to control matters seems to have been the extraordinary decision of Trinity House to extinguish the Lizard light! They felt it made life too easy for the wrongdoers. King James I himself did nothing and, through his neglect, allowed the British Navy to rot.

'The South coast ports were sordid with sailors, begging and dying by the road.' There is a familiar ring about the 'bawlings and impatience of these people, especially their wives, whose tongues are as foul as the daughters of Billingsgate.'

Despite these hazards more and more men flocked to the French or English Channel quaysides to enrol on the merchant adventure. Some of them, opportunely, took along small items of their own to barter for twice their price in foreign ports. The jeans with which a man may bargain today, were, in those times, a roll of Breton linen or calico or maybe some West of England cloth. Wages increased but so did the risks, and the rivalry exploded between better paid, private merchant-men and the Navy's seamen who received half as much, if they were lucky. Around this time 'slops' – official issue clothing – were introduced: canvas jackets, trousers and waistcoats although they were not uniform. All this led to a state of anarchy in the Channel with everyone doing as they liked – including the Dutch and the Turks at the expense of the merchant fleet. No one was content.

Nowhere was this blurring of roles more expertly exploited than in St Malo which, by the seventeenth century, had become the City of the Corsairs. Today, reading a Malouin guide book, the visitor may well feel uplifted by the pride of modern townsfolk in those citizens who, long ago, undoubtedly made their beautiful town, Venice of the Channel, the '*Porte des Indes*'.

It seems appropriate that such a colourful place should have pro-tected itself with a dramatically ferocious, and unique, police force: the Dogs of the Watch. This pack of fifty English mastiffs was let loose at night after *Noguette* (curfew) rang out and the gates to the city ramparts were closed. André Thevet said of them in 1575, 'extremely ferocious and furious dogs that no man would ever have the courage to stand up against and they wander round and round the town all through the old night'. They were recalled at dawn with a copper horn, fed on leeches and then shut in kennels, now remembered in the street names *Venelle aux Chiens* (Dogs' Alley), and later in the *Cabane aux Chiens* at Le Sillon. These dogs are believed to have devoured many a thief whose dismembered bodies were found on the shore.

Towards the end of the seventeenth century de Vauban, the great engineer and naval architect, redesigned and modernized the densely populated medieval city which consisted almost entirely of wooden houses with overhanging gables. In their place he built the dignified houses of the *Quartier Dinan* (later called *Californie*) which are best seen from across the bay at St Servan, rising from behind the walls of St Malo Inter Muros, often silhouetted against a blood-red sunset. These are the splendidly important homes made possible by the exploits of such men as Duguay Trouin, the greatest of all the corsairs.

Now only a very large pet, the English mastiff's bulk and strength and its characteristic of being difficult to train indicate how fearsome it would have been in St Malo at night in the 1570s. (Barnaby)

The corsairs of St Malo, or *Armateurs*, had grown fat and prosperous on their pickings. For although they were not allowed to pillage or sink any captured foreign vessel and had to hand over one tenth of the spoils to the Lord High Admiral of France, two thirds of the remainder was theirs – one third to be divided between the captain and crew. Some corsairs bought themselves a place in heaven with gifts to the Malouin church, but it was a dreadful life made tolerable only by the possible rewards. Whilst at sea there were five meals a week, usually bacon and beef alternately, with wine and cider before an attack. There was seldom a surgeon on board but always a priest, and in between trips life might be lightened a little by the prostitutes of the *Rue des Moeurs* (morals).

The seeds of the great Puritan adventure – the voyage of the *Mayflower* with the Pilgrim fathers to America – were sown in the kitchens and cafés of the Dutch town of Leyden. There a small group of English farmers and agricultural workers had settled in the hope that they would find a greater freedom to worship in their own way than in Jacobean Britain; but though they had religious freedom they could not find work in a largely maritime nation, and gradually they turned to thoughts of a new life in a New World.

Of course, there were colonists already settled in Virginia: Captain John Smith and a few hundred people had set up a settlement in 1607 and he had caused a sensation by marrying the Red Indian Pocahontas. So the Leyden community decided that they would do the same with the help, from London, of the Virginia Company. They were granted a licence by the King who rather liked the idea that they would support themselves by fishing ('it was the Apostles' own calling') and in 1620 a tiny band of thirty-five people set sail for Plymouth in Devon, in a ship called *Speedwell*.

Even this part of the journey was fraught with problems. They docked first in Southampton where some sixty-seven other passengers joined them from all over Britain (the name Pilgrim Fathers was not adopted till the more flamboyantly romantic late eighteenth century). At Southampton a merchant ship, the 180-ton *Mayflower* joined them, but shortly after setting sail the *Speedwell* developed a leak, and the expedition had to put in to Dartmouth for repairs and when eventually she sprang a second leak beyond Lands End, both ships returned to Plymouth.

The *Speedwell*'s passengers had to transfer to the *Mayflower* but some forty people had to be left behind. The transfer of all the goods and chattels, furniture and food from one ship to the other, took ten days. One hundred and one men, women and children were to embark on that Atlantic crossing divided into 'Saints' and 'Strangers'. The 'Saints' were the residue of the Leyden Community who were hoping for great things for their children in the New World. The 'Strangers' were ordinary passengers, servants and a group of men who had indentured themselves for seven years to pay for their passage. No one came from Plymouth.

Down on the quay that day of September 6th, 1620 the little ship was watched sadly by a small group of those who had had to be left behind and a collection of local people. Edward Winslow, one of the Pilgrims, wrote in his diary: 'Wednesday, 6th September. The winds coming east-north-west, a fine small gale. We loosed from Plymouth having been kindly entertained and courteously used by diverse friends there dwelling.'

And so began the voyage which was at the time unremarkable, but was in fact to prove the most significant expedition in British colonial history.

Probably the most momentous departure which ever took place at Plymouth. Others had already settled in the American colonies, millions were to follow, but pride of place in history is given to this little ship, the Mayflower, *and its passengers, setting sail on Wednesday 6th September, 1620.* (Mansell)

The handsome young Charles I never put a foot right for Protestant Channel folk. His reign started off badly with the arrival of his fifteen-year-old, Catholic French bride, Henrietta Maria, sister of King Louis XIII, at Dover in 1625. The arrangement smacked of some double dealing behind the scenes with France. It was even rumoured Charles had turned Roman Catholic. Her household was to be Catholic and, as France had no navy, Charles was asked by Richlieu to lend her a Royal Naval vessel and seven merchantmen. To the indignation of the crew these ships were used when the Duke of Buckingham was sent in 1627 to La Rochelle to help French Protestants who were blockaded in their stronghold there. The Duke was an admiral with no sea knowledge, no administrative experience and little political sense; he achieved nothing and returned to Portsmouth having lost 4000 men.

King Charles levied ship money on the whole resentful country in 1635, trying in vain to raise revenue for his ailing Navy; he billeted soldiers on the already poverty-stricken coastal towns. All this lost him the support of most of the Channel towns and the Navy too. With more foresight he might have seen that it was neglect of his ships and his sailors which eventually would cost him his head, for when the Civil War broke out in 1642 the country's greatest asset, the Navy, was on the side of Cromwell.

His grandest gesture towards the fleet he had inherited was, like other Kings, to build a ship bigger and better than any before. She was called *Sovereign of the Seas*, a name destined to rekindle a sense of pride in British sovereignty over the Straits between Dover and Calais. Though she carried 100 guns she was not to be sovereign of any seas. She was little more than a royal three-tier extravaganza, designed and built by the great Pett family. A record 1637 tons, weighed down with gilt carvings of Victory, Jason, Hercules, Neptune, sea horses and miscellaneous kings, she was a riot of Greek gods, busty ladies and floral fantasies, all entwined with animals enough to sink the Ark. From these florid, over-exuberant carvings known as 'gingerbread', came the expression for excess: 'gilt on the gingerbread'.

The Sovereign of the Seas, *1673* (BBC Hulton)

The Elder Brethren of Trinity House in their august wisdom, solemnly disapproved. They said, 'The art or wit of man cannot build a ship well-conditioned and fit for service with three tier of ordnance, and since there is no port except in the Isle of Wight could harbour so large a ship it followeth if she be not in port, then she is in continual danger, exposed to all tempests, all storms that time shall bring. In desperate estate she rides in every storm; in peril she must ride when all the rest of her companions enjoy peace and rides safe and quiet in port.'

Even so she lasted fifty years, having been flagship in the Battle of Barfleur against the French in 1692. Samuel Pepys had happy memories of the time in 1661 when he hid, with a lady friend, in her lantern!

It was poetic justice perhaps that one of King Charles's rebellious Channel subject's last memory of that handsome royal head, was seeing it stuck between the bars of a window in Carisbrooke Castle on the Isle of Wight. He had taken refuge there at the end of the Civil War to the dismay of the Governor, who treated him well at first, but then imprisoned him. On March 20th, 1648 Charles tried to escape through the window. Acid and files were needed to free him. Eventually, in November, 2000 soldiers were sent to take him to London for execution.

The waters of the Bay of Reville, on the little known eastern coast of the Cotentin peninsula, lap nonchalantly in summer on beaches that barely mark where the equally peaceful plains slip secretly into the sea.

At St Vaast La Hogue the great ramparts and the tower on the Île de Tatihou are also monuments to the splendid imagination of de Vauban. To the north too he laid the foundation for the future naval bases of Cherbourg, which he called, over-optimistically, 'tomorrow's Channel Inn', and Le Havre. He improved the spectacular Fort La Latte in St Malo, surrounded on three sides by water, and made it virtually impregnable – except to Tony Curtis, who hurled one-eyed Kirk Douglas from its ramparts on to the rocks in the film *The Vikings*!

St Vaast is now a peaceful place, undisturbed by memories of the naval disaster when the French fleet under Admiral de Tourville on its way to reinstate James II in England, was annihilated by an Anglo-Dutch fleet. Unaffected by the influx of tourists and *plaisanciers* its only outward sign of conflict can be seen on ship window notices urging the oyster fishermen to take guard against foreign yachtsmen who it is feared will destroy their traditional livelihood.

The Dutch wars which followed Charles' execution were economic; they never had the same passion or traditional enmity of the British wars with France. By then there were far too many Dutch and British residents living and marrying in each other's country. Charles himself had encouraged Van Dyke and Rubens to paint at his Court. The wars were the inevitable result of Dutch expansion and her persistent infiltration of British colonies throughout the years of the Civil War. Eventually the Dutch were bringing more profit to Amsterdam from Virginia and Barbados than were the British to London. By the time Cromwell took over enough was enough. It was clear that the way to safeguard British interests across the Atlantic was by control of the Channel itself. There was no longer room in the Narrows for two such competitive powers.

Cromwell began a huge programme of naval expansion. The Navy was always popular because it did not threaten civil liberties, but few people knew or cared about conditions – few had seen a ship or even a picture of one.

Two Navigation Acts were passed which effectively forbade foreigners from trading with British Colonies. Their purpose was to further 'the increase of shipping and the encouragement of the navigation of this nation which, under the good providence and protection of God is so great a means of welfare and safety of this commonwealth'. There was to be no foreign trade with colonies and no foreign carrying of goods into English ports. Foreign ships might bring in produce of their own country but not others. English ships and seamen took over these roles.

The Dutch ignored the Navigation Acts and so the first wars ever to be fought entirely at sea were conducted within sight of the shores of England and France. In the meantime, France, still under the great *eminence grise*, Cardinal Richelieu, and during the ending of the reign of the golden King Louis XIV was quietly becoming more and more wealthy and powerful on land, and again by sea. Politics, not religion, was now the driving force.

There is a saying amongst French naval authorities today 'It can't be done. Colbert did not order it.' The influence of Jean Baptiste Colbert (1619–1683) is undisputed. He *was* the navy. A statesman and politician, protégé of Mazarin, whom he succeeded, he became *Ministère de la Marine* in 1669 and powerful in almost every department of government except war. He was a 'man of marble', severe, relentless and often unpitying. He is most remembered for his establishment of a professional Navy, at a time when the great marine defence engineer de Vauban was at the height of his eminence. Together they transformed the situation on the Channel for France and really for the first time the French Navy was a force for the British to reckon with. De Vauban warned, even then, of five good invasion landing beaches in the Cotentin, one of which was to become better known as Utah beach in 1945.

Colbert initiated the system of *Inscription Maritime* to replace the 'press': a tempting package to encourage young men to enjoy military service with all kinds of perks when their spell of duty was over. The Commander at Le Havre was instructed to keep his ships brightly painted and clean to attract the right calibre of men.

French attitudes to trade were still somewhat superior; it was regarded as a demeaning, if necessary, affair, and efforts to stimulate interest were made by encouraging noblemen to trade without losing their titles as had been the case before. At the beginning of the reign of Louis XIV, in a world total of some twenty thousand ships, only six hundred were French, so the building of merchant ships was encouraged with offers of a £32 per ton carrying capacity subsidy. Vincent Cronin says, in his biography of Louis: 'For ten years not more than two or three French war vessels had been seen on the sea; all naval arsenals were empty, all vessels reduced to 20 or 22, a number of which were not even fit for action having fallen to pieces.'

Louis decided to rebuild. Three million pounds annually was set aside and French seamen forbidden to work for foreigners. Trees were numbered and felled in a huge systematic programme of shipbuilding and, ironically, an English master shipbuilder was employed. By 1667 France had fifty men of war; by 1671 it was over a hundred.

While Colbert was improving the quality of the men, de Vauban was building them safe harbours from which to work. Despite his name, Sebastien le Prestre de Vauban, he had humble origins but is respected by military historians worldwide for his exuberant revolution of French fortifications. His fortresses are works of art and he was a master of detail. A robust hefty man with a strong jaw and steely blue eyes, he was tough on himself but humane to others and he loved France. Dunkerque in his hands was transformed from a wretched fishing village into a superb harbour: 'the most grand and beautiful design of fortification in the world'. It was all destroyed by the British at the end of the Dutch wars. Truckers stranded today in the desolate desert around Dunkerque Harbour would have reason to wonder, if they knew, 'de Vauban where are you now?'

Jean Baptiste Colbert (1619–83), who created the French navy in the 1670s, by Geille (BBC Hulton)

Louis XIV was imaginative in other ways. He had ideas, with his growing navy, of competing with Britain and building up his own Empire. The population of Canada at that time was not much more than that of a large French village, scattered along the St Lawrence river. So he sent out some three hundred men annually and with them about a hundred young ladies known discreetly as *Les Filles du Roi* (the King's maidens). Their departure fron Honfleur was personally supervised by Marie Thérèse herself who saw to it that the chosen few were '*sans rien de rébutant à l'éxterieur*', as well as being '*saines et fortes pour le travail de campagne*' (that they were not personally repugnant and were healthy and strong for farming work).

Their treatment sounds reminiscent of the slave sales: ' ... these vestals were piled one on the other in three different halls where bridegrooms chose brides as a butcher chooses sheep. There was wherewith to content the most fantastical in these three harmes; for here were to be seen the tall and the short, the blonde and the brunette, the plump and the lean; everybody in short found a shoe to fit him. At the end of a fortnight not one was left. I am told the plumpest were taken first because they could resist the winter better.'

John Evelyn was commissioner for Kent and Sussex to provide for the sick and wounded during the second Dutch war (1665) but long before this he was writing and recording his French travels in his diary.

John Evelyn (1620–1706) the diarist, engraved by T. Bragge from the original by Kneller (Mary Evans)

March 23rd 1642.
We passed all along by the coast, a very rocky and rugged way which forc'd us many times to alight till we came to Haver de Grace, where we lay that night. The next morning we were admitted to see the Citadel which is both very strong and regular and in regard to its situation altogether impregnable; it is also excellently stor'd with artillery and ammunition of all sorts, the works furnished with faire brasse canon; the allogiaments of the Garrison very uniforme, a spacious place for drawing up the soldiers a pretty Chapell and a faire house for the Governor. The Duke of Richlieu now being in the fort we went to salute him ... that which I took more especiall notice of was this motto upon the canon, out of the Prince of Latine Poets Ratio Ultima Regnum ... when we were done here we embarked ourselves and horses ... to a town called Honfleur which dissembogues the Seine into the sea.

This was an age of passionate diary-writing which captures better than any other the flavour of life afloat. The Rev Henry Teonge, for instance, who slipped his debtors by running away to sea, wrote, having arrived off the cliffs of Dover from London after *three* gruelling weeks, 'no life at the shore being comparable to this at sea, where we have good meate and good drinke provided for us and good company and good divertisements; without the least care sorrow or trouble ...

punch and brandy since I came on board have run as freely as ditchwater'. Needless to say the seamen did not have it so good!

The writings of Edward Coxere are really the life-story, from his fourteenth to his fifty-second year, of an intrepid and humorous Kentish merchant seaman, who served many masters, was taken and imprisoned by the Turks and converted to Quakerism after the Restoration by Edward Burrough and Samuel Fisher.

In the year 1647 I was about fourteen years of age. I was sent over to France to learn the French tongue, which was the first of my crossing the seas.

From Dover to Boulogne in France, and from thence I was carried in a wagon to Havre de Grace, which was about a week's journey. Being safely got there, the French boy's mother, which was left at my father's house in exchange for me to learn English, came to the house where I was, there being two other English boys with me who came on the same account to learn the French tongue. My French mother, as I then called her, understanding that I was in exchange for her son, with that she kissed me and got me soon home to her house, which was a brewhouse. She being a widow, her father, who I then called grandfather, managed the affairs of the brewer, who was a fine ancient man, a Roman Catholic. They would be speaking to me in French, but I was like one dumb, and my mind not well satisfied for all my new kindred, for their loves did not balance with the trouble of mind I had in being so far from home amongst such as I could neither speak to nor understand.

My French mother soon got me a father; she married with the King's attorney, so that my kindred increased. He had several daughters, and lived at a town called Montivilliers, seven miles in the country, where he carried me. But, I being not willing to stay, I soon got home to my French grandfather again, and chose rather to live with him than with my fine kindred. My mother proved not so kind to me as she appeared at first, which discouraged me very much, especially I not being able to speak for myself for about two months' time, but like a dumb boy making signs (as when I would to sleep I would shut my eyes and lay my head on my hand) so long till I began to despair; it seemed so hard for me to learn. For my credit lay very much at stake, for most of my friends had so good opinion of me, which concerned me the more to have as much of it as I could. But by degrees I got one word after another till I did begin to tell a French story, and when I was entered I got courage in hopes to save my credit and satisfy my friends.

At eleven months' end I was sent for home to England, my father having an account of my improving my time. When I came home I was examined by a French merchant in the French tongue, who gave my father an account that I spoke it as well as if

I had been born in France, which gave good satisfaction to both father and mother. After I had been home some time, care was taken to put me to a trade. It was concluded on to send me to Middleburg in Zealand to be a wine-cooper. I being sent over, was not there above a week. I met with one of my countrymen who asked me if I would go home again. I consented to it. I steered my course for England again. My friends wonder to see me, asked the reason why I came back. I could give little account but 'did not like'; so got no credit by that voyage.

Twice being clear of his man-of-waring and being at home, I shipped myself for Rochelle with William Tucker of Dover for forty-three shillings per month in a vessel called the *Christopher*, laden with red herrings. We sailed out of the pier in company with three other vessels, *Alexander White, William Grigorie, John Qwin*. When we got sight of the Isle of Wight we were taken in a sorry storm so that *Sander White* was forced ashore about Beachy, *William Grigorie* forced ashore by Shoreham, *John Qwin* lost at Dover pier-heads putting in again there. Report was that above forty ships was lost that storm between the river and the Isle of Wight. We were very badly fitted with an old vessel and materials, as sails and rigging, as also a drunken master, for in the night our mainsail blew to pieces, our blocks fell down about our ears, the ropes and strops being rotten, so that we were in a very great strait.

The master lay then drunk in his cabin and did not turn out. I bid the boy tell him the sail was blown away. He said he could not help it, but lay still when we were in a perishing condition in all appearance, the storm being then so violent. We through God's providence, without the help of our brandy-drinking master, kept from suffering shipwreck and being whelmed up in raging seas; this being in the night-time, in the morning we were by the storm drove on the French coast near Guernsey. The master then turns out and, finding us in a strait without a mainsail, orders us to get the main-topsail down. I and one more went up and got it down with no small difficulty, we being in such a tottered condition, our ropes so bad, and the tumbling of the vessel, that they below still looked when I should a been thrown over abroad, being out at the leeward arm. The meanwhile our master sat down at the cabin door with a stone bottle of brandy between his legs to give us a dram when we came down; but a fortunate sea, as I may call it, hove him and the bottle to leeward and broke it to pieces. So then for want of brandy our master was kept sober, so that then we had some help of him, for he was able enough when sober.

We stood towards the English coast and got well into Plymouth, but withal we were so leaky that we were forced to pump for our lives day and night all this while. The danger we went through this voyage is hard to be uttered, before it was ended. When we got into Plymouth, our work was to stop leaks. Our master then got to drinking again, and his tone was then we were bewitched. We were all of us too wild and little considered the mercies we received, but look large liberty when ashore in drinking and sporting as the manner of seamen generally is.

We being a-drinking together at the sign of the Dover Castle, coming out of the house fell in among a parcel of press-masters' seamen, who got hold of me, asking what ship we did belong to. We told them the name of a man-of-war, which was a lie, but so it was that it happened to be the same ship those pressmen did belong to. In this we were betrayed, and I was held fast, but not so fast but I broke from them, it being in the evening, and lost my consorts and pressmen too. But my consorts did make their escape too, so that we met together again.

John Evelyn described his Channel crossing of August 13th, 1650.

When I came to Dover where I had not so much as my trunk opened; so at 6 in the evening we set saile, the wind not favourable, I was very sea sick, coming to anker about one o'clock; about five in the morning we had a long boate to carry us to land though at a great distance; this we willingly entered because two vessels were chasing us; but now being almost at the harbours mouth through inadvertancy there brake in upon us two such huge seas as had almost sunk the boat I being neere the middle up in water; our steeres man, it seemes, apprehensive of the danger was preparing to leape into the sea, and trust his swimming, but seeing the vessel emerge, put her into the peere, and so God be thanked we got wet to Calais where I went immediately to bed sufficiently discomposed ... next morning I marched under their protection to Boulogne. Twas a miserable spectacle to see how these tattered soldiers pillaged the poore people of their sheepe, poultry, Corne, Catelle and whatever came their way.

The Dutch wars lasted about twenty years. The only territorial gain for Britain came through Cromwell's Treaty with Cardinal Mazarin in France against the Spanish Netherlands. The treaty won Dunkerque for the British and three Flemish provinces for France, thus establishing the modern Franco-Belgian boundary. Dunkerque was a short-lived gain, since Charles II could not afford to keep the town, and resold it to Louis XIV after the Restoration in 1660. On the whole, the wars do not stir the imagination with great names or exploits, apart perhaps from that of Van Tromp who is reputed to have tied a broom head to his mast as a sign of having 'swept' the English from the Channel, nor did the wars run as deep in the hearts of most ordinary people as hostilities with France. But like all wars, to the people living amongst them they were real enough.

The first battle of the Dutch Wars was graphically described by Dr Fitche, in 1898, in *Fights for the Flag.*

A spectator standing on the wind-blown summit of Beachy Head on the afternoon of May 19th, 1652, would have looked down on a great historic scene. In the famous strait beneath, some sixty great ships were engaged in the fiery wrestle of battle, and the sullen, deep-voiced roar of their guns rolled from the white English cliffs across the strait to the dunes of Calais, faintly visible through the grey haze. But the fleets engaged were in point of numbers strangely ill-matched. Running westward past the Downs before a fresh breeze came a great Dutch fleet of fifty ships under the flag of Van Tromp, the most famous of Dutch admirals. Beating up to eastward to meet them was an English fleet of fifteen ships under Blake, who was in no sense a seaman, but who comes next to Nelson himself in the greatness of his sea exploits. It is easy to picture the scene ... the antique-looking ships, short-bodied, high-sterned, snub-nosed, the bowsprit thrust up at a sharp angle and carrying a tiny mast with a square sail at its extremity. A modern seaman would gaze amazed at the spectacle of a seventeenth-century fleet, luffing clumsily into line, or trying to claw to windward.

And yet the fighting quality of these clumsy fleets was of a very high order. These Dutchmen, heavy-footed, solid, grim, were in the seventeenth century, to use the phrase of a French writer, 'the Phoenicians of the modern world, the waggoners of all seas'. They were the commercial heirs of Venice. The fire of their long struggle for freedom had given to the national character the edge and temper of steel. They had swept the Spanish flag from the seas. The carrying trade of the world was in their hands. They fished in all waters, traded in all ports, gathered the wealth of the world under all skies, and, as far as marine qualities were concerned, might almost have been web-footed. Holland today is a land without ambition, comfortable, fat, heavy-bottomed. In the middle of the seventeenth century Holland proudly claimed to be the greatest naval power in the world, and by daring seamanship, great fleets, famous admirals, and a world-encompassing trade, it went far to justify that boast.

Great Britain had just finished her civil war, and the imperial genius of Cromwell was beginning to make itself felt in foreign politics. The stern and disciplined valour of his Ironsides, that triumphed at Naseby and Worcester, was being translated into the terms of seamanship. The Commonwealth, served by Cromwell's sword, and Milton's pen, and Blake's seamanship, was not likely to fail in vigour by sea or land. But there is always a flavour of sea-salt in English blood, an instinctive claim to sea supremacy in the English imagination. England in 1652, released from civil strife, was feeling afresh that historic impulse,

and was challenging the Dutch naval supremacy. The Commonwealth claimed to inherit that ancient patrimony of the English kinds – the sovereignty of the narrow seas, and the right in these waters to compel all foreign ships to strike the flag or lower the topsail in the presence of a British ship. Behind that question of sea etiquette lay the whole claim to naval supremacy and the trade of the world. The fight off Dungeness on that May afternoon . . . was really the beginning of the struggle betwixt two maritime republics for the mistress-ship of the seas. To quote Hannay 'the greatest naval power of the day, and the greatest naval power of the future' were measuring their forces in the tossing lists of the narrow seas.

In this his first great naval fight Blake showed an individual daring like that of Collingwood when he bore down, far ahead of his column, on Villeneuve's far-stretching line at Trafalgar. In his ship – the 'James' – that is, he outsailed his squadron, and met alone Van Tromp's compact line, with its swift-following jets of flame and blasts of thunder as each ship in turn bore up to rake the British admiral. But Nelson himself never showed swifter decision or cooler daring as a leader than did Blake when

he unhesitatingly led his fifteen ships to meet Van Tromp's fifty.
… For four hours the thunder of the battle rolled over the sea.

Even in that early day, however, the British gunnery had those qualities of speed and fierceness which, somehow, seem to belong to it by right of nature; and, as night fell, the stubborn Dutch gave up their attempt to force the strait, and, leaving two of their ships as prizes, stood over to the Flemish coast; while the British, their flagship dismasted and with shot-battered sides, slowly bore up to Dover. It is characteristic, however, of the tireless and silent energy of Blake that, as war had now broken out, he instantly commenced to sweep Dutch traders off the seas. From every quarter of the compass Dutch ships, richly laden, were creeping homeward, unconscious that war had broken out; and Blake's frigates, instantly taking possession of all the trade routes, sent them as prizes up the Thames in scores. The British, in a word, showed themselves both nimbler-witted and nimbler-footed than the Dutch.

A year later the Dutch fleet was finally destroyed and Van Tromp was killed. The right to salute was conceded in home waters. The third and last Dutch war broke out between 1671–1674.

The first battle of the Dutch Wars in May 1652 has no name. No battle honours to credit the bravery of Blake and his sailors, outnumbered here by the ships flying the tricolour of the Dutch Republic. (BBC Hulton)

Few of the carefree walkers, striding the South Downs Way behind Arundel realize that this was once a royal highway to freedom. During the Civil War, after the execution of Charles I, the Channel coast was almost entirely against the new King. Only Cornwall remained Royalist and was Charles II's contact with France for munitions. So when he went into hiding in 1651 with Parliamentary troops hunting him high and low, there was no port along the coast prepared to sport a boat to help him escape. At Hambledon on the Surrey/Sussex border he made secret contact with Royalists Colonel George Counter and Lord Wilmot. Having cropped his blond hair and slept a night in the beautiful, timber-framed house, St Mary's, at Bramber, they set out over the Downs with their bad-tempered looking 'servant'. Considering the number of posters offering £1,000 reward – and Charles II's height of 6 feet 2 inches, it was amazing that no one spotted his true identity.

They crept, almost bush by bush down into Shoreham on the bleak, scantily-populated coast, where they met a local shipmaster, Nicholas Tattersall, who owned a coal ship *Surprise*. Tattersall recognized his client immediately and upped his price of £50 to take 'two special friends – who have been engaged in a duel and there is mischief to be done'. The King spent that night cooped up in the comparative safety of the ship's little cabin, stuck out on the mud. At 7 a.m. the tide rose, the winds filled the sails and they set off for France on a calm sea. An hour later soldiers galloped into the creek – they were too late. Once out on the sea Charles devised a scheme to hoodwink the crew because Tattersall needed an alibi if he were going to divert to Fécamp. The crew were to be bribed by Charles to make them change course, so that the two 'merchants' could go to France to 'settle debts'. To this day the people of Fécamp celebrate the anniversary of his landing.

When Charles was restored to the throne, Nicholas Tattersall sailed that boat up the Thames and Charles, with humour that three hundred years later would have appealed to Winnie the Pooh, re-named her the *Royal Escape*.

The Clerk of the Acts of the King's Ships in charge of rebuilding the navy of Charles II was a poor, but honest young man of twenty-seven who knew nothing at all about ships. His name was Samuel Pepys and he had just made his very first sea journey to bring back the King.

Of all the Channel crossings made by any monarch few have been recorded with such vivid honesty as the return of Charles II. Nothing seems to have escaped the enthusiastic eye of Samuel Pepys; his record of that riotous mission and first footing in Holland is spiced with the kind of gutsy gossip that sells national tabloid papers today.

The outward journey was kept busy by painters, and workmen and tailors refitting the austere Cromwellian craft into a ship fit for a king. The name was changed from *Naseby* to *Royal Charles*, and her figurehead, representing Oliver Cromwell trampling six nations underfoot was burned, to the delight of the crowd. In its place was put a £100 Neptune.

Once in Holland, Pepys and the crew decided to make the most of

Samuel Pepys (1633–1703) diarist and 'saviour of the navy'. An engraving by Kneller. (Ann Ronan)

their stay, and in true tourist style they 'did the town'. They visited galleries, bought presents and got very drunk. So drunk in fact that he recalls 'I lay down in my gown upon my bed and slept till the 4 o'clock gun the next morning waked me, which I took for eight at night that night; and rising to piss, mistook the sun rising for the sun setting on Sunday night'.

After several days at this pace the King and his entourage were ready to embark – not an easy task for there were so many Dutch spectators crowding the shore there was hardly room for passengers to get to the ship. There were two dukes, the Queen of Bohemia, Princess Royale and Prince William and much merrymaking all day till it was time to sail in 'most happy weather'.

Says Pepys, 'All afternoon the King walking here and there, up and down, quite contrary to what I thought him to have been, very active and stirring . . .'

Charles II landing at Dover 23rd May 1660 after the painting by Adrian Van der Venne. 'The King . . . was received by General Monk with all imaginable love and respect. Infinite the crowd of people. And so into a stately coach there set for him, and so away through the town towards Canterbury.' The Diary of Samuel Pepys. (BBC Hulton)

139

'Upon the quarter deck he fell in discourse of his escape from Worcester. Where it made me ready to weep to hear the stories that he told of his difficulties that he had passed through travelling four days and three nights on foot every step up to his knees in dirt with nothing but a green coat and a pair of country breeches on and a pair of country shoes that made him so sore all over his feet that he could scarce stir . . .'

By Friday, May 25th, after two days of feasting and lively discourse the company prepared to land at Dover. 'The King and two Dukes did eat their breakfast before they went', says Pepys 'there being set some shippe diet before them only to show them the manner of the ship's diet, they eat of nothing else but pease and pork and boiled beef'. About noon the brigantine was there ready to carry him . . . 'I went and Mr Mansell and one of the King's footmen with a dog that the King loved that shit in the boat which made us laugh and me think that a King and all that belonged to him are just as others are. . . . The Mayor of the town came and gave him his white staff, the badge of this place which the King did give him again. The Mayor also presented him from the town with a very rich bible which he took and said it was the thing he loved above all things in the world, the shouting and joy expressed by all is past imagination.'

Of course Samuel Pepys was not a Channel man: he was a Londoner through and through, but he pops up time and time again on professional visits to keep a watchful eye on his coastal charges.

During his time first as Clerk and then as secretary to the Admiralty dockyards he became a permanent part of the naval scene. Portsmouth had been the first town with a dry dock as long ago as 1495 but there was no regular dockyard labour force until the seventeenth century, when expanding trade and a boom in shipbuilding made better facilities imperative. Pepys oversaw, and costed this expansion. At Portsmouth, in addition to the dry docks, there were building slips and a wet dock, storehouses, timber yards, workshops, blacksmiths, mast ponds, victualling and slop stores, rope walks and stores for guns and ammunition. There were upper and lower stores, upper and lower hemp houses, a block loft, rope maker's house, office and nail loft canvas room, hammock room, kettle room, iron loft, tar house, oilhouse, sail loft, top maker's and boat maker's houses. Labour problems were much the same as today and there were constant refusals of one craftsman to do the work of another.

One of the greatest changes in ship design in the seventeenth century was in the building of sterns. They began to use 'round tuck' planking, sweeping in a long curve to the transom at the after end of the lower deck. The long, low beak at the fore-end of the ship became short and upward sweeping. Pepys himself took a great deal of interest in new techniques and design and encouraged designers and kept meticulous records of their work. He reformed the Navy Board and gradually brought it all under civil control, and became not only the first great civil servant but, as Sir Arthur Bryant has said, 'the saviour of the navy'.

Charles, with typical, wholehearted, good humour, was the first monarch to enjoy the sea for its own sake.

John Evelyn recorded in his diary 'I sailed this morning with His Majesty in one of his yachts or pleasure boats, vessels not known among us till the Dutch East India Company presented that curious piece to the King'.

The 'curious piece' was a yacht called *Mary* – a little craft which had been developed for use amongst the canals and dykes of Holland and which Charles had first admired when it transported him to join the British fleet for the Restoration. The Dutch seized an opportunity for goodwill and made the King a gift. He wrote a warm thank-you: *'maintenant vous avez encore rafraichie Noste memoire pour un nouveau present d'un yaugh, des plus jolys et des plus agreables a Noste humeur qu'on auroit pu inventer'*.

He immediately ordered an even better home-made copy from Pett the shipbuilder which he said was a 'pretty thing and much beyond the Dutchman'. Because there was no galley aboard, whenever the King went racing he was accompanied by a cook-ship to supply his meals. From this very simple beginning evolved the sport which has now transformed the Channel and created a whole new industry of boat builders and marina developers and attracted a breed of people who race and sail for pleasure.

France under Louis XIV had become the most glamorous cultured nation in Europe – not for nothing was Louis called *Le Roi Soleil* – and not surprisingly was he admired by pleasure-loving Charles II.

It was said of Charles that if there was to be a choice between the cost of a woman or a ship, the woman always won. Louis knew what he was doing when he despatched the beautiful Madame Louise de Kérouaille as a spy to the English Court, a post for which she was well-paid by becoming the King's mistress and Duchess of Portsmouth. The caution-to-the-winds, moral revolution, after the uneasy pedestal upon which Cromwell had placed Britain, made late seventeenth-century life a great deal more relaxed and entertaining despite the wars. After all, they were far away at sea, and most people were oblivious to the hardships still suffered along the coastline. The sight of bodies dressed in black floating in the Narrows were not really remarkable for all that they had been dragged from church to fight. Such happenings were a local affair.

Eventually the wars fizzled out largely because England was exhausted by the Plague and the Fire of London and broke. Charles did not enjoy war but his wish to keep the peace and his sycophantic admiration for Louis XIV really laid the foundation for eventual conflict with France. He was not averse to playing 'poor cousin' in order to keep Louis' favour. The Treaty signed secretly in 1670 at Dover stirred up once again the not-so-dormant British hatred of the French, and eventually created counter demands for alliance with the Dutch. For there lay a Treaty within that Treaty, in which Charles promised to try to return England to Catholicism and to lend the

James II by Samuel Cooper (1633–1701) his short reign, 1685–88, was threatened by his half-brother, James, Duke of Monmouth, whom he executed. (BBC Hulton)

James Scott, Duke of Monmouth (1649–85) (BBC Hulton)

English Navy in support of French operations against the Dutch. He was also to receive subsidies from Louis to make him independent of the British Parliament (and so a satellite of France). Such personal decisions, taken without the backing of his Government, were anathema to Protestant people and so the old dog would not lie down. The last years of the Merry Monarch's reign were clouded by increasing public fear that he was hand in Catholic glove with Louis and all was far from well also across the water, in France.

For a few years the French and English continued to indulge in sporadic war in the Channel, and France attacked Holland in a battle which made Prince William of Orange a national Protestant hero. This fatherless, childless, asthmatic had one real enemy, France, and he was to use Britain in his designs to destroy her.

Charles's brother James came to the throne in 1685 and it was not long before the threat of Catholic domination had caused a minor revolution in Britain. Protestant Monmouth landed at Lyme Regis in May, 1685 with a force of 4000 untrained rebels, but the attempt collapsed. In 1689 the Dutch Prince of Orange, married to James's daughter, was invited by seven leading nobles to lead a rebellion. His 'invasion' was watched by crowds lining the beaches around Dover and Calais to see the huge fleet made up of Swedes, Danes, Prussians, Scottish and French Huguenots sail through on its way to Devon. There was a 'Protestant Wind' blowing that November 3rd, which carried the sound of trumpets and drums from the decks of the fleet to the excited spectators.

In France the mood was apprehensive. The idea of an Anglo-Dutch alliance was not at all a happy one. William's gamble was enormous, and again the weather decided the toss, for the same wind that blew William through the Straits, held Lord Dartmouth, James II's Admiral, trapped in the Thames Estuary. He lost a day and never caught up. On the morning that William was stretching his legs on English soil, Dartmouth was becalmed at Beachy Head. Even the Dutchman King, who believed as a Calvinist in destiny, must have been astonished at his good fortune.

Most of the soldiers landed on the grass-edged Churston Cove between Elberry and Brixham and struggled up the wooded valley behind it, to what is now the Torbay Coast Footpath. William himself came ashore in old Brixham harbour. Amongst the spectators on the quayside was a fisherman called Varwell who seized the opportunity for acclaim, for since the tide was out the King had to be piggybacked over the mud into his new Kingdom. It had been an exhausting journey, in which some five hundred horses had died *en route*. The steps on which William climbed have long since gone, but the stone onto which he first stepped has been incorporated into a granite column on the new pier.

The people of Brixham were jubilant and made up a special ditty to welcome the King:

And please King William your Majesty
You be welcome to Brixham Quay
To eat buckhorn and drink bohea [a special tea]
Along with me
And please Your Majesty.

King William was yet another foreigner who did not like Britain and used the crown for his own purposes. His Queen, Mary, daughter of the new exiled King, seems to have been equally opportunist, for on February 22nd, 1689 John Evelyn wrote once more:

> I saw the new Queen and King, so proclaimed the very next day of her coming to Whitehall, Wednesday 15th February, with wonderful acclamaition and general reception, bonfires, bells gunns etc. It was believed that they both, especially the Princesse would have showed some seeming reluctancy at least of assuming her father's crown and made some apologie, testifying her regret that he should by his misgovernment necessitat to the Nation to so extraordinary a proceeding, which would have showed very handsomely to the world (and according to the character given of her piety and consonant to her husband's first declaration that there was no intention of deposing the King but of succouring the nation; but nothing at all appeared.
>
> She came into Whitehall as to a wedding, riant and jolly, so as seeming to be quite transported; rose early on the next morning of her arrival and in her undress (as reported) before her women were up ... lay in the same bed ... where the late Queen lay and within a night or two sate downe to play at Basset as the Queen her predecessor used to do.

William III (1650–1702) As Prince of Orange he made peace with England after the 3rd Dutch War, and he supplanted the Catholic James II in the Glorious Revolution of 1688. (Ann Ronan)

James fled to France with his new baby son, and Louis XIV eventually declared war on Britain and her new 'illegal' monarchs. At La Hogue, in 1692, on those peaceful shores that had launched Norman William's invasion fleet, the Dutch William destroyed the French fleet under Admiral Tourville, on Britain's behalf. Though few ships were lost La Hogue was a maritime massacre from which the French Navy never really recovered. It was the seventeenth century Trafalgar.

During the Dutch wars the first simple efforts at manoeuvres had been attempted. This kind of activity was beyond the skill of the merchant seamen, so during this period The Narrows became the training ground for professional sailors, trained from boyhood for fighting at sea, and the birthplace of a new kind of ship built for defence only and unified for the first time as a full scale Royal Navy.

The sailors, trained under Lord Anson were known at first as the English Maritime Regiment. They were paid by Parliament and were sea-soldiers capable of fighting on land and on sea. They joined, unlike the merchant navy men, for life. The Duke of Albany's Maritime Regiment of Foot as they were known became by 1672 'The Marines'.

Fierce hand to hand fighting portrayed by West during the Battle of La Hogue off the east coast of the Cherbourg peninsula when the Dutch King of England, William III, defeated the French fleet to ensure the exile of the Stewarts and the dominance of the English in the Channel.
(BBC Hulton)

'If ever the hour of true danger shall come to England they shall be found to be the nation's sheet anchor'. So said Earl St Vincent in 1823.

In their famous yellow coats and broad brimmed hats this force won for itself a unique place in the hearts of the British. Over the next three hundred years from their bases at Plymouth, Portsmouth and Deal they were sent to restore peace around the world after riots and uprisings. Two thirds of the assault force on D-Day were marines, from whom Churchill founded the Commando units to carry out irregular intelligence raids on the French coast. Churchill knew that the rough, tough history of the Marines made them ideal material. So, the Royal Marine Commandos became a Channel Regiment born and bred, chosen not only for their military skill but for their brains and individuality too. They cut their teeth on the beaches of France during that War.

Today Commandos are trained at Lympstone in Devon, to be loners, self-reliant and resourceful, able to cope in any terrain, be it desert, jungle, mountain or sea, anywhere in the world.

The Royal Marine School of Music at Deal trains men to an extraordinarily high standard of professionalism and appearance for the all-important task of morale-boosting. The massed bands of the RM have appeared at ceremonials world-wide marching to the music of

The uniforms of the marines from their origins as the Duke of Albany's Maritime Regiment of Foot to their Victorian heyday. Present uniforms are much less glamorous, and much more practical. (BBC Hulton)

> A life on the ocean wave
> A home on the rolling deep
> Where the scatter'd waters rave
> And the winds their revels keep.

Fishing:
a Dog's Life

They scooped the very bread from out our hands, boys,
There's nothing that these pirates have to fear.
The seas that tumbled round our homeland
For thousands now of years have served us well.
Why should we be so beset by brigands
Who legally are sending us to hell?

Chorus: You shoot your nets on either hand,
You bait your line with caviar,
You might just as well remain on land, boys,
There's no more fish out where you are.

Contemporary Lament
by Brenda Wooton
(To be fair, though, it could have been
sung by her Breton counterpart, Alain Stivel.)

It is the challenge of the sea itself more than its harvest, more even than the rewards that harvest can sometimes bring, which has, since time began, lured men to pit their wits against impossible odds, and go-a-fishing. A farmer tends and loves his land but has a close relationship with his livestock too; the fisherman who knows and understands every submarine valley, hill and cavern is somewhat less lyrical about his catch. It is a means to an end. The end is the sea. Time and time again in the pubs around Mousehole, or Penzance you will hear 'it is a dog's life' – but still they go.

There is a romantic delight for visitors in Cornish villages clustering like barnacles around a crack in the cliff at the end of a single tortuous road, once impassable in winter and today impossible in summer. Freshly painted in the spring, ready for the summer visitors, these converted fishermen's cottages were once wave-battered, dark, cold and high with the stench of pilchards in the fish cellar on the ground floor. Most of today's Channel fishermen live in modern, council houses on the outskirts because they cannot afford the price of romance. The reality of Cornish (or Dorset, or Sussex) fishing life was less than romantic; and all for a product the British do not like.

Queen Elizabeth I had to pass a law encouraging her Protestant subjects to eat more fish. 'Fish on Friday,' was literally a God-send for Catholic fishermen.

Nowadays the south coast consumes less fish than anywhere else in Britain, according to the Ministry of Agriculture and Fisheries, and much of that comes from far afield, and is served in newspaper. If you want to buy fresh sardines in Cornwall, you must catch them yourself. At least the fishermen of Fécamp, who controlled the fishing grounds of Hastings in the Middle Ages, can be gratified (despite their diminishing returns) by the exquisite, sculptural, window display offered up by the Poissonière.

The heyday of the Channel fishing was in the eighteenth century when every little port and harbour was a-bustle with flapping sails and rattling carts; net-making and repairing; hammering, chiselling boat yards; buying and selling; and made rich with the smells of new rope, tar and fresh, or not so fresh, fish. Each had its own specialities, its own sense of pride and personality.

On March 1st the farewells were said, wives, mothers and daughters lined the quayside on both sides of the water to watch their men folk leave for a gruelling six months stint in the rich fishing grounds of Newfoundland. This was not Channel fishing, but it concerned Channel fishermen and was an adventure which affected the daily lives of those villages for over three hundred years.

In 1634, the peak period, about five hundred boats and eighteen thousand men annually set sail – racing across the Atlantic to establish the firstcomers' right to the role of 'Admiral' for the season. From the fortress town of Granville, on the wild, granite coast of the Cotentin, some one hundred and ten ships, four thousand men, headed the same way. The French, who had plentiful supplies of salt from the Bay of Biscay, were able to pickle their catch on board whereas the British were forced closer to shore and pickled the fish on land. Nearly all their catch was sold, even then, in Europe where the demand was for fish to meet Roman Catholic religious requirements.

The British boats were closely followed by 'sac' boats, often from Dartmouth, who picked up the cargo and returned to sell either the fish itself *en route* in France, Spain or Portugal, or the cod liver oil to soap manufacturers in Britain. At the end of a season one ship might have caught a quarter of a million cod. This was a highly-skilled, three-way, mercantile operation on which the fishing of Brittany and the West Country prospered. The last crew sailed from Dartmouth for Newfoundland in 1907.

While the deep sea boats were away, inshore fishermen struggled on their precarious way. The French, having won the long-distance monopoly of Newfoundland fishing, were never again so active along their own coastline, and though the sounds and smells, and hustle and bustle along the evil Breton coastline was, on the surface, much the same as that in Britain, it was never as commercially important. Each stretch of coast developed its own particular speciality.

In Cornwall, for centuries, the staple diet was pilchards, fresh in summer, salted in winter. Pilchards made up the filling for the original Cornish pasty – the tin miners' sandwich.

Stargazy Pie is one of those traditional dishes that many have heard of, but few people – outside Cornwall – have tasted. Originally it was made from pilchards, which are simply mature sardines. Shortly before the First World War, the vast shoals that arrived each year off the Cornish coast changed their migratory pattern and disappeared into the Atlantic. This caused great hardship to Cornish fishermen, who sold pilchards for smoking and canning, and for untold generations had obtained fish oil from them. A minor offshoot of this disaster was that the pie was made with herrings instead. You can make it with sardines too.

Today, pilchards are once more available, though in much reduced numbers. Stargazy is so named because the fishes' heads protrude from the crust – a remarkable piece of culinary ingenuity. Though the heads are not eaten, the oil contained in them drains back into the fish during cooking. This oil would be lost if the heads were removed first.

Every August the look out, 'huer', was posted on the cliff-top watching for that dark shifting cloud in the sea. As they came up Channel he cried out 'Hevva, hevva' to alert the waiting boats that their prey was heading east.

Daphne Du Maurier recalls, with passion, the pilchard dawn of her twentieth-century childhood.

> What has happened ... is it fire ... is it flood. ... What are they shouting and crying outside our windows. They hurry us from the house to the cliff's edge and all Mullion is assembled there, pointing, shouting, staring down to the troubled waters in the cove ... governess, nurse and nursemaid, visitors like ourselves to Cornwall who have never in the sanctum of the nursery or school-room soiled their hands with fish, scream in our ears, 'the pilchards are in, the pilchards are in'.
>
> The water is a seething mass of fish struggling to escape and the men in boats and on shore are laughing, shouting ... pilchards ... pilchards ... pilchards, the primitive turmoil of a Cornish world gone mad.

A scene that must have been repeated back and back through time.

Conger too was an important item of food in the West Country and large quantities were exported to Spain and Portugal as early as the reign of King John. The trade fell off during the long years of the Napoleonic wars, chiefly because of the scarcity of fish, there not being enough to satisfy the home market. 'Conger douce', as it was called, was prepared by cutting the fish flat through their length and sewing the pieces together with twine to form a continuous sheet. This was then stretched on a framework without salt or other preservative until dried – 'in wet seasons much loss and more offence to the noses of townspeople accrued from so very coarse a process'. This delicacy was grated and used to enrich soup.

Conger rarely take a bait by day or on a moonlit night, and never touch tainted bait. The 'boultys' or 'boulters', had a snood 5 to 6 feet long at every 2 fathoms with a tinned hook baited with cuttle or pilchard. The long line was stretched and moored, its position marked with a buoy, the snoods having many separate cords to prevent the fish escaping by gnawing the line. The best grounds lay 30 to 45 miles from land on sandy bottom; conger were here coloured white and ran to enormous size, many exceeding one hundredweight. In littoral gullies the colour was a rich, purplish-black. 'Once a boat not infrequently brought in 1,000 pounds weight in a night's fishing'.

For centuries there was great pride and tremendous individuality in the boats that were built to cope with the varying conditions of almost every landing ground, and the fish to be fished. In Brixham there were the Dandies, the Bumble Bees and the Hookers – all part of the world's first trawling fleet developed there during the eighteenth century to take advantage of the flat, sandy bottom of Lyme Bay where sole, in particular, lurked. Sole was the rich man's pleasure, and so the fisherman's profit, but gained at the expense of scale-sore, bleeding hands.

In fashionable Brighton, where fishermen were arrogantly forbidden from the beach to please the new, elegant, nineteenth-century holidaymakers, they were the renowned 'Hoggies' and in Hastings, where the fishing community spirit is so strong that it has survived on the shelving shingle despite lack of shelter or anywhere safe to land, the medieval looking luggers lie like stranded whales – the last beach-moored fleet in Britain.

Edgar J. Marsh in the *Inshore Craft of Great Britain* has described the Victorian beach at Hastings.

> The beach presented an animated scene. A big catch, landed an hour or so back, lies on the pebbles with a half circle of buyers assessing its worth to them; some whiskered old men with stove-pipe hats or billycocks stand beside younger fellows in caps, most with hands in pockets and a nonchalant air as the auctioneer starts the sale. A mystic sign, probably unknown to the fishermen standing nearby, tells who is bidding for their night's work.
>
> Close by are lines of hawkers' flat carts, the horses quietly munching in nosebags, and dozens of hand carts belonging to less affluent cadgers and a smart van or two owned by the leading fishmongers. Drawn up on the shingle are luggers and punts, a few with very meagre catches on display. In the background the tall, tarred net sheds and the Fishermen's Church, and on the skyline the ruins of Hastings Castle. Men from one lugger are hurriedly shaking their nets over the bulwark, hoping that prices will not fall before the buyers reach them. Other boats lie bows-on to the beach, men hastening with baskets of choice fish, trusting to catch the eye of a manager from one of the big hotels out betimes to secure prime quality fish for his visitors.

Having given its name to the best known battle of British history Hastings has seemed reluctant to change much over the years. The people now dress differently, the houses have changed but the boats are still beached on the Stade and the tall wooden net sheds in this engraving can still be seen today. (BBC Hulton)

It is an anachronistic place this 'Bulwark Shore'. The seventy remaining high rise 'net shops' on The Stade at Hastings are also the last of their kind – a curious Tudor outcrop of three-storied, tarred, wooden, storage sheds. Further round the shingle headland at Dungeness, in the shadow of the monstrous power-station is an even stranger echo from the past – the Denge Community.

The Denge Community was founded, who knows when, but well over a hundred years ago, by two families: the Tartes, from Cornwall and the Oilers from France. They are there still, clinging to a way of life that has been overtaken by the power-station in whose shadow they live. For generations they have manned the Dungeness lifeboat, men and women alike, launching it down the precipitous beach; they have fished off the wrecks and today live in converted railway carriages and self-built, wooden homes, with atmospheric names such as 'Windwhistle', on the very edge of the wilderness. It is a wild place for tough people, but now their children are at school and there is television, their inheritance must be threatened.

The scene grows more tarry and ropy, more like old Peggotty and his upturned boat. Huts, fishermen's sheds, boat houses, a few bare looking innes, a lifeboat station and a lighthouse; these are the features of this nomansland that has crept up out of the sea since the Middle Ages.

The natives often move about with bits of board tied to their feet like snowshoes to ease their passage over the shingle. They are called buckstays or baxters. Everything looks so flat, so shallow, it is a surprise to find when reaching the sea that it is blue and deep quite near the shore. Vessels of some size can approach and anchor there sheltering from the storms. It is unreal indeed to stand in this strange nomansland watching the piled up waters of the sea as it carries to and fro a constant traffic of ships ... set miraculously as the Jews were in their crossing of the Red Sea, on the scarred bed of the Channel waiting for the awful moment when the waters shall break their unnatural tension and come tumbling back.

The lives of coastal families were regulated by the fishing season. There was a ritual on land common to all fishing families, French or British and a richness of sea-lore too. Every village had its own traditions and fishing yarns to be yarned of an evening and there is a linking thread between them – the sound of the sea.

If something works well why change it? The long life of the net sheds of Hastings is a tribute to the imagination of those who, hundreds of years ago, devised this method of storing and drying nets.
(J. Allan Cash)

May 1st was important to Brighton fishermen for if the beginning of the mackerel season should chance to fall on it this was regarded as a lucky omen and the boats would put out to sea bedecked with flower garlands. But in any case, on whichever day the mackerel were first sighted there would be celebrations on the beaches off Market Street and Bedford Street on the afternoon before the boats left. This they called 'Bendin' In' or 'Bread and Cheese and Beer Day' ... and was last held in 1896. Big baskets of hot bread were brought to the beach ... with baskets of round red cheeses, barrels of beer for the men and ginger beer for the children – all free to the fishermen from the masters of various boats. Sometimes too there was a Punch and Judy show.

The Folklore of Sussex
Jacqueline Simpson

There are grandfathers still in Sussex who recall the excitement over the arrival there of the herring. 'We watched them from the beach come bubbling up the water. What magic too, in those rare still nights looking along the nets in the moonlight to see the lit buoys bobbing under with the weight of maybe five cubic yards filled with herring behind a 26 foot boat.' Less romantic the nights when such overloaded boats sunk in stormy seas, dragged down by the very weight of the fish.

The pilchards are no longer fished, perhaps because the young fish (sprats) are more popular, though their offal is suspended in 'rubby dubby' bags to catch 'rough dogs' or small sharks which are sold to the Brighton scampi market. The Brighton herring have disappeared and even the mackerel have been threatened by over-trawling. In Brittany, where fishermen are as traditional a part of the coastal scene as menhirs and doily-patterned churches are inland, seashore farming of seaweed became an alternative activity for the men who lived by the sea. *La Récolte des Guems* was for fishermen a harvest festival. Their laden, horse-drawn carts have trundled from the past and are even today an important, if surprising, feature in the pungent Breton lanes. Seaweed is an important twentieth-century fertiliser; but once again ecology rears its beautiful head, for the greedy removal of those vast, red, ever-shifting, floating islands could also mean the end of the fish's food supply.

France's greatest Channel harvest today is not fished at all. Oysters, eaten at Cancale after a stormy voyage, were supposedly the inspiration for Debussy's three sea poems *La Mer*. Oysters were never the prerogative of the French and have always been at the centre of yet more rivalry. Oysters found off the Cornish coast delighted the Romans and they were found in abundance around Cornish estuaries at Frenchman's Creek and Helston, and these, according to many a connoisseur were creatures of infinite superiority. British oysters, claims a London gourmet restaurant, are the best in the world. The French are thin in taste and not so fleshy, but because the golden palates of the rich demand oysters as a delicacy, the vast beds around the mudflats of Cancale, which once produced oysters to command for Louis XIV, have come into their own again. That exquisite, ancient taste of the sea has, in its turn, conformed to twentieth-century demands and been introduced into Britain from St Vaast, not only as pâté but, unbelievably, sausages!

Traditionally, oysters were fished by red-sailed boats but these have been replaced in Cancale and other *parcs* along the coast by a rough, wooden raft known as a *chaland* which glides across the vast mirror of the Bay St Michel to wait for that extraordinary tide to drop. As the tide drops the oyster fields can be seen marked out by boundary fences sticking above the water and by skilful manoeuvring the *chaland* is shuffled into position, settles in the mud and the oystermen slip down into their personal territory to work ankle-deep in the cool, oozing mud.

However, oysters are threatened in France as they were in Britain by a disease, Bornamnia, by pollution and by the effects of marine development. The local paper of St Vaast has been full of petitions protesting against pollution. The fishermen are as unhappy today about visiting *plaisanciers*, who disturb the water, as they once were about the arrival of The Black Prince on their shores.

To counteract the Bornamnia virus the French are importing a Flat Pacific oyster, and are not averse to a little verbal sabotage, by feeding the Press with sad stories about the death of the British oyster. Not so; in the Duchy of Cornwall the fifth generation of oystermen is busy sailing its beautiful work-boats and punts. Fal oysters are bright green from the old copper mine workings and have to be sold for soaking in the metal free waters of Helford or Penryn where they become 'white', and delicious.

The story of fishing in such a confined area as the Channel could have been one of a band of several countries working in a common cause, united by the sea upon which they depend. After all it is nearly impossible to define exactly the boundaries of ever-shifting water, nor is it possible to control the movement of the fish that swim in it. They are a common resource. But fishermen are stubborn loners, not given to unions, so the story has been one of individuals struggling for survival.

Fishermen – French or British – face the same storms, the same currents, the same dangers, wet and cold. This is the last, great, hunting activity of man. But in the English Channel those dwindling numbers that do continue to fish, are largely clinging to a way of life, rather than a credible living. There is still a living to be made, but for the lone operator there are easier ways of doing it.

The advent of the Common Agricultural Fisheries Policy has been an attempt to organize, to farm co-operatively, the fish which are a common resource to all nations. The Fisheries Policy does not, of course, apply only to the Channel, but it is in the Channel that the old rivalries hold good, despite the fact that it was in the Channel that the vexed question of fishing rights was resolved, when the two governments agreed limited access for some French boats to certain waters between 6–12 miles, and exclusive fishing up to 6 miles off the British coast. There is a strong feeling in the bars around Mousehole that, when it comes to Channel fishing, the British are gentlemen among thieves – that the opening of territorial waters to foreign fleets is a baring of the British fishing breast for certain death. 'Since there's nothing left on their side of the Pond they'll all rush over here'.

Fish conservation cannot be managed in a purely national context, for fish which have been caught, fully grown, in the waters of one country may have been spawned in the waters of another. Neither the Cod, nor the Herring, nor the Haddock are born British or French citizens, but move in when they are ready. The Channel is therefore heavily dependent on conservation in foreign waters. So quotas are necessary but hotly disputed. In the Channel the Fish Patrol Squadron, a branch of the Royal Navy, keeps an eye on unlicensed fishing and mesh sizes (to control the netting of small fish), and they are respected by the French government too. Even so there is a reconnaissance map drawn up regularly by the Ministry of Agriculture and Fisheries which clearly shows pirates within the limits, and certainly there are fishermen managing to sell their catch direct to Russian factory ships in mid-stream and so making greater profits.

To co-ordinate all these historically disparate concerns the EEC has

While the British navy prepares to defend the Channel against the Russian navy, the Russian fishing fleet send factory ships to Falmouth to buy up the catches of the local fishermen. Defence interests are one thing; commercial interests are another.
(Barnaby)

established co-operatives around the Channel, which also administer compensation to fishermen of about 60 per cent of the price at which the fish is taken from the market when fishing is banned. These co-ops, such as that in Brixham are a direct link to Brussels, but it has a hard task keeping the peace in Britain even, between interests of already rival ports such as Plymouth ('a shambles', says Brixham) and Newlyn ('all sewn up', says Plymouth).

The fishermen of England – the fleet for whom so many proud, lusty shanties have been sung – cornerstone of the British maritime image, fish 4% in the Channel. The French take 30%, and the Dutch, so well-organised and commercially adroit, take 57%.

Of all the great Channel fishing ports only Newlyn, where they have built a brand-new fish dock, retains a thriving business and runs a buying and selling co-operative. And at the heart of that is one family – the omnipresent Stevensons. 'The local Mafia' is muttered by some sole operators on the quayside, where the Stevenson name stands out on all the trawlers and trucks.

If it is true at all, the family of Wm. Stevenson represents a very benevolent Mafia and offers security to many men. From their brown, Dickensian office overlooking the sea, with its dusty ledgers and Victorian pay-out cubby-holes, they run a multi-million pound business on feudal lines. A rich family, headed now by two brothers, one of whom was so shy, locals say, he used to pay for his girl friend to go into the pictures and sit in the car outside to wait for her. One hundred and thirty years ago their grandmother owned two pilchard boats. Now Wm. Stevenson and Sons operates a private family of trawlers and control some hundred and thirty boats plus another fleet of trucks and a freezer company. 'We sell more fish from this office than the rest of Devon and Cornwall put together.'

Their story is one of dogged success at a time when most fishermen complain the industry is scuppered. Exporting 85 per cent to France and Spain, the Stevensons seem to be going from strength to strength; buying and selling, they are geared to ward off the modern pirates of Penzance – the fish-and-run fleets of France, Spain and especially Holland.

Because there is no dole in Spain, dependence on fishing there has been responsible for the huge size of the Spanish fleet – now the biggest in the world – and problems over entry into the EEC. As it is, say fishermen in Cornwall, there have been seventy Spaniards fishing at a time under flags of convenience in British waters. Two years on that scale would have cleaned out the entire quota.

Though there is probably scope for the small, efficient boat-owner ferrying his catch across to France, most have discovered, like the caravan-site farmers, that there is easier money in holidaymakers, and many of the younger men prefer to take trippers out to fish for their tea in waters which once launched grandfathers towards the deep-sea hunting grounds.

> Think of those wild winter nights when a shout was scarce heard above the roaring of the gale, the grinding of hulls, the crash of falling spars, and the thunder of slatting canvas as sails, torn from their gaskets, were blown to ribbons. Suddenly the darkness is lit up by the eerie light of blue flares and the dull boom of minute guns is heard from one of the lightships, to be followed soon by a shower of stars as rockets burst in the sky, telling sorely-tried mariners that help is on the way. The wind shrieks and howls, blowing like the wrath of God, rain comes down in torrents, huge breakers are crashing in on the steep beach, grinding, sucking, pushing the shingle in all directions as a dog scatters a flock of sheep, the yeasty foam running back between the pebbles, to be driven in again as the next sea breaks.
>
> What a maelstrom into which to launch an open boat. Yet that was the backcloth against which the Deal boatmen played their noble part in the saving of life and property.
>
> Spray stings the face and reddens the eyes as the men lean against the force of the wind; spume, spindrift and fragments of seaweed drive far inland, up the narrow alleys into the open country where tall elms bend in torment from the lashing they are taking. Groups of men hurry along the beach to make up the crew of lugger or lifeboat, in many a home anxious women hand

food and warm clothing to their loved ones, whilst frightened
children cling to their skirts, wondering what all the noise and
excitement is about, little realising that in years to come they will
recall with pride being on the beach when their father's lugger
saved an exhausted crew.

Deal Boats and Boatmen
Edgar J. Marsh

The same craft were used for 'hovelling', the ancient skill of
salvaging anchors from wrecks and supplying them to drifting ships.
Sometimes three or four would race to the sands, for the profits from
such activities were great, and, of course, this same spirit found an
outlet too in the equally skilful craft of smuggling. It was a full-
blooded place whose reputation for breeding longshore 'sharks' was
justified but well-earned.

It is hard to be sure if the Goodwins have been a bane or a boon to the
men of Deal. Of all the Channel's forgotten places, Deal today is
maybe superficially the more forgettable, certainly to the undiscern-
ing. But stay awhile, sitting in one of the small chrome and plastic tea
shops on the front and look out over that water which has witnessed
the life and death of much history. Here in this curious left-over
outpost, whose planners have determinedly fought the building of
multi-story shops, is the essence of the Channel.

Ruthless courage, crafty opportunism, heartbreak and home-
comings, patriotic passion and smuggling merge here – the white cliffs
of Dover later became the island symbol – but it is Deal and the people
of the 'bulwark shore' who shared it.

Despite all the advances in techniques since the fishing net was developed thousands of years ago folk still have to mend the mesh by hand, as here in Deal. (J. Allan Cash)

The Channel Islands:
the Story in Miniature

I love this island lone and wild,
Where England, freedom's child.
'Neath its old flag, doth right maintain.
Victor Hugo

La Houllée, Richeroche, La Conchée, Plât Ile, La Genetaie. These are the islets of the Chausey group within the Channel Islands, of which few French and even fewer British people will have heard. A romantically lonely, mostly uninhabited string of fifty-three islands belonging, unlike the rest – Jersey, Guernsey, Alderney, Herm and Sark – to France. They are a beautiful, blue, granite necklet strung across the Bay of Avranches, astonishingly fertile with wild flowers and cottage gardens. Peaceful because of the absence of roads, they are a marine biological paradise at low tide when the waters drop leaving fifteen square miles of sand, pebbles and varech beds exposed for exploration.

It is as though someone had written the name of Chausey in invisible ink in the history books. But it is there for those with the curiosity to discover it. The rest of the Channel Islands, those belonging to the British Crown, are themselves little understood by the majority of their mainland compatriots. Although tourism today has topped £200 million they are almost as remote in the minds of most British as the Falklands. Potatoes, tomatoes, woolly jumpers, cows and *Bergerac* are about as far as the public knowledge extends.

Victor Hugo's assessment seems inescapable: 'They are portions of France which have fallen into the sea and been picked up by England', but he is wrong. Geologically they did not fall – they were cut off by changing sea levels. Historically it was England that was 'picked up' when Duke William assumed the title of King. To this day the Islanders like to feel that England belongs to them rather than the reverse and the traditional toast 'to the Queen' is, in fact, 'to our Duke'.

Each island has always cherished its individuality. They are astonishingly different geologically, and consequently sociologically and politically. You will find few books by residents studying their combined role, for the Jersey man does not acknowledge Guernsey or vice versa and the tourist offices today are determinedly independent. Guernsey is not even represented in London.

It is this sense of nationhood which has underwritten their story – understandably wishing to be Norman when convenient and British when not, but always being Islanders above all. It is astonishing that, lying so close to each other, their histories have never fused. Guernsey alone was occupied by the French in the Hundred Years War.

The Toad (Jersey) was traditionally the refuge for Normans, The Donkey (Guernsey) for Bretons and they lie, with The Cow and The Crow (Alderney and Sark) in a sea which the French claim is not even the Channel. This, they say, is the Atlantic. So the 'Channel' Islands are a microcosm of Anglo-French history; an enigmatic symbol. They are the pivot of the story.

In his *History of the Island of Jersey* the Rev Philippe Falle says 'We are apeculiar to the Crown, a parcel of the Dominion of the Crown of England yet not, nor never were a parcel of the Realm of England'. The Islander describes himself as a citizen of the UK, Islands and Colonies. Norman French was, until recently, in regular use and is still the official language of the State. It is still much in evidence in place names, and flourishes amongst the many Norman French Societies. Follow the coastal roads and you will see on the sign posts a fascinating progression from Viking, to Norman, to Norman French to English ... *etacq* (cape), *mielle* (sand dune), *guet* (watch tower), *dicq* (embankment). To speak mainland French was at one time considered snobbish. Many familiar family names – Carteret, Ollivier, Mauger – are Norman; the legal system is based on the Norman *Loi Coutumier* and the ancient right of appeal direct to the British Sovereign the *Clameur de Haro*. This entitles a wronged person to cry on the site of the tort *'Haro, Haro a l'aide mon prince on me fait tort'* and so have his case tried in the Crown Court.

So, although allegiance to the Crown is solid, the internal affairs of each island are not subject to English Parliamentary rule nor are they represented in Westminster. Because of their strategic importance they have had to protect their rights and customs first from Normandy and then from Britain but it was really at the end of the Hundred Years War that they established the present 'States' and moved from royal administration to real self-government.

Today there are two separate Bailiwicks, Jersey, the largest, and Guernsey which includes Herm, Alderney and Sark. Each has its own legislative assembly, government (in Jersey the States, and also in Guernsey the States) and court of law. In practice this means for instance that capital punishment is law (though no one has been hanged since 1959); the wearing of seat belts is not. In international affairs the islands are represented by the UK. The Islander is not subject to British tax laws nor is he subject automatically to military service in times of war.

Jersey was probably accessible by road as late as Roman times for the final breach with the mainland is thought not to have occurred until around 2000 years ago. Many millions of years ago the Cotentin peninsula itself may have been an island within which they were all incorporated and only two hundred years ago Herm was linked to Guernsey. Certainly the rocks from which the Channel Islands are formed are unimaginably old – but vary in age and method of formation from island to island. Some, visible today along the south coast of Guernsey, were created in the very depths of the earth's crust, others, like the black patches on the pale grey gneiss (a metamorphic rock) of Alderney, came later.

Much later, only about seven hundred million years ago, volcanoes spread a layer of ash over what is now Jersey and this can be seen in the multicoloured striped rocks of l'Islet in Bouley Bay and the cemented remnants of ashes, rock and lava at Archinondel and Mont Orgeuil. Jersey even has its own miniature Giant's Causeway of red hexagonal blocks formed by the lava flow. During the Debensian period, about eighteen thousand years ago, the Channel Islands had become out-crops in a vast plain left behind when the sea level dropped. Turbulent streams and rivers (whose beds are still visible to the submariner around the islands) dissected the plateau and bitter winds blew yellow, loamy dust from the ice sheet of northern Europe which covered Jersey, Guernsey and Sark and left the rich fertile soil of today. By about 4000 BC the sea had risen and drowned most of the plains and thickly wooded countryside just as it had already done in the eastern Channel. Jersey, Guernsey, Alderney and Sark became islands separated forever from mainland Europe. The curious genealogy of many millions of years is clear to trace, not only in the superbly varied scenery of each Channel Island, but even in the different coloured stone of which their homes and monuments are built.

Archaeologically speaking too, each island has its own identity. Jersey alone is known to have been occupied at the time when early Palaeolothic man was moving into northern France, for the hand axes with which he hunted the woolly rhino, the elephant and a small deer – zeuner (*cervus elaphus jerseyensis*) which was unique to the island – were discovered in a cave at La Cotte de St Brélade together with layers of food, thousands of flake tools and the bones of dismembered carcasses which made this a site unrivalled in Europe.

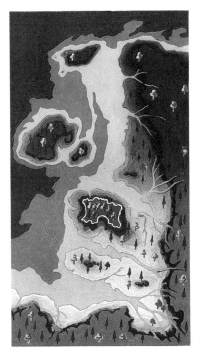

About 9000 years ago the encroaching sea had cut off Guernsey, Alderney and Sark but Jersey was still part of the mainland, covered in and surrounded by thick forests. (Department of Postal Administration, Jersey, C.I.)

By 4000 BC Jersey is almost isolated. The sea level would gradually rise by another 40 feet reducing the island to its present size. (Department of Postal Administration, Jersey, C.I.)

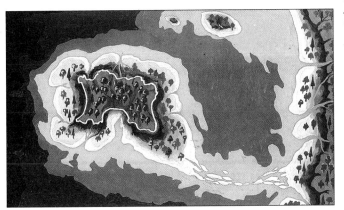

The best-known memorial to prehistory are the megalithic tombs such as that at Dehus, Guernsey, which are circular (unlike those in Wessex) and feature an extremely rare sculptured menhir representing a mother goddess or fertility figure.

The Bronze Age came to the sparsely occupied islands around 2000 BC and by the time the Roman influence reached the Channel shores Celtic and classical culture were fusing and there are signs (in emergency hidden coin hoards) of unsettled times in which the islands became 'stepping stones between the Celtic people on both sides of the Channel'. But at the first stage, as in earlier periods, the link was more strongly with mainland Europe and the archaeological excavations have gone hand in hand with those of Brittany rather than those of Britain.

The Dark Ages in the Channel Islands were as dark as they were anywhere else. Eventually Christian missionaries, such as St Samson, established churches there, and, as in other parts of the Channel, tried to adapt local folklore to Christianity. He offered medals to children to stay away from the traditional Midwinter Festival (which the church adopted as Christmas).

But eventually came William who had inherited Normandy from the Viking Rollo and who, in turn, conquered England. Under William were established many of today's arrangements such as exemption from British tax laws – which has been responsible for a large increase in immigrant population especially in recent years – and the very strict property rules – any EEC resident wishing to buy or rent property must submit to a stringent examination to prove his admission will benefit the Islands. When eventually King John lost control of Normany itself he retained the Channel Islands under the British Crown as they have been ever since.

In the years between the Norman Conquest of Britain and the Hundred Years War there was confusion in the Islands which were loyal to the Crown but largely dominated by Norman landowners and Norman churchmen. It was King John who confirmed the Islands' traditional customs and liberties 'from time immemorial'. He confiscated estates of the pro-French 'Norman' lords and he restored the rights and possessions of the abbeys and churches, knowing that the spire of Coutances Cathedral could be seen from Gorey Castle and that 'one may twice in a day cross the sea between us and them'. But most importantly he removed the Island's dependency on centralized rule from Rouen by the appointment of a warden as the personal representative of the King of England, Duke of Normandy, to administer the revenues, and to hold courts and assizes.

Even so there was constant friction as the British tried to control their spirited Island subjects with difficulty; one appointed Warden, Otto de Grandison, ruled from France and did not visit the Islands until he was ninety years old and they were on the point of rebellion.

At the beginning of the Hundred Years War the Islands were in a key position. In 1336 they were used as pawns in an attack by David Bruce, son of Robert the Bruce of Scotland, who was in exile in France at the time when Edward III and Philip of France were flexing their muscles at the outbreak of war. Because of their importance the King made a declaration in 1341 which was to settle their government for centuries.

> Considering how faithfully the beloved men of our Isle have ever maintained their loyalty towards the Kings of England, and how much they have suffered in defence of our rights and honour we concede for ourselves and our heirs that they hold and retain all privileges, immunities, and customs granted by our forebears or of other legal competency and that they enjoy them freely without molestation by ourselves, our heirs and our officers.

This ensured their loyalty throughout continued upheavals of history. Each island continued to exercise its own particular form of independence. The events of mainland history did not always affect each island equally and though in 1483 it was agreed they should be neutral in time of war – Protestants, Catholics, Yorkists, Lancastrians – the French and British have in turn dominated separately. During the Civil Wars, for instance, Jersey was Royalist and Guernsey Roundhead, and when Protestant William of Orange eventually prohibited trade with France, Jersey smugglers met their customers at Ecrehous rocks, while Guernsey men sent their goods to England.

> The Islands were ever a strategic rendezvous for the lawless and the outcast having better anchorages than the mainland opposite.
> *The Channel Islands*, Lockley

During the fifteenth and sixteenth centuries the clicking of needles might well have drowned the voice of the preacher in church. With growing prosperity, especially in Jersey, there was a tremendous boom in the wool trade and the Islands' reputation for fine knitted goods was established. Mary Queen of Scots went to her execution wearing a pair of Jersey knitted stockings.

From 1600 the Rolls of the Jersey Royal Court showed that the knitting of stockings had become an established industry for both men and women. So much so that in 1606 a law was passed forbidding anyone to knit during the harvest and vraicking (seaweed gathering) seasons. By 1617 inspectors were appointed to ensure 'quality control' and to see that only three-ply wool was used.

Most of the raw material was, in fact, imported from Britain and did not come from the famous four-horned sheep of which none are now left in the wild, though there are some in Gerald Durrell's Jersey Zoo. By 1637 there were six thousand knitters in Jersey alone, making six thousand pairs of stockings weekly. Mostly these were sent to France – England preferred waistcoats – and for two hundred years the trade brought in considerable revenue to the Islands. In 1899 John Stead described

The Dexterity and Expedition with which they dispatch a Pair of Stockings are almost incredible. To them Light and Darkness are indifferent. A woman seen walking without a Stocking in her Hand is stigmatized with Idleness. So attached are they to this Employment that they have appropriated to knitting the Name of Work (i.e. *oeuvre*, from which is derived the verb *ouvrer*, to knit). In Summer they assemble in large Numbers, and sit in A Ring under the Trees, which make of all the Roads a continued Avenue; and the Avocation must be urgent that can call them from the Social Party. In Winter, a Number of Houses send forth their Fair Ones, '*nocturna carpentes pensa puellas*', sitting on soft Rushes, carefully picked and dried for that purpose. There '*seros hyberni ad lumnis ignes pervigilant*', and from the Close of Day till Midnight, An Universal Activity prevails. Nor let it be imagined that these Hours are dull and tedious. They indulge their native Mirth in innocent Recreation, and the Song of Festivity forbids the Intrusion of Melancholy. The young Men, returned from their more hardy Occupations of the Day, repair to those cheerful Meetings. There, seated in the Middle of the Ring, they pay their Offerings at the Shrine of Beauty, and yield their Soule to the Impulse of Love, which is here generally attended with an Innocence and Simplicity unknown in larger Countries.

All that remains today are archive reminders of the picturesque Jersey, Norman-French words that grew from the wool trade. A *bergethie* a sheepfold, a *gardeaux de brebis* a shepherd, *touoser* to shear, *la treme* natural wool. The phrase *du fi d'ichin* was Jersey wool; the word for lambswool, *de l'angn'lin*. But above all the method of Jersey knitting is still jealously protected by the local Women's Institute.

Life in the Islands was hard for many people. The seigneurs and richer families lived well enough in solid stone houses, with the characteristic Norman, round arched doorways. Usually there was an outside stair up to the second floor and two fixed features – the bed, the *lit d'fouaile*, and a large family table. Peasant farmer–fishermen were on the whole self-supporting, there were a few artisans and craftsmen and a great many *pauvres*, landless and unemployed living in hovels.

Apart from knitting, the Newfoundland fishing trade was the best hope for the poorer people, whilst the more wealthy looked eastward towards trade – even today Jersey has a thriving tea-blending business.

Throughout the wars with France the Channel Islands were a thorn in Napoleon's side.

These two islands are the despair of France, at the breaking out of each war through their remarkably active privateers. The habit of encountering the dangers of the sea renders the natives very brave. They have well-disciplined regiments of militia, excellent marksmen. They are always in a state of warfare against the customs house officers of the two kingdoms, now against the French commercial marine. A population of this character greatly enhances the natural strength of these islands.

The Governor of Cherbourg

Consequently, although they were constantly threatened, the wars brought considerable prosperity to the Islands. Napoleon raged: 'France can no longer tolerate this nest of brigands and assassins. Europe must be purged. Jersey is England's shame'. But with increased defences came more men, garrisons to supply and more income all round. Peace in 1814 was a mixed blessing.

The nineteenth century was for the Channel Islands – as for everywhere else around the coasts of Britain and France – an exciting time of change and development and growing prosperity. Improved communications made a new industry possible: tomatoes or love apples as they were called. Alongside tomato-growing there blossomed a flower- and bulb-growing business too, and flowers were sent on the new steam packets to Covent Garden. Today from the air Guernsey dazzles the eyes, for the Islands appear hooded by glass.

Guernsey from the air can look like the Glass Island. (Aerofilms)

Many islanders went abroad. William Cody, 'Buffalo Bill (1845–1917), was descended from the Jersey family Le Caudey. Others came as tourism became fashionable, and the Islands also attracted many celebrities to settle there. In the extraordinary house called *Hauteville* in St Peter Port Guernsey, with its garish furnishings, Victor Hugo wrote *Travailleurs de la Mer* and took cold showers in the nude in public! The dedication on his statue in the Candie Grounds is taken from the dedication '*Au Rocher d'hospitalité et de liberté à ce coin de vieille terre Normande ou vit le noble petit peuple de la mer à l'Ile de Guernsey sévère et douce*'. ('To this rock of hospitality and liberty, to this corner of the old land of Normandy, where lives the noble little community of the sea, to Guernsey, harsh yet gentle.')

Jersey links with the famous Victorian portrait now known as 'Bubbles' are less well-known. John Millais, who became President of the Royal Academy, painted a portrait of his grandson and was appalled to discover it had been sold by a magazine to the manufacturers of Pears soap and retitled. Millais also painted a portrait of Jersey's most famous actress – Emile Charlotte le Breton, better known as Lily Langtry, mistress of Edward VII.

During the First World War each of the Islands contributed manpower to the fighting forces but the War itself was a long way away. The Second World War was a different matter for they became the only part of the UK to be occupied by the Germans. The British government had to conclude that their defence was impossible and at the end of the Phoney War the Islands became victims of the kind of clumsy ill-conceived decisions that characterized so much of the early months of the War.

According to Charles Cruikshank in his book *The German Occupation of the Channel Islands*,

> There was no precedent for the island occupation. A fact which critics of the Islands' administration would do well to remember. They had no experience of conducting even friendly negotiations with a great power since the UK had always been responsible for their external relations. Overnight they were abandoned to their fate. They awoke to find themselves dealing on equal terms with the greatest military power the world had known.

They were to become a part of Hitler's Atlantic Wall and their occupation marked the end, in Hitler's view, of the British Empire.

The Islanders were – even in the minds of the British Government – out on a limb, and though the Islands were demilitarized it did not seem to register in Whitehall that there could be a threat of invasion, or even that it would make much difference if there was. The Channel Islands were of no strategic value to the Germans or the British, but Hitler made of them sensational propaganda value. Evacuation of those residents who wished to leave, and of holidaymakers who had even been encouraged to take a break from Britain during the Phoney

War, was chaotic and only on Sark, where La Dame ruled with a rod of iron, was there any cohesive action. In fact almost nobody left Sark. Six thousand six hundred people went from Jersey out of a population of fifty thousand, and seventeen thousand out of forty-two thousand left Guernsey. No one was left on Alderney. Those who were there remember burying their silver and valuables in the garden and leaving their homes and their possessions, apart from two suitcases, with only overnight warning. On 28th June the Germans bombed St Helier and St Peter Port, whereupon the BBC announced demilitarization and the Germans decided to invade.

The Islanders were now helpless pawns. Their propaganda importance was quite overestimated by Hitler. There is little doubt that Churchill would have abandoned them if their loss might have won the war, and many times throughout the duration they were, unbeknown to themselves, exposed to reprisals, especially when the practice commando raids put them in great danger.

It was Churchill's strategic judgements, rather than his concern for the Islanders, which saved them. 'Operation Blazing' would have destroyed them all, but it did not happen because of the likely loss to the RAF. Relief food for the Islands was forbidden although undoubtedly the collapse of the German garrison would have meant revenge attacks.

The enemy arrival in fact passed off fairly smoothly and the Germans took great trouble to behave correctly and with concern; the Island authorities were allowed to continue their rule, with German approval, and to act as a link, or buffer, between the occupying forces and the people, with a view to ensuring as little suffering as possible.

In 1941 the 'toad', the 'donkey' and the 'crow' became Jakob, Gustav and Adolf – the code names for Jersey, Guernsey and Alderney when the Organization Todt, under Dr Todt, was sent to start a programme of military reconstruction. At the outset the OT was formed of non-combatant workers, but when political prisoners and POWs were drafted in, the situation changed, and the fifteen thousand workers were treated ruthlessly – especially on Alderney where contact with Islanders was non-existent for they had all left. Rations were at starvation level, dysentery was rife, and many died of deadly nightshade poisoning as desperate men ate the temptingly deceptive berries.

Charles Cruickshank tells of the words of a German soldier at the time:

> The mixture of people on the Island has been increased with the arrival of Russian civilian workers, smelling sour, dressed in rags, often barefoot and wearing peaked caps. We see their rigid and melancholy silhouettes everywhere. I attribute their condition partly to insufficient food, and partly to their wooden-soled shoes. The most pitiful Frenchman is a cut above them. An Arab, about to leave the Island hoping to join the Foreign Legion, said he would liquidate four hundred of these types in

an hour ... The Russians beg for cigarettes when one meets them. They follow us home waiting to pounce on stubs.

By 1944 most of the OT had gone to build Hitler's Atlantic Wall. There was, of course, much suffering, especially hunger, because it was hard to grow enough food to support the increased population, and as the war continued so people became more and more hungry. Ration books were issued, but when eventually two official brothels were opened in Guernsey with two men and thirteen women from France, the French Government refused to supply food from France on the grounds that they weren't 'heavy workers'. Within two weeks of the German invasion Churchill changed course and decided to hit back. He sent a telegram: 'If it be true that a few hundred troops have landed on Jersey or Guernsey by troop carriers, plans should be studied to land secretly by night on the Islands and kill or capture the invaders. This is exactly one of the exploits for which the Commandos would be suited ... Pray let me have a plan'.

The plan – codename 'Anger' – proved, like many plans conceived in anger, to be a disaster, though Churchill hoped that it might at least be a valuable lesson in amphibious warfare. Everything went wrong. The boat was not big enough, they misjudged the tides, and misread the compass directions (two years later when Lt Philip Pinney landed successfully on Sark and climbed into the Dame's bedroom, he was greeted by the welcome 'Thank goodness to see a decent-sized man at last').

In fact the Commandos learned their craft during these quick raids on the mainland and Islands. They became known as 'the steel hand from the sea'. They landed from motor launches (one of which was affectionately known in the Channel Islands as 'the little pisser') and the aim was to keep the Germans constantly jittery.

For the first two years of the occupation life was on the whole monotonous, both for the Germans and the residents, but in 1942 Hitler decided to use all the English-born residents as hostages and they were shipped away to internment camps in Germany. The anxious Council of Jersey and the Controlling Committee of Guernsey continued as they had throughout the occupation to maintain some semblance of reason and to negotiate with the Germans – their resignation would have served no purpose and would, in the end, have brought worse trouble to the Islands. They did their best to monitor and control the operation and to achieve exemptions on compassionate grounds. Appeals were ingenious – the illegitimate son of the native islander who had been born and cared for after his birth in England was turned down; so was a man who claimed to be doing war work – bottling beer for the German Army. The Germans failed to understand the complex character of the Islands and assumed that the British Government would place higher value on English, rather than 'colonial' born islanders. When the hostages went, records Charles Cruikshank: 'They were magnificent and England can be proud of them; they sang and joked on their way to the quay and for all the world seemed to be going on a great picnic'. Altogether about two thousand men and women and children were shipped away.

After the liberation of what Churchill called (somewhat curiously in the circumstances) 'our dear islands' and the reform of the Islands' constitutions, a number of influential businessmen came to power and rehabilitation was set in motion. Within only a few years the economy was booming, tourism flourishing and both Jersey and Guernsey became the base for financiers and merchant banks. Today:

> Jersey stands slightly aloof from the other Islands, sophisticated, bustling with life, appealing to wealthy residents and tourists, but retaining a strong agricultural element. Guernsey ... less sophisticated but with a more relaxed atmosphere; some wealthy residents and fewer tourists. Alderney, windswept and bleak when the sky darkens and the wind blows and the sea is whipped into the future is independent, free and easy. Sark, beautiful and tranquil is where time stands still and Herm like a lost south sea island.
>
> *Portrait of the Channel Islands*
> Raoul Lemprière

The others, accessible on occasion by boat, remain remotely romantic, uninhabited havens for wildlife.

Tourism, on which the Islands lean so heavily, has brought its problems, with an influx of some 8 visitors per single resident each summer. But for all that the British Channel Islands are on occasion visible from the mainland of France, and there is a Gallic flavour everywhere, the French are *still* not tempted onto British soil. Eighty per cent of tourists are British, two thirds of the remainder French. Equally few British penetrate the not-so-far-away Chausey group. Yet despite the overloading which sometimes threatens to sink the little Islands, the workaday life of residents carries on much the same; tourism is welcomed, but not allowed to disrupt business: a highly beneficial bonus that does not diminish the Islanders' independent determination to keep themselves afloat through industry, commerce and agriculture.

On the occasion of the United Kingdom joining the European Economic Community, special terms were negotiated for the Islands, and were defined by a protocol to the Treaty of Accession. Under these terms the Islands are included within the European Economic Community for the purpose of free movement of industrial and agricultural goods. To that end they are required to apply the common external tariff, the agricultural levies on imports from third countries and certain parts of the common agricultural policy. Other provisions of the Treaty of Rome, including those relating to the free movement of persons, capital movements, and the harmonization of taxation and social policies, do not apply to them. As well as being relieved of some obligations under the Treaty, the Islands are denied some of the benefits. In particular, the Islands do not have access to Community funds in support of agriculture, while Islanders who do not possess close ties with the United Kingdom have no rights of free movement within Community countries for the purposes of employment and right to establishment. They do, however, maintain traditional rights of free access to the United Kingdom labour market.

Once again the Channel Islands have marked their independence by achieving the best (or worst) of both worlds – standing half in, half out of the EEC.

The Eighteenth Century:
In – and Out – like a Lion

On the night of November 26th–27th 1703 the Channel was ravaged along all its coasts by a tempest which has been recorded as the worst in its history. Forests were uprooted, the Eddystone Lighthouse blown down, men-of-war wrecked, eight hundred houses and four hundred windmills destroyed in Britain alone and thousands of lives, including fifteen hundred seamen, were lost.

That storm was a turbulent beginning for the eighteenth century Channel, a century which was ended with equal ferocity with the Revolution – the deluge Louis XVI forecast with '*aprés moi, le déluge*'.

The focus of history, the great events of power politics, national jealousy and industrial and social revolution moved inland. Wars were waged and battles fought in foreign lands and on far distant seas. In Britain, and later in France, improvements in agriculture followed by industrial expansion began to move the source of work and money to the towns whilst better health care, doctors and diet sparked off a population explosion which sent many restless artisans and craftsmen in search of homes and work elsewhere, often in the New World.

With good Queen Anne on the throne (1702–1714), relying heavily on the Francophobic Duke and Duchess of Marlborough, life was peaceful enough in Britain. Not so in Europe where much turmoil and suffering was caused by the power struggles of nations, terrible winters, cattle disease and hunger. The peasants' lot was not a happy one, and everyone longed for peace.

At the start of the century the Channel landscape was largely undeveloped and the quality of village life declining. By the end the English coast at least had developed something of the peacefully prosperous air of Constable's paintings, with fields and orchards enclosed by hedges and many new trees planted. All this was possible because the landed gentry became interested in gardening and more involved in their estates. Tenant farmers were not always so fortunate.

The sea which had always been a place of work or war began to provide for the rich a new found pleasure: a means of escape, a poetic inspiration for writers and artists, therapeutic for body and mind. The English passion for travel now became a reality for some of the expanding middle classes too, helped by better roads and transport. By the end of the century quick-thinking tradesmen, fishermen and impoverished working folk of all kinds were ready to exploit the obvious goldmine on their beaches.

The sea was their salvation for it provided a brand-new source of income and jobs. From being a resort of kings and princes, the eighteenth and nineteenth centuries saw the Channel grow into a playground for the Victorian masses. In order to enjoy the excitement of travel they were prepared to put up with the inconvenience of 'abroad' being full of foreigners.

As long ago as the eighth century, when Alcuin of York was working in the rowdy court of Charlemagne, the Archbishop of Palermo – the Counsellor to the King of Sicily – the Bishop of Chartres and the Abbot of L'Aumane were all English. An eighth century Pope forbade lay women and nuns to make the journey from England to Rome because 'there is not a town in France or Italy where there is not an English harlot or adulteress'. Much later in 1474 enough pilgrims were crossing the Channel for William Way to write a travel guide packed with useful tourist tips; 'Also y consel yow to have wyth yow oute of venyse confettyunne ya confitatyus, laxactyvvs, restoratyvys, gyngever ryse fygys, reysebes gret and small wyche schal do yow gret ese by the wey, pepyr saferyn clowys maeys a few as ye theng nede and powder dekke.'

By the eighteenth century it was France and especially Paris which led the sparkling social and cultural life of Europe in this 'age of elegance'. It was to France that noble and middle class British families began to send their daughters to be finished, their sons to be polished and their elderly into genteel vegetation. In the intellectual hothouse of the Paris salon there grew a new and surprising Anglomania; a growing interest in British philosophy and writing. But in general the enthusiasm which was carrying overcrowded packet boats full of sea-sick travellers from Brighton or Folkestone did not sweep the French in the opposite direction.

They felt they were (and still are) in the mainstream of Europe. Voltaire made the crossing, so did Chateaubriand. But social contact was a one-way affair. True, a few seventeenth century children had been sent from Boulogne to learn English in Kent. True, escaping aristocrats sought shelter along the south coast. But nowhere along the wilder shores of Dorset or Devon would you ever have found thriving colonies of French emigrés as you would have found the English, still so very English, well-settled and happily cooking kippers in Dinard, Granville, Dieppe and Boulogne.

The eighteenth century love affair with France involved incredible hardship *en voyage*. A crossing to Calais or Boulogne necessitated the final indignity of being carried ashore across shallow beaches by professional porters who charged profiteering prices and often dropped their customers. It was clearly worth it for nothing, not even the Revolution, stopped them. If the French usually came to Britain *in extremis* the British went to France for fun.

The best known of eighteenth century travellers were the young men and their bearwards (tutors) on the Grand Tour. These were little more than our own student backpackers, perhaps more parentally

supervised and certainly far less well-behaved. For these spoilt young men were too immature and too rich on the whole to benefit greatly from the intellectual feast offered them.

Instructions given by the father of Lord Herbert to his tutor, the Reverend W Coxe, and Captain Floyd before their departure on the Grand Tour.

Avoid Drink, Gaming and all improper Connections, and move away directly, if necessary on their account.

Attend to Economy.

Wear no embroidered or laced Cloaths, except Regimentals. . . .

Young French Officers the worst of the Company.

Mouth Water. Tooth powder and Pomatum receipts. Teeth looked over abroad by skilful Dentist Spring and Fall. Flat Saddle from Wilton (one Horse with it and fire off from, and leap over Bar, every day with Floyd, everywhere) Running Snaffle and Bit.

Thick tennis shoes, & Flannel Socks for Lord Herbert and never play without them, or Fence, on account of foundering.

Lord H: learn to dress his own hair, to bleed and put on a Horses Shoe occasionally.

Lord H: to speak something now and then before Mr Coxe and Floyd in English.

The indignities suffered, if not iniquities committed, during Grand Tours by grand people were a source of inspiration for cartoonists. These happy Italian peasants are not helping our hero to a better view of the Bay of Naples and Vesuvius. They are helping themselves to his baggage. (Mansell)

Much more observant were the genuine travellers, the writers and diarists who commented on the human scene. Arthur Young, the agriculturalist was appalled by conditions in Brittany before the Revolution.

The country has a savage aspect; husbandry not much further advanced ... which seems incredible amidst enclosures; the people almost as wild as their country and their town of Combourg one of the most brutally filthy places that can be seen; mud houses, no windows and a pavement so broken as to impede all passengers but ease none; yet here there is a chateau and inhabited. Who is this Monsieur de Chateaubriand the owner, that has nerves strung for a residence amidst such filth and poverty. [It was Réné de Chateaubriand's brother.]

The poor people seem poor indeed. The children terribly ragged, if possible worse clad than with no clothes at all. A beautiful girl six or seven years old playing with a stick and smiling under such a bundle of rags as made my heart ache to see her. One third of what I have seen in this province seems uncultivated and nearly all of it in misery.

This was certainly an exaggerated picture but there is no doubt that French agriculture lagged far behind the British and had not yet benefited from the agricultural revolution.

Tobias Smollett, who, with his French wife, ventured abroad for his health, caused an uproar in France after the journal of his trip was published. He was caustic about much of France – but Boulogne he liked.

Living here is pretty reasonable; the markets are tolerably supplied. The beef is neither fat nor firm; but very good for soup which is the only use the French make of it. The veal is not so white nor so well fed as English veal; but it is more juicy and better tasted. The mutton and pork are very good. We buy our poultry alive and fatten them at home. Here are excellent turkies, [*sic*] and no want of game; the hares in particular are very large, juicy and high flavoured. The best part of the fish caught on this coast is sent by post to Paris in *chasse marines* by a company of contractors like those of Hastings, Sussex. Nevertheless we have excellent soles, skates, flinders and whiting and sometimes mackeral [*sic*]. The oyster are very large and coarse and rank. There is very little fish caught on the French coast because the shallows run a great way from the shore; and the fish live chiefly in deep water; for this reason fishermen go a great way out to sea, sometimes even as far as the coast of England. . . .

The shop keepers here drive a considerable traffic with the English smugglers whose cutters are almost the only vessels one sees in the harbour of Boulogne, if we except about a dozen of those flat bottomed boats which raised such alarms in England in the course of the war.

Indeed they seem to be good for nothing else and perhaps were built for this purpose only. The smugglers from the coast of Kent and Sussex pay English gold for great quantities of French brandy, tea, coffee and small wine which they run from this country. They likewise buy glass trinkets, toys and coloured prints which sell in England for no other reason but that they come from France, as they may be as cheap and much better finished of our own manufacture. . . . It is certainly worthwhile for any traveller to lay in a stock of linen either at Dunkirk or Boulogne. . . . I have made provision for shirts for one half the money they would have cost in London.

. . . the poorest tradesman in B. has a napkin on every cover and silver forks with four prongs which are used with the right hand there being little occasion for knives for the meat is boiled or roasted to rags.

The French beds are so high that sometimes one is obliged to mount them by the help of steps and this is also the case in Flanders. They very seldom use feather beds but lie upon a paillasse or bag of straw over which are laid two or sometimes three mattresses. Their testers are high . . . and their curtains generally of thin bais red or green laced with tawdry yellow in imitation gold.

In some houses there is no such thing as carpet to be seen and the floors are in a very dirty condition. They have not even the implements of cleanliness in this country . . . everything shows a deficiency in the mechanic arts. There is not a door nor a window that shuts close. Hinges and locks and latches are of iron and very coarsely made.

The French welcomed the British travellers as a transfusion for their dying communities; romantics, such as Chateaubriand, discovered in *le seaside* a source of poetry and pleasure. The French, at first pretended they were only concerned for their health, but before long they too were flinging their clothes aside and frolicking, like the skinny-dipping English, in the briny. Victorian pruderies were yet to come.

The French have often, to British amusement, been obsessed by health; sea cures or *Thallasouperie* are major attractions even today in the glossy brochures of Deauville and Dieppe where palatial salt water centres draw wealthy hypochondriacs to relieve their aches and pains.

William the Conqueror was one of the first, they say, to use the sea as a cure for a drunken soldier, by making him imbibe the salt water. It was also thought to be a remedy for dog bites and the story of Fanor, favourite dog of Henry IV, is worthy of the pet loving British. Fanor was bitten himself by a rabid rival and so sent to Dieppe where he was taken for a dip amidst splendid welcoming celebrations laid on by Sieur de Signogne – 'who loves me loves my dog,' the King had said.

In 1761 three ladies in waiting to Marie Antoinette, Madame de Ludres and Mesdemoiselles de Coetlogon and Rouvroy, were bitten by a rabid dog and also taken to Dieppe where they were pulled, naked, kicking and screaming into the sea.

Where did it all begin? To be honest, it began in Scarborough, Yorkshire and not on the Channel at all. The Spa had for some years been an honourable and fashionable health centre and in 1660 a Dr Wittie claimed that the sea there 'cured gout dried up superfluous humours and killed off all manner of worms'. By 1730 Scarborough had become the first true seaside resort.

When people were clothed, literally, from head to foot, even in summer, the glimpse of a naked body ensured a high sale for Rowlandson's cartoons, even in such an apparently innocuous scene as here at Scarborough, the original seaside resort. (BBC Hulton)

But in 1736 the Rev William Clarke wrote from the village of Brighthelmstone in Sussex from whence a packet to France had just been started, 'we are now sunning ourselves on the beach at Brighthelmstone, such a tract of sea ... such regions of corn ... but the mischief is we have little conversation beside the *clamor nauticus*. . . My morning business is bathing in the sea and then buying fish: the evening is riding out for air, viewing the remains of old saxon camps and counting the ships in the road and the boats that are trawling. The lodgings are as low as they are cheap: we have two parlours, two bed chambers, pantry etc. for five shillings a week and if you will really come down you will not fear a bed of proper dimensions.'

Michelete in Boulogne called Dr Richard Russel the 'Inventor of the Sea', and in truth he was. Not even the worthy Doctor could have imagined that his pompous treatise *Dissertation on the use of sea water in Diseases of the Glands*, would prove to be the launching pad of a hugely profitable international industry.

' … a perfect repose of the body and calmness of the mind is to be observed before the use of the cold bath. The blood must be prevented from flying to the head and the bowels must be sound.' He spoke, ironically, of the detergent effect, unaware no doubt, that if nothing else, the disinfecting of those lice-ridden, unwashed ladies and gentlemen was an achievement.

Sea and sand are now synonymous with sunshine. At Brighthelmstone in the 1780s the sea was the sole beneficial element. The cartoonist's sympathies echo modern feelings about eccentrics who bathe in the sea on cold windy days. (BBC Hulton)

He insisted that visitors drank sea water, in large quantities, probably diluted with beef tea or milk. He bought himself an imposing, redbrick house on the front at Brighthelmstone and local opportunists immediately saw that ailing visitors could be more profitable than fish.

> Admiring ages Russel's fame shall know,
> Till ocean's healing waters cease to flow.
> (contemporary verse)

But alongside all this fashionable ill health was also emerging the irresponsible, earthy sense of fun which was to have its head in the often decadent eighteenth century.

> You prudent grandmammas, ye modern belles
> Content with Bristol, Bath and Tunbridge Wells,
> When health required it, would consent to roam,
> Else more attached to pleasures found at home
> But now alike gay widow, virgin wife
> Ingenious to diversify dull life
> In coaches, caravans, and hoys
> Fly to the coast for daily, nightly joys
> And all impatient of dry land agree
> With one consent to rush into the sea.　　　(Anon)

The picture was a little less than dignified. The cartoonist Rowlandson made these often naked, seaside cavortings into the eighteenth century equivalent of the smutty postcard. Ladies could, if they wished hire a special bathing dress and were not permitted to walk unclothed to the beach. But bathing machine respectability did not become commonplace until about 1750 and then caused queues and scuffles between waiting bathers. Some people even sent their footmen on horseback into the sea to stake a claim.

Wisely, bathing machine owners built waiting rooms, and these eventually became a focal point for news and gossip. With bathing machines too came the notorious 'bathing women' – seaside ogres who ruled the nervous and bludgeoned the unruly with fearsome authority. They were tough. Standing, often for hours on end, waist deep in the sea, their excessive skirts and bonnets incongruous beside the swimmers whom they had stripped of their dignity. John Constable the painter called them 'hideous amphibious animals'. Of them all, Martha Gunn of Brighton whose notoriety has been recorded in a best-selling Toby Jug, was probably most known. Her gravestone records: 'she was particularly distinguished as a bather in this town for nearly 70 years'. Certainly she was a favourite of the Prince of Wales and when eventually she grew too fat, she was made a beach superintendent and was there on duty at six each day.

There is much good evidence now that women can tolerate extreme conditions better than men, and fat women, such as the Prince of Wales' favourite bathing woman, Martha Gunn, were examples of this in the 1740s when they spent all day in the sea assisting the rich and famous to benefit from short dips in the briny. (BBC Hulton)

Gradually, better houses and lodging places were built to accommodate the visitors … though there had been an element of adventure for the aristocracy in playing at being peasants. But nothing was good enough for Viscount Torrington who complained, 'that the infirm and the upstart should resort to these fishing holes may perhaps be accounted for, but that the healthy owners of parks, good houses and good beds should quit them for the confinements of dirt and misery appears to me downright madness'.

But when Royalty too began to dip its toes in the Channel the flood became a torrent. First was George III, who was sent to Weymouth to recover from a bout of madness.

His Majesty entered the sea in 1789 to the accompaniment of *God Save Great George Our King* from a band in the neighbouring bathing machine. All Weymouth was agog and all the streets and the people were decked out in local slogans.

The Princess Mary did not share his enthusiasm. 'The place is more dull and stupid than I have words to express … Sophia and me do not intend to honour the sea with our charms this year.' George III also went to Sidmouth in Devon, Princess Amelia his daughter discovered Worthing and Queen Caroline went to Southend. 'Majesty moving over the face of the earth inspires them with fresh influence.'

But Brighton was the brightest jewel in the seaside crown, and Brighton was to dominate the social sea front from the Prince of Wales' first visit in 1783. From the beginning Brighton responded to the challenge. There was no Pavilion then, no Royal Crescent. He met Mrs Fitzherbert there, and in the romantic poverty so beloved of the aristocracy he set up home in a Sussex farmhouse. Like Marie Antoinette, who dressed up as a dairy maid at Versailles, royalty in Britain developed a rustic yearning for the simple life – in principle. Brighton became a degenerate centre of exhibitionist excess. Brighton alone along the channel coast even began to attract a few aristocratic visitors from France – acclaim indeed. In 1764 Gwilly Williams spoke of 'extraordinary exotics, barbers, milliners, barons, who arrive on almost every tide'. They went horse racing and they loved the sophisticated life by the sea, so Brighton became the first, and last, town to be accepted as smart by the European noblesse.

In 1788 two momentous events occurred in Europe. The French Revolution began and the conversion of the Prince Regent's simple farmhouse into the marine pavilion, which was embellished and transformed into Brighton Pavilion and has spellbound visitors ever since with its opulent vulgarity.

The Princess Lieven wrote later 'I do not believe that since the days of Heliogabalus there has been such magnificence and luxury. There is something effeminate in it which is disgusting'. Cobbett was vicious about 'the Kremlin' as he called it.

Take a square box the sides of which are three feet and a half and the height a foot and a half. Take a large Norfolk turnip, cut off the green of the leaves, leave the stalk nine inches long, tie these round with a string three inches from the top, and put the turnip on the middle of the top of the box. Then take four turnips of half the size, treat them in the same way, and put them on the corners of the box, then take a considerable number of bulbs, of the Crown-Imperial, the narcissus, the hyacinth, the tulip, the crocus and others; let the leaves of each have sprouted to about an inch, or more or less according to size of the bulb; put all these pretty promiscuously but pretty thickly on top of the box. Then stand off and look at your architecture.

Like it or not the Pavilion was, and is, the most extraordinary building along either Channel coast, although it was later almost overshadowed by the nightmarish aberration of a nineteenth century eccentric Alexandre Le Grand at Fécamp. This is now known as the Palace-factory home of Bénédictine, the world-famed liqueur, and is even described by the official Bénédictine publicity brochure as 'something that might have been conceived in the delirious brain of the mad King Leopold of Bavaria ... an army of pinnacles, arcades, arches ... this forest of notched arrows reminiscent of the mysterious park of the Sleeping Beauty.'

The anonymous work of hundreds of craftsmen over hundreds of years created the style of the great ecclesiastical buildings of Europe. The attempt to recreate that style at Fécamp in the Abbey Factory where Bénédictine is distilled, has produced another rich man's folly. (Alain Bouhier)

The Palace was built to house the factory for Le Grand's own dream of reviving the lost medieval drink loved by Francis I and originally made by the Bénédictine monks. Today the near-celestial scent of some twenty-seven herbs used in the making of the liqueur wafts through the huge halls and up the stairways in uneasy contrast with the vulgarity of its surroundings.

The French Revolution stirred the adrenalin in many an English man. Europe could never again be the same and ordinary folk everywhere began to flex their democratic muscles. In Britain they were shocked by the bloodshed. Its effect on the Channel was dramatic, especially for those at the eastern end where they received the full flow of emigrées escaping the horror of the guillotine. They poured into every village along the coast of Kent and Sussex dressed as sailors, maybe hiding in barrels, crouched inside coils of rope.

Who better known than the notorious Sir Percy Blakeney. 'They seek him here, they seek him there, those Frenchies seek him everywhere. Is he in Heaven, is he in Hell, that demmed elusive Pimpernel.'

The Scarlet Pimpernel, first in the line of great British spies was the creation of the Baroness Orczy in the twentieth century. The sentiments are entirely those of the smug British twenties but they are not so far removed either from the historic attitude of the British to the French. The Pimpernel himself belongs to the violent period of the Sans Culottes and the Casquettes Rouges, when the streets of Paris ran red and the news from over the water made 'every honest Englishman's blood boil.'

After the execution of Louis XVI and Marie Antionette in 1793, an ambitious, missionary zeal for the conversion of Europe to these new ideas gripped France. She declared war on Britain. The Grand Tour ground to a halt, schools stopped exporting British students, there was no further horsemanship at Angers. Pontement Abbey where the daughters of the Hobart, Annesley and de Ros families were being finished was turned into a barracks and it became illegal for British families to make the cross-channel journey without a special permit. This did not stop them trying and many were fined for bribing foreign captains to take them on board. Fishermen and smugglers kept contact alive but they did not often dare risk human contraband.

It was through smugglers that Napoleon kept himself informed during his 'Continental System' blockade of English ports.

The Grand Tour, not suspended until 1801, was resumed after the Revolution and the British visited again the country their rulers and politicians had decreed for so long was the enemy. They made the journey, usually from London to Paris, by diligence, arriving at Dieppe after noon on Sundays, Tuesdays, Wednesdays and Thursdays.

For many years, according to a contemporary observer, 'the road to Paris was very lively not only with diligence carriages and post chaises but also with the passage of royal personages, ministers, diplomats, messengers of the King, lords and ladies, travellers of all sorts and condition, in a ceaseless coming and going between the two great centres of civilisation'. Besides the Royal passengers of France and the Messagers General, an English diligence also served between Paris and London. One of the earliest of the packets took sixty ladies to Calais. Such dedication they must have had! One traveller, Thomas Manning, wrote to his grandfather:

The tide having ebbed we were obliged to land without entering the inner harbour to Boulogne. It was night before the sluggish boat that the mariners sent could officially land us all and a strange landing it seemed to me. The boat rowed towards the nearest shore till it ran aground, which happened in the midst of the breakers. In an instant the boathead was surrounded by a throng of women up to their middles and over, who were there to carry us ashore. Not being aware of this manoeuvre we did not throw ourselves into the arms of these sea nymphs so instantly as we might, whereby those who sat at the stern of the boat were deluged with spray. For myself I was in front and very soon understood the clamour of the mermaids. I flung myself on the backs of two of them without reserve and was safely and dryly born on shore, but one poor gentleman slipped through their fingers and fell head over heels in the sea.

Napoleon's British Visitors and Captives 1801–1815
J. Goldworth Alger

Persons from London and other parts are flocking down to Torbay, though they know that Bonaparte is not expected to land, and that they cannot go on board the Bellerophon; but they can row in boats round the vessel, and occasionally catch a

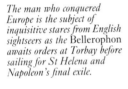

The man who conquered Europe is the subject of inquisitive stares from English sightseers as the Bellerophon *awaits orders at Torbay before sailing for St Helena and Napoleon's final exile.*

glimpse of him. He is the greater part of the day in the stern-gallery, either walking backwards and forwards, with his hands behind him, or surveying the shipping and shore through a glass. In general he keeps alone, Bertrand and Lallemand remaining at some distance behind. Captain Maitland is more frequently with him than any of his suite, and he pays him great attention. He is in good health. He passes but a short time at his meals, and drinks but little wine. Coffee is frequently served up to him on the deck. When he first came near the land about Torbay he is reported to have exclaimed '*Enfin, voila ce beau pays!*' (At last, here is this fine country), adding that he had never seen it except from Calais and Boulogne. All seemed to treat Bonaparte as an Emperor who appeared as one in thought, walking at a very steady pace, quite upright, now and then stooping a little to look through portholes at the vessels alongside. His person altogether gives one the idea of a strong man. At six o'clock the bell rang, dinner was announced and he went below followed by his attendants. Our jolly tars, with their usual good humour, put out a board chalked 'He's gone to dine'. He remained, however, not much more than half-an-hour when another board announced his reappearance on deck where he resumed his walk in the same spot, occasionally with a child and conversing with the ladies.

Contemporary Torbay newspaper report.

This was the nearest that Napoleon ever came to the shores of Albion. Just as Hitler ear-marked Dover Castle, in a flight of fancy, for his residence, so Napoleon had dreams of becoming a British citizen. Whilst the *Grande Armée* was assembled at Boulogne he even had the temerity to strike a medal in France which said *Frappé a Londres* (made in London). The Emperor, whose legend had scared so many English children at bedtime, sailed out of history from Torbay to the South Atlantic island of St Helena.

Only a very short interlude from Napoleon's adventures belongs to the Channel, but what a story of brinkmanship it was.

Napoleon, who pronounced his name Italian style, Napolĕonĕ Bonapartĕ, the tempestuous, furniture-flinging Corsican child assumed, when adult, that Britain, like everything else he wanted, was there for the taking. But, brilliant general and often charismatic host that he was, and though he became Emperor of most of Europe, he forgot two important obstacles: the British and their Channel. He underestimated the first and knew nothing about the second.

On the one side there was the prematurely aged William Pitt who emerged briefly from a lonely, monastic retirement in Walmer Castle near Deal, the bleak official residence of the Lord Warden of the Cinque Ports, to train a local 'home guard'. Further round the coast on the Downs above Brighton, society turned out to watch the Prince of Wales taking the salute at a 'Royal Tournament' and mock battle with about seven thousand troops. Everywhere seaside bands of volunteers clubbed together and drilled themselves into a rustic army that would have been about as effective as Napoleon's untrained navy.

Across the Channel, eyeing the coasts of Britain from the plains above Boulogne and feverishly amassing his *Grande Armée* was the sabre-rattling Napoleon himself. With a telescope each could have watched the antics of the other – who could have foretold the winner?

Though the naval battles which gave Great Britain the right to claim 'Britannia Rules the waves' were fought far away, the ships and the men who fought them were launched through Channel waters.

Through most of the eighteenth century there was very little improvement in the design of war ships. Nelson's *Victory* was more like one of 1558 than she was like a craft of a hundred years later. In 1719 the Navy Board, being satisfied with existing vessels, laid down a fixed scale for the dimension and tonnage for ships of each class which left no room for design-initiative or the possibility of adapting the displacement to the increasing weight of armaments. So, as French ships grew better, the English fleet stood still, though the quality of the seamen themselves did improve considerably. After the Revolution when the French guillotined most of their finest officers the British fleet was again supreme.

The employment of generals in both the navies of France and England; Blake, Monk, Chateau Renard and in Holland Opdam, meant that a more military style of maritime warfare was adopted. That is, fighting in line (linear), rather than the each-to-his-own method as before. In 1748 officers in England were given full uniform for the first time. It was an unbelievably fancy affair of ornately embroidered waistcoat, frock coat with long lace cuffs and a three-cornered hat. How they maintained a smart appearance in the face of a strong sou'westerly is a mystery. The basic colour of blue, which was to become standard for navies worldwide, was chosen by George II in a fit of admiration for the Duchess of Bedford whom he watched riding in a trim habit in the park. Admirals were also allowed thirty servants, captains four per hundred crew including barbers, musicians and boys to train as officers. The ordinary sailor had to wait another hundred years before he was uniformed.

When a man joined the navy, probably at Portsmouth or Plymouth, he was given a ticket but was not paid on the voyage, only on return. Food was appalling. Hawke once wrote to his Plymouth quartermaster:

> The beer brewed at your port is so excessively bad that it employs the whole time of the squadron in surveying it and throwing it overboard ... a quantity of bread from the *Ramilles* will be returned to you by the *Elizabeth*, though not altogether unfit for use, yet so full of weevils and maggots it would have infected all the bread come on board this day.

A somewhat cynical poem lamenting the neglect of the men after Hawke's defeat of the French says:

> Ere Hawke did bang
> Monsieur Conflans
> You sent us beef and beer
> Now Monsieur's beat
> We've naught to eat
> Since you have naught to fear.

Since the time of Cromwell the ordinary sailor was by law allowed a share in the spoils of captured vessels. It was this motive that spurred on many men to participate in such a desperate and dangerous life. Needless to say the rewards for the crew were little more than beer money whereas Captains and Admirals were well able to build fine houses for their families. The inspiration for their bravery was more often the thought of the reckoning at the end than their country's glory; the principles may have been less than patriotic but the results they achieved were without question.

In 1745 Commodore Anson sailed into Spithead after years at sea round the other side of the world, with the 60-gun *Centurion* – the sole survivor of a squadron sent out to attack the Spanish in the Pacific. His story is a graphic portrayal of what it really meant to be a sailor in the eighteenth century and behind the single line entry in the history books is an ordinary everyday story of navy folk in all its human drama.

That expedition was ordered to leave Plymouth in November 1739, but as ever there was a shortage of manpower. So someone (it could surely not have been Anson) 'pressed' five hundred Chelsea pensioners into service – old men no longer fit for war. But they were not so frail they could not walk – and many of them did – out of Plymouth as fast as they could. So, to make up the numbers, two hundred and ten marines (so new they had not learned to fire a gun) were taken aboard, and with this motley crew and some two hundred seamen short, Anson embarked. They left the cliffs of Devon for four years of every disaster and torment fate could hurl at them. But when eventually the little ship struggled back she was carrying 1,313,843 pieces of eight, 35,682 ounces of silver – enough to make Anson wealthy for life and give every survivor of the voyage a healthy bonus. Though hundreds of men had died the trip was a tonic to the navy, and when Anson himself later became First Sea Lord, his personal experience encouraged him to reform the navy's administration.

The Hogarthian misery of the press, which terrorised the narrow streets of the south coast towns was outclassed in the early part of the century by the French galleys which were floating concentration camps. The people of Dunquerque viewed their return up Channel from the Mediterranean each winter with mixed feelings for they spewed into the town an evil, sinister atmosphere. They were stinking, insanitary coffins, one hundred and forty feet long and open to the sky.

Life on board when the galley was at sea was a sort of Hell's picnic, for there was really no accommodation for anyone. For the convicts there was, of course, no question of sleep; the petty officers did the best they could on the forecastle head, the soldiers huddled into the hold or under the deck awning if the weather was fine and even the officers had no sleeping place except on their camp chairs under the poop awning. And so crank were the ships that to avoid the risk of capsizing, the awnings could only be spread in the finest weather. Cooking facilities were primitive and as no one ever washed the ship crawled with vermin from stem to stern. From below came the constant crack of whips on bare flesh, screams of pain and savage growls . . . those who died, or even fainted at their post were cut adrift from the bench and flung overboard. They were fed on wine soaked biscuits as they rowed.

The Splendid Century
W. H. Lewis

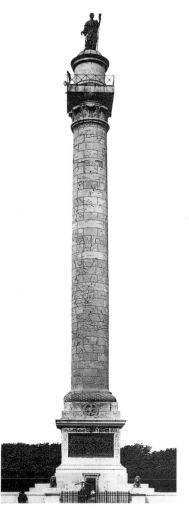

Rather than have him gaze longingly across the Channel to an England he could not invade, those who erected the statue of Napoleon above Boulogne have him looking back across France to a Europe his armies did conquer.
(Popperfoto)

These *galériens* were men condemned to over twenty years for religious or criminal offences: many were Hugenots.

When the galleys rowed into Dunquerque each year they were allowed ashore to ply their trade, so the streets swarmed with quack medicine sellers, wigmakers, desperate thieves and murderers, clock menders, tailors and, if a man had nothing to sell, he was forced to knit stockings, or be flogged. In the winter months at least, with the officers and captains gone from the galleys they could organise makeshift sleeping accommodation.

Whilst at anchor the galleys were stripped and refitted and the ammunition and guns for next season stowed aboard. About April new convicts arrived, chained together in fives, on foot from Paris . . . those, that is, who had survived the four hundred kilometre walk through bitter cold, the standing for hours on end naked in the open, the beatings and the hunger. They would never again eat, sleep or work apart and would spend their time under the dreaded *nerf de boeuf* – a bull's penis used as a whip. The *galériens* appalling lot was not eased until the beginning of the nineteenth century with the coming of steam.

Napoleon's *Grande Armée* remained encamped above Boulogne for two years. Its monument stands bleakly in the middle of a featureless *parc* approached on all sides by long straight avenues. Napoleon atop has his back, appropriately, to the Channel he always refused to acknowledge.

His first plan to distract the English navy and entice it away from the Channel failed. He had organised 'decoy' raids on Ireland, the Caribbean and West Indies hoping to draw the fleet from the Straits but the British Admirals saw through the scheme and did not give the order. Then the wintry seas also began to batter his hopes. His ships were neither strong enough nor large enough and he had totally underestimated the temperament of the Channel currents and tides and the amount of time it would have taken to get all his men and transports across. In the meantime the British had themselves been effectively blockading French ports everywhere. There was no way Napoleon could ever get his soldiers to sea, and eventually he was diverted by inland problems and thoughts of his own coronation.

During the winter of 1803 there was a very sniffy exchange of correspondence between Napoleon and George III, whom he familiarly addressed as *mon frère*, at which the British Government stylishly demolished his arrogance by addressing their reply formally 'To the Head of the French Government'. In 1804 he proclaimed himself Emperor.

Not until August 1805, after a series of complex encounters in various parts of the world, was Napoleon back at Boulogne ready for invasion. But the army was not. There were far too many ships in the harbour to be embarked on one tide and Napoleon's dream of controlling the Channel for six hours, which he said would give him control of the world, was clearly not possible.

After the Peace of Amiens in 1802, Nelson had been sent to hold the French fleet in the Mediterranean and Collingwood to the wild and dangerous Bay of Biscay where, in a masterly feat of seamanship, he plugged the French exit from Brest and deprived Napoleon of his much-needed escort for the *Grande Armée* over the Straits. Month after month they stayed there in conditions that exercised superbly their skills of navigation, ship-handling and resistance. Here was a problem for the French, for they had atrophied in port, resting and preserving their strength, whilst the British were constantly on their toes.

Meanwhile the English fleet lurked off Ushant in wait for Villeneuve with whom Napoleon expected to join forces. Villeneuve, however, lost his nerve and went in the opposite direction, so Napoleon, with no support by sea and tremendous problems welling up behind him in central Europe, changed course and marched his army off to Germany instead. On 19th October 1805 Villeneuve reappeared and two days later the French Navy was totally defeated at Trafalgar.

The threat was over, the Martello Towers that were being thrown up all around the coast were completed but never used. When Cobbett visited Hythe at the end of the war he treated them to his customary scornful attack.

> 'These ridiculous things which I dare say cost five, perhaps ten thousand pounds each.' He was equally critical of the Royal Military canal which was dug, and still runs, across Romney Marsh between Hythe and Rye. 'Those armies who had so often crossed the Rhine and the Danube were to be kept back by a canal dug by Pitt, thirty foot wide at the most?'

When it was all over and Napoleon had eventually crossed the Channel he wrote, while on board the *Bellerophon*, to Lord Keith:

I solemnly protest here before Heaven and before Men against
the violence which is being done to me against the violation of my
sacred rights in taking away my liberty by force. I came freely
aboard the *Bellerophon*. I am in no way a prisoner. I am the guest
of England. I came here at the suggestion of the Captain himself
who had orders from the Government to receive me and take me
to England with my followers if that would be agreeable to me. I
came in good faith to put myself under the protection of the laws
of England. Also, sitting on board the *Bellerophon* I am at home
with the British people. If the Government, in giving orders to

the Captain of the *Bellerophon*, to receive me and my suite hadonly wanted to draw me into a trap, then he has forfeited his honour and disgraced his flag.

If this action takes place it will be in vain for the English to speak to Europe of their laws, their loyalty and their liberty. Faith in Britain will be lost in the hospitality of the *Bellerophon*. I appeal to history. She will say that an enemy that has for twenty years fought the English people came freely in his misfortune to seek protection under her laws – what more shining proof could he give of his esteem and confidence? But how did they reply in

When the Warden of Dover Castle said in 1880 that the French would invade England through the Channel Tunnel he must have known of this drawing published in France in 1803 after Napoleon had suggested a candlelit tunnel under the Channel. The Battle of Britain seems to have been thought of at least 137 years before it entered history. (Topham)

Two little men whose gigantic personalities and enormous strategic abilities on land and sea respectively dominated the struggle between their two countries. Napoleon is shown in a detail from Orchardson's painting On Board the Bellerophon; *Nelson after Hoppner.* (BBC Hulton)

England to such magnanimity? They pretended to extend the hand of hospitality to this enemy and when he gave himself up in good faith they sacrificed him.

Napoleon and Nelson never met. What a confrontation of giants that would have been. The white-haired thin-faced Nelson and plump dark-haired Napoleon, both under five foot.

Some of the tender moments of the great British Naval warrior's life were spent dining with his beloved Emma, Lady Hamilton, and sometimes her unsuspecting husband, at the Three Kings in Deal, now renamed The Royal.

Nelson's glory, the achievements which brought him international fame among a spectacular galaxy of men such as Rodney, Howe, Keppell, Cornwallis and Collingwood came late in life between 1793 and his death aboard the *Victory* in 1805. It is not really surprising that though Portsmouth today guards his flagship the *Victory* with jealous pride there is fiercely contested rivalry for the honour of her presence between the town which waved him farewell so many times and Chatham, the dockyard which built her.

The tiny Admiral saw the Channel as a small though vital part in a far wider naval strategy for Britain. He knew that to protect British insularity he must protect the Western Approaches and divert or distract any fleet rounding Ushant and so eventually threatening the Straits.

During this time the British also developed the naval flintlock, a method of firing a gun which replaced slow matches and, in speeding up the rate of fire, made it that much more effective. The carronade too was a deadly short-barrelled gun made at the Carron Ironworks in Scotland and not used by the French. Most important, under Nelson the Navy revised and improved its signalling standards. Before 1782 there had only been a very rudimentary method of signalling between ships, but in 1800 a system invented by Admiral Sir Hope Popham was adopted, using flags to denote numbers and letters. In the days before Trafalgar, Nelson's commanders used hundreds of flags to keep the Fleet in touch with developments.

All these developments came together at a time when the British fleet was commanded by a man that everyone loved and respected. His humanity, generosity and understanding made him a formidable figurehead. It was a recipe for success that the French with their inept, naval leadership and rotting ships could not hope to match, and indeed it resulted in the end of war at sea for ninety-nine years because there was no one left to match the British. They, not Napoleon, had held the Channel and so the mastery of the seas.

Smuggling:
a Community Enterprise

The professions of fisherman, merchant, customs officer and smuggler were interdependent and all too often indistinguishable. Everyone was involved. In each coastal community resentful priests, doctors, publicans supported the struggle against the authorities and duties they imposed on the trade from which villagers had, traditionally earned their living. In the Channel, British and French smugglers, fair traders or 'owlers', had a perfect practice ground for four hundred years until, in the eighteenth century, they reached the peak of their skill and their power. From then on, in fact until Victoria established a somewhat more moral tone, the secret coves of Cornwall echoed of a night with the crunch of boots; on Romney Marsh lowered voices could be heard against the sound of muffled oars and inland gangs of vicious thugs were prepared to mug or kill even women and children who stood in their way. Sometimes there were two hundred men on the beach at a time landing tea, brandy or tobacco.

Admiral Vernon wrote to the Admiralty in 1745:

> I cannot but think it is a seasonable time to suggest to Your Lordships that there are in the town of Deal no less than 200 able young men and sea-faring people who are known to have no visible way of getting a living but by the infamous trade of smuggling, many keeping a horse and arms to be ready at all calls.
>
> At Dover it is conjectured that there may be found 400 at a time ready to smuggle, Ramsgate and Folkestone 300 each and it is conjectured that from the town of Folkestone itself a thousand pounds a week is run over to Boulogne ...
>
> This smuggling has converted those employed in it first from honest industrious fishermen to lazy, drunken profligate smugglers and now dangerous spies on all our proceedings for the enemies daily information.

The enemy was, as ever, the French who, although they were not averse to a spot of local smuggling too, never got themselves organised on the same scale as the British. There was not much that Britain had to offer them apart from gold, or maybe wool. During the Revolution part of the port of Dunquerque was set aside for the smugglers to bring in about £10,000 worth of gold coins a week to boost the threatened French economy.

Special boats – the Guinea boats – manned by about thirty-six oarsmen, were built in Calais and with a speed of nine knots were very difficult to catch. There was an illegal camaraderie which flourished ironically when the two countries were officially at war and trade was obstructed across the Channel.

'Owlers' ran wool across to Europe returning with wine or tea; and during hostilities deserters from both sides were smuggled out, despite the armed efforts of the customs men.

Owling was the name given to the smuggling of wool – largely from Kent – and probably because of the hour at which it was conducted. In 1698 the Wool Act, which decreed that wool owners within ten miles of the Kent or Sussex coast had to account for their fleeces, was successful to some extent, except that export smuggling declined so import smuggling increased.

With the passing of time the smuggling story is seen through the romantic, rosy telescope of novelists and artists.

> Twas midday before the first body was cast up, when the sky was breaking a little, and a thin and watery sun trying to get through and afterwards three other bodies followed. . . .
>
> Then I felt something that told me he was coming and saw a body rolled over in the surf . . . between us we drew him up out of the running foam and then I wrung the water from his hair, and wiped his face and, kneeling down there, kissed him.
>
> . . . Sea and stones had been merciful with him and he showed neither bruise nor wound but his face wore a look of great peace. . . .
>
> They stood for a while looking in silence at the old lander who had run his large cargo on Moonfleet beach and then they laid his arms down by his side and slung him in a sail and carried him away. I walked beside and as we came down across the sea-meadows the sun broke out and we met little groups of school-children making their way down to the beach to see what was doing with the wreck. They stood aside to let us go, the boys pulling their caps and the girls dropping a curtsey when they knew it was a poor drowned body passing; and as I saw the children I thought I saw myself among them . . .
>
> Return of Elzevir Block to Moonfleet Village
> Landlord of the Why Not whose son David was killed
> by the Revenue men.

SACRED TO THE MEMORY
OF
DAVID BLOCK
Aged 15, who was killed by a shot fired from the *Elector*
Schooner, 21st June 1757

Of life bereft (by fell design),
I mingle with my fellow clay.
On God's protection I recline
To save me in the Judgement Day.

There too must you, cruel man, appear,
Repent ere it be all too late;
Or else a dreadful sentence fear,
For God will sure revenge my fate.

Inscription on David Block's tomb in Moonfleet.

The customs men whose task it had always been to make a stand against smuggling were established in Saxon times by King Ethelred. He decreed a regular tax on wine and it became the 'custom' for merchants to hand over a portion of their wages in return for the right to trade. The men who levied these dues were called Customs men. After the Conquest there was, inevitably, a big rise in the consumption of wine by the new Norman rulers and a levy in kind 'the prisage' was established to supply the King and Court. King John it was who eventually organised a national customs service in Britain which, in its basic form, has survived to the present.

Probably the best known of all customs officials was Geoffrey Chaucer in 1374, whose father and grandfather before had been Controllers in Southampton.

But it was virtually impossible to control what came to be called 'fair trade' when men of such standing as Sir John Gilbert, Richard Grenville and Hakluyt were all using the West Country towns as free ports, and there was little resistance. Not until the reign of Charles II was it considered necessary for the Customs men even to have boats in order to keep an eye on ships at sea. At the same time the service was expanded with a policing force to include land waiters, tide waiters and coast waiters as well as the notorious Riding Officers whose job it was to patrol the cliff tops on horseback and root out smugglers haunts, but as they were mostly in the pay of the smugglers they met with little success. In any case opposition only made the contra-bandists more determined.

The eighteenth century version of our modern 'sus' laws was introduced in 1745 and said that any person found loitering within five miles of a navigable river might be considered a suspicious person and probably deported, whipped or hung. 'Any boat built to row with more than four oars found upon land or water within the counties of ... Kent or Sussex shall be forfeited and every person using or rowing in such a boat shall be fined £40.' If an offender was not caught within six months the whole county could be fined. These penalties applied only to British subjects so women fled to France when pregnant to give their babies French nationality.

The smugglers then used their centuries-old sailing skill to design especially fast boats to outwit the cumbersome revenue cutters.

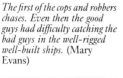

The first of the cops and robbers chases. Even then the good guys had difficulty catching the bad guys in the well-rigged well-built ships. (Mary Evans)

Tricks were used to disguise the boats in all manner of skilful ways. Some like the *Daniel* and *William* carried two sets of sails in different colours, others like the Dutch *Sarah Jacobe* were able to switch gear to become a cutter, trawler or sloop at will. Their cargo too was camouflaged, barrels were painted white and hidden in caves in the chalk cliff near Birling Gap, hollow masts contained spirits; brandy kegs were slung under keels; tobacco was woven into hawsers and one cargo was hidden beneath a layer of stinking sprats that kept the customs men at bay.

Anyone who was anyone was part of this scene. Landed gentry, the clergy, everyone – it was almost impossible to find a jury that was not involved or a magistrate ready to convict his friends. Even the preventative officers themselves were open to bribery. In 1735 farmers in Kent were forced to raise labourers' wages during harvest to stop them defecting to the smuggling business. A tubman or batman (so named because of the wooden bat they carried to beat up customs men) earned one guinea for a night's work, at a time when the weekly wage might be 10 shillings at most.

Said Sir William Musgrave, Customs Commissioner, 'They never ride out except on their own private business and they fabricate their journals. Some of them are agents and collectors for the smugglers and they are not resolute enough to prove any serious obstacle to large bodies of armed smugglers.'

Violence and organised gang warfare outstripped anything we know today. The men of Hastings, or 'hatchbacks', were feared by all for their idiosyncratic method of chopping their enemies on the back with a hammer. One night in 1768 the notorious Ruxley Gang had boarded a Dutch vessel in mid-Channel in the pretence of trading, and had killed the Captain. Two hundred Inniskillen Dragoons were secretly sent to Hastings to round up the offenders and rescue the mayor who was suspected of spilling the beans. A Man-o'-War and a cutter stood by offshore since removing the prisoners overland would have run the risk of reprisals. Of the thirteen men eventually convicted four were sent to execution dock. Success stories were more common ... and Arthur, 'King' of the infamous and most savage Hawkhurst Gang made a fortune of over £50,000 and built himself a fine house. The Hawkhurst Gang terrorised the coast from Kent to Poole in Dorset and it was said they could muster five hundred men in an hour and that frightened farmers everywhere hired them horses and barns for storage.

Signal lights were important to smugglers, particularly unofficial lights. (Mary Evans)

Events on the night of October 6th 1747 were just the stuff upon which the Hawkhurst Gang built their reputation. Even now it is not too hard to recreate the drama of that night, when a shoemaker named Daniel Chater from Fordingbridge, Sussex, escorted by an elderly Tide Waiter, William Galley, stopped at *Rowlands Castle Inn*, Havant, on their way to Chichester. Daniel Chater had been amongst the cheering villagers who gathered to watch the Hawkhurst Gang pass by with a team of tea-laden horses. They had broken into the Custom

Organised crime has a very long history. In 1745 the Hawkhurst Gang in Dorset were well organised. Having lost their illegal cargo to the Revenue men they broke into the Customs House to steal it back and carried it off on a team of pack horses. All this for a shipload of tea! (Mary Evans)

House at Poole to recapture the cargo of tea which the revenue men had seized from their smuggling cutter *The Three Brothers* in September. But Daniel Chater made a grave mistake: he recognised one of the gang, Jack Diamond, known as Dimer and, although Dimer had passed him some tea, the £200 reward offered for information leading to an arrest proved too much.

So Chater was being taken to Chichester to testify when he, in turn, was spotted by a Mrs Payne who tipped off the local smugglers. That was to be the end of Chater; the innkeeper would not allow such deeds on his premises so the two men were tied to horses and galloped out into the countryside where they were beaten. Galley, an old man, lost consciousness and was buried alive; Chater had his ears and nose cut off and was then tipped into a well and pelted with rocks.

But this outrage did bring about the downfall of the Hawkhurst Gang for one by one they, and the innkeeper, were tracked down, tried and executed.

Even so, public sympathy still was with the smugglers. Popular songs such as *The Poor Smugglers Boy*, *The Smugglers Bridge* and *The Attack on Dover Gaol* turned them into folk heroes.

Last Monday between two and three thousand gallons of spiritous liquors, which the Revenue Officers of this town and neighbourhood had seized within the last three or four years (and which it is thought, had it been sold would have fetched upwards of six hundred pounds) were by them consigned to the Kennel, in a manner that produced a scene highly entertaining to the spectators; for the hour of action was no sooner arrived than there appeared a great concourse of people, composed of men, women and children, from five to fifty years of age, some of whom planted themselves at the entrance of the passage from whence the fountain of Aqua Vitae was played off (and frequently, to increase the fun, high in the air) with uplifted pails and open mouths, to catch what they could of it in a pure state, before it reached the ground; while others less delicate in their pursuits, formed on one knee, a regular line on each side the gutter (which they had previously bayed up with slub) and with pots, pans, porringers and pipkins, fell eagerly to work in ladling up its contents, and happy were they who could obtain the most full buckets of this rare puddle; a little time, however, convinced us that what they saved had not been wholly committed to their wooden vessels ...

Local newspaper 1788

In the mid-eighteenth century three-quarters of the tea and half the Dutch gin drunk in Britain was brought in by the side door. A Government pamphlet *Advice to the Unwary* alleged that at Dunkirk a distillery had been built for the sole purpose of smuggling Geneva gin to Britain and that £40 million of silk and brandy was part-exchanged for wool.

'Genuine Crow Link Gin' – sold openly in the London shops – was brought in at the notorious Crow Link Gap in Sussex, near Birling Gap.

It was the war with Napoleon which finally spurred the Government to take more effective action against the Fair Traders. Maybe they were shamed by some observations of the Emperor Napoleon whilst in exile on Elba.

They did great mischief to your government. During the war all the information I received came from the smugglers. They are people who have courage and ability to do anything for money. They had at first a part of Dunkerque allotted to them to which they were restricted but as they latterly went out of their limits, committed riots and insulted everybody I ordered Gravelines to be prepared for their reception where they had a little camp for their accommodation. At one time there were upwards of five hundred of them in Dunkerque. I had every information I wanted from them. They brought over newspapers and despatches from the spies we had in London. They took over spies from France, landed them and kept them in their houses for some days, dispersed them over the country and brought them back when they wanted. They assisted the French prisoners to escape from England. The relations of French prisoners in your country were accustomed to go to Dunkerque and make a bargain with them to bring over a certain prisoner ... they

offered several times to bring over Louis and the rest of the
Bourbons for a sum of money but they wanted to stipulate that if
they met with an accident or interruption to their design they
might be allowed to murder them. This I would not consent to.

Letter dated 4th August 1815
Quoted in Keith Papers

At all events in 1809 the Preventative Water Guard was formed with
23 cruisers and 42 boats along the Channel and threw a cordon
around the coast. This Water Guard was the direct ancestor of the
Coast Guard, though the name Coast Guard was in fact first used in
France where the *Garde de Côte* was employed first in the eighteenth
century, solely to look out for wrecks. Smugglers were tackled far
more fiercely by the Navy and today the French coastguard system
remains an integral part of the armed forces, with armed patrol boats.

After the Napoleonic Wars the Preventative Water Guard led in turn
to the British Coast Blockade; formed in 1815 and being a military
organisation, these 'warriors' as they were called, made use of the
Martello Towers built all along the south coast to ward off threatened
invasion. Each of these was under the command of a naval lieutenant
helped by a team of mostly elderly sea-dogs acting as shore-based
lookouts. They wore smocks over their uniforms and carried distress
flares for emergency signalling, but it was still a dangerous life
exposed to attack.

In 1822 the Prince Regent finally merged all these overlapping and
expensively run groups into one independent Coast Guard under the
Board of Customs. Then in 1829 instructions were published which,
for the first time, were to encourage a new attitude among the men.

'When a wreck takes place on any part of the coast under the charge
of the coastguard every individual on the spot or within reasonable
distance is to use his utmost exertion to save the lives of persons on
board.'

The Coast Guard became a rigorously disciplined, but still armed,
body; men at Fowey had all leave stopped after three successful
smuggling hauls in a year. They were all also forbidden to have shares
in a public house or trade in any way. Neither could they own a boat.

Conditions and pay generally were appalling. 'It was enough to kill a
horse and only a strong man could stand it.' Those housed on boats
were seldom allowed on shore unless driven there by a storm. Whole
families were sometimes housed in these watch vessels – three cabins
to a family; the wives cooked on a communal stove and went ashore on
Fridays or Saturdays for the weekly shop. On shore, families with six
or seven children were crammed into tiny cottages, often built in
dangerous locations, miles from other habitation or shops.

These are the pretty cottages which ecstatic estate agents now sell for
fancy prices to dewy-eyed weekenders and holiday makers.

But for all that, the Coast Guard was becoming an increasingly
brave, well-behaved force throughout the nineteenth century; the

emphasis was still on training as a naval reserve rather than on life saving. In 1856 the Admiralty even issued instructions:

'It is to be understood that the Admiralty does not accept any responsibility for the inadequacy of the system of life-saving arrangements that may exist.'

As a back stop, teams of enthusiastic volunteers – in typical British style – were trained by the Coast Guard to do the best they could in an emergency; but by this time the earlier function of the force – that of stamping out smugglers – was no longer top priority, for smuggling had ceased to be profitable on a large scale. Gradually the British public began to develop a personal involvement with this caring organisation in a way the French never really did.

During the World Wars, Coast Guards were called on to serve and showed great bravery, especially in mined waters. But between the wars began the great growth of *le Seaside* along the Channel coasts of France and England. Motor cars and railways brought people *en masse* for their holidays. Their inexperienced enthusiasm often led them into trouble, and so presented a new challenge for the lookout man.

The Coastguard Act of 1925 gave Britain its first force devoted

As the Revenue men became better organised they obtained information and they could attack the smugglers, arrest them and sieze the contraband. In the end the 'trade' declined for lack of profit, not lack of opportunity. (Mary Evans)

primarily to coast watching and rescue that was to set a pattern for the next fifty years. The Coastguard himself became a professional, dedicated to his job; usually an ex-mariner with the sea in his blood. A familiar, reassuring figure, linked in the minds of people with a sense of nationality and patriotic pride, he became a symbol of our island personality, even if people inland were not quite sure what he did.

The French Connection. Les Douaniers *of Dunkerque* make the front page.

The Crest of the Wave

Is there, amongst the tumbled gravestones in a corner of Avranches municipal cemetery, a faint aroma of hot scones and home-made strawberry jam? For here, in this long forgotten last retreat, lies the British Colony which, like so many others around this Channel coast, flourished and then faded in the nineteenth century.

They came from Chester, from Canterbury and Royal Tunbridge Wells. They built their churches, imported priests, founded their own clubs, such as the Victoria, and pursued quiet studies in the respectably genteel way of Cranford folk. Their contribution to local literary and scientific study is recorded in the *Revue d'Avranchin*, be it the gift of some fossils for the town museum or the identification of the 'chinchille' a little blue flower seen in the garden of the Misses Oldershaw, or the donation of books 'of religious inspiration' such as *Shall We Know Again*, by their author, a Mr M R A Taylor of Warrington.

Why they came at all is an enigma, but they were well received and their departure was often poetically regretted in the *Revue*.

'With the Autumn depart both the swallows and the English.' (There is no distinction between Ireland, Wales or Scotland.) 'Avranches is again depopulated and its English colony, so worthy and numerous is diminished. There remains only an Admiral, a rector and a General.' That Autumn of 1876 a Mme Dubic, *née* Winship, departed – for another life. Her majestic height, her intelligence and her Scottish wisdom are praised in the *Revue* – she came, they said from the Athens of the North (Edinburgh) to the Athens of the Channel!

There are no pilgrims now to their dishevelled resting place; someone has cut back the elderberry tree that pushed its way between the cracked headstone of the Rev Ryde Meldrose – a civic attempt to keep the British in line with the rest of this carefully tended site. A riot of ormolu and wax lilies, edged between neat gravel paths, rises sharply up the hill above the motorway until, ironically, at the top, blindingly white in the sun, are the sharp reminders of another community who came to stay – the British war dead who gave their lives in 1945. From Henry II to the present, the phantoms of Albion linked hands around Avranches.

Of course Avranches was not alone. At the end of the Napoleonic wars curiosity overcame the British middle classes again and they poured back to France. 'The idle captives of the land of fogs shook their damp wings and prepared to take flight towards the regions of pleasure and brightness.'

The lure of France was then, as now, too strong. Samuel Rogers said 'Ours is a nation of travellers. None wants an excuse. If rich they go to enjoy, if poor to retrench, if sick to recover, if studious to learn, if learned to relax.' It was all so foreign. Many settled, others came simply to stand and stare.

Trevelyan said 'Since Tudor times the influence of the sea had been strong even in upland villages, no one of which is more than 70 miles from a tidal estuary. To the old maritime influence was now added in full measure, the colonial. Our island people were in some respects the least insular of mankind. To Europeans we appeared insular because we were not continental. But our experience and opportunities were greater than those of folk in other lands.'

One of the travellers who first enjoyed the delights of wandering off the beaten track was Thomas Adolphus Trollope, the elder brother of Anthony, who enthusiastically undertook what were then quite adventurous journeys into the wilds of France. 'He might as well have been in darkest Africa.'

> The country which the following pages are intended to portray is not large in extent, nor very important by position ... but it must be remembered that the inhabitants of this remote province [This is Brittany!] though certainly not the only remaining lineal descendants of the ancient Celtic race, are yet by far the most perfectly preserved specimen of it. To the student of man and his history the Breton peasantry present an object of observation as interesting and suggestive as the fossilized remains of extinct races of organized beings can to the physiologist.

Later he describes the mysteries of making crêpes.

> In this farm-house which was larger and better, in every respect, than that of our friend at Tregastel, we had an opportunity of witnessing the whole art and mystery of making crêpe, or *crampoosh*, as it is called in Breton.
>
> A bright wood fire, constantly supplied with bits of dry, light, fuel, was blazing on the capacious hearth, and, supported on two tripods in the midst of it, were two circular iron plates, about eighteen or twenty inches in diameter. Near the hearth stood a large tub, full of a sort of thin gruel, made of sarrasin flour and new milk; and beside it a wooden bowlful of little balls of butter, about three quarters of an inch in diameter. One of these was seized by the fair fingers of the neat-handed Phillis, who was presiding over the manufacture of the *crampoosh*, and hastily rubbed over the surface of one of the plates, upon which a cupful of the gruel was then poured. This quickly acquired a degree of consistency. Another ball of butter was rubbed on the surface of

it, and the half-formed cake was then most dexterously turned, by means of a long, slender, wooden spatula, kept for the purpose; and in about half a minute one *crampoosh* was finished. It was then whipped off the plate with the same instrument which had served to turn it, and added to an immense heap of its predecessors.

This operation was going forward with great activity on both the plates on the fire, and the quantity made seemed quite enormous. But they explained to me that they only made crepe once a week, and that the quantity I saw was, consequently, the whole week's stock.

The cake, when taken from the fire, is in some degree crisp; not sufficiently so to be stiff like a biscuit, but of a consistency halfway between that and a pancake, and as thin as a wafer. I had not much admired the crêpe when eating it stale, in the farm-house at Tregastel; for it loses all its crispness when cold, and becomes leathery and damp. And the peasants fold it up, and keep it in large closely packed heaps, which makes it worse. But I went on devouring with much relish the hot *crampoosh*, fresh from the fire, as the laughing girl, who was making them on her knees before the hearth, handed them up to me, hanging over the stick, with which she turned them, and thought that fresh crepe and new milk made by no means a despicable meal.

In many ways the French were far more insular in outlook than even the British. The truism that France was the centre of the world was acknowledged by most French: they felt no need to travel, except perhaps, for their health, but even then they did not go abroad. Many books were published warning travellers of the danger of such activity and advising, for instance, that journeys should only be taken on medical advice – perhaps correctly, for the French lagged a long way behind the British in road and railway building! Hotel building, when it occurred, was mainly for foreign visitors – the splendid edifices of the Victorian English seaside were not to be seen on the north coast of France. Nor was there any equivalent to Thomas Cook, the Baptist missionary who founded his firm to run Sunday school outings and who, in 1867, took the first organized party across the Channel to the Paris Exhibition for £4.55.

Until the present time, the upper and middle classes, both of Great Britain and the Continent, are the only classes who have come to London. The multitudes have not yet made their appearance; but when the price of admission shall be reduced to a shilling, the excursionists will rush in by the cheap trains from every part of the United Kingdom, as well as from the Continent. Paris will land its thousands per day upon our shores; and the workers of Sheffield and Birmingham, of Manchester and the West Riding, of Glasgow and Belfast, and of countless other industrial towns and districts, will pour their teeming myriads into the great cosmopolitan metropolis, to carry away with them, there cannot be a doubt, a remembrance of pleasure and instruction to last them for the remainder of their lives. For six months or more, the intelligent mechanics of our distant towns have been clubbing their weekly shillings and pence for this rational purpose; and among the many interesting spectacles which London will offer shortly to foreigners, none will be more interesting than the visits of these hordes of working men – the men who made the Exhibition what it is, and who, we fervently hope, will derive the greatest advantage from it.

Illustrated London News

The building of the Pavilion at Brighton at the end of the eighteenth century had been the inspiration for a rash of new development along the length of the English south coast. Hastings, Margate, Weymouth, Bournemouth and Torquay began to blossom elegantly in those years after the Revolution. Architecture, which before had taken no account of the sea, began to turn about and face this newly discovered asset.

When the middle classes began to follow the working classes down to the coast they needed suitable accommodation, hence the building of such hotels as the Lord Warden at Dover in 1840. (Mary Evans)

Palatial hotels such as the *Lord Warden* at Dover were the pride of their time; there were 150 guests at the opening banquet. This 'most sumptuous place of entertainment in the Empire', with its chandeliers, 150 bedrooms, salt and fresh water baths and dining rooms is now the Head Offices for British Rail. How are the mighty fallen!

It was years before the French were to adopt the same idea and when the artists, Benjamin Haydon and his friend David Wilkie, joined the first stampede to France in 1815 they reported that Dieppe 'turns its back upon the sea as if in disgust at the sight of an element on which the country had always been beaten'. It was an old-fashioned place way behind most other resorts. Small wonder, maybe, that the French there had an underlying apprehension about the English who insisted on invading their country. Dieppe itself had been almost totally demolished by British bombardment in 1694 and only piecemeal repaired. At the beginning of the nineteenth century the harbour was falling down and though the houses had been rebuilt with hewn stone from the crumbling town walls and ruined churches, the architect had forgotten to supply them with staircases and these were added as a ragbag afterthought, often externally! It was not a town where gentle-folk would settle, indeed British links with Dieppe had always been with an eye to profit, not culture. Even so it was excitingly foreign, and there was a sense of mutual curiosity between the Dieppois who habitually gathered to stare as the packet came in from Britain and the tourists who were astonished by the contrast with their new, fashionable, south coast resorts. For a start the women wore 'fancy dress' – in Britain even the working folk had never sported a national costume – and since most of the men of Dieppe were away fishing in Newfoundland, it appeared to be a town for women only. They were a colourful bunch, their short, calf-length skirts in bright colours clashing with their baggy blouses, topped by the curious mediaeval white coiffe at the neck. They hauled in the boats, humped the passengers ashore, landed the fish, wheeled it in barrows to the market and yelled their wares on every corner, and clattered in their clogs. The reserved Protestant British were taken aback too by the overt signs of gloomy Catholicism everywhere – the crosses, the wayside shrines, the cavernous churches and the glimmering candles.

It was the Duchesse de Berri, widow of the assassinated Louis XVIII who first brought to Dieppe a little of the panache which was attracting the smart set to Trouville. Hardy English visitors had already caught the eye of the commercially-minded administrators of the town. They could see which way the ozone was blowing. For years the sea front had been used as a municipal rubbish dump. In 1822 they transformed this into a promenade with a little Casino: they removed the gun batteries, which were tactlessly pointing across the Channel, and introduced a travelling library, a card and billiard room, dress hire and dancing. Because the beach sloped so steeply, bathing machines were not possible but the *guide baigneurs* were there in striped matelot jerseys to help swimmers into the water. However, it was all rather primitive, until Marie Caroline, Duchesse de Berri bought a house on the front.

She was what the French called *jolie laide* – a euphemism for plain – but she was an enthusiast and she entered into the spirit of the new age with gusto, swimming, boating and partying. So much so that the

Casino was renamed *Bains Caroline*. By 1825 there were enough British settled in the town, mostly between the Chateau and the road to Paris, for that area to be known as the *Quartier Anglais*, and for them to have a church of their own and a Consul. With the British came a new prosperity – all gaily set against a backdrop of music by Rossini, who stayed there for several summers, and the romantic paintings of Turner, *The Changement du Domicile* caused a stir for being unrealistic at the Royal Academy Summer Exhibition in 1825.

The Chapman family, originally from Brighton, were typical of those who wove their lives into that of the Normandy coast and to some extent the Breton, during the nineteenth century. There were Chapmans trading wine, cattle fodder, flour and timber. They led comfortable lives with servants who were astonishingly hard-working, probably because the Chapmans paid more than the French nobility, who still abused their peasants.

When eventually the railways came to Dieppe in the 1840s – long after they were well-established in Britain – it was an English engineer, Joseph Locke, who went over to mastermind the project and an English company, Thomas Brassey and William McKenzie, who secured the contract for the Paris connection. The company moved to Normandy and a Cornishman, William Buddicom, set up a foundry to make the carriages and wagons which the French it seems were not geared to tackle. So yet another British army, this time of tradesmen and navvies, spilled into Normandy and generally disgraced themselves on calvados. Many of them married French girls and settled, and the English stamp was left in a way the French themselves have probably forgotten: in a country where cars drive on the right, trains run on the left.

After the trains came Queen Victoria herself, on the first ever Royal Tour. The Queen adored France, and spent several summers on the Mediterranean.

The Queen went to stay as a guest of King Louis Philippe at the magnificent newly restored Chateau d'Eu which had been relinked by canal to the sea under the guidance of an English engineer, Packham. It was a splendid visit and in 1844 Louis Philippe returned the compliment by making a state visit to Britain. So began a high level *rapprochement* between the two countries. The *Illustrated London Evening News* recorded the event enthusiastically:

> On Monday evening [7th October 1844] his Majesty King Louis Philippe reached the picturesque town of Tréport. All the houses were illuminated, while the wives and daughters of the fishermen lined the way from the quay to the border strand, where lay the royal gig, each holding a flaming torch; the effect was most striking from its cheerful and primitive simplicity. During the King's embarkation, the marine band played away merrily; and the sound over the waters, coming with the effect of the light upon the waves, the rockets in the air, the cheering of

the sailors, and the shouts of 'Vive le Roi' from the shore, formed a most beautiful and affecting scene ...

On Tuesday morning, the guns of the *Queen*, a 110-gun ship, at Spithead, began to boom in the distance, announcing the coming in sight of the squadron of the eagerly expected Sovereign, which event occurred at a quarter to eight. The French squadron came on slowly and majestically, each ship of war saluting as it advanced, and each battery in turn taking up the salute. From the moment she anchored at Portsmouth, the *Gomer*, which bore his Majesty, was an object of riveted and eager attention, nor was this steam-frigate unworthy of such curiosity. She presented an aspect at the same time imposing and interesting. Her form is admirable; the wide expanse of her spotless deck, her masts, yards and rigging show she has been the pet handiwork of the French shipwrights, and that she is the favourite of her captain and crew, who manoeuvred her in silence, and with a most seamen-like celerity and ease. Below she has all the character of a floating palace – the drawing rooms are as convenient as they are magnificent; that in which the King received his visitors has its sides lined with crimson velvet, whilst in every direction you behold tables of the rarest woods and luxurious *causeuses* and sofas lined with yellow satin.

There were, of course, intellectuals and writers who came too and wrote about Britain, and others like Hippolyte Taine who wrote without coming at all. Their interest and admiration of the British way of life was carried back across the Channel to the Paris *élite* where English fashions were worn, and the English Dandy became the ideal. Horse racing and the Jockey Club, Kate Greenaway and Anglo-American Bars were all cross-Channel imports of the time. Franglais began, the linguistic hybrid which can be traced from 1820 (Dandy), 1826 (corned beef!), 1837 (pyjama) through to 1885 (five o'clock tea) and 1902 (lavatory). Even so the average Frenchman still felt, like Montesquieu 'the French cannot make friends in England'. They regarded the English as 'the provincials of Europe, self-sufficient, suspicious of continental ideas, unaffected by what they saw abroad and incapable of marrying with any other race.' Gentility was merely an effort to overcome historical boorishness. Emile Boutmy who studied the comparisons at the Paris School of Political Sciences towards the end of the century came to the conclusion, although he was an Anglophile, that France was better off without English protestantism and materialism. 'In England power and intelligence are very developed but the heart is arid.'

An anonymous granite cross, set bleakly on a promontory overlooking the sea on the solitary rock of Grand Bé, off St Malo, bears the inscription, *un ecrivain francais*. The *ecrivain* was the great romantic Anglophile writer François René de Chateaubriand who was, perhaps, one of the first whose spirit was fired by the Channel he loved

Great romantics such as Chateaubriand spend their lives making dramatic statements. His last wish was to be buried here, by the sea, at St Malo – dramatic to the end. (Popperfoto)

with such passion. He was born on a wild night in 1768, in a room overlooking the site of what was to be his grave some eighty years later. The life between was one of epic grandeur, spanning two continents and two centuries; an adventurer, a politician, a poet, a diplomat, a philosopher, a truly 'noble savage', always dominated by his first masters, the wind and the sea.

As a child Chateaubriand was haunted by the sea; he was taken to church in St Malo to kneel among old sailors; he listened, enthralled, to the chanting of the hidden nuns rising from St Victoire above the thundering of the waves on the rocks. He played alone on the beach of Le Sillon, the strand that connects old St Malo loosely to the mainland, and built sandcastles there. In his *Memoires d'Outre Tombe* (Recollections from Beyond the Grave) he wrote, 'How often since then have I thought myself building for all eternity castles that have crumbled faster than any castles of sand'.

Much of the time was spent in the claustrophobic company of his terrifying father, his mother and his sister in the Chateau of Combourg soaking himself in the writings of romantic, melancholic Rousseau, the ballads of Ossian and the poems of Gray. In May 1793 he joined many exiled French in London, which he grew to love and stayed for seven years giving French lessons. There he suffered the peaks of literary acclaim and the depths of personal despair at the loss on the scaffold of both his brother and sister-in-law. Eventually he was drawn back to France, where he became politically powerful and before he died he negotiated with the Government for the site of his lonely tomb in order that he could 'continue my dialogue with the sea'.

Flaubert, visiting the grave some years later, wrote: 'He will sleep with his head turned towards the sea, in this tomb built upon a reef. His immortality will be like his life, deserted by his fellows and surrounded by storms'.

Towards the end of the century as the railways opened up vast areas of inland America, and especially Canada,. more and more young hopefuls decided to pit their wits against the wild in North America or in Australia. The same spirit was moving young people in Europe and many of them crossed the Channel first to Britain - especially to Southampton. There was a special transit camp outside the town where emigrants waited for the liner.

The *Illustrated London News* reported:

> On Monday April 8th 1844 one hundred and sixty five souls, men, women and children, embarked at Deptford on board the St Vincent of 628 tons, preparatory to sailing the following day for Plymouth, where she will receive all who may be assembled there from the western part of England; from thence she will proceed to Cork, and take in emigrants from Ireland, quitting the last-mentioned port on the 16th of April, for Sydney.
>
> The depot at Deptford is a building fitted up and arranged with bed-places, bedding, etc., in distinct apartments, separating the married from the single, and a large dining hall, where the emigrants get their meals. Here they continue collecting between the periods of sailing of the respective ships, and all are expected to be present two days before the day of embarkation. On Monday the St Vincent received her living freight on board from the depot, and they were immediately counted off into messes of eight or ten each, and victualled for the day. Between one and two o'clock we witnessed the spectacle of taking the first meal, and it certainly was a most interesting scene. The married people were very decently attired, though not so much so as the single, for in several instances, amongst the latter, both male and female, there were indications of gentility in dress and manners that caused surprise.
>
> The apartment of the unmarried females was rather dark, but still there was light enough to show several really handsome countenances and good figures, whose departures from Old England seemed to cast a reflection upon the bachelors they left behind. If there is any gallantry in Sydney, many that we beheld cannot be long after their arrival without husbands.

The pace of life began to accelerate and, as the internationally competitive world opened up by the Industrial Revolution became obsessed by speed on land, merchant sailing ships from Britain and then from America, still armed, began to race backwards and forwards

The Royal Yacht Victoria and Albert *passing the Needles, an illustration from the* Illustrated London News *quoted opposite.* (Mansell)

through the Western Approaches. As the wooden steam paddle-boats rocked and rolled their way between Britain and France, sailing craft were also streamlined and enlarged until a ship might have 30 square sails and 15 fore and after. The ratio of length to beam began to resemble the superbly sleek proportions of the Viking drakkars or the Venetian galleys and by 1840 when the Royal Mail decided to subsidise the development of steam boats the way was open for a worldwide network of communication – much of it Channel-born.

The arrival in Folkestone of the Indian Mail from Bombay was described in the *Illustrated London News*. 'In approaching this port the vessel hoists a signal of the Mail called a "Whiff" or pennon tied at the end in a knot to give notice to the Harbour Master and the railroad authorities to have all things in readiness to speed it on its flight to the Metropolis. The answer to these signals from the pierhead is made by a double white light as shown in our engraving. Immediately on the

Mail signal being observed, the indefatigable Mr Faulkener, makes the necessary arrangements for its reception. . .'

The Queen, herself a dedicated traveller, used the Royal Yacht for her journeys to Europe and the Isle of Wight, and so declared her own confidence in progress.

Our artist has engraved the Royal Yacht *Victoria and Albert* passing through the Needles for Plymouth, on the morning of Tuesday week [18th August 1846]. There was a heavy sea throughout; the Queen remained on deck the whole of the passage.

We subjoin the details of the interior of the Royal Yacht, with the recent alterations. The Royal Apartments occupy the after-part of the yacht, and comprise the Dining-room, the Drawing-room and the Bed and Dressing-rooms. The Dining-room occupies the entire stern from side to side, and is lighted from the stern windows, from side windows, and a skylight in the centre. It is 20 feet in length, by 22 feet breadth, and 7 feet 7 inches in height. The panel work is of a dark colour, with gilt mouldings, Sofas (the under part of which is used for lockers) are attached to the circular stern. The chairs are plain mahogany and green morocco; one of them, with brass knobs and spikes on the feet for security, always stands on the starboard side, and is appropriated for the Queen. A circular table, but which may be extended to dine 18 persons, stands in the centre. At the sides are ivory hand-holders to catch hold of when removing from place to place when the vessel is in motion.

The Drawing-room is 24 feet long, 12 feet 6 inches broad, and 7 feet 7 inches high. The paint work is lilac in colour bordered with gold beading. It has three windows in the side and is also

The dining room of the royal yacht as described in the Illustrated London News *alongside.* (Mansell)

lighted by strong prismatic glass works in the deck. The chairs are curiously formed to double up, said to be invented by George IV. There is a circular table in the centre, and a square table at each end, as well as a side table, the whole having raised brass work round the edges to prevent anything from rolling off. Two handsome and commodious easy chairs stand abaft and a sofa on either hand. Against the vessel's side is a pianoforte, a Brussels carpet covers the deck, and the whole is extremely simple. On the starboard side of the passage, opposite to the Drawing-room, is the Royal Bed Cabin and Dressing-rooms.

Illustrated London News

It was some years before the travelling public really considered steam as reliable as the packet sailing boats and were to begin making the journey with their personal carriage strapped to the deck. Mid century passengers arriving at Dover or Folkestone would have found a choice of hard bargaining owners plying their trade and boosting their respective merits which were, by modern standards, minimal! In Dieppe the quaysides were thronged with women equally anxious to lure visitors to hotels of dubious quality. With no stabilizers the boats pitched and rolled their oil-smelling way over the water, paddles thumping, engines roaring and white enamel bowls placed neatly along the decks. Creosote on a lump of sugar was a favourite remedy for seasickness. Stabilizers were not fitted until 1923 and even as late as 1938 a serious journal was reassuring 'death has never been known to occur from sea sickness'. The torture lasted anything up to $2\frac{1}{2}$ hours from Dover to Calais, but to the hardy seafaring British this must have been part of the adventure. From Brighton it was far worse. At least at Shoreham passengers were able to step ashore from the boat onto a landing stage. The Victorians also discovered the joys of inshore pleasure steamers, with the building of that great British institution – the pier. The first was built at Bournemouth in 1861.

Because of inefficient engines, coal consumption meant that no ship could manage the longer journeys under steam alone. Isambard Kingdom Brunel, the great engineer-designer, died just two days before the launching of his greatest project which changed all that. On June 17th, 1860 *The Great Eastern* set off on her maiden voyage from Southampton. Brunel had said 'Nothing is proposed but to build a vessel of the size to carry her own coals on the voyage' and he contracted to build a boat 'no less than five times as large as any ship previously built'. This juggernaut was 692 feet long, 120 feet wide and was designed to carry 400 crew, 800 first class passengers, 2800 second class and 1200 third. On her maiden voyage she took 40 passengers who had each paid £75 for the trip over the Atlantic. The original idea was to use her for the round trip to Trincomalee in Ceylon but she never made the journey because her owners ran out of money before she was finished and sold her for the North Atlantic run, on which size did not matter anyway!

The Great Eastern was far too large to go through the Panama Canal, too large for most harbours, she rolled horribly and she was a financial disaster, but she paved the way for the passenger liners which were, before very long, to transfer the elegant life of the new palm court hotel to the sea itself.

By this time passenger boats and liners were equipped with electricity, individual cabins, lounges and all the social cachet and palm court paraphernalia of hotels. The century had begun with a handful of steamship owners who had achieved in a hundred years what had taken five hundred years of sail. The Free Trading policies of the Victorians had opened the world market (though they were killing British agriculture). On the Continent protective duties had been imposed, and the British ship owners took advantage of their freedom; food was imported from all over the world as were raw materials which in turn helped the export of manufactured goods from those materials. British coal was King and the merchant seaman was by now a highly trained professional apprenticed to the ship owner and examined by the Board of Trade. Mainstream Channel was dominated by the British cargo ships, and the inshore waters were busy with beautiful, red-sailed barges, ketches and schooners carrying minerals, china clay and timber round the coasts in competition with the railways.

So, just as pressures were building on land, this increased traffic on the sea made the need for greater care and control and greater awareness of the value of life imperative.

Although the demise of Napoleon had left Britain undisputed controller, not only of the Channel, but also the seas worldwide, the Navy itself did not take quickly to steampower. For fifty years after Trafalgar, military ships in France and England hardly changed their appearance. The Navy was run by reactionary elderly Admirals and the French Navy was virtually non-existent. Palmerston said that the arrival of steam had thrown a bridge across the Channel over which thirty thousand Frenchmen could pour overnight.

The French introduced steam to their battle fleet with the *Napoleon* designed by Stanislas Dupuy de Lome. She was a huge 235-foot, 92-gunner with a top speed of 13.8 knots. Soon after the British went one better with the converted *Sans Pariel* and newly built *Agamemnon*.

The only real 'hiccup' in the peace was caused by the far distant war in the Crimea which was really not a British affair at all but which brought the British and French into a temporary brief alliance, and radically changed the appearance of warships.

Scenes along the Channel beaches at the time of the Crimea would have illustrated only too well the still dishevelled state of naval organization. Improvements there had been, but the need for urgent mobilization against Russia caused a crisis.

British sailing ships were too large and there were still not enough professionals to man them. When Queen Victoria came down to wave them off in 1855 from the Royal Yacht, her salutations were returned by a ragbag of volunteer crooks, convicts and reluctant coastguards who objected to the unaccustomed discipline and even to wearing regulation clothes – 'pusser's slops'. It was a war for which they had no heart and though the public insisted on covering it all in glory there were two distinct types of song being sung that year in the pubs of Portsmouth.

'Britannia, the Pride of the Ocean' was the official party line and public mood:

> Now the grog, boys, the grog, boys bring hither
> And fill fill up true to the brim,
> May the memory of Nelson ne'er wither
> Nor the star of his glory grow dim.
>
> May the French from the English ne'er sever,
> But both to their colours prove true,
> This Russian bear they must thrash now or never,
> So three cheers for the red, white and blue.

More accurate perhaps about the mood of the men was:

> So into the War they drag us willy nilly,
> Oh! I've no patience with them, they're so silly,
> Bringing upon such expense and trouble,
> Already there's the income tax made double,
> No hides – our boots and shoes will soon be frightful,
> Oh! I declare it makes me feel quite spiteful,
> Our pitch and tar will be as dear as leather,
> Tar? Yes, I'd tar him – that bold Czar – and feather him
> From being feathered, guards and gates may bar him,
> But let Jack Tar pitch into him he'll tar him,
> Oh! the nasty abominable bruin,
> I hope and trust we're paying for his ruin.

All along the Channel, ships from the *Mesageries Maritime* (post) and the merchant fleet were requisitioned and because there was no war to be fought at sea it was discovered that small ships with engines were far more practical to manoeuvre in small harbours and so began the era of the small, steam-driven gunboat. First again, the French also built *La Gloire*, an ironclad warship in 1859 followed immediately, of course, by the *British Warrior*.

The *Warrior* was a revolutionary ship. Built by Scott Russell and Isaac Watts, she was iron throughout, armour plated $4\frac{1}{2}$ inches thick along her 208-foot length. She had a top speed of 14.3 knots and, most important, she could carry 850 tons of coal, more than any other ship in the world. Within ten years of her launching the Royal Navy had 30 ironclad ships of the line, all different, all experimental, testing different shapes, accommodation and armaments. The new ships also forced a rethink about such basic needs as toilets, which on the wooden ships were slightly less than convenient – four thousand men could queue to get at twelve primitive holes in the side and by day the official 'sweepers' were left to tidy up. The Navy was on the move after fifty stagnant years.

> Ding clash dong bang boom rattle clash boom rattle clash bang clink bang dong bang clatter bang bang BANG. What on earth is this, or soon will be?
>
> This is or soon will be the *Achilles* iron armour plated ship. Twelve hundred men are working at her now, twelve hundred men working on stages over her sides, over her bows, over her stern, under her keel, between her decks, down in her hold, within her and without, crawling and creeping into the finest curves of her lines, wherever it is possible for men to twist. Twelve hundred hammerers, measurers, caulkers, armourers, forgers, smiths, shipwrights, twelve hundred dingers, clashers, dongers, rattlers, clinkers, bangers, bangers, bangers.
>
> *The Commercial Traveller*
> Charles Dickens

In 1885 a third of the world's sea-going ships were British, including four fifths of the world's steam ships. France had fallen to fifth place (and the French government was giving subsidies to sailing boats as late as 1902 in the belief they had a greater future). The Channel was becoming a motorway for non-stop traffic *en route* to somewhere else. The east and west coasts and harbours of Britain came into their own with their easy access to canals and railways and so to the industrial heartland. Apart from Southampton which, after a lapse of nearly three hundred years, began to expand as an outport for London, the Channel towns of Britain had little role in this mercantile bonanza. Their importance lay more in their strategic position as a bulwark against France. For although there was, on the face of things, peace, never did the British allow themselves to trust their traditional sparring partner.

The two countries continued to flex their muscles across the water and every few years some event, great or small, would give them the opportunity to come out of their corners but they never exchanged blows. There were near misses: when in the 1830s Belgium declared independence from Holland to the delight of Britain and the fury of France; when Count Orsini made a bomb in Britain and took it over the Channel to assassinate Napoleon III; and when there were fishing rows over Newfoundland in the 1880s. Trouble was probably avoided because of the strength of the British Navy based in the newly expanded, naval dockyards of Portsmouth and Plymouth. In France,

Le Havre had become the second largest commercial port after Marseilles but there was no Channel military base to compare with Portsmouth or Plymouth.

Lord Palmerston's decision to build a string of anti-French forts along the Channel coast was viewed in retrospect with some contempt. These massive structures were descendents of Henry VIII's beautiful seaside castles, but were already obsolete by the time they were finished, and were destined to be known as Palmerston's follies.

Today they are curiosities no more. School-children play hide and seek in the chilly, labyrinthine catacombs that riddle the cliffs of Newhaven. Behind the 100-foot cliffs, where the ice cream vans park and hundreds of unsuspecting day trippers roast on the shingle, is the beach entrance to the precipitous passage which climbs inside the chalk to the main Fort.

In 1862 a young Royal Engineer, Lt John Ardagh, booked a room in the Bridge Hotel and went to carry out a cliff top recee. Two years later work began and by the summer of 1871 the first troops had moved into the ten-acre fortifications, which were used as a training base and garrison. In the front line of two World Wars it was finally abandoned to the seagulls in 1948. For fourteen years it was the forbidden haunt of adventurous schoolboys until in 1962 it was finally handed over to the public at a colourful occasion, Operation Double Ceremony, to be managed by Newhaven Urban District Council. They sold off much of the land for development. It says something for the English affinity to the sea that the Sealink Ferries glide impressively past the windows of the flats which were constructed near the east side gun casement peering down across the harbour entrance.

The Fort itself was bought by Lewes District Council in 1979 and by dint of superhuman local effort restored from rubble-ridden dereliction to its original state and converted into a vast tourist complex.

Approaching the coastline by sea in the second half of the century, dramatic changes were visible. There was still a busy bustle of inshore traffic – china clay leaving Fowey from the new mines at St Austell and coal coming round the Kent coast to be landed at Hastings. Down at Falmouth, the most westerly Channel port, the quay punts went out to meet the merchant vessels and deliver messages which had arrived by the new-fangled electric telegraph. For boats that had been so long from home this service was greatly welcomed and 'Falmouth for Orders' became the first stop of returning craft. From Falmouth, too, the cutters set out with new clothes to sell to gentlemen who did not wish to return home in travel-stained garments. Many of the little steam tugs acted as towing boats to help the larger craft into harbour. But the greatest bustle was caused by building: building of defence works, piers, harbours and, of course, houses to accommodate the workers, and hotels to accommodate the holidaymakers.

It was happening in France too on a smaller scale. The statue of Napoleon on horseback on Cherbourg seafront has on its plinth yet another of the Emperor's grandiose pronouncements: 'I will recreate at Cherbourg the wonders of Egypt'. Like many of his other prognostications it did not quite come about, for Cherbourg never really justified the title once given to it of 'tomorrow's Channel Inn'. Although it became a port of call for the great transatlantic liners, when that trade died at the end of World War Two Cherbourg was relegated to the status of a bus stop to the south.

Even so as the ferry purrs in past the eastern end of Napoleon's harbour today the 3300 metre 'digue' three miles out to sea built as a protection against the merciless nor'westers, is indeed a wonder. It is the massively impressive ancestor of the Mulberry harbour, created by man on an inhospitable shore. Started in the reign of Louis XVI a series of many hundred colossal cones, stuffed with rubble, were sunk over the years to form an island base for the breakwater. When Napoleon's remains were returned from St Helena in 1840 to Cherbourg it was still not finished but he would surely have been well pleased with his maritime monument. What might he have felt about the nuclear submarines being built in the Naval Dockyard?

Napoleon's grandiose promise to Cherbourg is recorded for all to see on this statue. (Topham)

Over in Southampton the construction of the Royal Pier opened the harbour to the larger ships of the period and gradually, as the rail network spread, Southampton began to grow. The Peninsular Steam Navigation Company, the Royal Mail Steam Packet Company, the Union Line and P & O were all based there, and though initially most of the transatlantic passenger traffic went from Liverpool and Bristol, by the end of the century the Empress Dock was opened and Southampton became the only port able to house the monster liners that were being built. Southampton was the first all-steam port.

Accidents were commonplace but none more eerie than the 'death' of the steamer *Victoria* which sank in thick fog off the Point D'Ailly nine miles west of Dieppe in 1887. Among her passengers appropriately was Mrs Bram Stoker, wife of the creator of Dracula.

In the early hours of the morning of April 12th the lighthouse keeper at Point D'Ailly woke to see a pea-souper over the Channel, and an alarming silence. The fog horn which habitually warned shipping off the headland was silent and the assistant keeper fast asleep. In the meantime the *Victoria* from Newhaven, with 94 passengers, including a party of nuns and a crew of 25 on board, was creeping along the coast. With no warning horn, Captain John Clark mistook his position and the *Victoria* went grinding onto the rocks. There was no immediate need for alarm but there was panic among the passengers. They ignored the Captain and pushing and shoving – men before women – crowded into the lifeboats only to be hurled into the sea when a woman's scarf became entangled in the mechanism. The other two lifeboats drifted round to Fécamp, while mothers and babies clung to driftwood. At Quiberville local folk in the hotels on the front were woken to provide drink and blankets for the frozen frightened

Capt. Boyton with suit, paddle and sail ready to cross the Channel – on his back. (BBC Hulton)

The boat to Boulogne passes Capt. Boyton going the other way. (Mary Evans)

survivors, and spectators gathered on the beach to gaze aghast at the debris on the shingle: hats from Luton, burst boxes of frozen mackerel and clothes. The bodies were taken to the morgue in Dieppe. But as the wrecked vessel sank and her planking burst open a cargo of black crepe – destined for the widows of Normandy – floated away from the hold and gradually became entangled around the masts and funnels of the *Victoria* so that as she finally went down her outline was shrouded in bizarre, mourning drapes.

A furious row broke out between the French and English who blamed each other for the tragedy. The French said that if they had run the ferry the accident would not have happened. The British, more justifiably, blamed the sleeping keeper.

Concern for life was not solely a matter for officialdom. There were a growing number of individuals bending their minds to various aspects of safety and lifesaving and the Channel was an excellent testing ground for ideas, which have mostly sunk without trace.

Five months before Captain Matthew Webb astounded both French and British by swimming the Channel in 1875 just for the hell of it, an American, Captain Paul Boyton, made the crossing to test a revolutionary invention. Wearing his specially designed, inflatable, life saving suit to which was attached a tiny sail mounted on a socket in his foot and a steering paddle as a rudder, he had reached South Foreland from Boulogne after twenty-four hours in the water. The phlegmatic Captain Boyton, of the United States Atlantic Life Saving Service, set out on his audacious journey on Saturday, April 11th with the blessing of Queen Victoria herself. It was the second attempt – a first from Dover had failed. He wore a navy, serge suit under his outfit to prove its waterproof qualities. An hour and a half before Boyton entered the water the steamer *Prince Ernst* set sail from Folkestone to rendezvous somewhere in the middle and accompany him, with a boatload of sceptical journalists alongside. It was a hard paddle, during which he tucked into beef sandwiches and green tea until about 2.30 in the

morning he saw the welcoming fire that some fishermen had lit on the North Foreland beach to guide him in. The Queen, who had watched a test run at Osborne on the Isle of Wight, sent her congratulations, and the Press acclaimed his contribution to safety at sea.

When Queen Victoria reviewed her fleet at Spithead in 1887 a transformation had taken place which was to move the Navy in body and spirit forward into the twentieth century. The Royal Reviews of the Fleet have always been a mirror of change. The Isle of Wight, like a cork in a champagne bottle neck had watched history fizzing down the Solent past its shores. For it is here, by Spit Sand where the channel into Portsmouth Harbour divides from the main road up to Southampton that the British Fleet has for some four hundred and fifty years shown itself off to its Monarch. Holinshead says Henry VIII was the first 'having a desire to see his Navy together, rode to Portsmouth'. Most recently came Queen Elizabeth II.

The Royal Reviews of the Fleet at Spithead became a matter of national pride, although in the early days they were to some extent an excuse for monarchical merrymaking. Charles I and James I went down and, of course, the sea-loving Charles II, who actually put to sea with his Fleet and had to be disembarked at Torbay in a storm. Charles could not be kept away from the sea and was always popping down to see how things were going. Queen Anne became Lord High Admiral for a time but avoided making the journey, so did George I and George II who liked neither the sea nor Britain, so was not surprisingly, disinterested in the British Fleet. But George III in his Royal Barge was the first to organize a fully formal Review of the Fleet and 'triple discharge of cannon' salute in June 1773 to acknowledge their achievements during the Seven Years War with France.

'Sailor Billy', later King William IV, really allowed the sea to go to his head and treated the Navy rather like a personal toy. To the irritation of the Lords of the Admiralty he had a habit of 'borrowing' their ships and setting off down the Channel without asking permission. Even so, as Lord High Admiral, he was towed by one of the very first steam ships *Lightning* against the wind and came 'into harbour in a beautiful manner amidst the cheers of thousands of most respectable people assembled on the lines and beaches.'

It was, naturally, wise Queen Victoria who really appreciated the importance of the Navy and made the Royal Reviews a regular state event. Under Victoria they became, like the Russian May Day parades in Red Square, a show of force, extravagantly iced with pomp and ceremony. In 1845 she went to see the last-ever Review comprising sailing ships alone. By the time of the Crimea, the Fleet was a motley collection of screw and paddle-driven. The use of torpedoes accelerated the need for iron hulls. At the Golden Jubilee in 1887 all Her Majesty's ships were made of iron and the largest, the *Inflexible*, at 12,000 tons had 24-inch thick armour plating. In 1894 the *Turbina*, which must have been a *Concorde* of the sea in her time, could have sped past at 34.5 knots, the first-ever ship with turbine-driven engines and the fastest ship afloat.

The changing appearance of the Fleet. In 1865 the British Admiral's flagship, a magnificent wooden warship, takes the salute at an Anglo–French review. In 1887 the royal yacht, during the Jubilee Review, steams past a fleet of iron ships but sail has not yet given way to steam. In 1911 the battleship Neptune *leads the Fleet to its anchorage for the Coronation Review.* (BBC Hulton)

Perhaps the saddest occasion of them all was in 1901, when the cortège carrying the old Queen's body on its way to burial from her beloved Osborne on the Isle of Wight steamed past a fleet stretching in single line from Cowes to Spithead.

There have been many reviews since then as the shape and style of the Channel Fleet has altered drastically. When Queen Elizabeth last came she saw much smaller and deadlier ships and submarines powered by gas turbines and atomic reactors. Yet, although the style of Channel shipping is so different, the British love of traditional ritual has left the form of Review unchanged. As the Sovereign passes the ships are manned and a Salute is fired. After dark the Fleet is lit up. In the past the bells rang and gunports were opened to show a blaze of light; now it is a matter of flicking a switch to illuminate the ships.

How much Her Majesty knew about the men who served her is hard to say, but by mid-Victorian times in the public imagination the sailor had become an exotic figure – the Blue Jacket synonymous with ideals of patriotism, Queen and Country. Songs were written about him and sentimental pictures painted. This kind of romanticism never happened in France, a fact which is confirmed by the lack of written material about the human face of the Navy. The shelves of any good public library in Britain are stacked with enthusiastic records of every aspect of the life of Jolly Jack Tar. In France you may delve into book after book without finding any popular record of the Navy, let alone the men who served.

It is a romantic view, of course, because for the man below-decks life was still tough. The be-pigtailed, tobacco-chewing mariner had no tenure of service – when he was not needed he was discharged – unlike the officers, who were still largely the sons of gentlemen or the Marines. So, to compensate for his lot, he drank; the drunken sailor was one of the spicier sights in the south coast ports. The cutting of the rum ration between 1830 and 1850 did much to improve conditions, plus the introduction of more and better clothing, the easing of punishments and the introduction of libraries aboard ships. Every reform brought the Navy a little nearer to the idea of employing a permanent crew.

The bare bleakness of the mess-deck, with its long range of plank tables and stools, had as little suggestion of physical ease as a prison cell. It was damp and chilly in a cold climate, and damp and hot in the tropics. It was swept by searching draughts if the ports were open, and nearly pitch dark if they were closed, glass scuttles not having been invented. It was dimly lit at night by tallow candles inside lamps at long intervals, and as there were no drying rooms it reeked of wet serge and flannel in rainy weather. In short the living quarters of the mid-Victorian, blue jacket, stoker or marine were as widely dissociated from any ideal of a home in the usual sense as could well be imagined.

Moreover, he was always in a crowd by day or night. His work and his leisure, his eating, drinking, washing and sleeping were all in crowded surroundings. He swallowed his bully beef and hard tack, his pea soup, 'copper rattle', and rum, at a mess table so congested that he had absolutely no elbow room and scarce space to sit. He washed himself twice a week on deck at the same time as he washed his clothes, in the two tubfuls of cold water which formed the allowance for the whole twenty-five men in his mess, in the middle of a splashing mob at other tubs all round; and he slung his hammock at night among hundreds of others so tightly packed that they had no swinging room however much the ship rolled. Even in the head he had no individual privacy.

Hurrah for the Life of a Sailor
John Winton

There was continuing effort too in this time of peace to improve the quality and even to train the sailor in his craft rather than rely on the haphazard tuition of individual captains or not.

In 1830 the first gunnery school had been established in Portsmouth harbour – aboard the sailing ship *HMS Excellent*. The memo which the Admiralty sent to the C-in-C Channel marked an unsuspected, at the time, dawn . . .

Their Lordships having had under their consideration the propriety and expediency of establishing a permanent corps of seamen to act as Captains of Guns as well as a depot for the instruction of the officers and seamen of His Majesty's Navy in the theory and practice of Naval Gunnery at which a uniform system shall be observed and communicated throughout the Navy have directed that with the view to the formation of such an establishment that a proportion of intelligent young and active seamen shall be engaged for five or seven years renewable at their expiration with an increase of pay attached to each con-secutive re-engagement from which the important situation of Master Gunner, Gunner's Mates and Yeoman of the Powder Room shall hereafter be selected to instruct the officers and seamen on board such ships as they may be appointed to in various duties at the guns in consideration of which they will be allowed 2 shillings per month in addition to any other rating they may be deemed qualified to fill, and will be advanced according to merit and the degree of attention paid to their duty which, if zealously performed will entitle them to the important situation before mentioned as well as that of Boatswain.

John Winton

It was a gigantic step forward; words such as 'permanent renewable' and 'merit' had never before been used in connection with the Navy.

As ever, alongside the serious business of history, ran local initiative. As the tide ebbed a red warning flag was run up the *Excellent* mast to warn that firing was about to begin. Over on the shore the unbelievably named 'Grub' family would strap wooden 'ski' boards to their feet and prepare to skim out across the mudflats in search of the used shot, which they dug up with specially designed tools and resold to the Captain for as much as eleven shillings. It was a profitable business.

Eventually the wooden sailing ship was replaced by a shore-based *HMS Excellent* on Whale Island.

Gradually parts of Dieppe were cleaned up, an English garden with roses planted by the new casino modelled on the Crystal Palace and Dieppe, like the rest of the Norman coast, began to attract a stimulating, often controversial, community of writers, artists and musicians. They were mesmerized, not only by each other's company, but also by the space, the light and the subtle half tones, which are there still for those who come, in the twentieth century '*à la recherche du temps perdu*' of the nineteenth. The Riviera attracted the brash and exotic; in the north it was a more insidious, gentle affaire.

Monet said '*la mer est la toile du fond de mon existence*,' (the sea is the protective web around my very being) and asked to be buried in a buoy in the Channel, but was, in fact, buried at Giverny near his famous water lily garden.

The Impressionist school of painting, with its shifting, irridescent patterns and philosophy 'light is the principal person in the picture' had its roots in the countryside around Le Havre. The farmhouse of *la Mère Toutain*, where they gathered from time to time to drink cider through the years. The young Boudin, son of a pilot met the fifteen-year-old Monet there with the painter, Jongkind, Isabey, Millet, Manet, Rousseau and later Dufy. Their world remains.

The Cotentin writer Barbey d'Aurevilly writing at the time described; '*J'ai été élevé dans l'écume de la mer, cette mer de Manet m'a pris dans ses vagues et je me suis dit que je la connaissais.*' ('I was brought up in the sea spray, this sea of Manet's took me up in its waves and I felt that I understood.')

In Jean Roman's evocative portrait of Normandy *Toute la Normandie* he opens the modern travellers' eyes to the countryside along the coast.

The Normandy sea alone is not for painters, whom she has impregnated with her waves, it is also the sky and the images; the damp sand the irridescent light, the grey and silver games of the rain and sun. With the most Norman of all painters, Eugène Boudin, born at Honfleur, died at Honfleur, you cannot be sure if he has taken his colours from his native land, or whether he has in fact given them, but every where seems signed by him. In the *Musées* of Honfleur or Le Havre the paintings of Boudin and Jongkind seemed not to be paintings so much as windows onto the sea and into space ... this acid green lawn at the Deauville racecourse – it is a Dufy … this restaurant table where on the pale grey marble a golden coloured sole make the vivid yellow of an open lemon sing – that is a Braque.

Along the beaches and in the richly pastoral countryside they explored and agonized new depths of understanding. As the artists threw new light on their world, so the writers – Baudelaire at Honfleur, Balzac at Bayeux and Marcel Proust at Vabourg – were observing the *Comédie Humaine*. Their descriptions of provincial life are so sharply, and sometimes painfully, evocative of a France that has passed and yet is so nostalgically familiar, and timelessly moving.

In part one of *A La Recherche du Temps Perdu* (Swann's Way) Proust speaks of visiting the seaside:

> My grandmother, who held that, when one went to the seaside one ought to be on the beach from morning to night, to taste the salt breezes, and that one should not know anyone in the place, because calls and parties and excursions were so much time stolen from what belonged by rights to the sea air … there are tints in the clouds this evening, violets and blues which are very beautiful are they not, my friend? Especially a blue which is far more floral than atmospheric, a cineraria blue which is surprising to see in the sky. And that little pink cloud there has it not just the tint of some flower, a carnation or a hydgrangea? Nowhere, except perhaps on the shores of the English Channel, where Normandy merges into Brittany have I been able to find such copious examples of what you might call a vegetable kingdom in the clouds … in that Bay which they call the Opal Bay, the golden sands appear more charming still from being fastened, like fair Andromeda, to those terrible rocks of the surrounding coast, to that funeral shore famed for the number of its wrecks where every winter many a brave vessel falls victim to the perils of the sea.

Anyone who was anyone at the turn of the century around Varengeville, just outside Dieppe, found themselves in the novels of Marcel Proust. The Prousts were friends of the Mallets who still live in a curiously out-of-time Lutyens house there, where Braque has his cliff-top grave. Few of the visitors who wander round the sweet disorder of this English garden and admire the modern owner Robert Mallet's efforts to establish a fragrant, and in Normandy unique, *pot pourri* of a Garden Centre are aware of the connection. But family life at *Parc des Moustiers* has a chaotic, un-French openness which must have its roots in those sparkling *fin de siècle* gatherings.

It is rare for the French to open their doors to strangers. The nearest most foreigners come to Norman family life, especially aristocratic family life, is through the rusting, green, wrought-iron gate guarded by the statutory *chien mechant*. Not here the street life of the doorstep gossips of the south. But at *Parc des Moustiers* visitors wander through the Mallet home while the children play, and a never-ending stream of callers stay for lunch. It is all less *élite* than perhaps would have pleased the Prousts, but if British, stately-home owners can stay afloat by sharing their past with the present, why not the French?

The elderly Mme. Mallet admits that she is considered an eccentric by the French who tend to come to look at her. 'You remember, *Upstairs, Downstairs*? Well, since we opened this place I'm downstairs.'

Over in England as the exuberant working classes discovered the delights of the day trip and summer holidays by rail the gentry were increasingly inclined to slip over to the still quietly cultured coast of France. The idea of holidaying did not emerge there even for the bourgeoisie until the early 1900s and for the workers hardly at all. Even today the neat, new houses along the northern coast of France usually provide a second home for comfortable Parisian families and are deserted in winter.

There were fewer paddlers in France then, but there were rafts for diving, superb wicker stools with footstools and striped awnings everywhere. The sands were often laid over with matting, or, as at Deauville, with *planches* to protect the feet. It was all very civilized and restrained, like listening to the sound of the sea in a shell.

> You can sit with an awning stretched above your head and look drowsily over the sea ... opalescent and full of soft changes and you can chat with as many of the *beautés des plages*, Polish princes and distinguished artistic people as you happen to know. There is the Prince de Sagan, with his irreproachable button hole; the Comtesse de Greffuhle is sitting on the *estalade*, Massenet and Saint Saens are on the chairs yonder; Cleo de Mérode, the beauty of the opera, is taking her bath wearing the prettiest little black socks, yellow gloves and thin, many twisted, gold chains around her neck. All round you in the sun is a flow of soft dresses mostly in sharp clear colours, and delicious hats.
>
> Simona Pakenham

The beaches of Britain were alive with pierrots Punch and Judy shows and donkeys ... the bucket and spade era was under way. Gradually progress pushed west and Brunel's bridge over the Tamar opened Cornwall for exploration. By then the railways had reached everywhere else but even so there were large areas of undeveloped coastline largely because, since the novelty had not worn off, the Victorian family was still content to arrive at its destination and relax there. Railways, unlike the cars which were to follow, made few demands on the countryside.

In Brighton, the extraordinary Magnus Volk, whose house had the first electric light in Britain and who was himself a pioneer of electric engineering, built the splendid Brighton and Rottingdean Seashore

Electric Railway. It was extended twice and later, in 1897, he created the Daddy Long Legs – a fantastic bus on stilts which ran through the sea. There is a similar contraption still working across the shallow waters between Bigbury and Burgh Island near Plymouth – there the tide rushes in from both sides and half the fun is to get trapped on the island where the atmospheric pub's scrumpy is worth waiting for.

Magnus Volk was also the first person to be honoured with an export order for a car: his electric car was bought in 1888, by the Sultan of Turkey who wrote, 'Please specially to my address one electric carriage. The price mentioned in your despatch will by paid by means of the Ottoman Bank.'

By the end of the century the signs of pressure on the coastline were already there, for the population of Southern England came to regard the sea, and the Channel in particular, as their inheritance. They came to settle in larger and larger numbers and also to retire – which never happened in France. The essentially British flavour of genteel, residential hotels and stucco, bed and breakfast, boarding houses saw its origins in those golden Victorian and Edwardian summers and led to the reckless speculation which desecrated so much between the Wars. Peacehaven on the South Downs (originally to be named Anzac, the 'home fit for heros') should be preserved as a nightmarish reminder to future generations of a speculator's dream that went badly wrong. Torquay and Bournemouth which rose, literally, from a marsh, did better.

Bathing machines had a long and useful life keeping the beaches safe for citizens and visitors. But for the bathing machines, St Leonards in 1905 has all the appearance of a modern seafront.
(BBC Hulton)

The French created Deauville, but most development was, and is, contained. There are miles and miles of the Norman-Breton coast today which are clear of building and unspoilt.

Deauville did not exist in 1860. Cows meandered peacefully across the marshes and were willing models for the artists summering in Trouville. In that year the Duc de Mornay, a Belgian banker Monsieur Donan, and an English Doctor wandering over those marches, had a vision. They saw a whole new town created specifically for the *gens chic* of Paris to amuse themselves; a town of straight, broad avenues and gracious houses. They built a railway and a racecourse to draw the clients away from Trouville – the first time any town had been purpose-built from scratch. The result was most curious. Deauville today is the down-town Trouville. Though the tourist office would have it otherwise, its sumptuous hotels and extravagant, eccentric houses do not have the *cachet* of the elegant, discreet Trouville with its bougainvillea-shrouded cliff tops.

The imposing seafront of Deauville. (Aerofilms)

In Deauville everything is on stage. The architectural fantasies dreamed up by over-indulgent Parisians, stand eyeless and shuttered for most of the year. The whole place appears like a vast theatrical set waiting for the curtain to rise on just one month in the summer. Then the smart visitors pour in: Prince Charles to the racecourse, British women's magazine readers on cookery courses. In 1910 Eugène Cornuche, casino proprietor at Trouville, built another at Deauville which attracted the Casino society and Deauville became, for a while, the most elegant town in the world, a favourite haunt of Maharajas, Princes and the Duke of Windsor.

Perhaps it is not surprising that since the British *élite* were not able to hold their own on shore and the towns were becoming more and more the refuge of the hoi polloi, society took to the boats. After all, a British King, Charles II, had discovered the delights of yachting.

Cowes, easily accessible on the Isle of Wight, had four tides a day, acres of open water and, especially important, a tradition of skilled boatbuilders who had learned their trade as the builders of fast, smuggling luggers and even faster revenue cutters.

The wealthy began to grace Cowes at the beginning of the nineteenth century and organized regattas to amuse themselves. In 1815 they had formed the Royal Yacht Squadron and owned a small fleet of armed boats on which they played sailors. They evolved a code and a ritual which transformed the whole affair into an exclusive club, in which members had to submit to discipline if necessary – even flogging. Despite the gilt-edged tone of the RYS, in its early days it was concerned with sport, rather than society. Many other clubs were started for the lower orders and regatta watching became a seaside pastime. But when the Prince of Wales, who came regularly to Osborne with his mother, the Queen, was made Commodore the tenor changed. Cowes became a court.

Louis Napoleon, King Alphonso of Spain and the Kaiser all came to Cowes. There, in the bar of the RYS were heard the first murmurings of unease, as the Kaiser flaunted the rapidly growing strength of the German navy, a fact that was alarming Europe. When the season was over the royal sailors moved on to Cannes, the 'Mediterranean Cowes' as Edward unsympathetically called it.

There are many different kinds of *plaisanciers*, heirs to that Cowes Week style, now pitting their variable skills against the complexities of the Channel, though on the best days only twenty per cent of the marina population ever leaves harbour. Most boat owners use their craft in much the same way as a caravan: it is a floating weekend home, no more.

For the more serious sailor the Channel is either a race track, or it is a cruising ground. There are those for whom offshore racing has, according to Dick Kenny in his book *To Win the Admiral's Cup*, 'replaced tiger hunting, a solitary sport for men with deep pockets. A glamorous world.' It is they who whip around the eternal Channel triangle, starting at Fort Gil Kicker, past the Portobello Buoy in the

*West Cowes in the 1840s,
'Westward of the Castle,
looking towards Egypt', and a
busy little place in its day.
(Mary Evans)*

Solent, to Brighton and over close enough to the French shore to smell the Gauloises, and back. That kind of race is a weekend sport and gets you to the office on Monday morning. It is anathema to the cruising yachtsman who would not dream of missing out on a meal and a bottle of wine (or two) in Cherbourg.

The Channel has nurtured such exciting events as Cowes Week itself when the Solent is a forest of gold and silver masts, but also the demanding *Admiral's Cup*, started with a view to enticing international yachtsmen to race in British water, and the breathtakingly beautiful *Tall Ships* race. It has attracted sailing men and women of the calibre of Uffa Fox, Chichester, Chay Blyth, Clare Francis and the only sailor Prime Minister, Edward Heath. From France has come Eric Tabarly. But on the whole the wind-tide patterns have once again given the British the edge over the French, for on their side of the Channel the phenomenal tidal race makes 'the buoys steam past'.

New ways of getting around were becoming more popular and as the holiday-making public became more familiar with their surroundings they began to walk, cycle and eventually to motor, and so, of course,

guide books became necessary. Most famous of these – and still a joy to read – was that by Karl Baedeker, a German. The Baedeker guides roamed the whole of Europe but each has a distinctly high-minded tone.

Sailing off Cowes in the 1860s. (Mary Evans)

Of hotels in France he says: 'Hotels of the highest class, fitted up with every modern convenience, are found only in the larger towns and more fashionable watering places, where the influx of visitors is great. In other places the inns generally retain their more primitive, provincial characteristics, which might prove an attraction rather than otherwise were it not for the shameful defectiveness of the sanitary arrangements ... it is therefore advisable to avoid being misled by the appellation "Grand Hotel" which is often applied to the most ordinary inns. Soap is seldom, or never, provided.'

Of the British hotel he declares: 'As compared with Continental Hotels English hotels may be said as a rule to excel in beds, cleanliness and sanitary arrangements, while their cuisine is on the whole inferior . . . the culinary art of hotels off the beaten track of tourists seldom soars above the preparation of plain joints, steaks, chops, vegetables and puddings ... In hotels not lighted throughout by gas should supply candles on every floor and not just at the foot of the staircase.'

Whatever the attractions of travel or Paris were for Dumas, he was always drawn back to the sea. He quotes Byron: 'Oh sea, the only love to whom I have been faithful'. He wrote much of the *Dictionnaire* at Roscoff in Brittany, and some in Normandy at le Havre, where he met Courbet and Monet. He loved the shrimps and *bouquets roses* (prawns) of that coast, and invented a soup – *potage a la crevette*, shrimp and tomato bisque – for them.

Nowhere is there a more imaginative, graphic appraisal of French and British standards than in Baroness Orczy's famous book *The Scarlet Pimpernel*. It was written in the self-satisfied twenties, after the Treaty of Versailles, but its sentiments could equally have belonged to the nineteenth- or eighteenth-century traveller.

> facing the hearth, with his legs wide apart, a long, clay pipe in his mouth, stood mine host himself, worthy Mr. Jellyband, landlord of the *Fisherman's Rest* ... Mr. Jellyband was, indeed, a typical rural John Bull of those days when our prejudiced insularity was at its height, when to an Englishman ... the whole Continent was a den of immorality and the rest of the world an unexplored land of savages and cannibals ... the coffee room indeed, lighted by two well polished lamps which hung from the rafters looked cheerful in the extreme. Through the dense clouds of tobacco that hung about in every corner, the faces of Mr. Jellyband's customers appeared red and pleasant to look at ... the London–Dover coach started from the hostel daily and passengers who had come across the Channel and those who started for the Grand Tour all became acquainted with Mr Jellyband, his French wines and his home brewed ales.

What a shock it must have been for Marguerite, Lady Blakeney, wife of the Pimpernel, to find herself expected to eat at the French equivalent of Mr Jellyband's establishment – *Le Chat Gris* a wayside inn at Cap Gris Nez.

> The paper, such as it was, was hanging from the walls in strips: there did not seem to be a single piece of furniture in the room that could by the wildest stretch of imagination be called 'whole'. Most of the chairs had broken backs, others had no seats to them, one corner of the table was propped up with a bundle of faggots where the fourth leg had been broken.
>
> In one corner of the room there was a huge hearth over which hung a stock pot with a not altogether unpalatable odour of hot soup emanating there from ... on the bare walls with their colourless paper all stained with varied filth there were chalked up at intervals in great bold characters the words *Liberté, Egalité, Fraternité*.
>
> The individual who had come to the door ... was the owner of this squalid abode ... an elderly, heavily built peasant, dressed in

a dirty blue blouse, heavy sabots from which whisps of straw protruded all round the shabby blue trousers and the inevitable red cap with the tricolour cockade that proclaimed his political view. He looked with some suspicion at the travellers muttered '*sacrés Anglais*' and spat upon the ground.

Sailing off Cowes in the 1980s. (Picturepoint)

The *Méfiance Cordiale*

The signing of the *Entente Cordiale* in 1904 was enthusiastically encouraged by Edward VII whose personal *entente* with the French had been a lifelong passion. From the time he was fourteen he crossed the Channel more than any other monarch, captivated not only by the sparkle of Paris, but by the warmth of female hospitality which always awaited him *en route*. In Dieppe, his first port of call, the tall, thin house of ill repute still stands, a silent witness to the frailty of a King and his hopes for closer understanding between the two countries.

The *Villa Olga*, or *Villa de la Mystère*, was the residence of the beautiful Olga Alberta, daughter of the Duchess Caracciolo, and, it was whispered, of Albert Edward, Prince of Wales. The Duchess was at the centre of a scandalous *ménage à quatre* which was enough to keep respectable society such as Lord Salisbury at the other end of the *plage*, or even out of town. But not the Prince. He was a frequent visitor. Simona Pakenham has described the 'deplorable' English taste there. 'The chintz-covered furniture supplied by Maples, wicker chairs ... pictures framed in bamboo ... photographs of royal persons ... superbly crested notepaper and inkstands and a butler who constantly replenished your glass'. The Prince himself always arrived by yacht and tried to slip in unnoticed by mooring outside the Quai Bérigny and rowing ashore.

But the *entente* was never more than a pious hope and the cordiality always lukewarm. The idea was to link France and England in friendship but the Channel was ever too wide for that. When war was declared in 1914 France still felt Germany could have been halted had England openly declared unity with her in the months before. She would not.

To tell the story of global wars within living memory can only trivialize their impact in a book that is 10,000 years long. But the Channel role as a 'double agent' within that story should not be forgotten. It was the moat which kept Hitler out. The strip of water which had historically separated Britain emotionally from Europe and kept the French and English at each other's throats has always been and remains an *agent provocateur*. The traditional dislike, even hatred, of Anglo–French governments during the period between 1904–45 affected so many vital decisions that invasion threats apart, events might well have been very different if it had not been for the Channel in between.

British policy throughout that period was to manipulate the two rival powers of Germany and France, in order to maintain a balance. But as a consequence she weakened the wrong one, and for much of the time seemed unsure who the enemy was.

The rise of Germany in the fifty years after the Franco–Prussian War had been astronomic. She was an upstart, with no naval tradition yet she wanted to rule the seas. During that time British sea power was used to keep open world trading routes, rather than as a weapon of war and so gradually German naval strength began to catch up. France had the finest army in Europe but virtually no navy.

In 1906 newspapers in Portsmouth were humming with news of the launching of a revolutionary ship. She was a battleship armed entirely with 12-inch guns, driven by turbines and capable of 21 knots, the

The name could not have been more fitting, but it had been used before. The Dreadnought *was one of Nelson's ships at Trafalgar. In 1906 it meant exactly what it says – we fear nothing.* (BBC Hulton)

Dreadnought. Because she was so advanced she made the rest of the British fleet redundant, and so ironically gave Germany a better chance of catching up.

This is the man, Admiral Sir John Arbuthnot Fisher, who dragged the Royal Navy into the twentieth century. (BBC Hulton)

The *Dreadnought* was an up-to-date ship. She was the first ship where the crew lived aft, and on her steam trials she could do 21 knots and when she was going 21 knots and you were aft down the mess deck she would shake about. Even the ditty boxes would go up and down. She was Flagship of the Home Fleet, Admiral Sir William May and his wife was up there in a yacht. She used to like to see the sailors in No. 5s . . . a deck suit . . . and winter or summer she used to like to see the sailors so winter or summer we were always in Number 5s. We used to get up in the morning about half past five, a quarter to six. We used to fall in on the poop and then away we would go and clean ship, it was in Portland in winter, sanding canvas, holystoning the decks, trousers up to your knees, sometimes for an hour and a half before it got light, and then wash down with the hose. Everything was always wet.

Seaman Gunner Stanley Munday, R.N., c. 1907

Masterminding this new aggressive approach to the Navy was a ferocious, power-mad, hatchet-man, Admiral Sir John Fisher, known as Jacky Fisher. His motto 'get on or get out' was followed by 'scrap the lot' and that was exactly what he did, when he became First Sea Lord in 1904. Jacky Fisher had already disbanded the training ships, founded two colleges for officers – at Dartmouth and at Osborne on the Isle of Wight – and extended training from one and a half to four years. He so bullied everyone that by 1908 seven *Dreadnoughts* were being built as well as armoured cruiser destroyers and submarines. Perhaps the Navy needed a tyrant to wake it from its traditional conservatism, but no one takes kindly to a man who calls his opponents 'yellow admirals' or 'bathchair harriers', and in the end he went. But in a few tempestuous years he had jerked the Navy into the present.

In the middle of all this Blériot flew the Channel. No one in Britain or France then – or in the next thirty years – saw the aeroplane as an instrument of war which would leave ships again free to defend the Channel and transport troops and ammunition to the scene of battle.

People had been attempting to bridge that gap for generations. In fact the first men to fly the Channel were a five foot Frenchman, Jean Pierre Blanchard, and an American physician, John Jeffries, in 1785 from Dover to Calais in a balloon. In 1903 Orville Wright made the first powered flight which led in turn to a crop of experiments and fatalities. Then, in 1909, The Daily Mail offered £1000 for the first pilot to make the cross-Channel flight in either direction.

This was an event in its time as significant as the moon landing. Yet only one man, the local policeman P.C. Stanford, saw Blériot land on the cliffs west of Dover Castle so there were almost no pictures.

With breathtaking *sangfroid* the Customs officer said that any attempt to impose Customs regulations on anyone engaged in aerial navigation would only bring the Department into ridicule. He wrote in his report:

> I have to report that M. Blériot with his monoplane successfully crossed the Channel from Calais this morning and landed in a meadow on the East side of Dover Castle about 2 miles from our watch house shortly after 5 a.m. having occupied 35 minutes in crossing. I visited the spot where he landed at 6.30 a.m. and got into conversation with an individual largely interested in the Wright aeroplane who gave it his opinion that although airships will never come into commercial use there are great possibilities in store for them and I think that a time may come when this Department may have to treat their arrival seriously and take steps to ensure that no opportunity be given for Revenue interest to suffer through indiscriminate landings of airships in this country.

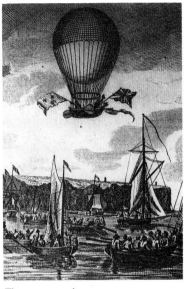

There was more than one revolution in the air in the 1780s. It is fitting that a Frenchman, Jean Pierre Blanchard, and an American, John Jeffries, should have heralded the coming changes with a flight across the Channel in 1785. (BBC Hulton)

Blériot's main concern at the time was that his tweed suit, cap and khaki jacket was inappropriate apparel for the brouhaha unexpectedly awaiting him at the Lord Warden Hotel. He was offered a suit from a French friend which had the ribbon of the Legion of Honour sewn on the lapel and protested that he could not possibly wear an unearned decoration. He need not have worried – a telegram arrived at breakfast time announcing his appointment by the Government of France as Chevalier.

So France, and shortly Britain, were airborne, and the stage was set for an era which was eventually to be dominated by the sky not the sea and where radio propaganda, used for the first time, was fired backwards and forwards over the Channel like bullets.

After the assassination of Archduke Ferdinand on June 28th, 1914, and the subsequent declaration of war by Germany on Russia, the British cabinet hoped that Germany would agree to limit hostilities and keep the Channel clear. This, as ever, was paramount in the minds of the British. Anything was possible provided that the island was secure behind its watery portcullis. When Germany declared war on France the British still hoped for neutrality: after all the Royal family was embarrassingly closely related to Germany but was bound by the *Entente Cordiale* to be friendly to France.

It was the German invasion of Belgium, rather than friendship for France, which jerked the British into the war, to defend the coastline upon which her freedom depended. The French resented the dragging of feet, and despite the British who died on their soil in the trenches, there are reputable French history books who manage to relate the war story without mentioning that the British were there at all.

The Channel itself saw very little of that war. On both sides young men vanished to fight and did not return but war fever was peculiar to the British, perhaps because the country had been at peace and untroubled by internal upheaval for a hundred years. Boat after boat ferried Britain's 'best boys' to their deaths in the trenches, cheerily waved on their way by wives, sweethearts and mothers. It was – at the beginning – a lovely war.

For the French it was yet another hideous struggle to hold their own on a continent where their boundaries were perpetually threatened by shifting power struggles and changing political fortunes. In the end there was no end. Marshall Foch said Versailles would only mean cessation of hostilities for twenty years. He was right.

Along the shores of Northern France the repose of English afternoon teas was at first undisturbed. Children played on the sands, *gentilles* misses trailed admirers over the golf course at Dieppe. Simona Pakenham who grew up there says there was certainly talk of war, and much heart searching between local domestics and their mistresses. Then, as now, the French working classes were politically aware and delighted in argument, and the great question of the moment was directed at their British neighbours: 'Will the English honour the *Entente Cordiale?*'. Those English, whose lives had been remarkably smooth, could not remember the nightmare of the Franco–Prussian war; they had little fear of the Germans and could not see that beautiful summer ending.

Then on July 31st the walls around the town were suddenly plastered with posters announcing general mobilization, and overnight *les salles Boches* briefly became *les salles Anglais*.

On August 3rd, the Germans declared war on France, and the English were not 'with them'. It took the invasion of Belgium twenty four hours later and the threat to the Channel, rather than love of France, to break their isolationism from Europe. The British joined the fray on August 4th with a fleet of 24 battleships and cruisers compared with the Germans' 20.

According to David Howarth in his engrossing story *Sovereign of the Seas*:

> A long period was just beginning in which the proud and most splendid fleet was slowly proved to be an illusory weapon which could hardly ever fight the battles it was designed for. The British had to have a battle fleet in 1914 because the Germans had one; the Germans built one because the British had one. And the British still had one with much less reason when the Second World War began in 1939. But even in the First War, it was a puzzle to find a positive enough use for it to justify its enormous cost. Its main function was as it had been in 1804 the dull and inglorious chore of simply existing in order to keep the enemy fleet in port.
>
> In both wars the British had more than enough of the greatest ships, the visible symbols of strength. It was not only the Navy that took a pride in them. Everyone did and many people in

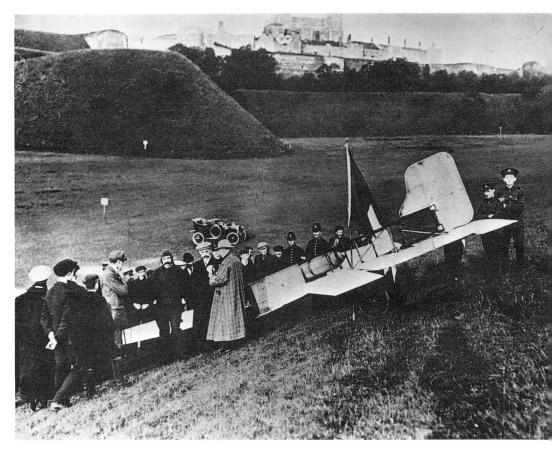

retrospect still do. But they took too much of the Navy's money, manpower, shipyard and dockyard space and Britain came nearer to losing both wars through lack of the smaller humbler ships which could do the work the battleships could not do.

Maybe Admiral Fisher – sacked after a row with Churchill – had the last word. 'To build battleships, ... so long as cheaper craft can destroy them ... is merely to build Kilkenny cats unable to catch rats or mice. All you want is the present naval side of the Air Force. That's the future Navy!'.

It was, indeed, the smaller humbler ships of the Dover Patrol that held the German might at bay in the Channel and provided a backstop for the Grand Fleet which was successfully blockading the Germans in their home ports from the North Sea. For two years, until Jutland which both sides claimed as a victory, they faced each other like this and never met ... for despite all the modernization and sudden speed of development there was of course no radar and no means of knowing – any more than Nelson knew – where the enemy lay. During the War

The full significance of Blériot's flight across the Channel in 1909 was realized only 31 years later. Before then the two young soldiers by the tail of the plane may well have died, as Old Contemptibles, across the Channel in the trenches in France. (BBC Hulton/Picturepoint)

the British developed the first catapult which was able to launch reconnaissance aircraft. But the Germans developed the submarine against which they were powerless.

In Dover nothing was ready on August 4th. No airport or even landing facilities had been organized though the likelihood of air warfare had been obvious for some time. The first arrivals had to be staked to the ground up on Swingate Downs. The harbour itself, though extensively improved in the early 1900s, had been badly designed; there was no repair dock and the booms at the entrance were useless as they could be carried away by a high tide.

Dover is arguably our most important place – few countries have a town so clearly holding their fate in its hands. Yet though six of the most important sea battles in British defence took place within sight of the cliffs, it has given its name to none of them. In 1217 Eustace the Monk was defeated by Hubert de Burgh who said 'If these people land England is lost, therefore let us boldly meet them . . . '. In 1666 there was Sluys, and North Foreland in 1690, Beachy Head and of course the Armada itself.

It was the Dover Patrol which first gave the name of Dover a ring of glory. But in his book *The Dover Patrol* Admiral Sir Reginald Bacon reminds us 'The credit for the security of England lies in the English Channel and its tides but in the popular imagination the sea is forgotten and the land takes praise. That 20 × 20 miles of water is worth 5,000,000 cliffs of Dover. English men and women are rarely enthusiastic about the Channel, it is to them a cause of woe in peacetime when wishing to pass to the Continent, but it has nevertheless always been our best friend in war'.

The formation of the Dover Patrol was another of those endearingly amateur operations at which the British seem to excel and which are a perpetual puzzle to the French. A hotchpotch of fishing boats and redundant navy ships sail to keep the Straits clear of mines and submarines for the free-flowing movement of merchant vessels. Against them was ranged the might of the Navy collected in the North Sea ports of Germany and Belgium. Zeebrugge was the 'nest' of the submarine fleet, protected by a carefully-laid mine field.

The development of the submarine, that 'underhanded, unfair and unEnglish craft' and the destroyers in the years before the War was entirely disadvantageous to Britain; they were weapons of attack and Britain's conduct in naval affairs had always been defensive. It was essential to keep them out.

So, Rear Admiral Hood's first task was to assemble his extraordinary fleet, manned mostly by fishermen and many with only a rifle and a few rounds of ammunition apiece. In the first three years the trawlers swept for mines at the rate of two hundred and fifty miles a day about equivalent to sailing three times around the world. At the beginning there was one yacht and four armed drifters, by its end there were some 256 vessels who, using nets, microphones, depth charges, flares and the new spotting airships, not only kept the Germans out but also destroyed some 1,507 mines between 1915 and 1918 (in the same period and place the French destroyed 427). All this time they were under heavy attack whilst their friends were blown to bits around them. Although merchant losses in the Atlantic and North Sea were appalling, only one twenty-fifth of one per cent of the 120,000 merchant ships that successfully slipped through the Narrows were lost by mines. Through it all, the planes of the Royal Flying Corps, which became the Royal Air Force, zoomed overhead protecting boats and bombing aerodromes in Flanders.

The whole glorious episode was crowned by the raid on Zeebrugge on St George's Day in 1918; Zeebrugge lies outside Channel waters but it was to Dover that the heroes came back and in Dover that many of them are buried in St James's cemetery. Eleven Victoria Crosses alone were won on that day and the granite obelisks standing proudly on the cliffs above Dover and Calais are a constant reminder.

The success of the Dover Patrol was due largely to the fact that 'it was never static, always dynamic, forever experimenting and improving'. (O. G. Bavington Jones). It meant that most of the Channel coast saw very little action in World War I.

Of course Dover saw not only the hurrah departures but the horrific returns. In the first months of the War thousands of men, mutilated, sick and without treatment were brought back and the platform of Dover Station was stained with their blood. But down in Portsmouth and Southampton, and in the West country, the reality of what was happening had not clouded the great swell of patriotism. The public was protected too by a surfeit of propaganda. The departure of the first expeditionary force was made mostly at night and the cobbled streets echoed to the tramp of heavily-laden soldiers and rumbling waggons on their way to who knew where. They were welcomed on the other side by women with flowers. Most did not return.

When the Germans were defeated on the Marne in September it became clear that they would make for Paris and not the coast and there were some British residents who regretted their impetuous departure, such was the lure of France. By November, the air of calm was deluding them all and the British began to drift back. But life was never again the same.

'The children returned to a Dieppe that seemed to be in the grip of an occupation, though not by the enemy.' Khaki uniforms were everywhere, outnumbering the vivid red and blue of the French territorials. *Le pantalon rouge, c'est la France*, was the proud, but ill-advised boast; for red was an an easy prey in modern warfare. Plough horses trundled in from the fields carrying guns and ammunition alongside London buses with their destination boards still indicating Hampstead to Pimlico. The children had learned a few essential catch phrases too – 'are we downhearted – NO!'.

Simona Pakenham recalls 'the harbour was full of comings and goings of boats with provisions for the British Army, with munitions and coal, so many they had to queue for a place at the quayside to unload their cargo. Everywhere vans with English names on their sides, Peak Frean, Twinings, Schweppes, Huntley & Palmer, gave the soldiers the illusion that they had turned off onto the *Rue* into a side street of Piccadilly. English songs were being shouted from cafés and rather too many English tommies were having their first introduction to wine and brandy'.

Further north, in Boulogne, a party of fluent English-speaking French officers had arrived and booked themselves into the Hotel Christol, overlooking the harbour. They ordered merchants to clear warehouses of goods and on August 9th the first steamer arrived from Southampton bringing a detachment of the Argyle and Sutherland Highlanders, in kilts – to the delight of the locals. High on the plateau above the town, ironically in the shadow of the memorial to Napoleon's *grande armée*, preparations were afoot for the installation of a vast camp for the British Expeditionary Force which was later to be known affectionately as 'The Old Contemptibles' after the Kaiser referred to them as 'that contemptible little army'. Around each tent, in true British style, they planted gardens.

In Boulogne too the first European field hospital was established in the *Gare Maritime*.

The Mayor composed a poster to be pasted around the town. 'My dear Citizens. This day we see in our town the gallant British troops who come to cooperate with our brave soldiers to repel the abomin-able aggression of Germany. Boulogne, which is one of the homes of the *Entente Cordiale* will give to the soldiers of the United Kingdom an enthusiastic and brotherly welcome. The citizens are requested on this occasion to decorate the fronts of their houses with the colours of the two countries'.

All seemed to be going well. But then came the Marne and the casualties. Hotels, casinos and private houses were converted into hospitals and British wives were organized into war work caring for ghastly injuries and diseases such as they had never seen before, caused by the horrendous trench warfare.

After the Armistice social life across the Channel resumed its black bottomed jollity but the superficial camaraderie of the war vanished in the last puff of gunsmoke. The German fleet was destroyed – a victory enough for the British. The French, though, had their traditional fear of border violation and were never happy with the Treaty of Versailles which did not commit Britain to help France militarily and did not do enough to control Germany's territorial rights.

The British resumed their irrational wariness and anglophobia swept the French Government. The fact that from a much smaller popula-tion than Britain's, 1,500,000 Frenchmen had also died was forgotten – the lure of German markets for British trade ran in tandem with a fear of French revival. So in those years between the Wars Britain dictated the direction of events always in favour of Germany. The rise of Nazism should have been a warning to the British but it wasn't. Committed to disarmament, the British eventually signed an agreement with the Germans in 1935 behind the French back. Then in 1936 the Germans broke the Treaty of Versailles – which was always unsatisfactory from the French point of view – and reoccupied the Rhine. They were again threatening French borders.

For France Munich was a humiliating reminder of her dependence on British support, and fed the growing resentment which was capped by the disappointments of the Russo–German non-aggression pact in 1939. The French had wanted that to be an Anglo–French–Russian pact but the British, they said, dragged their feet, and an opportunity to stop the German expansion was lost.

Certainly, if you interpret the meaning of the phrase 'blood will out' to mean that inherited attitudes always surface, the inherited attitudes of eight hundred years had a great deal to answer then. The *Entente Cordiale* was never more than a *méfiance cordiale*. The events which led to 1939 arose, it is true, from the Treaty of Versailles, but were not helped by continual bickering by two countries who should have known better.

For a layman skimming the records of that time by far the most predominant impression is of petulance, quarrelling and mistrust. The personality of whole nations is so often judged by the character of the men and women who lead them and the fate of millions has to be dependent on the foibles, whims and mistakes of the few; history itself can be changed by a headache or a hangover. Though no one is in any doubt about Hitler himself, the behaviour of men like Pétain, Joffre, Churchill and Reynaud, 'the pocket Napoleon', seems sometimes inexplicable. Not without reason did Tennyson say 'theirs not to reason why, theirs but to do and die' of the men who served in the Crimea. His words could well have applied in World War II. Posters had united them in propaganda, but, though the ordinary men and women of France and England had shared such horrors, there was never any love lost between the men at the top, and for much of the time no one in Britain seemed at all sure even who was the enemy.

Many tides have risen and fallen since that sunny day of September 3rd, 1939, when children along the Channel coast began filling their buckets for the rather more sinister purpose of making sandbags. This time, ironically, because aeroplanes had become the predominant power in warfare, the entire Channel was to be drawn into conflict from Finisterre and Lands End to the Calais-Dover Straits; no more crabbing, no more sunset strolls along the prom, no more moonlight dips. The land was barricaded behind an obscene barrier of barbed wire, concrete and tangled iron which crept along the cliff tops and beaches and jutted menacingly from the sea itself. Those windows over the water shut their eyes behind shutters and even as far away as Cornwall people were punished for the unpatriotic behaviour of showing a candle in their windows after blackout.

But while such domestic upheavals as the evacuation of 125,000 sheep and 25,000 cattle from Romney Marsh to Hertfordshire and the West country were taking place and children were being moved unbelievably from the London frying pan into the Kentish fire, events behind the corridors of power had been moving in an alarming direction.

What happened during the period of the Phoney War, or, as the French called it *Drôle de Guerre*, is not widely known even now, not clearly understood. It is a story worth telling for whatever the verdict of history it was a tragic manifestation of the prevailing cross-Channel climate at the time.

For seven months the armies of France and England faced those of Germany and hardly a shot was fired, but France was already worried because the Expeditionary Force which had been shipped across the Channel was half that sent to support them in 1914. Britain had only half-heartedly introduced conscription in May 1939. The French were told that by May 1940 one Frenchman in eight had been mobilized, in Britain only one in forty, figures that were disputed by Britain, but believed in Europe. The British seemed to have complete faith in the ability of the French Army to hold its own. The French popular slogan at that time declared *'les anglais fournaissaient les machines, les francais leurs poitrines'*. It was a bitter and ultimately unfair reminder of the World War I jibe that the English would fight to the last Frenchman.

The British, now with Churchill as Prime Minister, were worried because the French Government, under Paul ·Reynaud, seemed as obsessed with confronting Russia as Germany. There was no co-ordinated policy either by air or sea and with the German break-through across the borders into France on May 16th morale was very low. Communications were appalling; messages upon which hung the fate of armies were either not delivered, not getting through or ignored. There was still though, despite the differences, an overall, outward show of unity – but then came Dunkirk. The British, faced by the threat of their army's destruction, decided to withdraw; the French faced with the extinction of their entire nation decided to fight on. At Boulogne the British garrison was evacuated, without inform-ing the French of its intention; at Calais the French officer in charge of British troops forbade their evacuation and by May 24th the allied troops remaining were squashed into a triangle with its tip at Grave-lines on the Channel. But no one, it seems, told the French that the entire British Expeditionary Force was about to pull out.

Meanwhile, in a chalk-walled underground chamber, constructed beneath Dover Castle by Hubert de Burgh in 1216 and now open to visitors, Vice Admiral Bertram Ramsay was ready to orchestrate *Operation Dynamo*. There, on the iron-railed balcony, Churchill looked across the water, wearing a tin hat, in style and mood echoing the spirit of Agincourt. On May 27th every craft that could put to sea, from rowing boats to the one-time pleasure steamer *Enterprise* sailed in the early dawn on a mission that was afterwards described as a miracle and as a disaster. It was both. In the next nine days those, often leaking, unseaworthy, boats, manned by dedicated but totally un-

trained men went backwards and forwards under constant bombardment. 'There was no pride and very little joy in that homecoming'.

Once evacuation by the British seemed inevitable, the French agreed to join the departure, 5000 men would be shipped over. But Churchill is recorded as having said, in a telegram to the Chief of the Imperial General Staff, 'every Frenchman embarked is at the cost of one Englishman'. In the event, a miraculous 338,226 Britons were saved though the French claimed only 100,000 of their soldiers got away.

According to a French eye witness on that terrible day:

> It was a grim spectacle; Dunkirk completely devastated, in ruins, sometimes being taken by storm by the waiting soldiers whilst German aviators swooped joyfully overhead. The town itself and its surroundings, formed a vast cemetery with cars and lorries overturned ammunition carts all burning, scattered among the dead bodies and growing piles of rifles and equipment . . . guns thundered without respite; from time to time the air was rent with bursts of automatic fire, groups of dazed soldiers sheltering in the wreckage of houses mingled haphazardly with civilians, watched helplessly as the few remaining edifices crumbled in clouds of dust.

The Withdrawal from Dunkirk by Charles Cundall shows the organised chaos which existed on the beaches throughout the days and nights of 27th May to 4th June 1940. (Topham)

243

An official French report also says:

A few British ships returned to Dunkirk to pick up French survivors but unwilling to approach too near the coast because of violent enemy bombardment, stayed at a distance from the beach whilst our soldiers were making violent efforts to get to them. Tired of waiting, the ships sailed back empty. One can imagine the feelings of our soldiers at seeing the last hopes of their salvation disappear over the horizon.

To be fair, the men of the *Militaire Francaise* were no sailors; they had no feeling for, and in innate fear of, the sea ... and many had to be cajoled and persuaded into the boats. Everywhere was chaos and panic.

Next day the Germans rounded up nearly 40,000 remaining French soldiers, and the French assumed that Churchill had abandoned them to fight alone. The loss of faith by both partners was one from which neither recovered.

In the next few days in order to preserve British resources and build up strength in preparation for a continuing war any further air or land support for France was stopped.

The vitriol poured out in private letters and telegrams on either side of the Channel was now worse than it had ever been. Clare Booth Luce noted the 'hatred of the British by the French growing by leaps and bounds'. Churchill said the French were 'lily livered' and Chamberlain thought the French generals 'beneath contempt'.

Events which followed at Tours on June 13th had little on the face of it to do with the Channel, but were yet another step in the extraordinary saga of a war that seemed to be raging between France and England, and were to have terrible consequences.

Churchill went across with the purpose of meeting the Supreme Council. In the confusion no one met the British party at the airport and they had to find their own way to Tours. Eleanor Gates, in her absorbing chronology of that nightmare year between September 1939 and 1940, *The End of the Affair*, recalls:

June 12th marked the opening stages of the French Cabinet crisis. The problems dividing the French Government were difficult but they could be formulated quite clearly. Was France to go on fighting a hopeless struggle or should the country lay down its arms ... If the latter was this to be achieved by an armistice or by a purely military surrender. If France was to opt for an armistice how was this to be reconciled with the March 28th agreement with Britain and if France continued the war how, where and under what circumstances was this to be done? The Supreme War Council ... failed to clarify the situation. Instead by the misunderstandings engendered there it inaugurated a period characterized by confusion, counter-orders and cross-purpose endeavours … It should have been devoted to an exhaustive appraisal of France's capacity to contribute further to the alliance. But because both Prime Ministers chose to play a waiting game and were less than open about what they wanted from each other the most important issues were dodged altogether and other embarrassing topics only hinted at. From such a meeting it is not surprising that the most various accounts have emerged which were, in turn, to provide rationales for the totally different paths taken by both nations.

None of this was helped by constant misinterpretations and French mistranslation of Churchill's terrible French. *Je comprends* is tantamount to 'I agree' – not, as he thought, to an expression of concerned understanding.

In the end when Churchill left, somewhat precipitately he was apparently not even aware there was to be a meeting of the French government in Tours the same day, so he met neither the cabinet, nor the Commander-in-Chief of the Fleet, Admiral Darlan, with whom he was about to cross swords so dramatically. He left behind a sense of shock and anger for the touchy subject of what to do about the French fleet in the event of French collapse had hardly been mentioned. Darlan needed Churchill's assurance of concerned support and instead he went home.

So France decided there was no option but to surrender, and Churchill's concern over the fate of the Navy became a crisis. Darlan, whose command of the Fleet was not yet affected, had already given Churchill his word of honour that he would not allow the Germans to gain control of the Fleet. But Churchill never acknowledged either Darlan's position or the importance of the Fleet. He was unconvinced. In a secret code the entire fleet, many of whom were based in the Channel, some in Plymouth and Portsmouth, were ordered to sail for the French or English colonies and 'if you cannot go anywhere else go to England'.

In those lovely summer days the French Navy tried desperately to evacuate the Channel ports whilst under constant attack, some ships they had to scuttle, and Churchill still complained that they were 'frittering away time'.

On 16th June came the Declaration of Union drafted by de Gaulle (now exiled in London and openly criticizing the French Government). It was approved by the British War Cabinet. It offered to unite Great Britain and France under a single government and give the citizens of both countries dual nationality; to provide joint organs of defence, foreign and financial and economic policies. The Prime Minister, Reynaud, was delighted, but the French Cabinet thought it was a sell-out to British colonialist ambitions and that France would become a satellite of the very country with whom she had wrangled for so long. Reynaud resigned, Pétain took over, and in the confusion two messages from Britain about the French fleet were never delivered.

Churchill was furious and began to make his own plans for the French navy. Says Anthony Hekstall Smith in *The Fleet That Looked Both Ways*, 'As the storm gathered in an effort to save ourselves we threw discretion and diplomacy overboard. Hour by hour, almost minute by minute, plans changed, decisions were altered.'

The entire French coast was still being evacuated of ships but the British resorted to tactics that barely seem possible now, bribing captains, local governors and newspapers in ports from Brest to North Africa (where the bulk of the French Fleet was defending the Mediterranean still). It was a farce.

The two telegrams (numbers 368 and 369 sent on June 16th) which spelled out the 'necessary precondition to the assent of His Majesty's Government to a French application for an armistice was that the French fleet should be sailed for British ports' were never delivered.

The signing of the Armistice on June 21st in a railway carriage appalled Britain – though the German terms were, in fact, surprisingly lenient. Page eight dealt with the fleet and did not demand its surrender. However, Churchill still had no faith in Darlan's word of honour so, having agreed to the withdrawal of the British Ambassador and the Naval Command in Bordeaux, he ordered that the French merchant fleet be seized. No one knew what was happening. For Britain, with a minute, ill-organized army, survival was now at stake, and the defence of the Channel in danger, should that fleet fall into enemy hands.

Ironically the Germans too wanted the French to scuttle for they were afraid that they were being double-crossed and were desperate that French ships should not fall into British hands! The French were being squeezed on all sides.

Then followed a decision which Admiral Cunningham later described as 'an act of sheer treachery which was as injudicious as it was unnecessary'. The British attacked the French fleet wherever it lay – in Portsmouth and Plymouth and in North Africa.

There were two old battleships, the *Paris* and the *Courbell* and two super destroyers the *Triomphant* and the *Leopard* in Portsmouth and about twelve hundred men aboard, ten thousand ashore. They had fought alongside the British and had made friends with the people in the town during their stay. Unknown to them the British had been using social gatherings on board as a means of learning ships' layout. The submarine *Surcouf*, a splendid new craft still on the official secret list, managed to get to Plymouth and was welcomed with trays of pink gins and bonhomie and in the meantime British ships from Spithead moved in on the pretext of protection.

What happened next is best described by an expert, Anthony Hekstall Smith, in a chapter called 'The Enormous Error'.

The Enormous Error

The masts of the ships and the roofs and chimneys of the dockyard buildings stand out against the sky that is beginning to lighten, for it will soon be dawn.

The sea breeze strikes cold, and the lone sentry at the head of the gangway blows on his hands to warm them, and peers at his watch.

1050. Another hour to go ...

With his rifle slung over his shoulder and his mittened hands thrust into the pockets of his greatcoat, the sentry takes a turn along the quarterdeck. Abreast of the after-turrets he stops to shelter under its lee.

Except for the lap-lap of the flood tide under the stern and the grumbling of a fender against the quay, there is not a sound.

The sentry moves again to glance over the ship's side.

An officer is hurrying along the quay.

A British officer ...

Unslinging his rifle, the sentry reaches the head of the gangway just in time to spring to attention as the officer steps on to the quarterdeck and salutes.

'An urgent message for the commanding officer. I must deliver it to him personally. Please take me to him.'

'*Bien, M'sieur. Suivez-moi*'.

As the sentry turns his back and moves across the deck, the officer raises his arm above his head. Then, drawing his pistol, he follows the sentry ...

Suddenly the deserted quay is filled with running men; armed men; sailors and soldiers; they appear from behind storage sheds, coal dumps and dockside railway trucks and from beneath tarpaulins in launches and picket-boats.

The first light of dawn glints on the fixed bayonets on their rifles as they race up the gangways ...

It is Thursday, 3rd July 1940. The time is 1300.

Operation Catapult had started.

One thousand sailors, five hundred Royal Marines and a battalion of infantry took part in the seizure of the French ships at Portsmouth, where Vice-Admiral Walker, Commodore of the RN Barracks, was in charge of the operation. In the words of the C-in-C, Admiral Sir William James, the plan went without a hitch.

Within minutes, led by the liaison officers well-acquainted with the layout of the ships, the armed boarding parties ran straight to their positions at the entrance to the messdecks, outside the officers' cabins, at every ladder and companionway leading to the upper deck, holding the crews prisoners in their own ships.

At Devonport, the operation followed exactly the same pattern as at Portsmouth, except that since there were more French ships, a larger number of troops were employed to seize them.

But at Devonport, things did not go quite so smoothly.

They did not go smoothly in the destroyer *Mistral* for when the boarding party rushed her, some of her officers managed to open the sea cocks and flood a number of compartments. Only after her commanding officer was threatened with having his men, locked in the messdeck, left to drown, were the sea cocks closed.

Things went even less smoothly with the *Surcouf*.

Not that Denis Sprague, leader of the boarding party, or Griffiths had any trouble getting aboard, for the sentry knew both by sight. And while Sprague followed the sentry to Martin's cabin, Griffiths opened up the forward hatch leading below, and then whistled for the boarding party.

It was not difficult to lock the sailors, still half asleep, in their quarters, or herd the officers at bayonet-point, into the wardroom. And, although he hated doing it, it was easy for Denis Sprague, followed by two ratings with rifles, to burst into Paul Martin's little cabin and tell him he was under arrest.

Martin reacted slowly to his extraordinary predicament, for he had been deeply asleep. Indeed, that night for the first time since leaving Brest, he had undressed and put on his pyjamas, determined upon having a good night's rest.

As he sat on the edge of his bunk, the scene in his cabin seemed part of a grotesque dream. Sprague standing there, pistol in hand, flanked by the two gaitered ratings gripping their rifles. Sprague telling him in a voice that was not quite steady, that he was under arrest. Demanding that he came ashore at once. In his pyjamas!

Martin insisted on getting dressed, and as he put on his clothes, watched closely by Sprague, his anger rose. Not against Sprague, who was so obviously embarrassed by the situation, but against the Commander-in-Chief, on whose orders Sprague was arresting him. The jovial, kindly Admiral, who but forty-eight hours ago had congratulated him on saving his ship from capture by the enemy.

My God! The perfidious British! It was not until Martin gained the wardroom with Sprague and the two ratings at his heels, that the full humiliation of the situation manifested itself.

There, helpless, bewildered and tousle-haired in their pyjamas, were his officers. There, was young Francis Jaffray, in his vest and underpants. There, too, were Lieutenant-Commander Griffiths, the Liaison Officer, his pistol hanging from its white lanyard, and the Marines with their rifles and fixed bayonets.

Sprague took a slip of paper from his pocket, and began to speak.

Since we could not allow the French ships to return to France, they were to be taken under our control, he explained, and for the time being the officers and men of the *Surcouf* must consider themselves under arrest. They would be taken ashore. Later, they would all be given the choice between continuing the fight with us or being repatriated.

It was at this point that Martin interrupted Sprague with a formal request that he be permitted to go on board the *Paris* to see Admiral de Villaine.

As Sprague hesitated, Martin said quietly: 'I give you my word that I will return immediately I have spoken with the Admiral.' Then, he added: 'And may I have your word that no-one will be removed from my ship until I return?'

Sprague nodded. 'You have my word, Commandant.'

Followed by Griffiths, Sprague accompanied Martin on deck.

'Take this officer to the *Paris*' he told a leading seaman. 'And bring him back,' he added under his breath.

As they stood watching Martin walk away, from somewhere inside the submarine they heard a shot fired.

Diving down the conning tower, they dashed for the wardroom.

Denis Sprague never reached the wardroom.

Seeing the Englishman racing towards him, brandishing his pistol, Bouillaut, *Surcouf*'s gunner officer, shot him through the head. Then Griffiths, half blinded by the haze of smoke filling the wardroom, fired at Bouillaut. But as he did so, he stumbled over Sprague's body sprawled across the threshold, and his bullet tore through Bouillaut's shoulder, hurling him against the bulkhead. But before he could recover himself, Griffiths was struck full in the chest by a burst of fire from an automatic, and fell to the deck, the blood gushing from his mouth.

His assailant was *Surcouf*'s doctor, who had dashed to Bouillaut's aid. And having shot down Griffiths, he emptied his automatic into the belly of a Marine sergeant who tried to bayonet him. As he crashed through the mass of fighting men, the Marine ran his bayonet through another Frenchman, whom he carried to death with him.

No one will ever know who fired the first shot on board the *Surcouf* or what caused it to be fired. In an atmosphere so tense with sullen resentment and so wrought with suspicion, a churlish order or a menacing gesture would have been enough to spark off the fracas that ended in a fight to the death between men who until a few hours before had been not only allies but friends. Submariners, who for months past had faced the deadly hazards of their calling fathoms deep in the Atlantic and in the mine-infested waters of the North Sea fighting a common enemy.

Amongst those who died that morning at dawn was Engineer-mechanic 2nd class Daniel. None of her crew had worked harder than he to save *Surcouf* from capture by the Germans, and so, perhaps, more than any of the others, his tragic end strikes the notes of treachery that run like a fugue through *Operation Catapult*. An operation that – Copenhagen not excepted – will go down in history as the worst blunder ever committed by the British Admiralty.

It may be argued that since thousands were involved in the seizure of the French ships in British waters, it is remarkable that so few were killed or wounded.

But was that seizure necessary?

The final humiliation of the officers and men came when, having been marched ashore, many of them with only the clothes they wore, they were herded into special trains and taken under armed guard to camps where they lived like prisoners-of-war behind barbed wire. The majority were sent to Aintree and Haydock Park, where the sailors slept under canvas and the officers on straw mattresses in the public lavatories. Others existed in equal squalor at Portsmouth, Harwich and Plymouth.

For the most part, the sailors were separated from their officers, who were eventually moved to the Isle of Man. But officers and men alike were deprived of correspondence with their families and bombarded with propaganda to join the Free French Naval Force.

Under such conditions, it is hardly surprising that they showed little enthusiasm for the cause and bitterly resented the moral pressures to which they were subjected. It is indicative of their prevailing mood that of one hundred and twenty-seven who had brought the *Surcouf* from Brest, only forty-three volunteered to return to her.

reprinted from
The Fleet that Looked Both Ways
by Anthony Hekstall Smith
by permission of the publishers
Blond and Briggs

At Mers el Kebir – which is not part of the Channel story but is, nevertheless an extension of the tragedy – the British also made the attack described by Admiral Sir James Somerville as a 'filthy job'. To make absolutely sure that the French fleet stationed in North Africa under the control of the 'collaborationist' government did not fall into German hands, the British sank it, killing 1297 French sailors. Arguments have raged around this terrible episode ever since and there can be no analysis in a narrative which aims not to judge but to explain the present in the context of past events. No one disputes that, right or wrong, *Operation Catapult* happened and that through its happening the Channel froze diplomatically. Just as well that the newspapers of the time were silent and the public unaware of the truth of what had happened.

Moat Defensive

A week after Mers el Kebir, the Battle of Britain, or rather the Battle for Britain, began in the air above the Channel. It was a fight such as no leader before Hitler had had to fight before a planned invasion, and he lost.

Like Napoleon, Hitler had gathered his fleet ready and as ever the British were not ready. Dad's Army is now an affectionate and gently ridiculed memory, but who remembers Dad's Navy? With virtually no army organized, civilians got on with the job of defence themselves. That summer everyone who had ever set foot in a boat became part of the Channel coast Front Line. Anyone who knew anything about the sea – fishermen, tugboat skippers, student oarsmen – and anyone who knew about engines from car dealers to garage fitters joined the patrol which chugged about the sea looking for Mr Hitler.

They were armed with a rifle, a pistol and a rocket each and an inordinate Canute-like confidence in their ability to stop the tide of events. The Great British Public were confident in the reassurances of the posters on every wall, under the caption 'Mightier Yet' which showed them pictures of the splendid battle line of warships protecting their future. It fooled Hitler too!

Meanwhile to protect the merchant fleet a new team of recruits had to be trained urgently. The RNVR cadets from Portsmouth and Plymouth were the young men who a hundred and fifty years ago might well have been pressed into service. In 1940 they were proud to volunteer and make a 'citizens' navy'. With the need for small ships to protect the merchant fleet, the opportunity for promotion and conditions of service made the challenge all the more tempting. Many of these men became part of the Coal Scuttle Brigade which escorted vital supplies of coal and merchant shipping through the straits in the early days. Night after night they worked against a chaotic nightmare of screaming Stukas from above and gunfire from the Calais batteries.

'The men on the colliers were helpless and vulnerable – working amidst gleaming, thumping machinery surrounded by steam pipes with only wafer thin plates between them and the sea outside. They did not know when they would be fired at. When shells arrived they knew that if the ship was hit they would instantly have the flesh stripped off their bones' (*The Coal Scuttle Brigade*, Alexander McKee).

It was much the same for the people in Dover. You cannot hear a shell coming and for four years they were in danger of being wiped out anywhere, any place, any time. The staff at Dover Castle today remember watching those flashing lights on the other side.

And on the other side ...

The skeletons are there still, overgrown into the heather and gorse backdrop of the Breton beaches – pill boxes, silos, ramps and gun emplacements now turned into bijou residences. All along the road to the Mont St Michel they stand, turned with the feverish twentieth-century passion for 'let's pretend' into comfortable homes.

The Bretons too had their Fred Carnos described by an American, Ida Treat, who lived on the Ile de Bréhat. For the French soldier in those days was as dazed and bewildered as were the British, by what was happening. 'Out in the lane the sergeant's men had finished unloading the cart and sat smoking in the grass, nearly all wore wooden sabots and their ordinary clothes, although some had added a vague military touch – a leg band, a broad leather belt and here and there a kepi. One little fellow had on a pair of stained and patched 'horizon' breeches, much too big that bagged about his bare calves like plus fours. Their uniforms, it seemed, were somewhere on the way together with their blankets and cotton sleeping bags.'

The heroism and unwavering determination of those people was hardly that of the 'lily livered' and, in Brittany particularly, where separatists had always been supported by the Germans, they were astonished to meet the most organized, effective and typically *têtu* resistance anywhere in France. For the Bretons may have been against French rule, but they were definitely not for German rule either! From the dangerous, jagged coast facing England, around the Bay of St Brieuc, they organized 'rat runs' of escaped prisoners and airmen over the Channel. Unsuspecting campers can lie here now in the Autumn when the gorse and heather is aglow, awed by the vastness and the changing light over a thousand creeks; they can bring their cars and clamber down through a specially constructed tunnel to a beach, today known as Plage Bonaparte.

Up there on the clifftop each batch of evacuees gathered when the message from England came through on the radio '*Bonjour à tous dans la Maison d'Alphonse*'.

Once together at *la Maison d'Alphonse* the message they dreaded from England was '*Denise ta soeur est morte*', which meant, quite simply, 'mission off'. The tension of organizing these escapes, the solidarity and the silence of the people in villages, like all villages, not used to keeping their own counsel, was remarkable. It has been vividly recalled in a book *La Maison d'Alphonse* by Rémy.

Job (Joseph Mainguy) and Tarzan (Pierre Huet) were in on all the operations. You remember, eh? The steady blue lamp at the bottom of the cliff far back in the cave and you, Job, with the torch with which you flashed the letters B or H in morse? The dinghies suddenly arriving without anyone hearing them and four English sailors in each? The password St Dinan Brieuc and the sailors unloading weapons, food, cigarettes, jerrycans of petrol, tyres, all in big suitcases. The airmen leaving, sometimes slipping into your pocket a message to be read when you got back to *la Maison d'Alphonse* – Long Live France, Trust in Us, We'll Be Back. The dinghies rowed off making for freedom but you had to head back towards the Germans with your heavy loads climbing the sheer cliffs. At the top, it was the minefield again, the white rags to be picked up so that the patrols did not spot them during the day while the corvette waiting for the airmen two or three miles offshore made for England. Do you know what the English called this operation because it went so smoothly? The Channel Bus Service!

This hatred of the '*Doryphores*' (colorado beetles) as the Bretons called the Germans, because they devastated everything in their path, was of course felt everywhere. But it did vary in its intensity and there is one aspect of the Resistance that wafts illusively through the story like the mists over the Viking beaches around St Marie du Mont. For here in the Cotentin, dislike of the British did not, of course, mean to be pro-German, but of all the coastline this is the place where you might possibly hear the admission 'our Germans were fine' and Germans returning on holiday now might agree 'this was a happy place for us'. After the war, town twinning with Germany in the Cotentin was easier than in other places, after all the war between them, unlike hostilities with Britain, had only lasted a short hundred years or so.

In Fécamp children soon got used to the Germans and were well-treated, shopkeepers did well – and the Benedictine monks did even better. In fact local folk remember their distress when a German troop returned from a Channel exercise horribly burned by British napalm poured on the water.

It takes such as Gilles Perrault, the writer, to observe 'maybe it was tactful that the Canadians came to Utah beach on D-Day. Liberation by the British might have been a bitter sweet affair'.

Genevieve was a child in Caen at the time, hiding from the Germans in the quarries hollowed out beneath the town by centuries of stone masons taking the rich, sunset-warm stone for the cathedrals of France, and Britain too. She described in the *Observer* in June 1984 the agony of disbelief that day when British bombers first screamed in over the beautiful city and began its systematic destruction. 'Not the British – they are our allies.' But it was the British. And though their reasons were strategically sound, the decisions of the military men in the Whitehall bunker were made in the remote way of those in authority who decide it is best to be 'cruel to be kind'. The bombing of Caen may well have been inevitable in the circumstances, but it was the British, once again, who were the destroyers.

People were screaming, dust, smoke filled the air, tiles falling from the roof, windows blown out, furniture crashing down. How long did the inferno last? An eternity. When it was over and we could stand up again we could not speak. Caen was burning, frightened people covered with blood, dirt, torn clothes and the bombers were flying away southwards. The trees around us had lost their leaves, limbs and bodies were hanging up in mutilated branches. Papa said we must leave the house. Maman refused. No, she was not leaving her house, the English were our friends, they did not want to kill French civilians. This raid was a mistake, they would not do it again ... Suddenly after 4.00 p.m. the bombers came back ... the inferno began again. This time we realized the English meant to destroy Caen and we were going to die.

There had been parties in most villages along the coast that June weekend for it was the weekend of the first communion for hundreds of children. Despite the occupation the region was peaceful, and supplies of fresh butter, fish and eggs were still available for farmers had been allowed to stay at work during the war. The intelligence chief for the area lived in a bicycle shop in Bayeux and as a Tour de France type was allowed by the Nazis to practise from time to time. When he received the now famous coded message 'It is hot in Suez', he set off on his bike to spread the news. Café owners, butchers and grocers stood by ready to destroy communications. Just before 9 a.m. the first of the invasion fleet was spotted, in black comedy, by a German soldier sitting in a doorless privy overlooking the sea. By then it was already too late; the Germans had been sure the invasion, if it came at all, would head for Calais.

In July 1984 former Associated Press photographer Ed Wright recorded the rebuilding which the French had wrought in Caen. (Topham)

The gently sloping beaches on which the Vikings had landed were ideal for the invading troops in June 1944, but a modern army needs massive supplies and massive supplies need a massive harbour; hence Mulberry, made in England, built in France. (BBC Hulton)

On the other side the assembly area around the Isle of Wight was a Piccadilly Circus – 5000 boats were on their way. You could have walked on their decks all the way to France.

The figures were staggering and are always worth imagining as you sit in the June sun on the hotel terrace at Arromanches overlooking the unending sands and the sinking iron blocks that are the tangible reminder of that day now so soon to fade with its heroes into history. Swimming in those seas alongside the khaki-clad ghosts, sunbathing with topless grannies whose sons died in the Resistance, is a surrealist experience. The panoramic museum at the opposite end of Arromanches Square says it all.

The model of the harbour you see here was made in New York in 1948 for the British Government which presented it, as a gift, to the Museum.

If you look at the top, on the right hand side you will see (painted in brown) is the pattern of eighteen old merchant ships and a cruiser all of which had seen many years service. They crossed the Channel under their own steam, and were scuttled by their crews nose-to-end on the Calvados rocks, which lay under the water. Thereby, they formed the first shelter behind which small units could unload their cargoes.

Immediately after this, the first pontoons known as *Phoenix* began to arrive at the rate of fifteen a day. These were made of concrete and weighed between 3000 and 6000 tons. Their

measurements were: length 220 feet, height 60 feet, width 52 feet. They crossed the Channel at an average speed of four miles per hour, being towed by three tugs, and when in position they were sunk like the old merchant ships on the Calvados reefs. There were 115 in all but only 40 of them, now in a very bad state, remain at the present time. They had withstood the battering winter gales for over thirty years when, in reality, they were built with the intention of serving for eighteen months. When completed, the breakwater they formed was seven miles long and the distance from shore was one mile and a half.

Only a few of the concrete pontoons of Mulberry remain, but nonetheless impressive in their solitude on the beach. (Topham)

The port itself was the size of Dover and the capacity of tonnage equal to that of Gibraltar.

At the same time as the building up of the outside breakwater, pierheads were established to unload the ships. These were floating platforms made of steel, at each corner of which were spud legs, four in all, which were lowered to the bottom of the sea where they adhered by pressure while the platform slid up and down according to the tide. The total length of the seven pierheads was 2300 feet. They were linked to the shore by floating roadways made of small concrete pontoons reunited together by Bailey bridges; the total length of each was about 4000 feet. There were four floating roads; one for light vehicles such as ambulances, command cars and jeeps, one for empty lorries going to the pierheads, another they used to come back when loaded; and one for heavy duty such as tanks, bulldozers and cranes.

In addition to these unloading possibilities, there were numerous barges as well as about 180 Dukws plying constantly between the ships and the shore.

Sometimes there were up to 280 ships at the same time in the harbour, so that on June 12th (six days after the landing) 326,000 men had been put ashore, as well as 54,000 vehicles of all sorts from jeeps to kitchens and tanks of 40 tons, and 110,000 tons of various goods.

To protect the harbour from aerial attack, a formidable defence by heavy machine guns and bofors guns had been established not only along the shore but on the ships and pontoons as well.

This was the prefabricated harbour which from the start contributed so much (and was one of the main factors) in the liberation of Europe.

First to be liberated were George and Therese Gondre who lived in the house at the beginning of Pegasus Bridge. Soon after, the sound of bagpipes over the water announced the capture of the bridge.

The events of that day were recreated in endless television coverage and recaptured by returning pilgrims on the 40th Anniversary in 1984. Why 40th? – because, of course, most of the heroes who survived and joined in the march past Queen Elizabeth at Arromanches would soon be too old to cope with such festivities and such emotion. As it was they paid homage in the superbly tended cemeteries around the coast, yarned to their hearts' content and recalled, for those who were too young to remember, the tender, funny and tragic moments of the Longest Day. The Canadians, the Americans, the British and Vera Lynn, were there on their respective beaches, but such are the shifts of history that the Russians, who formed part of the back-up that made it all possible, were not. They are now 'the enemy'. And the Germans, though they had no official part in it all, of course, were discreet observers, for German tourism is now big business in Normandy. In Brittany battlefield tours are a macabre draw – formally organized and commercially nostalgic with lobster omelettes such as were served in 1944 still on the menu. For the ordinary family tourist, the beaches where thousands of men died, offer superb swimming, there is sunbathing in the dunes and walks amongst the deep-cut, high-hedged lanes then so deadly for tanks. Caen has been beautifully rebuilt and is twinned with Coventry.

Postscript from *Autopsie de la Grand Bretagne* by Francois David.

> *Ils évoquent souvent 'the spirit of Dunkirk'. Cette image ne nous parâit pas signiative. Cet spirit a éxisté pendant la guerre parce que dans les circonstances du moment ils pouvaient difficilement faire autrefois. Les rescapés de cet épisode sont tout étonnés d'apprendre qu'ls ont été des héros et fait preuve de surhumanité. Parle-t-on en France pour évoquer la même attitude, d'un ésprit de Verdun?*
>
> (They frequently recall the 'spirit of Dunkirk'. This image does not seem to us at all significant. This spirit existed during the War because in the conditions of the time it would have been difficult for it to be otherwise. The survivors of this episode were astonished to find they had been heroes and had shown super-human qualities. Do we speak in France of the 'spirit of Verdun' to summon up such an attitude?)

The Busiest Waterway
in the World

> There'll be blue birds over
> The white cliffs of Dover ...

Passing through history, into the present tense, this is where the Channel begins and ends – below the sweet-smelling lawns of Dover Castle. From the impregnable, honey-coloured fortress, built by William I and earmarked admiringly by Hitler for his English home, you can see the Calais town hall clock and miles of Europe's coastline on a clear day. Red ferries, blue ferries, sliding in and out of the harbour; hovercraft bouncing back and forth; there are coastguards on the cliffs and down below fishing boats, pleasure boats, dredgers, tankers, cruisers, container ships, hundreds of thousands of people *en route* for somewhere else, all squeezed into that bottleneck. Before the war there were two crossings daily – now there are 110. They say this is the busiest waterway in the world – yet on a sunny day up there or gazing chin in hand from the broom-clad cliffs of Cap Griz Nez there is little impression of rush and bustle. No suspicion that there are modern pirates, smugglers and explorers or enemy submarines scudding beneath it all, or of the millions of folk who depend upon it for their work and their play. No hint of the network of organizations now pulling the two shores together, like stays, or the efforts to draw the cultural and economic laces tighter. For though the twentieth-century English Channel is an international trading freeway, it is also an Anglo-French leisure park, playground and nature reserve whose administration must be of mutual concern. For the British at least the Channel, even today, has strategic importance and is safeguarded by what the Royal Navy calls poetically 'The Offshore Tapestry' – this is the co-operative alliance of all those whose role it is to minister and protect the British seas.

Who would guess, looking along the cliff edge that the hub of it all is the white winged building, landing like a seagull on the highest ridge. There, thirty men and women, whose ancestors once patrolled the misty Kentish marshes, with no more than a lantern to scan the horizon, are manning some of the most sophisticated computerized radar equipment in the world, and control the movement of around 2500 ships a day. It is they who, with the co-operation of the French CROSSMA (*Centre Regionel de Surveillance et Sauvetage de la Manche*) keep the Channel working.

Not so long ago, sailing through the Straits was like riding a bumper car at the fair. Only twenty years back, on the 'dead man's watch' in the small hours of the morning, sailors relied largely on their eyes and the stars for sensing danger. However, with well over one million tons of oil a day and other highly dangerous chemical cargoes in transit, the stakes became too high. In 1967 the *Torrey Canyon* disaster cost Britain about £700,000 in dispersant detergent alone. In 1978 the beaches of Brittany were desecrated by oil from the *Amoco Cadiz*. The old-style coastguard had to be winched into the present. From 1961 to 1975 there had been a loss of £40 m and 107 lives. In 1981 there were only seven collisions and no loss of life or pollution. What had happened in between?

In 1972 the Channel Navigation Information Service (CNIS) was opened in Dover Coastguard Station under the jurisdiction of the then Board of Trade. Its aim was to advise and inform rather than police, and to work closely with the rapidly improving coastguard Search and Rescue (SAR) operations.

East-west ships were now asked to take the British coast and west-east followed the French shoreline, to be monitored by CROSSMA at Cap Griz Nez. Cross-Channel traffic, such as ferries, had to pass the main flow at right angles and specific inshore routes were allocated to fishermen and local operators. All vessels were requested to report their intended course at certain stated positions and two 'round-abouts' were plotted at congested junctions giving priority to certain ships. Many more owners themselves began to instal radar on board.

Long-range radar covering the seventy miles of the Straits began at Dungeness and Dover in 1976. This, combined with the frequent radio stations along and across the sea, meant traffic surveillance was greatly improved. So much so that both British and French authorities realized the need for larger, more efficient premises to match, and in 1979 the prize-winning, beautiful, aesthetically sensitive and outward-looking Langdon Battery was opened at St Margaret's Bay, Dover, housing a one million pound advanced data processing system. Its French cousin, slightly less well endowed, began operating in from its new premises in 1985.

The twelve visual display units with keyboards, enable operators to input and extract data associated with tracked targets, navigation marks and a large amount of procedural information – hazards, anti-pollution procedures, search and rescue facilities and administration details, such as telephone numbers and key personnel. They can even locate a translator to communicate with an Urdu-speaking master of a vessel in trouble!

In the same year that the Department of Trade formed the CNIS, the Marine Pollution Control Unit was established. The MPCU is now within the jurisdiction of the Department of Transport in London and works in close partnership with coastal Marine Pollution Control Officers who in turn liaise with local authorities and of course, the Coastguard on contingency planning. In 1983, Britain and France

were jointly contracted to safeguard the Channel in an agreement of North Sea coastal states at Bonn. Part of their responsibility is to implement MARPOL (legislation for the prevention of pollution from ships) and the new regulations which came into force in October 1983. These require all new ships to be fitted with pollution prevention equipment and existing ships to be fitted by October 1986.

Oil and the illegal discharge of chemical waste from ships is the main concern of the MPCU. But there are other vigilante groups such as Greenpeace and Keep Britain Tidy and the much smaller *Progres et Environment* in France, all equally worried about the horrific quantity of dangerous debris thrown on to the Channel shorelines with every tide. The English Channel today is a conveyor belt carrying the unwanted litter of Northern Europe, Canada and the United States between the Atlantic and the North Sea. Some of it is the flotsam and jetsam of war but mostly it is lost or wantonly jettisoned from ships carrying munitions or by unthinking people who see the sea as a rubbish tip. Much of it could be lethal.

Among all the electronic equipment of the operations room in the HM Coastguard Maritime Rescue Co-ordination Centre at Langdon Battery, Dover, including a status board showing the entire Straits of Dover, are old standbys such as box files, bulldog clips, and pencil sharpeners. (HM Coastguard)

Greenpeace, particularly, is involved in the controversial battle against nuclear waste and potentially explosive chemical cargos. According to them the French 'Windscale' at Cap de La Hague has a 5.5 km pipeline which is carrying huge amounts of radioactive material out to sea and dumping it in the wild waters which brought so many English kings to French soil at Roscoff. On this beautiful lonely ragged coast the French have sited not only a vast nuclear station but also the dockyard where her nuclear submarines are built. Greenpeace claim that there is a consequent higher than permitted level of radioactivity not only in fish but also amongst fishermen themselves. All the more worrying since La Hague also has, apparently, a history of accidents. Equally alarming are the quantities of highly explosive radio active waste carried in these congested waters, even, it seems on passenger ferries. Of course, official sources always say that precautions are foolproof but there are, clearly, many near misses.

Much Channel pollution takes the form, euphemistically, of litter on holiday beaches. Litter which is either thrown illegally overboard or is thrown up as the apparently endless flotsam and jetsam of war. There are certain permitted areas for legitimate discarding of munitions but losses are frequent and tide movements have been known to dislodge mines, torpedoes, shells and chemical warfare agents. The danger is not from the munitions themselves but from careless handling by unsuspecting holidaymakers and children. The use of metal detectors and the popularity of scuba diving has added to the risk, especially where there are wrecks loaded with munitions.

The work of organizations such as the Keep Britain Tidy Group, who run a Marine Litter Research Programme are an invaluable aid to public education and a guide to the safest beaches. According to Trevor R. Dixon, leader of the Programme, drugs ranging from aspirin to protozinc acid and plastic containers of lavatory and household cleaners and wine were amongst an alarming collection found on the beach at Sandwich Bay over one year. Such is tidal drift that countries of origin included North and South America, Russia, Africa and Scandinavia. A few years back 25 canisters of arsenic trichloride which, if exposed to air would have given off lethal fumes, were washed ashore on the south coast bathing beaches. In addition to human danger, there is, of course, huge economic loss to nets, water pipes and shopping. The Keep Britain Tidy Group would like to see the Channel designated a 'Special Area' in which the dumping of all solid waste is banned.

At first some captains felt that the new system was an intrusion by bureaucrats, a challenge to their inherited skills and nautical craftsmanship. Even a denial of authority.

A Shell tanker captain admitted, 'At first I thought the CNIS was eroding my expertise. It is the captain's job to get his ship home by the shortest, most economic route. Shipping lanes mean that isn't always possible – I have to follow someone else's instructions. But I realize now – it's a godsend'.

To some extent it did limit their options, especially in bad weather. For instance, ten years ago, if a ship carrying timber ran into winds, drenching her cargo on the port side, she could tack across the Channel in order to balance the list by soaking and swelling the starboard load. Good sea-faring practice, but now illegal.

Certainly when travelling from Jersey to Shellhaven on the Thames Estuary on one of the small 2500 ton tankers, the buffering protection of the coastguards and the CNIS is far from an intrusion. The half-hourly weather reports on Channel 10 VHF, 24 hours a day, the two-way flow of information between French and British shores which monitors the position of dangerous gas, chemical and oil cargoes, all enhance, rather than impede, the ship's progress.

How else could the captain know that, in the course of one night's journey, nine hazard lights and buoys would be out of action? Coast-guard observers keep a gull's-eye-view on such markers and report their failure to the appropriate authority. In France this is the *Services des Phares et Belises*, in Britain, Trinity House.

Sailors tend to live in a world apart, marooned as they often are for weeks on end, with surprisingly few personal contacts with other ships. Radio time is too valuable to waste on chat, besides, on such a cosmopolitan waterway, there is a language problem. They may pick up the agitated voice of a Japanese radio operator in trouble off Cherbourg and not really know what he is saying. The odd Russian epithet may sizzle down the line from a fish factory ship, but though the outline of certain vessels may become familiar over the years, their crews remain anonymous. This lack of understanding can be a nightmare to the foreigner which is why there is research afoot in Plymouth to develop a 'Seaspeak' international marine language, a nautical esperanto.

Meanwhile on the bridge the silent watchman plays 'chess' on his radar screen, marking his next moves on the glass with a special white crayon, shifting positions minute by minute and weaving his way through the astonishing snowstorm of moving dots that flutter confus-ingly before the layman's eye. He senses exactly where trouble threatens and even now with all these sophisticated aids his naked eye is as keen as ever it was. It is just that he does not have to rely entirely on it any longer.

Yet on the high seas sailors are curiously unaware of the way in which the CNIS – or even the Coastguard – operate. Few of them have seen inside the stations that watch over them. The voice of the mystery lady who gives them gale warnings as they pass, is a heartwarming bonus, 'she could have a date every night'. They know little of what she does or how she came to be there.

Even fewer of the 5000 ordinary people rescued from the Channel each year have any real inkling of the vast safety net that has been woven along the shores of France and England to catch them if they fall. To the frightened family adrift in a dinghy off the Tregastel rocks of Brittany or the master of a foreign grounded tanker, it does

not matter much how help comes provided someone somewhere does something – fast. That someone, initially, is the coastguard for he is at the centre of the 'Offshore Tapestry'. The RNLI, the French *Société Nationale de Sauvetage en Mer*, the Police, the St John Ambulance Brigade and the Armed Forces all stand by for emergency orders from the nearest MRCC (Marine Rescue Co-ordinating Centre). There are two of these on the British Channel coast – at Falmouth and Dover – and a peppering of smaller stations between. The CROSSMA stations look out from CROSS Gris Nez, CROSS Jobourg and CROSS Etel.

On receipt of a 999 call on land, the firing of a distress rocket at sea or a May Day call on Channel 16 VHF in Britain the buck stops there – with the Coastguard Duty Officer. The situation is not quite so clear in France.

All through a wild night in December 1982 a team of nearly forty men fought icy force 12 gales and mountainous seas off the Sussex coast to save the crew of a stricken Panamanian ship, the *Adoni*. With winds gusting at 55 knots, those on the exposed cliff tops were in danger, like those on the shore, of being swept into the sea and one of the lifeboats lost its radio when a wave crashed through the wheel-house. It was a typical rescue.

Next day papers told the exciting story, of course. The bravery of the lifeboatmen, the drama of the parted tow line, the agonizingly slow haul around the coast to the shelter of Newhaven harbour. None of them mentioned the role of HM Coastguard. None of them knew that when the captain of the stricken vessel ordered his men to abandon ship he was over-ruled by the Senior Watch Officer as 'conditions were far too dangerous with a Pakistani crew of unknown capabilities and a foreign skipper, I knew we should lose lives'.

This is the kind of split-second decision the modern coastguard is trained to make, decisions on which must hang the fate not only of a valuable ship but of the men too. He must know the strength of his own team and be sympathetic to the temperament of a cold, wet skipper who may be fearful for his job.

Down along the pine-scented shores at High Cliffe near Bournemouth, the Coastguard Training School, built in 1967 at a cost of some £300,000, looks more like a French camp site on a summer day. Here trainees come from all over the world to learn how it is done – the British way! To undertake a rigorous 9-month course and enjoy the small boy's dream – a unique simulator on which sea conditions or navigational hazards can be recreated and overcome in the comfort of your own individual cubicle.

Needless to say there are no cliffs at High Cliffe, they were eroded many years ago. So rescue exercises mean a pleasant day out at Swanage some miles away.

The Channel is unpredictable. Depths range from 20 fathoms in the Straits of Dover to 60 fathoms in the Western Approaches. Submerged prehistoric valleys and hills are often reflected on the surface as 'dirty water'. The unpredictable nature of this strip of water, now both a great international highway carrying Europe's richest cargo and a playground for the thousands of *plaisanciers* and holiday-makers pitting their often doubtful skills against the sea in little boats, has forced an effective, if uneasy, liaison not only with control but also with Search and Rescue between the English and the French.

In France MANCHEPLAN was formed to facilitate joint action in the face of a grave threat such as the sinking of the *Amoco Cadiz*. MANCHEX exists too, to arrange joint mid-Channel SAR exercises. Besides these formal arrangements there are regular, agreeably relaxed discussions in the pubs and bistros on either side.

It is essential in matters of life and death to be flexible and for territorial waters to be open so that whoever is best able to cope can act immediately. The British Channel Islands, for instance, have no coastguard and are cared for by CROSSMA at Cherbourg. British access to helicopters is greater than theirs and these are often called on by the French if speed is the main concern.

Sometimes in such cosmopolitan waters the onus of responsibility can, literally, shift with the tide. The cargo ship *Stirling Brook* lost power off the French coast on her way home to Sweden in 1982. She was offered a tow and refused, preferring to call on her owner for help. At that stage there was no emergency, only potential trouble. As she drifted helplessly across Channel shipping lanes, however, anxious coastguards along the Sussex and Kent shores began a nail-biting watch through the night.

With dismay they heard the master say that a tug had been ordered from Flushing. They knew there was no way that it would reach the endangered ship before she went aground at Dungeness, with all the attendant nightmares of loss of life, pollution, insurance and salvage. So without more ado a British tug was launched and saved the day.

Yet underlying all the official enthusiasm for a hands-across-the-sea sharing of resources there is still a traditional, historical, underlying wariness between the French and English men on the job.

The British coastguard is a civilian, an ex-mariner with the sea in his blood, a uniformed civil servant with the Department of Trade, backed up by a band of typical, amateur, trained volunteers. There are about 2000 part-time men and women along the Channel coast – teachers, nurses, building workers, firemen with daredevil spirit – trained in cliff rescue and life-saving techniques. They work on standby 24 hours a day from the two MRCC's now remaining on the south coast, at Falmouth and at Dover, and a peppering of smaller stations at Shoreham, Solent, Portland and Brixham under the command of the full-time officers.

To meet the need of more central modern organization many of the smaller stations have been phased out amidst protest from inshore fishermen and their wives. Aware of their vulnerability and dependence on the friendly local coastguard, with his intimate knowledge of hazardous creeks and rocks, they say lives are at risk. But even amongst the old brigade there are realists who admit nostalgia rules. At the tiny shoreline station near the dreaded Manacles off the Lizard you could see through the salted window when the sea was rough!

In France there is no benevolent institution. There are no auxiliaries and certainly no women!

Those manning the CROSSMA stations round Brittany and Normandy are national service conscripts; they are primarily sailors whose training comes in the line of duty, not at a special school. Whereas the saving of life is equally important, their methods consist, as ours once did, in policing the coast. They admit they are less 'soft' – especially after the *Amoco Cadiz* – and they feel the short, two-year period of service keeps their young men on their toes with no time to get bored.

Their patrol boat, *La Varence*, is even equipped with a gun which it has been known to use across the bows of a misdemeaning vessel. Certainly they have many more rules and regulations governing their own ships which they are prepared to enforce rigorously in the name of safety.

The workers in the look-outs are supplied by the French Navy who assumes control in the case of a serious emergency. But they are administered by the Civil Service – the *Affaires Maritimes* which is in turn part of the unwieldy Government Department of Transport. Overall is the *Prefet Maritime*, an Admiral who is responsible for day-to-day SAR operations. With two 'bosses' it is a rather cumbersome system and, therefore, because the French are on the whole unmoved by things nautical, they have never created a 'character' equivalent to our coastguard. The men of CROSSMA are not a familiar part of coastal life and there has been little attempt made to explain to the public what their function is, which means they have far less sense of personal involvement with the job.

This fragmentation tends also to result in a depersonalization of the rescue services in a way that is quite 'foreign' to the British. Just as there is no identifiable coastguard, neither is there a popular, volunteer lifeboat service supported as in Britain by public donations. There is a volunteer corps – rather like an auxiliary coastguard – trained in winter for summer inshore rescue work.

The need for lifeboats was accepted about the same time in both countries, in the early nineteenth century, when the National Shipwreck Institution was founded in Britain (1824) and in France the *Société Humaine des Naufrages de Boulogne*. In both countries, too, there was a lack of support until the 1860s when increased traffic made concerted action essential. This was the period of weatherbeaten, bearded old salts in oilskins clinging like barnacles to storm-battered boats, their bravery captured for posterity in sepia prints along with their buxom, nut-brown wives. The women who shared with the hazardous heaving and hoing of stubby boats up shelving shingle beaches and from javelin-spiked rocks. But passion for the sea turned the British lifeboat institution along a very different path from the French, for it remained totally reliant on voluntary contributions with no state help at all. 'It is the most efficient way of meeting the unpredictable demands of sea rescue.' The British lifeboat crewman is there because of his sense of humanity, his daring and his love of the sea. There is no financial motive and for this the British public rewards him with admiration and affection – and his organization, the RNLI, with generosity. The French lifeboat crewmen face equal dangers and act with parallel bravery but they are not equally cushioned in the warm esteem of the people they serve. A recent report from the President of the SMSM, which was formed in 1967, laments the poor state of finances compared with those in Britain and in Germany.

Both services are now equipped in the Channel with the latest boats and equipment and carry out joint exercises in water with the coastguards and CROSSMA. All the equipment in the world cannot overcome the shared danger, the hairline between life and death standing on deck as the lifeboat tosses and turns even on a calm day. The rail is as thin as the rope around the deck, the yellow suits are awash with spray; yet these indomitable little craft and crews can haul a hundred shipwrecked mariners aboard in seas so high they mask the sky, pitching and tossing the little boat 20 feet. And still they volunteer. The days may have gone when wives and horses hauled the boats up the shingle banks of Dungeness but not the dangers for those whose motto is 'Die we may, go we must'.

There are not too many lifeboat stations now where the familiar slipway launch is the prelude to a rescue.

This affection for the familiar here in Britain has led to a fierce barracking at recent modernization of the service. This has meant the closing of many of the small one-man stations and much more centralization to meet the needs of new technology. But especially in the West Country where fishermen feel that these cuts will cost lives, communities feel a great sense of loss. There have been petititons to 'Save our Coastguard' as far round as Newhaven in Sussex.

A few of the professionals themselves, who now work in the glass-cocooned warmth of such space-age centres as Langdon Battery, think nostalgically of the way things were. They admit there is a natural hankering among many of them on a stormy night to be down there where the action is, cold and wet and even frightened. But that is often the luck of the auxiliary now.

There is romance and a tremendous sense of power, of course, in their new role. For today's Coastguard is not solely a muscle man. He is a craftsman at the helm of a vast organization, yet sensitive as ever to any sea change, a movement of clouds, an unfamiliar shape on the horizon. Along the Channel especially, he is a magician with computers and radar with a greater responsibility to more people of all nationalities than at any time in the history of the service.

Sir William Monson, in about 1625, wrote:

> The principal thing in a pilot or coaster of our coast is to know where he is. By his first soundings his depth will give him light; and as he draws nearer the coast, either of England or Brittany, his depth will lessen, and by his lead he will take up sands by which he shall gather which of the two coasts he is upon, as also if he be shot into St George's Channel. The meanest mariner that trades to Rochelle, Bordeaux, Biscay, Portugal and Spain, knows more in this kind than the great masters and others that go to the East Indies and long voyages, because they make four or five voyages in and out of our Channel to the others' one, by which they gain daily experience of our soundings, coasts, marks on land, and the entrance of our harbours, which the others cannot do. The skill of a coaster is to know the land as soon as he shall descry it.

Reading the mariners' bible, *The Channel Pilot*, which describes every creek, every submerged sandbank, and pinpoints from the sea every church, house and factory chimney, is like looking at familiar places through the wrong side of the looking glass.

The thousands upon thousands of seaside visitors who venture no further than a day-trip in the *Skylark* have no conception of the importance to mariners, even in these days of radar, of places they take for granted. Visitors admiring Chichester Cathedral four miles from the sea can hardly be aware that its spire is clearly visible to traffic in the Channel. In the past, before the building of lighthouses, sailors depended for their lives on the existence of these 'day marks', as they were called. Windmills, even tree clumps, were protected and to remove them without replacement was an offence, and a look at some of the earlier editions of *The Pilot* takes you sailing back in history. Places like Shottenden Windmill on the Isle of Wight – 11 miles inland and 462 feet high – have long since gone. The clump of trees at Alverstoke, which the eighteenth-century Bishop of Winchester cut down, made the turning channel in Portsmouth ineffective – the famous Reculver twin towers known as the Two Sisters cost the local corporation £1260 to repair in 1807. The same year the tower of Plymouth old church was painted white because it was no longer distinguishable from surrounding buildings. Others – like Chanctonbury Ring, that mystical clump 780 feet up on the South Downs near Worthing – are eternal.

The twin towers of the ruined church at Reculver, on the site of one of the Roman forts of the Saxon Shore, are striking from the air, but even more outstanding from the sea. They are among the many sight marks used by seamen and pilots. (Aerofilms)

The ancestor of the modern pilot book was really *Wagenhaer's Atlas* of sea charts which became known simply as *Waggoner*. It was published in Britain just after the Armada, having already been a great success in Northern Europe. Before *Waggoner*, captains had managed with their own personal record of sailing instructions, called 'rutters', from the French *routiers*, and these were often passed father to son. In 1528 the first Rutter was printed in English to help coastal navigation.

Wagenhaer was extremely difficult to understand and in places reads like a modern Civil Service white paper:

> If you will enter at the east end of Wight keep the castle right against the lime-kiln that lies above Portsmouth until that Culver Cliff come within the point of the Isle, for then you shall have brought the Lime-kiln to the east end of Portsmouth which you must hold until the castle which standeth to the westward of Portsmouth do appear on the east side of the wood and then ply sometimes towards St Helen's Abbey keeping your marks in this sort, you shall then take no hurt on the Shoaldes or Sands. But if you cannot see the Lime-kiln then you shall keep the castle on the west side of Culver Cliff, until you have brought St Helen's church with out the point of the Island a ship's length. Then you freely sail; north west without danger of the Riffe or tail sand that lieth out. Then keep the square tower between the east end of Portsmouth and the castle until you may see the castle which standeth in the west side of Portsmouth, eastward of the wood: and so you may go inwards.

These signposts have always been, for the inshore seamen, the stepping stones to home, but for any vessel over 50 gross registered tonnage, the craft of negotiating ever-changing shoals and sandbanks, as a ship sails into harbour, has always been handed over to an independent, professional pilot who boards her for this purpose alone. The job of pilot is as old as shipping itself and his local knowledge and specialized skills are greatly respected. The Black Book of the Admiralty says:

> It is established for a custom of the sea that if a ship is lost by default of the lodeman (pilot) the mariners may, if they please, bring the lodeman to the windlass or any other place and cut off his head without the mariners being bound to answer before any judge, because the lodeman has committed high treason against his undertaking of the pilotage, and this is the judgement.

There was another reason why governments (here and abroad) preferred ships to be escorted by a local professional pilot – they did not want strangers getting to know anything of conditions that could be useful in war. The Charter of James II declares:

... and to the end, the channels, sand flats and rocks arising growing or lying in or near any of the seas or sea coast within, any of our dominions should, for the more safety and strength of our realm and kingdoms be kept secret within ourselves and altogether unknown to aliens and strangers of other nations.

The story of pilots, of day marks, lighthouses, buoys and lightships is woven inextricably into the story of Trinity House – a paternalistic and typically traditional organization whose venerable modern image is based on centuries of caring for the welfare of the mariner. It has no equivalent in France where pilots and navigational aids are the responsibility of *Phares et Belises*, which comes within the Government's Department of Transport and consists of representatives from a wide range of government departments and organizations concerned with maritime affairs. Its organization is complex and day-to-day running is the concern of the local *Services Maritimes*.

As in England, France was very slow to appreciate the value of lighthouses and it was not till Napoleon's time in 1806 that formal steps were taken and the *Services Phares et Belises* was born.

Trinity House was granted a charter in 1514 by Henry VIII, though it may have evolved from a medieval Guild of 'Godley disposed men who do bind themselves together in the love of Lord Christ in the name of the Masters and Fellows of Trinity Guild to succour from the dangers of the sea all who are beset upon the coasts of England to feed them when ahungered and athirst, to bind up their wounds and to build and light proper beacons for the guidance of mariners.'

In 1566, during the reign of Elizabeth I, the now Corporation of Trinity House was authorized 'to erect such and so many beacon signs and marks for the sea in such place or places of the seashore ... whereby the dangers may be avoided and escaped and ships the better come unto their ports without peril'.

Today, from the impressive headquarters near the Tower of London, the Master (HRH the Duke of Edinburgh), the Elder Brethren, who are elected from the Younger Brethren and carry the style Captain, and wear a full-dress Royal Naval Captain's uniform similar to that of 1880, run Trinity House. They maintain a fleet of lightships, pilot cutters, launches and a superb flagship *Patricia* and also have sole responsibility for all fixed and floating seamarks such as buoys, lighthouses and beacons. Trinity House also licenses approximately fifty per cent of pilots in Great Britain and these services are entirely self supporting, independent of tax payers' money.

Once upon a time being a pilot was tough. They lived out in the Channel on the cutters, sometimes with their wives doing the cooking, on a three-day rota, and running a cut throat race with each other to be first aboard an approaching ship. Aggravation between pilots and captains, who sometimes resented paying for the service was considerable. The pilots sailed the Channel looking for business and were frequently attacked or even kidnapped by hostile vessels.

Light towers, such as the Royal Sovereign, are not capable of being driven off station in storms and have much easier access through the helicopter deck, than the old lightships. (Barnaby)

Even today, when pilots are shore-based and on call, there is occasionally a problem. For with radar, modern aids and improved seamanship the need for such a service is sometimes questioned and some captains begrudge the cost of pilotage, so they vary in their co-operation. Climbing 60 feet up the side of a moving tanker from a bobbing launch can itself be a tricky problem and if the master is afraid and will not turn the ship around to give the pilot a lee (with calm water on one side) it can even be dangerous. Conditions are constantly changing and it is not possible for long-distance captains to keep abreast of shifting sands and changed currents; like the Managing Director of a company he must delegate. At Southampton, for instance, Cunard pay around £550 for the safe conduct of the QE2. Lack of cash has caused dredging problems so pilots must be especially diligent in their awareness of vessel loading and tide depths.

Standing with the pilot on the bridge of the QE2, or that of a Channel ferry (which may be exempt from pilotage because of the regular conditions of working), is oddly disturbing. The 65,863-ton QE2 (remember Brunel's *Great Western*? 1300 tons!) is now the only transatlantic luxury liner left. 963 feet long with a 30 foot draft – the 'wheel' by which this sleek sea monster is gracefully slid into berth, measures just a few inches. Though the chunky ferries are Dinkies by comparison, at least amongst the battery of radar screens and shiny knobs, they have something that can still justify the name of wheel! The *Royal Sovereign* lightship still named like a ship, rises provocatively from the Shards, seven miles off Eastbourne not a few miles from the best known and tested of all the lightships, the *Varne*.

The first computerization has blown out much of the romance of the lighthouses too though romance was probably only in the eye of the land-based beholder. Only twelve of the Channel lights are manned today of a total of ninety.

The rest are phantoms in the night, efficient but eerily empty, the comforting beam controlled not by a salt-caked keeper and his team but, like everything else, a land-based computer. The new flat-topped look is not the result of a gale battering. It means that relief comes by helicopter instead of by small boat through angry seas. The fog horn is electric. It is all very efficient but a new kind of poetry will have to be found to replace the old ...

It's not one gale, it's not two gales, it's not twenty gales tied together by their tails that frightens you. It's what comes after, when the wind's had two or three days to put a thousand miles of ocean into motion and turn it into what's called a heavy ground sea. That's what makes you afraid. It rolls the boulders along with it that are down there on the sea bed; and when it strikes them against the base of your tower the whole place quivers from its top to its toe. You can hear them, you can feel them, thump, thump, thump being thrown like that under the water against the foundation, rolling into it one after the other and making the tower shake with it too like all your teeth are going to be rattled out of your head. On and on it goes, on and on. And each one you feel you think it can't take one more thump like that, the next one for certain will be the one that'll bring the place down with a crash and that'll be the end. He'll have to have that experience to teach him to know the meaning of fear.

Channel lighthousekeeper from Lighthouse
Tony Parker

St Catherine's Oratory at Chale on the southernmost tip of the Isle of Wight was built as a lighthouse in the 14th century. The priest tended the brazier and prayed for those lost at sea. (Topham)

The first known lighthouse was the fifth wonder of the Ancient World, the Pharos at Alexandria. Built in 285 BC its beam shone from a 512-foot high tower over thirty miles of Mediterranean. Most of the Channel coasts remained in northern darkness throughout their early history. We know the Romans built a candle-powered Pharos on the cliffs of Dover because its shell is still there. But when attempts were first made to put some kind of warning beacons further west, to protect the fishing and merchant fleet, the efforts met with considerable medieval opposition. There was fear amongst villagers that lights would attract pirates and also might cut the number of foreign wrecks to plunder.

Originally lighthouses were privately owned with a view to extracting profit from passing ships. Although the very first Trinity House charter gave the owners some jurisdiction over the position and care of lights they did not win full control till the reign of William IV. In 1570 King James I granted a patent to Sir John Killigrew to build a lighthouse on the notorious Lizard Point overlooking the Manacles but local opposition was such that the idea was dropped.

The Manacles are a menacing reef of submerged rocks running out to sea. They rise, like stalagmites sheer from the sea bed, their teeth just breaking, dark and shiny through the swirling waters around the Lizard. If any place sends shivers down the hardiest sailor's spine, this is it. The claws of England – Land's End and the Lizard – have relentlessly crushed thousands upon thousands of helpless craft in their grip. Not till 1830 did bodies washed onto this coast have a consecrated burial, before that they were left to sink in the sand or be returned whence they had come. For this reason the coast was, so it was said, haunted by the ghosts of sailors condemned to wander through the stormy nights.

'There was a night in the eighteenth century when several hundred bodies were flung up into the crevices and leafless trees of a cove which is now known as Pistol Cove. The local folk beat off packs of savage dogs as they tried to bury the dead soldiers in improvised pits.' Wilkie Collins, the Victorian thriller writer, described the place and how when he walked through farmyard after farmyard he found no dogs, for they had since been outlawed by the villagers. One hundred years after that Daphne Du Maurier went looking for the place and found 'a small enclosure set about with stumpy willows, grotesquely shaped by the prevailing wind, the ground hussocky and rough …

*The original Eddystone
Lighthouse of 1698 reflected
the eccentricities of its designer,
Henry Winstanley, who died
when a storm swept away the
lighthouse in 1703 while he
was supervising repairs. The
second lighthouse, by Rudyerd,
had a simple design and
withstood the waves until
1755 when the oak tower
burned down. Smeaton's
tower, preserved at Plymouth
Hoe, was built of dovetailed
stone blocks and was replaced
because it was not high enough
and was being undermined by
the sea. Douglass's tower is
still in place today over 104
years after its inauguration on
May 18th 1882. (Below,
Ann Ronan; top left,
Picturepoint; top right, Ann
Ronan; bottom left, Ann
Ronan; bottom right, Mary
Evans)*

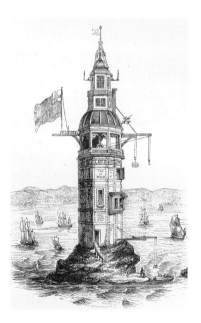

perhaps, as Wilkie Collins said, wild flowers grew here once and in his day, before the stumpy willows formed, the mound of the pit would have shown, now sunken with a century of winter rains. It was peaceful, untroubled, better than many other resting places for sleeping soldiers.'

Fifty years after Sir John Killigrew's death, his ancestor, another Sir John, tried again. His motives were not, like many lighthouse owners, those of gain. Trinity House itself advised against the granting of a patent, but because Sir John was a friend of the Lord High Admiral, work went ahead despite tremendous problems recruiting a labour force from hostile locals. In 1619 work was completed at a total cost of £500, and the coal fires were kindled at his expense for 10 shillings a night. Even so, despite the decrease in wrecks, ship owners refused to pay their dues even when the King himself decreed a halfpenny per ton toll on all vessels passing the Lizard. Eventually the light was pulled down and Sir John died a disappointed and impoverished man.

The first of the classic rock lighthouses was the Eddystone, standing on its pinhead outrock some thirteen miles off Plymouth. The light was first lit in 1698, and blown down by something rather fiercer than an 'eddy' in the great gale of 1703. That original creation, standing in the Channel like a fantasy from the inventive imagination of Heath Robinson, was little more than a folly – the weird imagining of the eccentric Charles Winstanley, showman extraordinaire and practical joker. The Eddystone was no practical joke and its conception resulted in a momentary Anglo-French rapprochement. Because France and England were at war while the lighthouse was being built, the Admiralty provided Winstanley with a protective warship but a French privateer attacked it, kidnapped Winstanley and took him to France. Remarkably, he was released on the orders of Louis XIV on the grounds that 'France is at War with England, not with humanity'.

Winstanley died, with his dream, during the great storm because he had insisted on being present himself to carry out urgent repairs caused by the gales. The building and its occupants disappeared without trace in the night in November 1703. He had established the principle that the apparently impossible can be achieved. Since then there have been only four lighthouses on the Eddystone Rock, the third of which, made of stone and based on the shape of the English oak, has now been re-erected on Plymouth Hoe. Today's building, constructed in 1882, has gone the way of so many and is no longer manned. Instead a light vessel, which proudly bears its name, is anchored one mile to the south-west.

There are others whose names shine like their lights over the pages of history and are as well known inland as they are to the men who owe their lives to them – Beachy Head, Dungeness, South Foreland.

Of all the Channel lighthouses, that which stands on the cruelly submerged 'Dover Rocks' off the coast of Brittany is most aptly named. Thirty miles offshore, it is the remotest lighthouse in Europe and probably symbolizes more than any other the possible peaks of

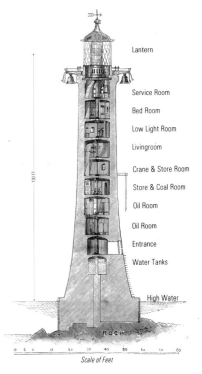

Lantern

Service Room

Bed Room

Low Light Room

Livingroom

Crane & Store Room

Store & Coal Room

Oil Room

Oil Room

Entrance

Water Tanks

High Water

ROCK

Scale of Feet

275

Anglo-French co-operation. The present Phare des Roches Douvres, which is 74 metres in circumference and 285 metres high was opened in 1955 and is the third of its name. The first was built in 1867, tombstone of innumerable wrecks about which Victor Hugo wrote:

> Aux roches Douvres, personne,
> Les Oiseaux de mer sont la chez eux …
> Des Roches Douvres on ne voit rien
> tel est l'isolement de ce rocher.
> Tout autour l'immense tourment des flots
> la rafale, l'eau, la nuit l'illimite, l'inhabite
> C'est la haute mer!

The second marked the northern limit of German naval activity during the War and was manned by the French under German direction. The light broke down suspiciously often, due, said the Germans, to poor French engineering – not, as was really the case on one occasion, to a spot of acid poured surreptitiously onto the electrical wiring by a French mechanic.

Escaping airmen were smuggled out by the Resistance to waiting ships and these had to pass the Roches Douvres, three hours out, on their way home. One night in 1944 the sea stole its victims from under the German nose when the corvette which had picked them up was smashed to pieces on the rocks of Douvres.

A plaque was set into the cliffs above the Plage Bonaparte at L'Anse Cochat, Brittany on 23rd June 1946. The carving shows an aeroplane in flames, a royal naval corvette number 503 *en route* for Dartmouth, and beneath it the legend 'In memory of 23 members of the Shelburn resistance team who died for France and of the crew of the British corvette 503 who died at sea.'

On the day in 1955 when the new third lighthouse was lit, writer Remy reflected in his book, *la Maison d'Alphonse*:

> I dreamt of those icy cold nights and gales in the winter of 1944 when the resistance team led escaping British airmen to the Plage Bonaparte so that they could get back to England and rejoin their regiment, and who were then taken out to the corvette offshore at L'Anse Cochat and the sea was there as it was at the Roches Douvres; this magnificent terrible sea, this treacherous cruel sea which would one day engulf the corvette 503 with her entire crew. Men change … wars pass but the elements remain …

The poetic drama of shipwreck, the terrible beauty, the shrieking winds, the crash of a hull on rock, the cries of drowning men has never been more sensitively and movingly recorded than by four generations of the Gibson family from the Scillies. Of course the Scillies

themselves are Atlantic islands, but the Gibsons' work has ranged around the Cornish coasts from the 1860s to the present recording 'the failed hopes, ventures and destinies ... the shattered monuments to countless generations of anonymous shipwrights and sailmakers, as tragic in their way as the vanished masterpieces of great sculptors' (John Fowles, *Shipwreck*). They tell of the insatiable public fascination with drama and disaster and the ghoulish thrill of tragedy and capture that moment in the story before the vultures swoop. For wrecks have always been a source of immense wealth both to the people eagerly scavenging along the shores on which the ships had foundered by fair means or foul, and to the official, organized and highly profitable salvage companies.

The wreck of the Noisiel caught between the claws of the Lizard and Land's End on Praa Sands in 1905. (Topham)

The Channel is a greedy sea and the stripped bones of a million ships have been sucked down into its cold dark waters. Through the centuries treasure hunters have explored their murky hulks and many have struck gold – sovereigns, jewellery and mementoes of a more personal nature.

Officially cargo from any wreck discovered in British waters below high water mark and within the three-mile limit should be reported to the Receiver of Wrecks in the nearest port. It is his job to locate the owner of any such objects and of the Customs Officer (often the same man) to check for customs Import Duty. So it is that undrinkable 'vintage' wine, maybe 200 years old, is processed in the same way as surplus plonk from the booze cruise.

After a year the Receiver must, by law, try to sell unclaimed goods, retaining 7½%, plus expenses. An excavation licence is required to disturb the sea bed or remove artifacts from a protected wreck but the sea cannot be patrolled all the time and so unofficial wreck hunting very often goes unchallenged, and is the bane of the marine archaeologists' lives.

Purists believe that such priceless treasure should be kept together, belonging to the nation and not become a source of personal profit. It is a grey area for there are also respected professional wreck hunters who finance expeditions from the sales of their discoveries. In Plymouth there is a reputable firm of auctioneers dealing in shipwreck treasure. A local patriot even auctioned the contents of his home to stop a £7,500 cannon from the Church Rocks Wreck being sold to America.

Even a tombstone can become a centre of curious debate. Sussex divers recently lifted a nineteenth-century memorial to a young mother and her thirteen-month-old baby from a Danish ship bound for the Virgin Islands. Their descendents requested the right to remove it from Britain and erect it, 200-years late, on the grave.

The complex and highly skilled work of salvage – as opposed to archaeological recovery – is set about with the problems of international maritime law and insurance claims, and is based on the principle established by Lloyds in 1893 'no cure – no pay'. So the stakes are high, and though a salvage company is in business for profit and may do well from another's misfortune, it also stands to lose. To some extent its work is parasitical but were it not for the salvage companies the Channel would be a far more dangerous place littered with submerged hazards and polluted by spilled cargo.

Archaeology is a form of salvage in retrospect. In the quest for knowledge it depends largely on the goodwill of commercial sponsors and government help and, though in the long term the rescue of historic wrecks brings profit through tourism, there is no sharing of trophies between those on the job.

Easily the most exciting of the Channel's great marine archaeological triumphs were the raising of Henry VIII's flagship *Mary Rose* from the grey waters of the Solent after 437 years and the gradual releasing from the sands at Bulverhythe of the Dutch merchant ship the *Amsterdam*.

The drama of the *Mary Rose* is well known. She was located in 1967 by a Portsmouth historian Alexander McKee who was the first to swim along her gun deck and see the sailors' skeletons still lying in their uniforms. His was the enthusiasm and determination which first set the project on its feet before it became a multi-million pound, international enterprise. The *Mary Rose* was a war ship full of probably useless gimmicks – a show piece. Her sinking was watched by a sixteenth-century weeping King and her raising was watched by several million television viewers and her submarine remains were explored by the enterprising twentieth-century Prince of Wales.

The *Amsterdam* was a merchant ship *en route* for the Dutch East Indies, which was blown onto the sands of Sussex in as 'violent a storm of wind as had been known in the memory of man'. The mutinous crew, drunk on the many thousands of bottles of Dutch gin and French wine on board, forced Captain Klump to beach the vessel in the hope that when the storm abated she would be refloated. But the *Amsterdam* sank into the sands of Bulverhythe in 1749, never to rise again. She is only one of nine historic wrecks lying at tide level, and visible at certain times, on the sands between Camber and Cuckmere Haven.

Modern Bulverhythe is a desultory, nowhere place; its low reddish cliffs and wave-battered promenade offset by lace-curtained beach huts overlook a bleak, shingly beach. This unmarked, wild spot was the place where William I landed (the stone upon which he is reputed to have eaten his first picnic in England is set unceremoniously outside Bexhill). Bolewarthethe, the landing place of the citizens, was an important limb of the Cinque Ports. It had a small harbour with a pier and wharves and was the execution place for local felons. All that has been washed away by heavy tides.

The Amsterdam, *caught, and preserved, in the sands of Bulverhythe on the afternoon of Sunday, January 26th, 1749. On the afternoon of Saturday, August 11th, 1979, the long process of resurrection and restoration begins.* (Barnaby)

It was not a place to draw the cheek by jowl crowds away from Hastings, until a combined team of Dutch and British archaeologists revealed that the curious ribs of a huge wreck that protruded from the sands at certain tides were those of one of Europe's most important sites. For, amazingly, when the *Amsterdam* ran aground with a loss of 68 crew, her cargo was never salvaged. The ship is said to have been 'loaded with money, bale goods [cloth], stores of all kinds of gold and silver, lace and wearing apparel and a great many thousand dozen bottles of wine'. It has lain protected in the sand all these years, an unprecedented record of eighteenth-century life and commerce, for when the great ship foundered she sank into a thick, clay layer just below the surface of the sand which poured into her hold. The tree roots which can now be seen on her eastern side are part of the forest which grew here at a time when the sea level was lower. Early seventeenth-century maps show an island here which is no longer marked in the eighteenth century.

What happened that night of the *Amsterdam*'s demise has been vividly recorded in a series of contemporary letters to the five-times Mayor of Hastings, John Collier, and include an account of the disgraceful weeks afterwards.

Sunday last in the afternoon a Dutch East Indiamen was drove a Shore at Bulverhith, and yesterday I rode down to see her, & from one of her Officers who spoke a little English I had this acct, that she was called the *Amsterdam*, of that place and Bound for Batavia, avt 700 Tons & 52 Guns & had when she came out avt two Months agoe Three hundred men, abt halfe of w'ch had been lost by Sickness & washed over Board, & loaded with money, Bale Goods, & Stores of all kinds. She was a new Ship, and had been all this time beating abt & never got beyond Beachy in her way. She struck in Pevensy Bay & lost her Rudder, and has laid of Bexhill at Anchor Severall days's. Some of the Hastings people got to her & undertook to Carry her to Portsmouth when the wheather would permit, But she could hold out no longer than Sunday.

She stands in a good place, & in appearance quite whole, & may do so for some months. But no possibility of getting her off. I Believe they will Save every thing that is worth Saveing, to the Great Disappointm't of the wreckers who come from all parts of the Country for plunder, there was yesterday: when I was there more than a thousand of these wretches with long poles and hooks at the Ends.

But all the Soldiers on the Coast are there, & Behave well at present – they keep the Country people off, & their officers keep the Soldiers to rights. They have Carried to the Custom house at Hasting 27 chests of money, & the other pt of her Ladeing will be Carried to Hasting as fast as it can be got out. One Chest was Emptied of its money by somebody, and, as it's said, was so before it came out of the Ship. But it's gone, by whome is not known.

I could get no certain acct of the quantity of money, some said threescore thousand pounds, others made it a great deal more, & others much less. The value of the Ship & Cargoe is uncertain, but two hundred thousand pounds was the general Estimate. There was three women on boards, who are now at Hasting. When I was down there were then abt forty Sick Men in the ship, w'ch they afterwards got out and sent to Hasting. I saw Sir Chs. Eversfield there, who told me he was down when she came on Shore, and that all the crew were Drunk, & so were all of them that I saw yesterday.

Letter from Mr George Worge to Mr Collier
28 January 1749 (two days after wreck)

I doubt not but you have had successive accounts of the Dutch Ship run ashore near Bulverhith, since which the care of the Sick Dutchmen, the plague of Quartering Soldiers, their & others thieving, has engrossed my whole time. This happening so soon after the *Nympha*, has destroyed the Morals & Honesty of too many of our Country men, for the very people hired to save did little else but steal. The Hoo people came in a Body, and carried off Velvette, Cloth &c. but on Warrants being issued, they submit to deliver all again. One of them stopped a waggon & called others to his assistance to rob it. I committed him to Gaol, & have since gott Mr Nicoll to take the Examinations again, and he has made His Mittimus for Horsham.

The Treasure of the Ship, amounting to nearly thirty thousands pounds value, being sent to London has eased us of a Company of Foot, who were the greatest Thieves I ever knew, they not only robbed at their ship, but their Quarters also. The Dutch Soldiers & Sailors robbed their Officers, as did too many of our own Town.

There was a Chest containing fifty Wedges of Silver, each weighing about four pounds & a half, broke open the first night, but by one means or another we have recovered thirty six & a gold watch, but a very little of the Gold & Silver Lace and wearing apparel. There are some Cables & Anchors, some Provisions, as Butter, Bacon, Beef &c. saved, also several Chests of Wine in Bottles, of which there is in the Ship a great many Thousand Dozen.

The Ship is so swerved in the Sand, that at high Water the Sea covers her, and at low, her lower Deck is under Water. They have endeavoured to blow up her Decks with Gunpowder, sometimes succeeding, at others not, the Powder being obliged to be putt under Water, but this Morning they blew up a great part of the lower Deck, and its thought the composition next the

Match being too dry, fired so quick that Mr Nutt the Engineer
perished . . .
P.S. The wine is French – if you would have any, please to let
me know, I fancy about one shilling a bottle will be the price.
Letter from Mr William Thorpe, Mayor of Hasting to Mr Collier
5 March 1749 (38 days after wreck)

Some of the survivors were sheltered in the isolated smugglers'
haunt the New England Bank Inn, with its winding path to the beach
and easy access to Bulverhithe Salts. The New England Bank was
demolished to make way for the London, Brighton and South Coast
Railways in 1854, but its cellars were re-discovered during building
works recently, with evidence on the walls of those shipwrecked
mariners. Others went to Filsham House, now a private house, where
they carved their names in the barn, unaware that in the secret passage
beneath them dogs were pulling carts laden with the pillagings of their
ship.

The Nautical Museums Trust is opening a Shipwreck Heritage
museum in Hastings. Visitors will be able to watch Channel traffic,
learn the romantic story of shipwreck and discover something of the
work of Trinity House and HM Coastguard's search which, hopefully, will ensure that archaeologists of the future will have fewer
trophies to find!

Ashore and Afloat:
the Channel Today

The English Channel is, so they say, the most expensive ferry crossing in the world. Would that the cost, around £3 a mile, always matched the comfort of *Concorde*, at about 34p a mile over the Atlantic. Although the British have so monopolized this strip of water they have, until recently, treated its crossing as an endurance test to be borne rather than enjoyed. Only in the last 10 years, under the watchful eye of the advertising men, have the ferry companies realized the potential pleasure in the journey itself and begun to woo the travelling public of Europe and Britain, and, just as important today, freight drivers who represent 26 per cent of traffic. Never before have there been so many perks to offset the horrendous price which they excuse on grounds of the seasonal nature of business. Each ferry has developed its own image and competes frenetically for custom. Choosing between them can be an adventure in itself, varying not only from company to company, but from ship to ship. It is not easy to create the atmosphere of the *Beau Monde* amongst a boatload of classless passengers in jeans, chip-hunting school-children and coachloads of over-indulged football fans and booze cruisers. But they are, at last, doing their best, and over 13 million people crossed from Dover in 1985. In the next ten years they will have to do even better in the face of competition from the Tunnel.

For much of the twentieth century the 'cattle trucks', as they were less than affectionately called, herded their long-suffering human cargo backwards and forwards over 'seas so rough', according to Jerome K. Jerome 'passengers had to be tied to their berths'. No wonder the French did not bother; they never had the same masochism as the British and the media men of the English Tourist Board were not yet at work on the French vision of the 'offshore island'.

Between the two World Wars services were chaotic and timetables unpredictable. According to Richard Garrett, a writer specializing in transport history, in the second class accommodation there were 'variety artists who had not made the top of the bill, commercial travellers with tired faces and shiny serge blue suits, returning seamen, hard up tourists and people being repatriated at someone else's expense. The gentry and members of the better-heeled classes had first class tickets. Many of them could afford the luxury of private cabins where they could drink champagne and suffer the torments of seasickness in private.'

It was just this shambolic neglect and inefficiency at a time when, by contrast, the luxurious Cunarders and the French *Normandie* and *France* were palm-courting their way over the Atlantic, which provoked a 'nice distinguished army type', Captain Stuart Townsend, to take matters into his own hands in 1926. His car was damaged during the crane loading and after many years of Channel use he suddenly felt enough was enough. After all, before loading, cars had to be drained of petrol, for which there was no compensation. The crane crews demanded tips all round, and for every car carried, passenger space was lost. He was sure he could do better. He did. The story is well-known.

He chartered a collier during the summer of 1928 with a capacity for 15 cars and 12 drivers, which still meant separating many passengers from their vehicles, and taking them by coach to the Southern Rail mail boat. But by undercutting the Southern Railway fare, by half, and permitting petrol to remain in the tanks, Mr Townsend's enterprise was popular. In the first year he made a profit of £50. Within the next two years the Southern Railway were forced to compete by reducing fares and then in 1930 the Townsend family bought a minesweeper *en route* for the breakers yard, renamed her *Force*, and converted her into the first purpose-designed car carrier, with room for 30 vehicles and 168 passengers. During that year she carried some five thousand cars chained under cover on deck and ventilated by fans. The twelve thousand drivers and their families travelled either at the forward end of the main deck or in the saloon. It was still no joy ride, but motorists were delighted if they could blot out the noise and dream away the journey in the cocooned comfort of their sleeper, and wake to coffee and croissants some hours later. It is a reflection of the 'poor relation' attitude to progress on the Channel that that minesweeper was still working in 1961 by which time jet aircraft were flying travellers around the world.

At the same time Southern Railway were about to achieve their dream, of a train which could be boarded at Victoria, shunted onto the boat at Dover and straight off at the other end. Efforts had been made since about 1889, after the building of the Eiffel Tower, to provide a luxury service for the rich between London and Paris, but somehow the rail part of the journey was always marred by the discomfort of the boat. Not until 1930 did the French give birth to a sadly brief period of stylish romance in cross-Channel travel, when the *Fleche d'Or* steamed away from the Gare du Nord towards Calais. She was made entirely of British-built Pullman cars and run by the *Compagnie Internationale des Wagon Lits des Grands Express Europeéns*. This was travel at its most dignified, cream and brown best. Three years later the Southern Railway produced her sister the *Golden Arrow* and these two great trains were linked by a specially-built ferry the *Canterbury*, a vision in studded leather and mahogany with a shiny brass class of her own. This was the age of the boat train. The pleasure of her company was expensive, but almost anyone who was anyone travelled in her, from

King Edward to Charlie Chaplin. Alas such exclusivity was not commercially viable and the time came when the Pullman had to be supplemented by simpler carriages for lesser mortals.

The very best service aboard the present generation of Channel ferries. (Townsend Thoresen)

After the Second World War everything was different. The Channel ports had been devastated. Plymouth, Southampton, Le Havre, Calais were flattened. France had lost heart and took longer to rally her spirits, so the south coast ports got off to a head start. Southern Rail became part of British Railways with Sealink as its shipping division. Competition grew between state and privately owned ferries. Sealink UK was privatized in 1984 and became Sealink British Ferries.

When Townsend's boat *Force* returned to service, cars still had to be craned on board at Dover, but at Calais there was a ramp so that they could be driven off through the newly cut doors in her side and up the ramp to the quayside. British Rail followed suit with the *Dinard* and then in 1950 Townsend launched the first drive-on drive-off vessel, hard pressed by BR's *Lord Warden* in December 1951. The *Lord Warden* could take 700 passengers and 120 cars and, joy, she had stabilizers. In 1965 came Townsend's first purpose-built car ferry and in 1965 the *Free Enterprise II* was the first drive-through ferry.

In 1066 when William I brought his Normans to Bulverhythe the native population of Britain totalled a few thousand. By 1956 it had reached 49.2 million and for the first time in its history the Channel offered a temporary escape route for masses of ordinary people on holidays-with-pay, daringly eager to sample the gastronomic delights and sanitary dangers of Europe. It was a curiousity not shared by the French for whom rumours of British weather, wine famine, draughty houses and tea with everything, proved altogether too much. So they stayed at home.

285

It is tempting to look backwards and lament 'nostalgia is not what it used to be'. Things have moved so fast in the last twenty years. The ghosts of the dear, dead days are there still at the Admiralty Pier end of Dover Harbour where everything has the musty smell of Victorian history. Even reminders of those heady forward-looking days after the Second World War can bring a lump to the middle-aged throat of those who, as the first excited tidal wave of ruck-sacked youth, faced a brave new world over the water. There could be no going back, and it all had to change to match the needs of an unimaginably large and sun-seeking public. But the past is never completely forgotten and growth is often built upon it.

The subdued lights and carpeted pillars of the former P & O ferry *Leopard*, now operated by Townsend, for instance, curiously echoes the spa-town elegance of her cruising ancestors. Gone are the cane chairs, the geraniums, the open fires and the deck games. In their place videos, television and the plastic props of a utilitarian age. But on the *Leopard* at least, the comfort and paternalistic care that character-ized the big, ocean liners has been grafted on to the more humble ferry.

It is surprising to find that one of the world's major ship owners once dabbled in the Channel. P & O began as the Peninsular and Oriental Steam Navigation Company in 1837 and soon became the Peninsular and Oriental Steam Company travelling through the Suez Canal to the East and the Panama Canal to the west. The red and yellow of Spain quartered with the blue and white of Portugal which flew on every P & O boat were a reminder of the founder's support for their Royal Houses during the civil wars of the early 1830s. In those gracious days when the 'sun never set' first class Poona-bound passengers left England Port side Out, Starboard side Home (hence POSH) in order to avoid the blistering heat of Egypt.

Not until 1967 did the company turn its attention to the short haul and, with a French partner, begin Normandy Ferries. The Dover Calais service opened in competition with Townsend and British Rail in 1976 and by 1979 as P & O held ninety per cent of the shares the French connection was dropped. Just about the same time Brittany Ferries was being founded at the neglected western end of the Channel.

By this time Townsend had been bought by the late Keith Wickenden who merged with a Scandinavian company to form Townsend Thoresen European Ferries. The turnover then was £100,000, today it is nearer £309.4 million.

In 1984 P & O Ferries were bought by Townsend Thoresen, and then there were three: Townsend, Sealink and Brittany Ferries. Three, that is, within the Channel limits. But in the meantime, just around the corner, where the Channel/North Sea boundaries are blurred, there was a new invasion, across seas once furrowed by the dragon ships of Vieul the Viking. Sally, the Viking Line, a Finnish 'upstart', by comparison with the others began operating from Ramsgate to Dunkerque in 1982 and in 1986 introduced what they claim is the most luxurious craft running between England and France. It would be churlish to be pedantic about their claim to Channel fame because the route they have chosen is inextricably awash with history. It skirts, excitingly, the Goodwin Sands, slipping away from Margate through parallel lines of marker buoys that make embarkation feel like a slalom course. On a spring tide and a clear day, travellers may spot the mast of one who did not make it but there is, luckily, little to indicate the menace of the treacherous shallow waters. The crew of the two Sally vessels have mostly learned their craft on larger, deeper, faraway seas but are drawn to the capricious nature of the Channel where the mood can switch from millpond calm to gale force in an hour.

The approaches to Dunkerque would be unrecognizable now to the retreating men of 1940 for the new harbour and vast area of reclaimed polder have desecrated that wild shoreline, 13 km away from the town itself.

The free enterprise versus state control wrangle has no end, but certainly whilst there is an option there is variety and, for better or worse, each ferry company has its memorable idiosyncracies. The Captain's fruit bowls, potted plants and bathroom scales on the bridge reflect the smaller personal quality of the line, which also lays on the most provocatively sumptuous, unending *smørgåsbord*. Better indeed that fings ain't what they used, pre-stabilizers, to be!

The acorns from which great oaks grow can sometimes be a very curious shape. The prototype of the Hovercraft was cobbled together in the early 1950s from two cat food tins, a vacuum cleaner nozzle and a pair of kitchen scales, by an inventive genius known as the 'father of the helicopter', now Sir Christopher Cockerell. It looked rather like a flying saucer and was derided by shipbuilders and aircraft manufacturers alike. Eventually Christopher Cockerell won the backing of the National Research Development Council and after that everyone wanted to get in on the act.

The first flight of the SRN1 Mark 1 took place in the shallow waters off East Cowes on the Isle of Wight and on June 25th, 1959 the craft made its first cross-Channel journey to mark the anniversary of Blériot's crossing.

Since those nail-biting days in home waters this Channel baby has grown up to perform amazing feats of adaptability in terrain all over the world from deserts to ice packs. But for users of its native waters, the Channel, it is still the 'alternative' way of getting to France and back. Most of the early problems have been overcome and today rough seas rarely halt a flight; for Hovercraft travel is akin to flying and this is the image the companies try to promote. Hoverspeed staff are uniformed hostesses, passengers are welcomed on board by the pilot who tells them of likely conditions during the trip. It is still noisy, but quick, at 60 mph and 6 feet above the waves the usual time between Dover and Calais or Boulogne is forty-five minutes.

There was, it seems, a French hovercraft some years ago, but it sank, without trace, and without successors.

The Onion Johnnie, like the knife grinder and the hurdy-gurdy man before, will soon cycle his way into the photograph albums of memory. Every August there are just one or two who pop their old, black bicycles into a truck and make the crossing to Portsmouth or maybe Plymouth; hardly a handful remaining from an annual invasion of hundreds who once poured into the coastal towns *en route* for the valleys of Wales, the Midlands, London and even the North of England.

The first record of an onion seller in Britain appears in 1350 when the Exeter customs rolls note the sale of *'onions et peaux de boeufs'* from St Pol de Leon near Roscoff. It was not until the nineteenth century, however, after the repeal of the Navigation Acts, that the onion sellers were part of the south coast scene. They were remarkable men, inspired originally by one Henri Ollivier, a peasant sailor who spoke only Breton and who braved all hazards on the twelve-hour crossing to take his produce to Britain. The golden age of the onion seller was the period between the wars when conditions were better and sometimes 'Mrs. Onions' came too, though curiously enough the independent-minded Johnnies were none too pleased about this development. They left their wives to spend the winter, often without water or gas, in derelict premises, empty sheds, old school rooms. They cooked, ate and slept like this, a lonely isolated life with little cheer and no wine. At their peak they could shift 12 tonnes of onions in six months – a talent that came to be known as a 'bell breaker'.

The special quality of the Roscoff onion was due to the local seaweed-enriched soil. For the people of Brittany, the *'recolte des guems'* – the annual beach harvest – was, and still is, woven into the pattern of their lives. At this time the lanes around are blocked by trundling horses and carts laden with the bronzy produce of the beaches. They lay it on the land by hand, as they still do most things in Brittany – sewing, weeding or harvesting, helped only by their horses.

But today's seaweed fertilizes the soil for a very different scale of agriculture. Though the peasants still own small strip farms of under twenty acres a family, they feed their produce into a central co-operative which, because of its more efficient marketing and distribution, can make more money for the individual. In return the stubborn *'têtu'* Breton farmer is subject to stringent standards which he does not always like – standards demanded by British chain stores. And

because the British are now growing their own onions, most of the men, and their sons, who would, a few years ago, have left home for six months in the year to make a reasonable living pedalling hundreds of miles a week on their *'gabarres'* are now driving juggernauts loaded with shallots to Covent Garden for Brittany's revitalized, computer-ized agricultural co-operatives. The exquisite, more subtle, taste of the shallot has been loved in Europe since Roman times, but is a recent export across the Channel, along with artichokes and cauliflowers.

The Onion Johnnie, with his rosy red strings, is a pungently symbolic link in the story of the *désenclavement de la Bretagne* and the changing face of freight. How extraordinary that in this long-suffering land with its roots in the culture of standing stones, and fairies, the road from Morlaix to St Pol passes the most modern market in Europe. There is not a vegetable in sight within the complex – which looks very like a four-star hotel – where buyers congregate for the day's business. This

Breton onions now come to Britain in containers and are bought in supermarkets. Fresh onions, bought on the doorstep off the bike, probably did taste better. (Barnaby)

is mission control, with an overpowering aroma of Gauloises. Each buyer is poised, finger on the button set into his desk, mouth by microphone and telephone, waiting for the computers to start the bidding. In front is an array of clocks and dials which report the produce available (probably phoned in by the farmer that morning), the prices and the bidding which is all done by the press of the button. Overlooking it all behind a glass panel as big as a cinema screen are the staff who record bids and buyers, and inform farmers of the day's proceedings. If the produce is destined for Britain, it will be on the overnight crossing to Plymouth and in the London supermarkets the next day.

Maybe most remarkable of all in this story of Breton revival, for a region not renowned for its go-getting, is the way it all came about. It was through the Economic Committee of Brittany that road systems were improved and the ferry company founded, which was not only to carry produce out, but bring visitors in. Brittany Ferries is the only French ferry company for a century that has lasted more than ten years, and it was started with the specific intention of integrating the marketing of people, places and produce. The booming success of the freight and tourist traffic has been responsible for the capital input behind the prosperity of Breton agriculture.

'Every time the Bretons have turned their back on the sea they have been poor. Every time they have worked with the sea they have become rich', says the Company Chairman. So just as the old ways in farming have been harnessed to new techniques so it is elsewhere. To survive, Brittany like so many other places, must market its wares '– and one of these is your English Channel'.

Without Brittany Ferries the region around Roscoff today would probably be a desert. Roscoff traders view the resulting influx of English tourists with some cynicism, since they feel abused by the visitors who spend little money and rush on to somewhere else. But since there are few restaurants and the guns on the church point at England, maybe it is not surprising!

In 1973 a converted tank landing craft left the newly-built deep-water ferry port at Roscoff with a number of freight vehicles carrying vegetables direct to the British market. But as on the banana boats and tramp steamers of old there was a demand for passenger accommodation on the return journey to the remote and exciting coast of Celtic France.

'We decided to open up the old Celtic trading routes through the Channel between Brittany and Cornwall, Brittany and Ireland and Britain and Spain. But talking with the teachers in schools we wanted to awaken a sense of history in the children of those countries to make them aware of their roots – and by encouraging this interest to bring them together'. From this simple start sprang the building companies, the travel organizations, the car hire company, all linked with Brittany Ferries. Much of the credit for the 750,000 visitors who pour into *gites, pensions* and camp sites of Brittany from Cornwall and Devon belong to the company that appropriately bears its name and whose roots are in the red soil of the Roscoff onion. The numbers of French who pour across in the opposite direction is, needless to say, fewer. The Bretons are comparatively poor still, and Roscoff is not on the route for anywhere they want to go – let alone Plymouth.

A pity really, for Plymouth, the host port in Devon, has been the magnificent, theatrical setting for British naval history and the curtain has almost never been rung down. There are more than forty Plymouths around the world – how can the world accuse Britain of insularity! The city has two rivers, the Tamar, that great divide between Britain and Cornwall, and the Plym. The Tamar provides a six mile long, deep water harbour entered through a narrow 500-yard opening, which is now protected by the extraordinary free-flying seawall, three miles long, built by Sir John Rennie in 1841. The Plym runs into a small enclosed harbour on the superb natural anchorage of the Sound. Plymouth suffered the destruction of 43 churches, 26 schools and the death of over 1000 people in 1941, during the last war, but even that did not deter this proud city and a sensitive rebuilding programme has been carried out.

The original Plymouth that Leland called 'a mene thing' was a small harbour at the mouth of the Plym, on what is now Sutton Harbour. The dockyard and arsenal were developed in the seventeenth century at Dock and Stonehouse and, in 1914, all three were merged to become the single borough of Plymouth. The oldest street, New Street, and its cobbles, survived the Blitz, as have many of the ancient houses. From on shore modern Plymouth is a spectacular city of wide avenues and fine architecture defiantly guarding a wild and remotely rocky coastline.

Above all Plymouth is a working, naval city dominated by naval presence at all times; the sprawl of housing estates that have eaten their way into the Dartmoor hinterland around the old city are almost entirely occupied by the Navy. The dock area with its ominous mountain of rusting debris from the Falklands War is growing all the time and the future looks as rosy as the onions that waft in on the *Armorique* or the *Cornaille*.

The presence of the Royal Navy in the Channel is very much in evidence, despite the fact that there is no longer a Channel Fleet. All ships of the Royal Navy come under the control of the C-in-C Fleet who runs what is known in the service as 'a dry ship'.

A shudder of pride or unease? It depends on your stance in the defence debate how you react to a first sight of the seas around Plymouth or Portsmouth but there is no denying their dramatic impact.

Portsmouth is the base for three aircraft carriers, two assault ships, 11 destroyers, six frigates, HMS *Endurance*, the ice patrol ship, HMS *Challenger*, the sea bed operations vessel and a squadron of seven mine counter measure vessels. Over the water in Gosport there are eight diesel-powered patrol submarines.

Through a fish-eye lens, a view of Plymouth over the new town towards the old harbour. (Topham)

Plymouth is the base for more than thirty frigates and a squadron of six nuclear-powered submarines of the Swiftsure class and for HM submarines *Trafalgar, Turbulent* and *Tireless.* These nuclear vessels have, since the end of the Falklands War, been undertaking patrols in the South Atlantic. The diesel boats operate with ships at Portland to give them anti-submarine training.

Of course, the whole idea of a submarine is that it *is* unseen, but the curious may find them berthed from time to time alongside HMS *Dolphin,* the submarine base at Gosport, and in the naval base at Devonport. Occasionally holidaymakers and Channel crossers may spot one entering and leaving harbour or out at sea in the Portland area or South of the Isle of Wight.

The navy may well be carrying out scores of different tasks in the Channel at any one time. Warships and their crews have to reach a high standard of fighting ability and in times of peace both equipment and men need to be kept ready, so there are regular training exercises.

These are often joined by foreign NATO navies, even French. For, although the French withdrew from the military wing of NATO in 1966, they go along as observers. Links with the Royal Netherlands Navy are much closer.

The Standing Naval Force Channel is NATO's mine counter measure force and has been extended considerably since its formation in 1973. Today membership is wider than the Channel countries and includes Denmark and North Germany. With up to ten ships it is now a mature operational squadron carrying out duties as far afield as the Mediterranean, the Irish Sea and the Baltic.

The Admiral in Charge of the French Channel fleet is based in Cherbourg and is under orders from Brest. 'We have in our mind so many borders to worry us that we are able to rely on the Royal Navy to protect the Channel', he says.

Until about 1970 the French navy was very shy of publicity and the people unaware of its importance. In the seventies the naval authorities woke up to the fact that if they were quiet about their abilities they would get no budget. So gradually they began to tell the press of their exploits and in the last few years, whereas army budgets have been reduced, the naval allocation has not. The fact remains however, that the young Frenchman is seldom drawn romantically to the sea.

Apart from military manoeuvres the RN can be seen at work on a host of other activities in the Channel. Ships of the Fishery Protection Squadron check trawler catches, hydrographic vessels survey the seabed, aircraft carriers embark sea harriers from the RN air station Yeovilton, minehunters look for crashed aircraft wreckage, or a frigate shadows a Soviet frigate on its way from Angola to the Baltic. At all times planes and helicopters from HMS *Culdrose* are on reconnaissance or taking part in Search and Rescue activities with the Coastguard.

What is it all about in these days of nuclear warfare? Does the Channel have any real importance, strategically any more? The answer appears to be 'yes'. The logic may not be too easy for the layman to understand with the image of the nuclear winter clouding the sky, but the offical viewpoint is quite categoric. 'Ninety per cent of reinforcements and equipment to sustain war in Europe would have to come from North America via the Channel. It is therefore as vital as it has ever been to defend that waterway. So in defence terms it is essential to maintain ships, to shepherd convoys, to take mine countermeasures and to act as a strategic interface between the maritime end of NATO and the land-air forces. The Channel is the crossroad of the two and presents a very complex and difficult job in tortuous navigational waters. The size of the navy may have shrunk overall, its skill and importance have not.

In the eighteenth and nineteenth centuries we were mostly preoccupied with France, and the Channel was the main area of concern. With the rise of Germany, the North Sea became the focus, and today the NATO navies are observing the gaps between Greenland, Iceland, the Faeroes and Britain through which the Soviet Northern Fleet would have to pass to threaten North Atlantic trading routes. We are no longer defending our little island, we are defending Europe.

On the commercial side the high-speed waterboatmen of the Channel, skimming backwards and forwards, are running a sophisticated, marketing battle to convince travellers that they offer the best, the biggest or the fastest and that their facilities and amusements are more tempting than those of anyone else: film shows, casinos, shops, childrens' clubs and competitions.

Perhaps the most critical of all the ferries' passengers are the newly elevated, roll-on roll-off lorry drivers; some two hundred and seventy drivers cross the Straits every day, and two hundred French drivers come here, mostly midweek because lorries are not allowed to drive in France on Sundays. Those who sit high up in their mod-con cabins like Lego men, survey the dock and ferry scene from such a different vantage point. Talk to a trucky about Dunkerque and you will learn it is a windy 'pig of a place' where you have to reverse on the boat and where there is no café for tea. The French *camionneur* has a really tough time.

They all like the camaraderie in the new silver service restaurants and the excellent food provided in their own lounges – a system that could smack of apartheid, but no one seems to mind, since it has been 'sold' as a plus for a valued client. Today there are even special freight ferries where the driver is given his own cabin. Just as well, for the lorry driver's lot is not always a happy one, and he deserves some encouragement. He can spend hours, even days, hanging around in port tied up in red tape and form-filling, and, if that is at the end of a 1000 mile journey, tempers are often frayed.

There is a kind of twentieth-century magic and mystery in those anonymous monsters beached in the harbour or packed in the hold. Who knows what they contain or where they are going? Pianos and ammunition for Italy, or swinging beef. This is the most dangerous of all and could be the inspiration for a horror movie: the carcasses of one hundred cattle swinging in time with the waves gather their own momentum and can overturn a lorry. They go out with steel pipes and return with lightweight toilet rolls. The stories of smuggling, subterfuge and sabotage which surround the truckers are no more than an extension of the good old eighteenth-century days when hollow masts and false floors kept the customs men on their toes.

Today, if there is smuggling, and of course no one knows of any first hand, it is likely to be more skilfully managed, since the Investigation Branch of the Customs has more power than the ordinary police. Instead of brandy it may be heroin.

Most of the huge amount of cross-Channel drug smuggling does not come on the lorries but, much as it always has, by small boats into sleepy coves and by air, concealed in heels, false linings, cosmetic tins and even stomachs. Drugs from London cross the Channel to the French ports too.

Of course the ferries are not the only freight transporters. Down Channel there are a few private specialists and since clearance times in the harbours are usually quicker than at airports, the Channel is the most efficient way of shifting Britain's freight to Europe and back. So there are always reports in the Channel local papers of possible new ro-ro ports at places such as Hayle in Cornwall (to Ireland).

Many of the drivers' frustrations are caused by particular demands of states within the EEC. Membership does not appear to have cut down the paperwork and regulations which change from year to year. All the ferry ports are managed differently and drivers have their favourites, rated according to the speed with which they can be on their way. Of course Dover deals with the largest number of lorries by far with 750,000 vehicles in 1985.

Clearance at Dover is about two hours and there are good eating facilities for drivers. The all-important turn-around time there has been reduced to seventy minutes and is still falling. Tourists and truckers alike are processed and controlled from Dover Harbour Board's observatory overlooking Eastern Docks, equipped with the standard battery of big-brother, closed-circuit television, public address systems, telex computers directing ship and shore (including a patrol boat outside the harbour), and ordering your car movements – there can be 1000 vehicles an hour in the peak season. The man with the cordless telephone waving you through is acting on instructions from an invisible, but all-seeing, controller and you are a pawn in their game, but it's better, by far, than the crawling queues of a few years back. Crossing the Channel from Dover is becoming more like a speeded-up movie. In the face of competition from the tunnel, the Dover Harbour Board is planning a £75 million development and reclamation over the next five years. Because of its geographical situation at the outlet of three river valleys, there is no room for expansion inland.

Dover, and her elegant neighbour Folkestone, 'strain side by side in the slips'. Folkestone is a beautiful if less known town with wide avenues and disproportionately grand hotels converted long ago into 'residential suites' for gentlefolk to ponder the palms and orangeries whilst retaining their soft-carpeted calm. Folkestone is overshadowed by the romantic history of its more famous neighbour. It has always been Dover and Folkestone, never Folkestone and Dover.

On the other side, Calais, flattened during the last War, lost some of its heart and its Frenchness. One wonders why Mary I was so upset at its loss! But since it is now France's leading passenger port, with well over five million passengers yearly, and 162 crossings between France and Britain daily, it has had to look to its port facilities. It has spent over £9 million on improvements, and has also altered the harbour entrance so that ships may come and go simultaneously. No more queuing in rough seas if the anchored ferry ran into loading problems. Calais now has the largest car ferry terminal in Europe.

Boulogne has built her reputation as the largest fishing port on mainland Europe but easy access straight from the sea to the quay makes Boulogne easy to enter and leave and for freight especially that makes Boulogne popular. Tourists may love lingering in the old Boulogne on their day trips, but for the lorry driver its delight is a speedy getaway to the south.

In comparison with the Dover/Calais and Folkestone/Boulogne crossings, Newhaven/Dieppe has the pleasantly simple atmosphere of

the way 'it used to be'. This is not so much a difference in the boats, as in the ports themselves. Newhaven has always had to fight for its life in the face of its own geography, constantly under threat from silting and with a problematic approach by road. Leaving Newhaven, down the narrow inlet to the harbour amongst the fishing boats, you can wave to the watchers on the harbour wall. It is real – a lot less like a satellite launching pad than the grander ports. The harbour authorities are sad. Partly because of the system of 'flags of convenience', whereby a country can avoid its crippling taxes by buying the right to trade under the flag of somewhere like Liberia; you hardly see a British cargo ship in Newhaven any more. Even the splendidly named *Albion Star* is German while Japanese ships bring tomatoes from the Canaries. But there are optimists who see the tunnel as an opportunity for the port which is four hours from France – the exact time lorry drivers are required to rest *en route*. They are also encouraged by Spain's entry into the EEC – a likely customer for Newhaven.

At Dieppe, too, the ferries sail from a quayside bustling with bars where travellers are immediately amongst families *en plein air*, dissecting mountains of mussels with the confidence of professional patho-

logists. Within five minutes of arrival in Newhaven you are in superb, fresh fish and chip country, at Dieppe it is mussels. *Vive la différence!* The much travelled writer V S Pritchett has described the new Dieppe with sentimental sadness. 'I first knew Dieppe years ago in the collar and tie age. When I sat in the café called the Tribunal there was an air of polite chatter. There were basketty chairs outside I seem to remember; today they are orange plastic.' Maybe, but the decor is still heavy oak, and red flocked wallpaper, terrible plastic flowers untouched by the cult of Americanization. This is ugly, old fashioned and wonderfully French, and there is still plenty to enjoy as you sit dipping your sugar lumps into bitter black *café*.

Just as Dieppe is small, so Le Havre is big, and an industrial town, like its twin Southampton. Le Havre lies at the mouth of the Seine, highway to Paris. Approaching the coast, as Henry V did in the fifteenth century, there is now an ugly sprawl of factories, warehouses and gas holders. Here is a world-record-holding tide gate, with a span of 67 metres which allows ships of a quarter of a million tons to reach the industrial zone. There is none of the dramatic beauty of that slow glide up the wide waters of the Solent, looking in parts like a Canaletto

Dover Harbour in the calm after the last war and before the organised chaos of today's daily rush to and from France. Photographed on August 22nd, 1946, with one camera in two different positions beside Dover Castle. (BBC Hulton)

vision. On the other hand, it is a well-planned, dignified, working town rebuilt after total demolition in August 1944 around the largest square in Europe.

As in Portsmouth, which now lures ro-ro and tourist traffic into its fascinating harbour, Le Havre is large enough to run boat trips to see the boats. These tours in Le Havre, to see the liners, the container ships and the tankers are the small (and not so small) boy's dream. In Portsmouth it is warships, great, grey, anonymous battleships, landing craft moving silently about their secret missions or simply riding at anchor – ready. It will be many years before the guides to Portsmouth Harbour forget that day in 1982 when the entire fleet became a Task Force and for the first time in over thirty years went into action. Whatever one's politics that memory makes them less of a static show.

Southampton has never developed an identity apart from the Docks and, as in Le Havre, the ferry is a bonus not a *raison d'être*. It has one of the finest natural harbours in the world, with a maximum tidal flow of only two knots, a maximum tidal range of 4.5 metres and the famous double tide which gives seventeen hours of rising and high water every day. Unlike other British ports, Southampton has not been affected by the decline of trade with the Commonwealth in favour of the EEC. Southampton is one of the six free trade zones in the UK where goods may be imported, processed and re-exported without paying duty or tax. Two things in particular have affected the post-war development of the port – the spread of the vast oil refineries along the New Forest shoreline, and containerization. The container ship is the modern merchant ship, a gargantuan floating raft maybe 1000 feet long. This mass movement of mixed freight is the cheapest and fastest by far. Twenty-six container ships today can do the work of 160 cargo boats of twenty years ago. They are a familiar sight in the Channel, dwarfing all else. All along the quay of any dock the containers stand waiting for departure. This is packing on a grand scale, loading and unloading of widely mixed cargo being carried out simultaneously on the instructions of computers. It saves about fifty per cent of costs and reduces the static time in a ship's working life from seventy-five per cent to twenty per cent.

There are a number of other, much smaller ports, Shoreham for example near Brighton, and Fowey in Cornwall, who do not rely on tourists at all and who are surviving and busy. The main road to Worthing conveniently runs inland at Shoreham and filters off much of the traffic, leaving an isolated, seaside strip with a character all its own, straddling nearly five miles of shoreline. The port and the village are surprising – Shoreham is a curious relic of far more elevated days. This was probably one of the main roads to Normandy after the Conquest, importing wine, exporting wool. In the Middle Ages it was an arsenal and a ship building industry thrived there. In those days the River Adur ran into the Channel at right angles and there was a huge inlet as far as Bramber, but with that dreaded easterly drift Shoreham was threatened with the same fate as Rye. The river mouth was

moving east by 118 feet per annum in 1759 and Shoreham was being stranded on a shingle beach. So the traders and the landowner (Duke of Norfolk) combined to open an artificial entrance with a lock, which meant berthed ships could stay afloat, and so Shoreham was saved.

The year 1957 was probably Shoreham's most exciting – when the building of Brighton Power Station necessitated the importation of 900,000 tons of coal a year and the port could not cope. The Electricity Generating Board agreed to help with a £3 million improvement. Together they deepened the channels, improved the locks so that they operate for five hours either side of deep water and extended the period during which vessels could enter and leave and improved capacity from 1500-ton to 4500-ton colliers. The Harbour Authority also decided to diversify – 'It was a very exciting time'.

With its picturesque village, Shoreham sits between the giants Brighton and Worthing, and with its emphasis on the importation of timber and wine, and especially sherry, it is a connoisseur's port. It has a rarity appeal. The wine comes in huge containers like oil and is no longer pumped ashore into barrels.

The Port itself is administered by the Authority which controls

Rye is one of the original Cinque Ports, but by October 1st, 1888, it had already been left far behind by the retreating sea. Almost one hundred years later the 'port' of Rye is even further from the sea. (Topham)

shipping and facilities and all profits are ploughed back into the business. Dockers and agency services are provided by private traders. It is a blend of private and public enterprise. 'This used to be such a gentlemanly business' but today every harbour is in competition and Shoreham has its sights set on a further 50 acres and greatly improved trade with the Mediterranean.

The Mission to Seamen is somewhat redundant today. Turnaround time is too quick for the sailors to get themselves into trouble ashore.

Shoreham Airport too has had a chequered history, built as it was on the somewhat swampy reaches of the river Adur; in fact in winter it used to flood. Its history is long and honourable, coming to the public notice when the first ever commercial freight flight took place on 4th July 1911. The cargo was of the new, electric light bulbs. The destination Hove – all of six miles away. That flight marked the beginning of a realization by businessmen that small, fixed-wing aircraft could provide a speedy way of getting them, and their products, to work and today Shoreham is the only remaining one of the first six pioneer airfields still operating as a public licensed aerodrome. Its new runway has overcome the muddy weather problem and there are now flights leaving regularly for the Channel Islands and the Breton coast as well as private planes travelling to Europe on business and Red Cross planes returning casualties from the ski slopes.

It is typical of Cornwall to weave romance into commercial success, and poetry around industrial desecration. The white cones that have exploded through the granite all round the edge of Bodmin Moor, the four hundred man-made craters, the icy, green pools, the gleaming, slippery roads are such stuff as financiers' dreams are made of and are one of Cornwall's most valuable assets.

China clay was discovered in Cornwall just as the bottom fell out of the tin market. In 1768 William Cookworthy, a Plymouth Quaker, opened a porcelain factory in Plymouth. The Chinese method of using kaolin (from their word for High ridge) to make fine porcelain had been a closely guarded secret since around 400 AD, but in the eighteenth century the knowledge reached Europe so that when Mr Cookworthy came across a particularly fine quality deposit near St Austell, Cornwall experienced a minor gold rush. Potters like Spode and Minton moved in, as did dozens of private speculators and created with their coming a way of life and a sub-culture like the tinners before them. Amongst their skills was wrestling – a sport in which for many years they challenged their counterparts, the china clay miners of Pleyber Christ in Brittany.

China clay, described in a nineteenth-century guidebook as 'a species of moist granite rock once so firm and tenacious has been reduced by decomposition into a soft substance not unlike mortar' is used mainly in the ceramics and paper industries (for glossy magazine pages) but also for paint and plastics, insecticides and fertilizers.

This is the land of Daphne du Maurier's *Jamaica Inn* where, as she says, 'wild flowers straggle across the waste, seeds flourish into nameless plants … seagulls hover … Cornishmen are wresting a living from the granite as they have done through countless centuries leaving nature to seal, in her own fashion with forgotten ground which, being prodigal of hand she has done with a lavish and a careless grace'. It is also the land of Dozmare, the 'bottomless' lake into which Excalibur was thrown by Bedivere. Unlike coal kaolin is hosed from the ground by jets of water.

About 2.75 million tons of china clay leave Cornwall through the Channel every year to more than sixty countries including, paradoxically, China. But then they also export sand to the Arabs. The EEC Group is the largest single producer in the world, working in conjunction with Pleyber through the port of Roscoff. China clay has made the pretty, little harbour of Par the busiest, small port in Britain and the deep-water inlet port of Fowey, leased from BR (surely the most beautiful industrial port), handles ships up to 10,000 tons.

Soon this extraordinary lunar landscape, created by men for whom scenery filled no stomachs, will be greened to merge with the moorland that surrounds it, in Britain's most extensive programme of replanting and conservation. The English China Clay Empire, founded on this 7000 acres of Cornish granite, is sensitive to Cornwall's dependence too on tourists. And tourists like their industry tame. Already some 61,000 trees of 47 varieties have been planted and 47 miles of fencing erected around new pastures to feed Soay sheep. Orange aubretia blooms on the slopes.

Holes in the ground are one thing. Holes in the sea present a different set of problems, out of sight and mind of most of us, until their presence causes a crisis, or even a disaster.

The sea bed itself is owned by Her Majesty The Queen and is administered by the Crown Agents, a rather lordly body with a proprietorial attitude to their office. It is they who grant mineral mining rights for oil and for dredging. For some reason the subject of dredging is never treated by the layman with the respect it deserves, for it is one of the Channel's most important, most controversial and, to those not connected with the sea, least known activities. Gravel, and its end products, is a highly valuable commodity which even today is beset with pirates.

For hundreds of years men anchored barges on inshore sandbanks, dug when the tide was out and hoped the weight would not sink their boats as the water rose. The story of Hallsands hamlet, near Start Point in Devon, tells the dangers of such lack of foresight. There is one house left at Hallsands today. In 1860 there were 37 houses and 128 people. It was a self-sufficient fishing community protected from the vicious storms of Start Bay by a broad shingle beach, Skerries Bank, about one kilometre offshore. The houses had clung to a 20-

metre platform cut by waves in solid rock and can still be seen in some of the more sheltered coves around the south-west coast. As the settlement grew, the houses were built on or across deep sand or shingle-packed clefts in the rock platform. In the 1890s the Royal Navy needed to extend Devonport dockyard at Keyham for the building of Dreadnoughts, and they needed 400,000 cubic metres of shingle. In 1896 an agreement was made which permitted the extraction of shingle 'from that part of the beach between high and low water marks of Start Bay and opposite Hallsands and Beeson Sands'. Great care was to be paid to threats to the foreshore or defences. Dredging began the following year and on average 1600 tonnes was removed every day, altering the beach so much that before long the low water-mark was further inland than the original high water-mark and villagers realized that their vital protective shingle bank was disappearing. There were questions in the House, and a local enquiry which ended in an offer by Sir John Jackson to the local community of £125 for every year dredging continued, plus a Christmas bonus. Then in the winter of 1900 the wild seas of the Channel beyond the sandbar broke through and battered directly on Hallsands perilous foothold. Houses began to collapse and the licence to dredge was removed. A long wrangle began, for it was now too late to save the village, and by 1903 Sir Jack had offered compensation of £3250 to which the local MP Colonel Mildmay added £250 from his own pocket. But that was not the end of the affair for in 1917 the seas broke through again and all remaining houses were severely damaged. A few were rebuilt over the years but the last person to live in the battered skeleton of a village was Miss Prettijohn who died in 1965. The tragedy had a beneficial spin-off for now no dredging is allowed within three miles of the coast.

The dredging boom has, not surprisingly, coincided with the post-war building boom in Britain. In France, they dredge in their rivers for a very different kind of shiny, flat pebble, and there is not the same hostility. Sea dredging is not permitted. What dredging takes place at Dieppe, upriver in Le Havre, or Calais, or Dunkirk is all being carried out by British ships. The French authorities did build their own dredger but when it capsized and men were drowned they seemed to lose heart. For British fishermen, and the yachtsmen of every nationality, those solid dredgers, so often flying the Dutch flag, are lurkers causing havoc to work and to play. Up at Newhaven there are regular confrontations between the fishermen who believe their fishing grounds are being destroyed and the dredgermen who say they are preserving the harbour.

The Channel dredging business began just off the Isle of Wight on what is known as Pot Bank and, although it has now extended along the length of the Channel, it is the island around which there is most argument. There are those on the local Council who claim the whole island is sinking because of it. Flying about the Channel regularly in a helicopter Robin Aisher, Chairman of Marley, a marina owner and fanatical yachtsman, views what is happening through the concerned lens of a camera. 'The gravel is whirling around all the time', he says, 'the Channel is unique in those shifting submarine hills and valleys but it is a constant hazard to the sailor and additional undermining by dredgers is criminal. West of the Isle of Wight the water is so clear you can see the bottom in an extraordinary way that never happens in France where it is all stirred up by the extreme tides – but the changes in sand bars and gravel beds all show up from above on the surface water and I keep an annual record of the movement'. His fear is that eventually dredging could counteract the huge coastal changes made by shingle drift during the storm of 1703 and that stretches of coastline could again be washed away.

Of course, the dredging companies do not see it that way and have surveyors constantly keeping an eye on erosion. They say that mostly they are dredging the old beach lines and river valleys. Besides, the other side of the story belongs to the constant battle against silting by many British ports. Much of this work is tackled by the Dutch who are particularly skilled because of their national obsession with drainage. In France many harbour works are funded by central Government where it is the responsibility of port authorities and that can come hard. Newhaven has to be completely dredged twice a year (for most of Sussex drains into the harbour) at a cost of about £1 m annually. Dover also spends £1 m, silt being dumped under licence at sea.

Seismic scans taken by geologists to show what is happening in Davy Jones' locker often reveal the marks of 'pirates' who have nipped in when the licensee is on his way home and illegally removed material.

Down on the seabed there are also undefined amounts of oil; the prospectors are all out there looking, probing and keeping their counsel. Along the English shoreline the vultures wait, hopeful that oil will bring prosperity. At what cost? ask the conservationists. Oil is there, and its existence could produce civil war in the south of England. There is a far greater awareness of the need for conservation in Britain today and organizations like the National Trust are actively up front monitoring progress.

Oil drilling began in southern England in the Isle of Purbeck in the 1930s and the first offshore well was B B Lulworth Banks No 1 drilled in 1963. Drilling in the Channel has always been beset by problems of weather, traffic and demarcation disputes with the French. The first speculative, regional, seismic survey run for an oil company to discover the structure and form of the rocks under the Channel was 'shot' in 1972 and the UK fifth round of licensing granted in 1977 included two blocks in mid-Channel ... one licensed to Hydrocarbons BP Ltd, the other to Conoco – both were dry.

The Kimmeridge Clay (Upper Jurassic), which is one of the most important reservoir rocks in the North Sea, has given its name to the Kimmeridge Field, discovered in 1959 in a small rock fold, impressed into a larger fold known as the Weymouth Anticline. The Wareham Oilfield (1964) is no longer producing but the Wytch Farm field north

Oil exploration in the Channel has proceeded quietly since the 1930s. As possibilities of a bonanza increase and decrease opposition waxes and wanes, but the sweet smell of oil profits may prove, as elsewhere, too seductive. (Topham)

of the Purbeck–Isle of Wight fault zone, which is a hundred million years old, is the one which has created most interest and most concern.

The hawks are hovering – watching with acute suspicion the activities of the J R Ewings, manipulating their toy rigs in London on the Channel map. The headlines are by no means euphoric. 'No job, no money, no control', they claim. One of the most controversial sites is once again around the Isle of Wight where the BP rig *Britannia* has sunk a well in Poole Bay four miles due east of the familiar Old Harry Rock. This field is a part of the Wytch Farm deposit on the beautiful

Studland Peninsula, which has itself been the scene of fierce conservationist lobbying. The two main contenders have been the National Trust which not only owns most of the mainland in the vicinity of Wytch Farm but also Brownsea Island in Poole Harbour, where it confronts the owners of nearly 31-acre Furzey Island, bought for £700,000 by BP. This is European Nature Conservation Diploma Country, awarded by the Council of Europe, where 'the conflicting interests of economic and agricultural development, recreation and conservation have been reconciled' – so far. It has been a combined effort between the Army, who have a number of ranges in the area, landowners, farmers and money men. But the sweet smell of oil could change all that and the vigilantes are out.

This is not a French problem; they really do not seem to have a great deal of luck in the Channel. They certainly do not seem to have any oil.

In September 1974 three large permit blocks were issued to a consortium comprising ELF–SNPA/BP–Shell: the Iroise permit NW of Brittany, the Amor permit West of Brest and the Mer Celtique permit west of the continental margin. Ten holes were drilled: all dry! Total cost: 600 million francs! Maybe this is why, it is rumoured in British naval circles, the French are not so bothered about the defence of the Channel?

Tourism is the largest employer along the Franco–British Channel shores. 'Le Relax absolu' – claim the television advertisments. So it is good to discover that the tourist boards on both sides are at last awake to their mutual heritage – the sea.

There is now regular consultation between and more imaginative marketing of the delights that might lure holidaymakers across the water in each direction. It has been a hard road for the English Tourist Board in particular, convincing the French that they would not starve or die of draughts if they set foot on British soil. Imaginative schemes like the Route des Pubs have helped. The French have been forced to get to grips with their plumbing but do not appear to be so anxious to exploit these links and tend to major their typically national pride on their gastronomical and geographical assets. There remains a delightful Frenchness about that coast which makes few concessions to foreigners, let alone the British. The tatty mini circus on the beach with its scraggy camels, the inevitable accordian, the bicycles made for four, the smell of breakfast pernod and coffee in the harbour cafes, all are such stuff as Monsieur Hulot was made of. It is not easy to compete with.

Ninety-nine per cent of British motorists have never taken their car across The Channel, an unbelievable statistic for those waiting patiently for their turn to pass through customs. But it is that ninety-nine per cent which is the target for the Channel's most potentially important industry – tourism. To compete with the cut-price package flights to the Costa Brava the regional tourist boards of Britain and France have been forced to get their act together in the last few years.

Although competition is considerable, parochialism is still sometimes a hindrance – nowhere more than the Channel Islands where the jealous individual islands might as well be a thousand miles from each other, and Guernsey is not even represented in London.

In Britain the National Trust has bought long stretches of the Channel coastline in order to protect and preserve its character and beauty for the public. The National Trust was founded in Britain in 1895, its aim 'alienation': for once the National Trust acquires a property it has the unique power to declare land inalienable so that it may not be sold or mortgaged and offers the highest form of protection available in this country.

There is no equivalent godfather in France where the coast is maintained by local authorities and promoted by the local *Syndicat d'Initiative*.

In 1980, to the utter disbelief of a romantic public, Land's End was sold by the Trehair family to a speculating tax exile for two and a quarter million pounds. The concept of paying, and dearly, to walk over a stretch of coast which perhaps more than any other stirs the imagination, caused an uproar. This symbol of loneliness, the figure-head of Great Britain, sailed into stormy waters. The local Penwith Council claimed a public right of way had been established by the thousands of pilgrims who, over the centuries, had walked to stand out on the headland of *Pen Von Las* (The End of the Earth).

The truth was that even such a national heritage costs a fortune to maintain and, as tourism expanded, so wear and tear became a problem. At the time at least one and a quarter million pounds was needed to halt the erosion of the 270 million-year-old rocks. The first and last house in Britain was falling into the sea.

So the tea shoppe, the hotel, the museum and the gift shops came along with craft workers, which meant a quarter of a million pounds in wages to local folk in a poor community. The story of Land's End moved into a new phase in its curiously undignified history for although it is breathtakingly beautiful – a cathedral of rocks in the sea – it has always attracted eccentrics, especially on the Land's End to John O'Groats jaunt – nudists, cyclists, Dr Barbara Moore, Jimmy Savile and Ian Botham.

Away from the car park and the coach tours the old public footpath edged with thrift still runs around the headland and those who walk it tend to turn their eyes away and out across 3291 miles of Atlantic – or is it the Channel? For, somewhere out there, where migrating birds begin their long journey to the sun, the English Channel is swallowed up by the great, grey anonymity of the ocean.

In 1965, when a survey was made of the 3000 miles of English and Welsh coast, it was discovered that already along the Channel coast almost nothing of note was left in Kent and Sussex. Enterprise Neptune was started by the National Trust as a vigilant campaign to wake the public and the authorities before it was too late and now they are the largest coastal landowners in the country.

Cornwall, Devon and Dorset owe a great deal to the National Trust policy which has evolved over the years and now includes the purchase of farms to protect the view of the countryside, as seen from the sea,

Land's End is protected from the attentions of wayward seamen by the Longships lighthouse. (Aerofilms)

The cliffs of the Seven Sisters in Sussex. (J. Allan Cash)

right up to the skyline. Before the last war R C Sherrif bought a pretty farm at Golden Cap, between Lyme Regis and Bridport, with his royalties from *Journey's End*, and in the 1960s he gave it to the Trust. The farm became a starting point from which they have built up an estate protecting six miles of the coastline. The Trust carried out its first rescue mission when it bought land at Birling Gap, the smugglers' hideaway at the base of a beautiful sweep in the Seven Sisters, because it had already become so tatty. They plan to improve, without sterilizing, this beautiful smugglers' inlet to encourage greater care by the visitors who already flock there.

One-third of the Devon and Cornish coast is now owned by the Trust, working closely with the Countryside Commission, who define all the long-distance coastal footpaths.

Twinning really arose from a need to heal the wounds left after the Second World War and both in France and England links with Germany were developed first. In the last twenty years, and especially since the creation of the EEC, the formation of twinning committees has become a thriving activity. Links across the Channel are growing, but their success so often depends on the enthusiasm of one man, or woman, who may well be married to someone from the other side and have a vested interest! There is also an element of healthy competition between towns and villages; if their neighbours have a twin over the water they may decide they must be missing out and twin up themselves.

Certainly the social intercourse is great and, indeed, has been criticized as a 'junket' for the authorities. This is hardly fair because most are careful not to use ratepayers money for their annual bonanza which, for all its benefits, is probably enjoyed by comparatively few middle-class people. The local brew has played a part in the rumbustuous success of Devon County's twinning, first with Calvados and then with Brittany, which culminates each year around the Devon County Show and the Caen Fair and has won for the county a Council of Europe prize. Everywhere in Devon, from the tiny village of Pughill (175 inhabitants) to Plymouth, twinned with Sept Vents, has links with somewhere: architects, priests, engineers, doctors and schoolchidren have been on exchange study visits. Bakers have made *croissants* in Devon, the Devonians ran a tea shop in Caen – though no amount of effort has persuaded the French ladies to form a French WI. Newsletters, historical pamphlets and journals, pass backwards and forwards, reflecting a considerable amount of bonhomie. In the jointly produced book *Nos Voisins d'Outre Manche* the archivists from the two regions have imaginatively assembled a manuscript record of regional links since 1066. It starts with William's confirmation, the endowment in France and England of the Abbey of St Etienne of Caen, country twinning, and passes through some of the historical exchanges such as Charles IX's appeal to French resistance against British Protestant invasion in 1652 and concludes with the county twinning charter.

The aims behind all this fraternization are, of course, better understanding but they are also clearly commercial and it is in the hardheaded world of business that the mass-market effectiveness of these exchanges may be queried. The Chambers of Commerce and the regional tourist departments seem to co-operate but it is doubtful if goodwill is enough to improve commercial attitudes between the French and the British. You will rarely find a Frenchman who says that he enjoys doing business with the British, or vice versa. On the other hand, the Chamber of Trade in Cherbourg employs an English 'Ambassador' who began his commercial links with France by exporting dolly mixture wallpaper! It is an uphill struggle all the way and a saga of distrust: the French, so they say in East Sussex, never reply to letters; the British, so they say in Deauville, are demanding, arrogant and rude. But twinning does no harm and may in time achieve a deeper understanding than a taste for *croissants* or knowledge of fish and chips.

One August day in the summer of 1902 a young man from Hastings found himself caught up in the festivities of Corneville sur Mer in Normandy. Edward E Clarke was a fanatical Francophile with a pointed beard and waxed moustachio and he was warmly included in the merrymaking which had been organised by a local society, the *Souvenir Normand*, the *Marquis de la Rochethulon et Grente*. The President d'Honneur was the Princesse de la Tour d'Auvergne. The *Souvenir Normand* had been founded to keep alive the memory of ancestral greatness. Edward Clarke was fired with enthusiasm and persuaded the *Souvenir* to hold its next celebrations in his home town of Hastings, surrounded as it also was by noble descendants of the Conqueror. So it was that in 1903, the year before the signing of the *Entente Cordiale* the French came to Britain and at Battle Abbey unveiled a marble *placque*.

Dieu aie!
Dans de champ historique de Senlac ou tomba le brave Harold le Saxon, 837 ans après la bataille qui donna à la Grande Bretagne la loi Normande, le Souvenir Normand, venu des bords de la Seine a proclame avec joie la paix des Normandies Soeurs. *

1066 – 1903
Stephanie la Tour d'Auvergne, President Mis de la Rochethulon et Grente, fondateur Jean Soudan de Pierrefitte, Vice President
20 Âout 1904

(* The Sisterhood of Normandy links the countries of Denmark, England, France and Sicily which have historic links with the Vikings and Normans.)

Today the Souvenir Normand is an exclusive, little-known, group, which stands apart from twinning organizations. It is an aristocratic affair, especially on the French side, of blue-blooded brothers and sisters. Bi-annually they come to lay a wreath on the Norman stone in Battle Abbey grounds and to listen to the rededicatory statement read in French and English at this ceremony.

Here on this historic soil where fell in combat so many of our forebears and where out of the evil of War arose a fusion of races which has brought lasting benefit to mankind:
  Let us in the name of God dedicate ourselves anew to the furtherance of friendship between our two great and allied Nations and pledge ourselves by our prayers and our work to strive unceasingly for the Greater Glory of God in the Development of Goodwill and Men and Peace on Earth.

The British return, as they did for the 900th centenary celebration of William's birth in Falaise, to be entertained in elegant style amongst the Norman chateaux. There are now branches of the *Souvenir* in other places where Norman influence was felt, in Denmark and in

Sicily, but it is the Anglo-French link which is strongest – a serious tryst between people who do not forget their common Norman ancestry and maybe see themselves, being descendants of William's *élite*, as on the winning side, French or British.

The ceremony is reported extensively in the French press – barely at all in the British.

'On a clear day you can see forever' and after 5000 years of crossing and recrossing in boats of increasing size it may yet take forever to bridge this gap between Dover and Cap Gris Nez and between the British and the French, even with a tunnel under the sea. (Popperfoto)

Postscript: Family Reunion –
the Link Made Concrete

We are in an Island, confined to it by God Almighty, not as a
Penalty but a Grace, and one of the greatest that can be given to
Mankind. Happy confinement, that hath made us Free, Rich
and Quiet; a fair Portion in this World, and very well worth the
preserving; a Figure that ever hath been envied, and could never
be imitated by our Neighbours.

A Rough Draft of a New Model at Sea
The Marquess of Halifax (1633–95)

It has been easier to land a man on the moon than to convince the
British that a tunnel beneath their Channel would be a good idea.
Since the first plan, for a candlelit tunnel for horse drawn traffic was
approved by Napoleon in 1802, the great majority of proposals have
been French. They have dreamed, for centuries, of ways to annexe
this offshore island, and so turn Britain into a European peninsula.
Their reasons have been as economic and political as our resistance
has been emotional.

Forming, as they do the blunt end of Britain, the bulwark shores of
Kent and Sussex have stood, historically, against 'the envy of less
happier lands'. It is hard to imagine less happier lands than they right
now. Ten thousand years ago Britain became an island, depending
time and time again for its defence on the people in this beautiful area.
Today they fear that their countryside will be wrecked and their status
symbollically challenged by the decision at Lille in 1986 to rejoin the
white cliffs of Dover with the grey cliffs of Sangatte. Even the French
concede that it is a momentous decision.

A century ago the French *Revue des Deux Mondes* said 'The day the
inauguration of the Tunnel will be celebrated, Britain will no longer
be an island – a stupendous event in the history of an island people.'

Now Mrs Thatcher has turned midwife, with President Mitterand as
her obstetrician, to what was called by Palmerston 'the longest
pregnancy in history'. Mind you, we have been here before. The
French Assembly approved the price of rail tickets for the tunnel as
long ago as the turn of the century, and here, in the 1930s a timetable
was published complete with platform numbers. The British have
joined in the game many times already – ten bills have been rejected by
Parliament. It was our Board of Trade who halted the original
tunneling in 1884 when they 'discovered' that the seabed below low

water mark and within the three-mile limit belonged to the Crown, though the foreshore did not. Once the burrowing reached that low water mark and was about to impinge on Crown property they stopped it. In 1974, after an election, Harold Wilson's Government reneged unilaterally after French and British workers had bored nearly a mile under the sea.

This time, however, the political will on both sides seems strong for what must be the most exciting engineering project of the century – even if the Great British public spirit remains unconvinced . . . so far. Guarantees are being built into the agreement which will prevent a repeat of 1974.

The design which pipped the others to the post is that proposed by the Channel Tunnel Group – an Anglo–French Consortium. It is for a twin-tunnel rail shuttle, like a submarine aeroplane carrying both cars and lorries.

Within seven years some 3600 cars an hour will be whisked at five-minute intervals from the 350-acre terminal at Sheriton in Kent to Sangatte near Calais in half an hour. Passengers will be able to stretch their legs and buy refreshments en route. Problems of traffic queues and customs delays, they promise, will be eliminated. Fares should be slashed, jobs boom. The French see British money reviving the flagging fortunes of Northern France and Paris, only $3\frac{1}{2}$ hours away, becoming the hypermarket for London. There is no great change of heart towards us though; only five per cent of Frenchmen come to Britain and in a recent poll fifty per cent thought the fixed link had already been built.

Despite the euphoria in many commercial and trading circles the CTG will have to work hard now to convince not only folk in the Garden of England that there won't be an horrendous snarl up on their doorstep, but also the people of Britain, who 'have not spoken yet', that they are not threatened by terrorists, invasion, asphyxiation and rabies, or a new Norman Conquest.

The greatest tunnel enthusiast of all time must surely have been the Frenchman, Thomé de Gamond, who in 1856 had visions of turning the great Varne sandbank into a mid-Channel port connecting two tunnels. It was not so different from the plan submitted by Euro-route in the recent contest.

Thomé de Gamond had no political or military ambitions for his country, and at the age of 48 would dive naked, 100 feet into the sea, with lint protecting his ears from pressure, four bags of flints as ballast and ten inflated pigs' bladders to take him to the surface after he had collected geological specimens from the sea bed.

Unfortunately, de Gamond died in 1877 a year before the first borings were made at Sangatte and celebrated in tremendous style at a banquet attended by the Prince of Wales. In 1880 the British followed suit with the number one shaft between Folkestone and Dover. It reached 74 feet and the tunnel was driven in for 897 yards. Number two shaft went down by Shakespeare Cliff and Colonel Beaumont's

The age of the Tunnel will be the age of the train – the electric train. Napoleon's candle-lit tunnel (which inspired the illustration on p. 187) and the thousands of drivers who would do it themselves face the same unsolved problem; how to ensure adequate ventilation in a 35-mile tunnel with combustible fuels. (Channel Tunnel Group)

boring machine (the head of which is still there) drove a 7 feet diameter tunnel for 2000 yards.

Reactions were as divided then as they are today. Admiral Sir Garnett Wolsey, Warden of Dover Castle, claimed it would be essential to conscript an army and place guns at the tunnel entrance. He asserted that the French would send soldiers, dressed as civilians, to invade us. Lord Randolph Churchill said Britain would no longer be *virgo intacta*. To give the French their due they did try to counter this criticism by designing a system of vents through which the whole thing could be flooded in time of war.

In fact, the tunnel became a tourist draw. The Beau Monde arrived for champagne parties and were entertained in elegant style amongst palm trees, in surroundings so clean that the ladies emerged with their dresses unsoiled.

For the last ten years hundreds of thousands of pounds have been spent by the rival consortia, eager for this extraordinary contract.

Surveyors, engineers, architects, politicians, local authorities, journalists, lobbyists and PR men and women have been beavering away. Now the die is cast. The Entente Cordiale faces it toughest test so far. For what began, all that time ago in the years before William landed, as a cross-Channel family confrontation has now become a matter of national identity and Pride. Who is annexing whom?

The British may yet be stirred to the thrill of the chase after technological achievement. Visitors to Dover may not, after all, find themselves aboard a ghostly *Marie Celeste* of a town. For rivalry, not rapprochment will be the spur to the pioneering spirit of old. In the meantime the planning goes on, pro-Europeans stand eagerly waiting for work to begin and the old tunnels stand blocked, blindly facing each other beneath the waves that wash either shore; symbols of an historical relationship that goes just so far – but so far no further.

Bibliography

This is not a comprehensive bibliography, merely an indication of areas of further reading.

GENERAL HISTORY
Barker, Sir Ernest *The Character of England* Clarendon.
Brandon, Peter *South Saxons* Phillimere.
Bryant, Sir Arthur *History of England* Collins.
Castries, Duc de *Kings and Queens of France* Weidenfeld & Nicholson.
Churchill, Sir Winston *A History of the English Speaking Peoples* Cassel.
Clark, Sir George *A History of Britain* W H Smith.
Clark, Sir Kenneth *Civilization* Gollancz.
David, Francois *Autopsie de la Grande Bretagne* Hachette.
Evans, Joan *Life in Medieval France* Phaidon.
Goldworth, J *Napoleon's British Visitors and Captives* Alger.
Hart, Roger *English Life in the Eighteenth century* Wayland.
Hibbert, Christopher *Agincourt* Batsford.
Hindley, G *Tourists, Travellers and Pilgrims* Hutchinson.
Howarth, David *The Year of the Conquest* Collins.
Innis, H A *The Cod Fisheries* Yale University Press (1940).
Jewell, Brian *Conqueror and Overlord* Midas.
Johnson, Paul *The Offshore Islands* Weidenfeld & Nicholson.
Johnson, Stephen *The Roman Ports of the Saxon Shores* Paul Elek.
Laurens, Ann *Britain is No Island* Cassel.
Lewis, W H *The Splendid Century* Eyre & Spottiswoode.
Lindsay, J *The Normans and their World* Hart Davis.
Lindsay, J *The Normans and the Viking Age* Hart Davis.
Morey, G *The English Channel* Muller.
Quennel, M & C H B *The History of Everyday Things* Batsford.
Rowse, A L *Tudor Cornwall* Macmillan.
Scott, A F *Everyone A Witness* White Lion.
Seignobods, C *History of the French People* Jonathan Cape.
Smith, Graham *Something to Declare* Harrap.
Trevelyan, G M *England under the Stuarts* Methuen.
Uden, Grant *Anecdotes From History* Basil Blackwell.
Victoria County Histories
Williamson, J *The English Channel* Collins.
Winchester, B *A Tudor Family Portrait* Jonathan Cape.

NAVAL HISTORY
Fowler, William *Royal Marines* Osprey.
Hargreaves, Roger *The Narrow Seas* Sidgwick & Jackson.
Haws, Duncan *Ships and the Sea – A Chronological View* Hart Davis.
Hekstall Smith, Anthony *The Fleet that Faced Both Ways* Blond & Briggs.
Howarth, David *Sovereign of the Seas* Collins.
Howarth, David *The Voyage of the Armada* Collins.
Kammerer, A *La Passion de la Flotte Francaise* A Fayard.
Ladd, James David *Royal Marine Commando* Hamlyn.
Mahan, A T *The Influence of Seapower on History* Sampson & Low.
Marsden, Peter *The Wreck of the Amsterdam* Hutchinson.
Mordal, Jacques *Twenty-Five Centuries of Sea Warfare* Abbey Library.
Read, H P *Trinity House* Sampson & Low.
Vader, J *The Fleet Without a Friend* New English Library.

THE TWO WORLD WARS
Bacon, Admiral Sir R. *The Dover Patrol* Hutchinson.
Cruikshank, C G *The German Occupation of the Channel Islands* Oxford University Press.
Keith Papers Royal Naval Society Naval Records Office.
McKee, Alexander *The Coal Scuttle Brigade* Souvenir Press.
'Remy' *La Maison d'Alphonse* Librairie Academique Perrin.
Turnbull, Patrick *Dunkirk* Batsford.
Warner, Philip *Invasion Road* Cassel.

SOCIAL HISTORY
Anderson, Janice *Victorian and Edwardian Seaside* Hamlyn.
Herms, Anthony *The Seaside Holiday* Cresset Press.
Pakenham, S *Sixty Miles from England* Macmillan.
Perrault, Gilles *Les Gens d'ici* J-P Ramsay.
Searle, Muriel *Bathing Machines and Bloomers* Midas.
Smith, Anthony *Beside the Seaside* George Allen & Unwin.
Whiteside, Thomas *The Tunnel Under the Channel* Hart Davis.

DIARIES AND CONTEMPORARY RECORDS
Anglo-Saxon Chronicles Oxford University Press.
Caesar, Julius *Caesar's Gallic Wars* Penguin.
Evelyn, John *Diary* Everyman's Library Dent.
Froissart, Jean *Chronicles* Macmillan (1913).
Hall, Helena *Sussex Dialect Dictionary* R J Acford.
LeGallo, Yves *L'Emigration Saisonniere Des Johnnies* Directeur du Centre de Recherche Bretagne et Celtique.
Meyerstein, E H N (ed) *The Adventures by Sea of Edward Coxere* Clarendon Press.
Pepys, Samuel *Diary* vols 1–11 Bell & Hyman.
Revue d'Avranches – Archives of the Bibliotheque of Avranches.
William of Malmesbury *Chronicle of the Kings and Queens of England.*

BIOGRAPHY
Champigneule, B *Rodin* Thames & Hudson.
Chateaubriand F R (trans R Baldick) *Memoirs of Chateaubriand* Penguin.
Edwards, Samuel *Victor Hugo* New English Library.
Williams, Neville *Henry VIII and His Court* Book Club Associates.

SHIPS, SHIPPING AND THE SEA
Adlard Coles, K *South Coast Harbours* Faber & Faber.
Bell, R G *Diaries from the Days of Sail* Barrie & Jenkins.
Bird, James *Major Seaports of the UK* Hutchinson.
Farr, Graham *West Country Passenger Steamers* T Stephenson.
Fowles, John *Shipwreck* Cape.
Garnett, Richard *Cross Channel* Hutchinson.
Goldsmith, George *Forgotten Ports of England* Carter.
Greenway, A *A Century of Cross-Channel Passenger Ferries* I Allan.
Harnack, E P *All About Ships and Shipping* Faber & Faber.
Jackson, G *History and Archaeology of Ports* Worlds Work.
Kenny, Dick *To Win the Admirals Cup* Nautical.
Larn, R and Carter, C *Shipwrecks on the South Coast* Pan.
Lewis, R *A History of the Lifeboat* Macmillan.
March, E J *Inshore Craft of Britain in the Days of Sail and Oar* David & Charles.
Mayne, Richard *Mail Ships of the Channel Islands* Picton.
de Rodakowski, Ernest *The Advantages and Feasibility of a Train Ferry Between France and England* (1905).
Thornton, E C B *South Coast Pleasure Steamers* T Stephenson.
Webb, William *Coastguard* H M Stationery Office.
Williams, Mark *No Cure, No Pay* Hutchinson.

TRAVEL
Brentnall, Margaret *The Cinque Ports* Gifford.
Bates, D *Companion Guide to Devon and Cornwall* Collins.
Coysh, Victor *The Channel Islands – a New Study* David & Charles.
Elsy, Mary *Brittany and Normandy* Batsford.
Grimson, J *The Channel Coasts of England* Robert Hale.
Hampshire, Kingsley Palmer *The Folklore of Somerset* Batsford.
Hay, D & J *The West Country from the Sea* Stanford.
Hillier, C *The Bulwark Shore* Eyre Methuen.
Hudson, K *English China Clays* David & Charles.
Lands, Neil *Brittany* Spur.
Lempriere, P *A Portrait of the Channel Islands* Hale.
du Maurier, Daphne *Vanishing Cornwall* Gollancz.
Mead, Robin *The Channel Islands* Batsford.
Parry, John *The Coast of Sussex* Longman (1833).
Roberts, Nesta *The Companion Guide to Normandy* Collins.
Roberts, Nesta *The Face of France* Collins.

Seymour, John *Companion Guide to South West England* Collins.
Spence, Keith *Brittany and the Bretons* Gollancz.
Spence, Keith *Companion Guide to Kent and Sussex* Collins.
White, Iris Bryson *East Sussex* Spur.